HOW TO JUDGE A HOROSCOPE
Volume Two

D1553530

How to Judge a Horoscope

Volume Two
VII to XII Houses

Bangalore Venkata Raman

Gayatri Devi Vasudev

MOTILAL BANARSIDASS PUBLISHERS
PRIVATE LIMITED • DELHI

Second Edition: Bangalore, 1982
Fourth Edition: Delhi, 1992
Fifth Edition: Delhi, 1995
Reprint: Delhi, 1997, 2000, 2003

ISBN: 81-208-0845-2 (Cloth) (Vol. II)
ISBN: 81-208-0848-7 (Paper)
ISBN: 81-208-0846-0 (Cloth) (Set)
ISBN: 81-208-0849-5 (Paper)

Also available at:

MOTILAL BANARSIDASS

41 U.A. Bungalow Road, Jawahar Nagar, Delhi 110 007
8 Mahalaxmi Chamber, 22 Bhulabhai Desai Road, Mumbai 400 026
236, 9th Main III Block, Jayanagar, Bangalore 560 011
120 Royapettah High Road, Mylapore, Chennai 600 004
Sanas Plaza, 1302 Baji Rao Road, Pune 411 002
8 Camac Street, Kolkata 700 017
Ashok Rajpath, Patna 800 004
Chowk, Varanasi 221 001

Printed in India
BY JAINENDRA PRAKASH JAIN AT SHRI JAINENDRA PRESS,
A-45 NARAINA, PHASE-I, NEW DELHI 110 028
AND PUBLISHED BY NARENDRA PRAKASH JAIN FOR
MOTILAL BANARSIDASS PUBLISHERS PRIVATE LIMITED,
BUNGALOW ROAD, DELHI 110 007

CONTENTS

PREFACE TO THE FOURTH EDITION

The third edition (wrongly printed as Second edition) of the Second Volume of HOW TO JUDGE A HOROSCOPE, dealing with Houses 7 to 12 was sold out within hardly a year after its publication, thanks to the keen interest evinced by the educated public in my writings on astrology.

The fourth edition herewith presented has been thoroughly revised and some paragraphs re-writen.

Credit goes to Motilal Banarsidass for printing out this edition attractively in short time.

It is my hope that the educated public will continue to evince the same interest in my astrological writings, as they have been doing for the past half a century.

Bangalore   B. V. RAMAN
13-12-1991

PREFACE TO SECOND EDITION

The first edition of the second volume of *How to Judge a Horoscope*, dealing with Houses 7 to 12 was sold out within hardly a year after its publication, thanks to the keen interest evinced by the educated public in my writings on astrology.

The second edition herewith presented has been thoroughly revised and some paragraphs re-written.

Credit goes to IBH Prakashana for bringing out this edition attractively, in a short time.

It is my hope that the educated public will continue to evince the same interest in my astrological writings, as they have been doing for the past half a century.

Bangalore   B. V. RAMAN
15–8–1982

PREFACE TO FIRST EDITION

The first edition of the first volume dealing with Houses 1 to 6 was published in 1941. For various reasons not worth mentioning preparation of the second volume had to be delayed all these years until my daughter Gayatri Devi Vasudev came forward a year ago and took up the preparation under my guidance. But for her assistance, the second volume would not have seen the light of day.

The second volume deals with Houses 7 to 12. It can be considered as more important than the first volume because it covers such important matters as marriage, occupation, etc.

The pattern of writing is more or less similar to that adopted in the first volume results of the disposition of the lord of a house in different houses, general combinations bearing on the house, results of different planets occupying the house and the time of fructification of such indications followed by a number of practical illustrations.

In fact the treatment of the seventh and tenth houses is so exhaustive that such details as the possibility and time of marriage, its break-up and re-marriage, nature of wife, her character, disposition, status, number of marriages, etc., have all been dealt with exhaustively.

So far as the tenth house is concerned - it is the pivot of the horoscope—whatever is astrologically possible to indicate the nature of profession in the present political, social and economic set-up has been explained as clearly as possible.

The other houses, *viz.*, eighth (longevity), ninth (general fortune, foreign travels, father, etc.), 11th (financial gains) and 12th (losses, spiritual advancement, etc.) have not been under-rated. They have also received due attention.

In the judgement of a horoscope an astrologer faces many a pitfall. How to overcome such pitfalls and arrive at a judgement have been explained with suitable illustrations.

The book has been illustrated with over 260 charts and is therefore of great practical importance to all those who wish to study astrology.

The first and second volumes covering the entire gamut of predictive astrology, especially in its practical aspect, will be found to be of immense use to all those who are interested in the subject—professors, amateurs and savants

I hope the educated public will extend to this volume the same indulgence it has done to my other writings.

Thanks are due to Messrs. P. N. Kamat and G. K. Ananthram of IBH Prakashana for bringing out this volume attractively.

Bangalore
7–8–1980

B. V. RAMAN

XI

Concerning the Seventh House

The 7th house mainly refers to marriage, wife or husband and marital happiness.

Marriage is a landmark in life. It is an institution founded on love and affection. But it is also a most complicated structure made up of a whole series of heterogeneous subjective and objective factors. Since we are concerned only with the psycho-astrological aspects of marriage, we shall exclude the objective factors of legal and social significance in our study.

Marriage is not an institution for brute sense-gratification. It is not a civil agreement that affects only the parties to it. It is the basis of the family and its dissolution as well as formation is a matter of social interest. It is the mould out of which the future generation comes out.

In our own country, marriage has been considered a sacrament and comprehends the equality of the partner in respect of Dharma (right conduct), Artha (financial position), Kama (sex relations) and Moksha (final emancipation).

Main Considerations

In analysing the Seventh Bhava, due consideration must be given to three important factors, viz., (a) the House, (b) the Lord, and (c) the Karaka, who in this case would be Venus.

There are the secondary considerations also, *viz*, the occupants of the 7th house and the planets associating with the 7th lord.

Results of the Seventh House Occupying Different Houses

In the First House : —The native may marry someone he has known since childhood or one who has been brought up in the same house. The wife or husband of the native will be a stable and mature person. He will be intelligent and capable of weighing the *pros* and *cons*. Afflictions to the 7th lord may entail constant travelling. If the 7th lord and Venus are afflicted, the native may be sensual and seek clandestine relationship with the opposite sex.

In the Second House :—The native will get wealth from women or through marriage. If afflicted, one may earn money through despicable means as trading in flesh, women, not excluding his wife. He may eat food offered at death-ceremonies (shraddha) and wander about seeking such food. If the second house is a dual sign and afflicted, more than one marriage is likely. If a maraka Dasa is on, the native may die during the period of the seventh lord. The person will have a wavering mind and will always be inclined sensually.

In the Third House :—This disposition gives lucky brothers who may live abroad. If afflicted the native may indulge in adultery with a brother's or sister's married partner. Affliction also gives misfortunes to co-borns. Female issues servive.

In the Fourth House :—Gives a lucky and happy married partner with many children and comforts. The native may have the benefit of high academic qualification and own many vehicles. If afflicted, domestic harmony may be spoilt through an immature and mean partner. The native may run into endless problems on account of his conveyances. If severely afflicted by the nodes and other malefics, the native's wife's character becomes questionable.

In the Fifth House :—An early marriage, the partner may hail from an affluent and well-to-do family. The wife or husband will be mature and an advantage to the native. If the 7th lord is weak, there may be no children. If severely afflicted, one may get issues through the adulterous conduct of the wife. If there are both afflictions and benefic influences on the 7th lord, the native may get only female progeny. Trouble to one's office superiors through foreign sources is likely. The native will possess good character.

In the Sixth House :—The native may have two marriages with both partners living. One may marry a cousin such as an uncle's daughter. If badly afflicted and the karaka Venus is also ill-disposed, one may suffer from impotency and many other diseases. The native's wife may be sickly and jealous by nature denying the husband happiness from marriage. If Venus is well placed but the 7th lord is afflicted, the native may suffer from piles. If Venus is weak but not afflicted, one may desert or lose one's married partner through some indiscreet act.

In the Seventh House:—If well placed, the native will have a charming and magnetic personality. Women will flock to him and seek him out for alliance. The wife or husband will be a just and honourable person coming from a family of reputation and social standing. If weak and afflicted, it gives a lonely life devoid of marriage and friends, and loss through marriage negotiations.

In the Eighth House :—When well placed, marriage may take place with relatives or the partner may be a rich person. Affliction causes the early death of partner while the native may die in distant lands. It gives a sickly and ill-tempered wife or husband leading to estrangement and separation.

In the Ninth House :—If fortified, the father may live abroad while the native may make his fortune in foreign lands. He will get an accomplished wife who will enable him to lead a righteous life. If afflicted, the father may die early. Married partner may drag the native from the right course (Dharmic) of life and he may waste away his wealth and suffer penury.

In the Tenth House :—The native may flourish in a profession abroad or his career may involve constant travelling. One will get a devoted and faithful wife or husband. The wife may also be employed and contribute to the native's income. Or, she may help in the advancement of the native's career. If afflicted, wife will be avaricious and over-ambitious but without sufficient capacity. Consequently native's career may suffer and deteriorate.

In the Eleventh House :—There may be more than one marriage or the native may associate with many women. If beneficially disposed, wife may hail from a rich background or bring in much wealth. If afflicted, the native may marry more than once, but one wife may outlive him.

In the Twelfth House :—There may be more than one marriage in the native's life. He may marry a second time clandestinely while the first wife is still alive. Or, if afflicted, he may marry a second time after losing the first wife by death or separation. But if the affliction is severe, the wife or husband may die or separate soon after marriage and there may be no second marriage. Death may occur while travelling or abroad. If both karaka and the 7th lord are weak, the native may only dream of women but never marry. The native's wife may hail from a servant's family. He will be close-fisted and generally poor.

These results occur if the 7th lord is placed in the different Bhavas. But they must not be applied literally to charts without considering the entire chart as a whole after assessing the strengths and weaknesses of the several planets.

Important Combinations

We give below important combinations on the seventh house drawn from standard and authoritative works.

If the 7th Bhava reckoned from the Lagna or the Moon be occupied or aspected by the 9th lord, or sign-lord or other benefics, marriage will be happy and the wife, a loving and fortunate woman. The 2nd, 7th and 12th lords in kendras (quadrants) or trikonas (trines), aspected by Jupiter, can ensure a happy marriage and a fertile wife. If benefics are placed in the 2nd, the 7th and the 11th houses from the 7th lord, the wife or husband will be able to derive all happiness with healthy and lucky children. If Mars and Saturn are in the 7th in Capricorn, the wife will be chaste, beautiful and lucky.

If the 7th lord and Venus are in even signs, if the 7th house is also an even sign and the 5th and 7th lords are not combust or otherwise weak, the person will have a good wife and children. If Jupiter occupies the 7th house, the native will be devoted to his wife. If Venus be in exaltation or own vargas or has attained Gopura or Vaiseshikamsa, the wife will be good and beautiful. If the 7th house be a benefic sign or if Venus as 7th lord be aspected by a benefic planet, the wife or husband will be devoted and charming.

If there are malefics in the 4th, 8th and 12th houses from Venus, or Venus is hemmed in between malefics, the wife will die soon after marriage. If there are malefics in the 7th from Venus, the marriage will be unhappy. Venus in the 7th for Taurus Ascendant threatens death to wife.

If the 7th lord is in the 5th or the 5th lord is in the 7th. the native may not marry, as if he gets married, childless. When the 2nd and 7th houses in the case of men and the 7th and 8th houses in the case of women are occupied or aspected by malefics, the loss of wife or husband happens. If the 5th or 8th lord is in the 7th, death of wife or husband occurs. Malefics in the 12th, 7th and Ascendant with the weak Moon in the 5th deny marriage or children. If the Moon and Venus are in opposition to Mars and Saturn, marriage is denied.

The Moon and Saturn in the 7th in a woman's chart indicates remarriage while in a man's chart, they deny marriage or progeny. Malefics in the 2nd, 7th and 8th from Lagna result in demise of married partner. The Sun and Rahu in the 7th cause loss of wealth through women.

Mercury in the 7th in Taurus or Jupiter in the 7th in Capricorn or Saturn and Mars in the 7th in Pisces are injurious to the life of the married partner. Mercury and Ketu in Lagna give a sickly wife Saturn and Mercury in the 7th indicate a widow or widower for a life-partner. If the Moon occupies the 7th house in a malefic sign or Navamsa, the wife will be wicked, mean and similar to a menial. If a strong Moon be in the 7th, the wife will be good. Ketu in the 7th gives a shrew for a wife while Rahu gives an outcaste woman.

If the 6th, 8th and 9th houses be conjoined with malefics and be also aspected by malefics, the wife of the native will indulge in adultery. If Saturn is in the 7th, or if the lord of the Navamsa occupied by the 7th lord be a malefic, or if the 7th lord or Venus be in a depression Rasi or Navamsa, the wife will be a wicked woman.

If weak and afflicted Venus be in the 7th house, the wife may be barren or the husband may be impotent. If Mars with a malefic occupies the 7th house, the native may suffer impotency caused by urinary problems. If Saturn and Venus occupy the 10th or 8th and receive no benefic aspects, the person will be impotent. If Saturn in a watery sign occupies the 6th and 12th houses and is devoid of benefic aspects, the native will be a eunuch. The following planetary positions cause one to be impotent :

1. Saturn in depression in the 6th or 12th house.

2. Saturn in the 6th or the 8th house from Venus.

3. The Moon in an even sign and Mercury in an odd sign and both being aspected by Mars.

4. If the Lagna, Venus and the Moon occupy odd Navamsas.

5. If Mars is in an even sign and the Lagna is in an odd sign.

6, The Sun and the Moon, Mars and the Sun, and Saturn and Mercury—if each of these planets of a pair is in an odd and even sign mutually aspecting.

7. If the 7th lord and Venus are in the 6th house.

If the 7th lord or Venus be conjoined with Rahu or Ketu and be aspected by a malefic, the native or his wife will be adulterous. If Venus occupies a Navamsa of Saturn or Mars and is aspected by Mars or Saturn respectively, the native's character will be questionable. If Saturn or Mars aspect Venus in the 7th house, the native will indulge in adultery. If Saturn, the Moon and Mars occupy the 7th house, both the native and his wife will be immoral. If the 2nd, 7th and the 10th lords occupy the 7th, the native will be a profligate.

If the Moon or Venus moving towards depressions be in a kendra in a cruel shashtiamsa and be aspected by or conjoined with a malefic, the native may commit adultery with his own mother. The same result occurs if the luminaries conjoined in kendras be aspected by or associated with malefics. The 4th house very badly afflicted causes similar results.

If Saturn in the 4th house be afflicted, the native will commit incest. If the afflicted Moon or Venus be in the 9th house, the native will violate his teacher's bed. The 9th lord and the Moon or Venus similarly afflicted give the same result. If Gulika with a malefic occupies the 7th house, or if the Sun be in the 7th house and Mars in the 4th, or if Mars be in the 4th with Rahu in the 7th, or if the 7th lord aspected by Venus occupy a sign of Mars, or if malefics occupy 3 of the kendras, the native's sexual behaviour will be coarse and crude like an animal's.

If the 2nd and 7th lords occupy their depression signs and benefics are placed in kendras and trikonas, only one marriage is possible. If Jupiter and Mercury are in Navamsas owned by the Sun and Mars, only one marriage is indicated. If Mercury in the 7th house occupies a Navamsa of Jupiter, the native will marry only once.

If the 7th lord and Venus be each in a common sign or Navamsa, the person will marry at least twice. If Mercury or Saturn be in the 7th with two planets in the 11th, two wives are possible. If the 7th lord be Saturn and conjoined with a malefic, the person will have many wives. Three or more malefics in the 7th, or Venus in depression, eclipsed or inimical sign with a malefic, or 8th lord in the 1st or the 7th, or the Lagna lord in the 6th, or a malefic in the 7th while the 7th lord with a benefic is in his inimical or depression sign, or the 2nd lord in the 6th and a malefic in the 7th give two wives or more.

If the 2nd, 1st and 6th lords be conjoined with malefics, in the 7th house, or if the strong 7th lord occupy a kendra or kona aspected by the 10th lord, or if the strong 7th and 11th lords conjoin or mutually aspect or occupy trines, the native will have many wives.

If the 1st or 7th lord be in depression or occupy an inimical sign or be eclipsed in Navamsa, the native will have another wife while the first is still living. If the 7th lord be weak and the 7th house be aspected or occupied by a malefic, or if malefics occupy the 7th and 8th houses and Mars is in the 12th house, or if the 2nd lord be weak while the 2nd house is occupied or aspected by a malefic, the native will have another wife during the lifetime of the first wife.

Planets in the 7th House

The Sun :—The native will be fair and have thining hair. He will have few friends and finds difficulty in getting along with people. Marriage is delayed and troubled. Fond of travelling, he will have loose morals. He likes foreign things. His wife's character will be questionable and the native will run the risk of loss and disgrace through women. He will incur the displeasure of the Government and suffer humiliation. He will be deformed.

The Moon—The native will be passionate and easily roused to jealousy. Mother may die while the native is young. Wife will be good-looking but the native will seek other women. Narrow-minded but sociable, he will be energetic and successful in life. He hails from a good family if the Moon is waxing and otherwise strong. He will suffer pain in the groins. He will be stingy. If the Moon is waning, he will always be quarrelling with his enemies.

Mars :—The native will be hen-pecked by his wife and submissive to women. Married life will have clashes and tensions or there may be two wives. The native will be rash and indulge in speculation. He will be intelligent, tactless, stubborn, peevish and unsuccessful.

Mercury :—A man of virtue and geniality, he will dress well and tastefully. He will have profound knowledge of law. He will be skilled in business and trade tactics. He will have writing ability and success through it early in life. Early marriage to a rich woman. Learned in mathematics, astrology and astronomy, he will be religious and of a devout temperament. Diplomatic but if afflicted, the native will be cunning and deceitful. He will have a good physique and looks.

Jupiter :—Diplomatic and kind-hearted the native gets a virtuous, good-looking and chaste wife. He will get good education and gains through marriage. He will be sensitive to others' feelings. He has a speculative mind and is a good agriculturist. He undertakes pilgrimages to distant places and is superior to father in his qualities. The native will possess good sons.

Venus :—Fond of quarrelling, sensuous and passionate, the native has unhealthy habits, and a happy marriage and devoted wife. He is fond of pleasure and drink, is suave and charming with winning manners. He has a magnetic personality. He has danger of loss of virility due to disease or excesses. He is successful in partnership with those of the opposite sex.

Saturn :—The native will be under the wife's control. The wife will be ugly or hunch-backed. He will have more than one marriage or marriage with a widow, divorcee or one advanced in age. He will be diplomatic and enterprising. He has residence abroad, a stable marriage and political success.

He will get honour and distinction in foreign lands, suffers from colic pains and deafness.

Rahu :—The native brings ill-repute to family, if a female. He will be unconventional and heterodox. He will have affairs with outcaste women or foreigners. His wife suffers from womb disorders. He eats good and rich food, has luxurious habits and suffers from diabetes, ghosts and the supernatural.

Ketu :—The native has an unhappy marriage with a shrewish wife. He is passionate, sinful, lusts after widows. His wife is sickly. The native suffers from cancer in the abdomen or uterus, if a female. He will suffer humiliation and loss of virility.

These results are modified by the aspects and associations received by the planet in the 7th house.

If the Sun is afflicted by Rahu, affairs with women may lead to scandals or loss of money on account of blackmail or similar trouble. If Mars afflicts such a Sun, married life will be strife-ridden and the partners will hate each other. In addition, the native may suffer from blood-pressure and a diseased heart. The body will suffer from excess heat which may result in piles and fistula. If the Moon afflicts the Sun, he may have no marriage at all and suffer from a wretched existence. If Mercury joins the Sun, he will be highly intelligent and tactfully deal with troubles accruing from Government or other sources. If Jupiter aspects or associates with the Sun, the partner may be a highly evolved spiritual soul and guide the native also. If fortified Venus be with the Sun, marriage will be marked by spiritual harmony.

If the Moon be influenced by Jupiter, married life will be smooth and happy. If afflicted Moon be with Jupiter, the native will have intrigues with widows but will put on a noble mask to deceive others. If the Moon be with Venus, it gives skill in dying, textiles, craft but if the same Moon is afflicted, the native may resort to unnatural methods of gratification. If the Moon and Rahu combine in the 7th, life will be intolerable with trouble from ghosts and goblins as well.

The following combinations have worked well in our humble experience.

If Venus combines with Mars and Mercury, the marriage will be stable and harmonious with both partners being successful and distinguished in their occupations. If afflicted, it gives extramarital affairs. It also leads to trouble and controversy due to writing or publishing obscene and degenerate literature. Venus with Saturn gives patience, stability in marriage and skill in dance and drama. If fortified, success on the stage or cinema can also be predicted. If afflicted, trouble through these same sources is likely. Venus and Jupiter give good children and a healthy and happy wife. If afflicted by Rahu or Mars, the native may indulge in immoral relations with preceptor's wife or elderly ladies. Mars and Venus give a weakness for gambling, resorting to dens of pleasure. If afflicted, living through these means and trade in flesh are indicated. If fortified, the partner will be loving but passionate and faithful. If Venus be afflicted by the Sun, the marriage will lack physical attraction, the couple assuming indifferent attitudes

If Saturn is afflicted by the Sun, stability of marriage is threatened. More than one marriage is also likely but this may also prove unsuccessful. Jupiter aspecting Saturn in the 7th gives stability but inner turmoil and resentment between the couple. If Mars afflicts, courts may intervene; or violence, such as suicide or murder, may destroy the marriage, provided of course there are other afflictions. If Saturn is with a waxing or strong Moon, marriage may take place with a widow; but if the Moon is further afflicted, intrigues with servant-maids and widows or an old decrepit, lecherous husband. If strong Saturn is afflicted by Rahu, marriage is with a well-to-do but irrascible, temperamental husband or wife. If Saturn is strong in his own constellation, the partner will later become pious and devoted. If Mercury afflicts Saturn, partner may be cowardly and deceitful; but if Mercury is beneficially disposed, marriage will be with one highly educated, refined and learned.

The mere occurrence of these combinations should not allow one to jump to conclusions. The aspects of other planets, not only as natural benefics or malefics, but also as functional benefics or malefics with reference to the Lagna must be taken into account. The strength and associations of the karaka and of the 7th house and 7th lord from the Moon must also be duly weighed before making an assessment of the quality of marriage.

This is especially so where the chastity of a girl or the question of the faithfulness of the husband is concerned. Such delicate issues must be resolved only after a very careful and diligent scrutiny of both horoscopes.

Time and Fructification of the Results of the Seventh House

The factors governing the Seventh House are (a) the lord, (b) planet or planets aspecting the 7th house, (c) planet or planets occupying the 7th house, (d) planets aspecting the lord of the 7th, (e) planet or planets in association with the lord of the 7th, (f) the lord of the 7th from the Moon; and (g) the karaka of the 7th Bhava.

These factors are capable of influencing the 7th house as lords of the Dasas (main-periods), as lords of Bhuktis (sub-periods) or as lords of the Antaras (sub-sub-periods) or the still minor periods.

The sub-periods of planets, capable of influencing the 7th house in the major periods of planets also capable of influencing the 7th house, produce results pertaining to the 7th house *par excellence* or of great intensity. The sub-periods of planets associated with the 7th house in the major periods of planets not associated with the 7th house can produce results pertaining to the 7th Bhava only to a limited extent. Similarly the Bhuktis of planets, not related to the 7th house in the major periods of planets associating with the 7th, can produce results pertaining to the 7th house only to a limited extent.

Where the 7th lord is involved in a powerful yoga, he is capable of producing in his Dasa or Bhukti, the results of the yoga relating to the 7th house. If the 7th house is severely afflicted, the 7th lord may, in his Dasa or Bhukti, cause destruction of the marriage or make it extremely miserable. If well fortified, it may give a successful, distinguished as well as happy marriage.

Nature of the Results

The general principles enunciated in regard to the six Bhavas in the first volume hold good in judging the seventh Bhava also.

During the Dasa of the 7th lord who is well placed, the native will enjoy the company of his wife and many pleasures with her. He will acquire new and colourful apparel, jewels, furnishings, beds and be healthy and radiant. He may go on pleasures—jaunts, excursions and travel abroad. Auspicious celebrations like marriages and similar festivities will take place during the Dasa.

If the 7th lord is ill-placed and afflicted, the native may suffer separation from his wife. The son-in-law may undergo a period of difficulty and strife. The native may get into trouble through affairs with women of ill-repute and wander about aimlessly. He may be stricken with disease in the private parts and come to grief thereby.

If the 7th lord is well-placed with the Ascendant lord in the 7th, travel abroad will be lucky. The native may prosper abroad and settle there itself. He may marry a lucky woman who will be very helpful. If the 7th lord combines with benefics, he may travel in a luxury-yatch or take up a job as a sea-captain. If the 7th lord is weak, one may be forced to beg in his Dasa. If the Ascendant lord be feeble, the period of the lord of the 7th house can be a maraka. If the Ascendant lord is placed in the 6th, 8th or 12th from Navamsa Lagna, travel in his period may be wearisome and profitless.

When the 7th lord joins the 2nd lord in the 2nd house, his period may fetch much money and wealth through marriage. Or marriage may take place with a working girl. The native may earn money in distant lands through agency and partnership business. If afflicted, the period may cause either the native's or his wife's death. If longevity is good, then since the 2nd and 7th are maraka places, the native may suffer separation from wife and much mental agony. If the 7th lord is in the 8th from Navamsa Lagna, the native's wife may not die but he may instead marry a second wife in some distant place. If the 3rd and the 7th lords combine in the 3rd house, wife may hail from a good family. The wife's father will be a man of fortune. During the sub-period of the 3rd lord, death or danger may befall a brother or sister. It may also give a second marriage. If the malefic influences predominate, the evil is intensified ; otherwise, not much need be feared.

Much travelling is indicated in the period of the 7th lord if he combines with the 4th lord in the 4th house. The native's life will be marked by domestic harmony and many auspicious events like marriages, engagements, etc., may occur. If afflicted, the native's mother may die or pass through a grave crisis. His education will begin paying, mostly in foreign lands. If fortified, he may obtain cars and other vehicles during the period of the 4th lord.

If a fortified lord of the 7th house is placed in the 5th house with the lord of the 5th house, wife and children will be happy and wealthy. If afflicted, children may die or mishps may befall them.   Marital life will suffer and wife may die or separate from the native.   This is specially so if the 7th lord is in the 6th, 8th or 12th from Navamsa Lagna.

If the 5th lord is in the 6th from Navamsa Lagna, children may be hospitalised for illness. If he is in the 12th, trouble through thieves and enemies to children is indicated. If the affliction to the 5th and 7th lords combining in the 5th is very great, children may be murdered. If the 7th lord combines with the 6th lord in the 6th, much evil is indicated.   The wife may suffer disgrace or some prolonged illness. Since the 7th lord is a maraka, it forebodes death or dangers to one's maternal uncle.   Trouble from lawsuits and debts may crop up. The native may lose quite an amount through theft or deceit. If benefics are also there, the evils will be mitigated and troubles may be only of a temporary nature.

The 7th lord in the 7th house with benefics is generally very favourable in his period. The native's life will be marked by a series of festivities and joyous celebrations. Marriage will

take place early in life. Wife will be beautiful with a good
social background. He may ecquire much wealth during this
period as a result of travels abroad. He will meet many influential people and these contacts will be advantageous to his
career. But if afflicted, the native may fall critically ill or suffer
various troubles. The period may bring in humiliation and
threat of being ostracised from society. The 7th lord in the 8th
will confer evil results in his period. The native's partner may
die or have serious health problem. He may get an opportunity
to go abroad but this may only create many difficulties and
problems. He may meet with an accident.

Fortune comes through marriage in the period of the 7th
lord if he is placed in the 9th with the 9th lord. The native
will undertake pilgrimages and give away much money in
charity. There will be an inclination to be pious and virtuous.
He will amass a fortune through just and honest means. He
will acquire property and enjoy every kind of comfort. The
wife will be a noble woman and lead him on the path of
righteousness. His work will prosper abroad. Fame and distinction will follow him. If the 7th lord in the 9th is afflicted,
the wife will lead him astray and away from his duties. He
will harbour ill-will and hatred for others and indulge in wicked
deeds. if the 7th lord is placed in the 6th, 8th or 12th
Navamsa, the evil results are greatly intensified.

If the fortified 7th lord is in the 10th with the 10th lord,
the native will gain much fame and reputation abroad. He will
be known for his generous and charitable instincts. His profession in the period of the 7th lord will flourish well
and he will obtain renown and distinction in his field of activity. His wife will be virtuous and respectable. If the 10th lord

is weak, the results will be quite contrary. If the 11th lord is strong, he will fare well in trade and partnership business. The business may expand well and even spread abroad. The native's elder brother may prosper well. If afflicted, elder brother may suffer losses. If the 7th lord has both benefic and malefic influences, gains from business will be moderate. If the 7th lord is in the 12th house and the karaka is also very weak, marital happiness will be lacking and one may lose one's wife through death or separation. If the 7th lord and Venus be both strong, wife may predecease husband only late in life. The native may go abroad but he will be unhappy there with constant troubles and worries. If the Lagna lord combines with the 7th lord in the 12th house with 12th lord both native and wife may reside abroad in the Dasa of any one of these planets, particularly of the 7th lord. If this combination has malefic afflictions, the native may along with his wife indulge in immoral acts and vicious pastimes. If the combination has benefic influences, the native may take to a life of spiritual discipline in the period of the 7th lord.

Timing Marriage

There are several methods suggested for timing marriage in classical works.

The lord of the sign occupied by the 7th lord or that of the sign occupied by the 7th lord in Navamsa are capable of giving marriage in their Dasas. Venus, the karaka or natural significator of the 7th house, and the Moon can also give marriage in their periods. The strongest of these lords gives marriage in his Dasa. The lord of the 7th house, if he asso- ciates with Venus, can also give marriage in his Dasa or Bhukti. The 2nd lord or the ruler of the sign occupied by the 2nd lord in Navamsa is also capable of conferring marriage in his Dasa. The lords of the 9th and 10th houses are empowered to give marriage in their Dasas if the earlier Dasas are fruitless. Marriage is also possible in the period of the planet with the 7th lord or the planet occupying the 7th house.

Another method is to add the longitude of the lords of the Lagna and 7th house. When Jupiter transits the resultant Rasi or its trines, it is favourable for marriage. The resultant obtained by adding the Moon's longitude to that of the 7th lord or its trines when transited by Jupiter can also give marriage.

Although there are several planets enumerated as marriage causing planets in their periods, due consideration must be paid to delay caused by other factors. Saturn's aspect on the 7th house and 7th lord both from Lagna and the Moon and on Venus delays marriage if the Dasa lord is not very strong. The association or aspect of the lord of the 6th, 8th or 12th on the 7th house, 7th lord and karaka also rules out early marriage. Primary importance must be given to the natal positions and Dasas and only secondary consideration to transiting planets.

Loss of Married Partner

Loss of wife and more particularly of the husband is of serious consequence in our society. Besides the emotional void created by the death of either partner, many other factors of nearly equal significance demand importance. The economical aspect apart, other practical questions such as running the household and bringing up the children arise. As such any horoscope should always be carefully scrutinised for loss of partner.

We shall give below some important combinations pertaining to loss of married partner and afflictions to married life culled from authoritative sources.

If the 2nd as well as the 7th house are occupied by malefic planets, death of wife occurs. But if the person concerned marries a woman with similar planetary afflictions, the mutual afflictions get neutralised and the couple will be blessed with children and prosperity.

If the 5th or the 7th house from the Ascendant or the Moon is occupied or aspected by a malefic, the native may not marry or if he marries, his wife may not live. If the Sun occupies Virgo which happens to be the Ascendant and Saturn occupies the 7th house, wife will die. If the 7th house is occupied by Mars, the wife will die. If the 7th lord from the Ascendant as well as Venus be fortified and occupy the 7th house and if the 7th house be strong and not afflicted, by aspect or association, by malefic planets, the wife and husban will die at the same time. If the 7th house has *karmuka* (an upagraha), either the native or his wife will die early.

If the 2nd and the 7th lords be associated with Venus or malefic planets and be badly placed, there will be loss of one or more wives depending upon the number of planets with them in *dusthana*. If Mars is in the 7th house in a Navamsa of Venus and if the 7th lord is in the 5th house, the native will lose his wife. If Venus and Mars conjoin in the 7th, the native will be bereft of wife. If the 1st, 7th and 12th houses be occupied by malefics and the weak Moon occupies the 5th, the native will have no wife or marry a barren woman. If Mars occupy the 2nd, the 12th, the 4th, the 8th or the 7th house, the native will lose, by death, his married partner.

Other Afflictions

If the 1st or the 7th house be occupied by the Moon in

depression with Rahu or Ketu or in a malefic drekkana such as Sarpa, Pakshi, Pasa or Nigada or in a Rasi-sandhi (junction of two signs), the native's wife will either go astray or be widowed. If the 7th house from Lagna in the case of men be a sign ruled by Mars or in an Amsa of Mars and if the 7th lord from the Navamsa Lagna be weak or with Rahu or Ketu, the wife will be rejected by the native, and she may become unchaste even when young. In the case of women if the Lagna be owned by Mars or in a Navamsa of Mars and if the 7th lord in Navamsa be afflicted as stated above, the native will be a servant-maid or go astray even as a girl and be rejected by her husband.

If the 7th house be occupied by malefics, the native will become a widow. If there be both malefics and benefics in the 7th house, she will marry a second time. If the 7th house be occupied by a weak malefic but aspected by a benefic, the native will be repudiated by her husband. If the 7th house be a malefic sign occupied by Saturn, the native will be widowed. If a malefic planet occupying a malefic sign representing the 8th house be aspected by a malefic planet at the same time, it results in the death of husband. If in addition to this the lord of the Navamsa occupied by the 8th lord is also a malefic the affliction becomes more intensified. If there are benefic planets in the 8th house, the native will predecease her husband. If malefics occupy the 7th or the 8th house and benefic planets occupy the 9th house, the native will live in happiness with her husband for a long time.

If the 7th and 8th lords join in the 8th house; if Rahu occupies the 7th house while the 7th lord is with the Sun aspected by 8th lord; or if Rahu conjoins Saturn and Mars in the 7th or 8th house, widowhood is denoted early in life.

If the 7th and 8th lords conjoin in the 12th house and the 7th house is aspected by malefics, it also leads to widowhood, If the 7th house and the 7th lord be subject to *papakartari yoga*, that is, being hemmed inbetween malefic planets, without any benefic influence, the result is loss of husband.

If Venus and Mars exchange their Navamsa positions, the native will be inclined to extra-marital relations. If Venus, Mars and the Moon occupy the 7th house, she will associate with other men with her husband's connivance. When the Ascendant is ruled by Saturn or Mars and Moon or Venus aspected by a malefic occupies it, the native and her mother will both indulge in harlotry. When Venus and Saturn occupy each other's Navamsas or aspect each other mutually, if the Ascendant in Cancer falls in Aquarius in Navamsa, the native will be highly lustful.

Summing up, the periods of the planets related to the 7th house in Rasi or Navamsa, or of Venus, or of the planets related to the 2nd house in Rasi or Amsa, or of the 9th or 10th lords or of the Moon, subject to other factors, are capable of giving marriage. Beneficial influences on the 7th house or its lord give happiness in marriage while afflictions by malefic planets cause misery, death or separation in marriage. The 7th house or Venus in dual signs gives more than one marriage.

The 7th House : The 7th house in Chart No. 1 is Pisces occupied by 5th and 6th lord Saturn. Saturn's presence as a malefic is not good causing affliction.

The Seventh Lord : The lord of the 7th, Jupiter, is in the 4th house in the 10th kendra from the 7th house. He is aspected by karaka Venus and malefic Saturn. Jupiter occu

Chart No. 1.—*Born 16-8-1937 at 8-31 a.m. (I.S.T) at 13° N, 77 E 35.*

Saturn		Ketu	Venus		Sun Venus		Ketu

Saturn		Ketu	Venus
	RASI		Sun Merc
	G I-10		
Jupiter	Mars Rahu Moon		Lagna

		Sun Venus	Ketu
Lagna		NAVAMSA	
Moon			
Jupit Merc. Rahu		Mars Saturn	

Balance of Mercury Dasa at birth : 6 years, 0 months and 8 days.

pies his moolatrikona sign Sagittarius both in Rasi and Navamsa. But in Navamsa he is afflicted by Rahu and exalted Saturn.

Kalatrakaraka : Venus as 2nd and 9th lord is beneficially disposed in a friendly sign in a quadrant. He is aspected by a benefic as well as 7th lord Jupiter and by Mars, a malefic being the 3rd and 8th lord. Venus is slightly blemished but quite fortified by Jupiter's aspect.

Considered from the Moon : The 7th house is Taurus, a benefic sign, aspected by the Moon and Mars and occupied by Ketu. Mars, by himself, would not be a malefic but his association with the Moon and Rahu afflicts him. The 7th lord Venus is quite favourably disposed as analysed above.

Conclusion : The 7th house is quite strongly disposed but the malefic influences are not negligible. The strength of the 7th lord Jupiter gives a strong-willed husband while the

Moon with Mars and Rahu makes the native self-willed. The afflictions result in temperamental clashes but the presence of Saturn in the 7th and Jupiter and Venus in mutual aspect result in a stable marriage with deep attachment between the couple.

Saturn's presence in the 7th house as the 6th lord causes delay in marriage. The Dasas operating during the period of marriageable age and after are of Venus, the Sun, the Moon, Mars and Rahu.

Recollecting the periods propitious for marriage, (1) the lords of the Rasi and Navamsa occupied by the 7th lord, (2) Venus, (3) the Moon, (4) the lord of sign occupied by the 2nd lord, (5) the 10th and (6) 9th lords and finally, (7) the 7th lord or occupant of the 7th house can give marriage in respective order in their periods.

The following planets in Chart No. 1 would therefore be empowered to give marriage in their periods :—

1. The lords of the Rasi and Navamsa occupied by the 7th lord—Jupiter, Jupiter
2. Venus
3. The Moon
4. The lord of the sign occupied by 2nd lord Venus— Mercury
5. The 10th lord—Mercury
6. The 9th lord—Venus
7. The 7th lord—Jupiter, the 7th occupant – Saturn, and the planet aspecting the 7th house—none.

The native's Mercury Dasa ends in childhood. The next Dasa that can give marriage is of Venus. Jupiter Dasa and Saturn Dasa operate very late in life. The Moon's period also comes rather late in life. Saturn in the 7th, no doubt, delays marriage but the strength of karaka Venus and 7th lord Jupiter cannot push it off too far. Venus would, therefore, be empowered to give marriage in his Dasa. Of the sub-periods of Venus, Jupiter, Saturn, Mercury and the Moon, Venus would be ruled out as being too early. Jupiter is the strongest of the remaining four contestants both by aspect, position anb lordship. Marriage occurred in Jupiter Bhukti, Venus Dasa in April 1961.

Early or delayed marriage is determined according to the times. At one time in India, marriages were celebrated of boys and girls at the tender age of 5 or 6 years. Later, as times changed marriages were celebrated a little later, perhaps at 10 or 12 years. In the 1960's, marriage at 25 was considered delayed while today it would be quite in order. Interpretation of a chart must always be made keeping in mind the background, period and society to which the native belongs.

The Seventh House : The 7th house Aquarius is occupied by Vargottama Ketu in Chart No. 2. It is aspected by 7th lord Saturn, benefic Jupiter and 4th and 9th lord, Yogakaraka, Mars. Saturn is 7th lord and his aspect on the 7th is a stabilising factor. Jupiter and Mars are functional benefics and their aspects fortify the 7th house. Ketu should give the results of sign dispositor Saturn or of Mars, both of whom are beneficially disposed. The 7th house has no afflictions.

The Seventh Lord : The 7th lord Saturn is placed in the 10th house in a benefic sign Taurus hemmed inbetween benefics, the Moon on one side and Jupiter and Venus on the other. The 7th lord is well placed.

Kalatrakaraka : Venus is in a friendly sign very close to benefic Jupiter and subject to a slight *papakaratri yoga* caused by Saturn and the Sun. But this malefic yoga is balanced by Jupiter's presence and the fact the Sun and Saturn are but the

Chart No. 2.—*Born 3-8-1942 at 7-23 a.m. (I.S.T.) at 13° N, 77 E 35.*

	Moon	Saturn	Jupit. Venus		Jupiter Venus	Lagna	Mars Moon Saturn
Ketu			Sun Merc.	Ketu			
	RASI		Lagna Mars Rahu		NAVAMSA		Rahu
	G 1-16			Sun Merc			

Balance of Ketu Dasa at birth : 2 years and 7 months.

Lagna and 7th lords respectively being, therefore, benefic to the Bhava and karaka concerned.

The 7th lord being free from afflictions and in a benefic sign gives a good-looking wife with respect for conventions indicated by Saturn. The 7th house having no afflictions gives a happy married life. Ketu, fortified in the 7th, is good but nevertheless gives some points of difference due to the wife's sensitivity in some matters.

As for the period of marriage, it occurred in August 1972 in the Moon Dasa, Moon Bhukti. (1) Venus and Mercury, (2) Venus, (3) the Moon, (4) the Moon, (5) Venus, (6) Mars, (7) Saturn, Ketu and Mars can give marriage in their periods. Ketu and Venus Dasas end early in life. Mercury Dasa does not operate at all. Mars and Saturn come rather late. Saturn's aspect on the 7th cannot delay marriage as he happens to be the 7th lord himself. Therefore, the Moon Dasa becomes effective. So also the Moon Bhukti.

Chart No. 3.—*Born 3/4-12-1953 at 5-17 a.m. (I.S.T.) at 13° N, 77 E 35.*

		Jupit.
	RASI	Ketu
Rahu		
Lagna Venus Sun	Saturn Moon Mercury	Mars

Moon		Mercury
Rahu	NAVAMSA	Lagna
Sat.		Venus Ketu
Sun	Jupiter	Mars

Balance of Jupiter's Dasa at birth : 14 years, 1 month and 20 days.

The Seventh House : Venus, the 7th lord, and the Sun, the 10th lord aspect the 7th house in Chart No. 3. There are no planets in the seventh house itself.

The Seventh Lord : Venus the 7th lord is placed in the Lagna with 10th lord the Sun. The Sun as a malefic but ruler of the 10th house, a kendra, becomes a functional benefic.

Kalatrakaraka : Venus is not only the 5th lord but also the natural significator of the 7th house. He is well disposed with 10th lord the Sun aspecting the 7th house.

Considered from the Moon : The 7th house is Aries aspected by 10th lord the Moon, 9th and 12th lord Mercury, Yogakaraka exalted Saturn and 7th lord Mars. The aspect of Mars as 7th lord is good but being from the 12th gives some moments of touchiness. However the combined aspect of exalted Saturn and 9th lord Mercury is powerful enough to ward off any problems.

Conclusions : The native is married to a chaste and devoted wife. This is particularly evident from the aspect of a blemishless Venus as karaka and 7th lord aspecting the 7th house.

The native married in May 1977. The following planets are capable of giving marriage in their periods : —

(1)   The lords of the Rasi and Navamsa occupied by the 7th lord Mars and the Sun

(2)   Venus

(3)   The Moon

(4)   The lord of the sign occupied by the 2nd lord Jupiter *viz.,* Mercury

(5)   The 10th lord the Sun

(6)   The 9th lord the Moon

(7)   The 7th lord Venus, no planets occupy the 7th, and the Sun as the planet aspecting the 7th house.

Of these factors Mercury would seem appropriate since all other Dasas begin very late. But Mercury Dasa itself begins rather late in life, that is, after 33 years. The chart has no indications for a late marriage. So, the planets in association with Mercury, that is, the Moon and Saturn would be the next choice. The Moon Dasa operates very late while Saturn Dasa occurs during youth. Saturn would therefore be capable of giving marriage. Venus Bhukti can be fruitful since he is the karaka as also the 7th lord aspecting the 7th and well placed. Marriage occurred in Venus Bhukti, Saturn Dasa.

The Seventh House : The 7th house in Chart No. 4 is Pisces occupied by the 11th lord Moon and Rahu. It is aspected by the 5th and 6th lord, malefic Saturn and another

Chart No. 4.—*Born 20-11-1950 at 3 a.m. (I.S.T.) at 18 N 55, 72 E 54.*

				Sat.		Lagna	
Moon Rahu							
Jupiter	RASI			NAVAMSA			Rahu
							Sun
	G I-84			Ketu			
Mars	Sun Venus Mercury		Ketu Sat Lagna	Merc. Jupit. Mcon			Mars Venus

Balance of Mercury Dasa at birth : 13 years, 7 months and 6 days.

malefic Mars, the 3rd and the 8th lord. There are no benefic influences on the 7th house which is considerably afflicted.

The Seventh Lord : The lord of the 7th house is Jupiter placed in a dusthana, *viz.,* the 6th house. He is aspected by no planet.

Kalatrakaraka : Venus is with the 12th lord Sun and Lagna lord Mercury aspected by malefic Saturn. He gets no beneficial influence and is quite afflicted.

Considered from the Moon : The 7th house is Virgo occupied by malefic Saturn and Ketu. The 7th lord Mercury is slightly better placed being with karaka but malefic 3rd and 8th lord Venus and 6th lord the Sun. The 7th house from the Moon also suffers affliction.

Conclusion : The native was married in September 1972 in Venus Dasa, Venus Bhukti. Applying the principles of

timing marriage this is quite in order. In August 1973 discord
between the native and her husband began. The couple separated in June 1974. Rahu and the Moon in the 7th are afflicted by Mars and Saturn, two powerful malefics for Virgo
Ascendant, causing the husband to dissipate his energies in
extra-marital affairs with women of ill-repute. All factors
relating to the 7th house being afflicted with no redeeming
beneficial influences deprived the native completely of any
marital happiness.

The Seventh House : The seventh house is occupied by
Ketu and aspected adversely by Mars in Chart No. 5. Mars as
5th lord is a benefic but he is in the 12th house aspecting the
7th house by his 8th house aspect which is very bad.

Chart No. 5.—*Born 8-10-1935 at 11-30 a.m. (I.S.T.)
at 13 N 10, 76 E 10.*

			Ketu			Lagna Ketu	
Saturn		RASI		Mars	NAVAMSA		Sun
Moon			Venus	Sat. Merc.			Venus
		GII-176					
Lagna Rahu	Mars Jupiter	Mercury	Sun		Rahu		Moon

Balance of Mars Dasa at birth : 4 years, 11 months and
20 days.

The Seventh Lord : Mercury is the lord of the 7th house
and is in the 11th house in a friendly sign but between malefics the Sun and Mars.

Kalatrakaraka : Venus is in the 9th house in an inimical sign aspected by malefic Saturn and with no benefic influences.

Considered from the Moon : The 7th house is Cancer aspected by Jupiter. The 7th lord Moon is hemmed inbetween malefics, Saturn and Rahu. The seventh is afflicted except for the aspect of Jupiter on the 7th from the Moon.

Conclusion : The aspect of Mars on the 7th house occupied by Ketu has resulted in violent clashes in married life. The 7th house from Venus is occupied by a malefic Saturn depriving happiness in married life. Only Jupiter's aspect on the 7th house from the Moon has prevented a complete break-up although life itself is miserable.

Chart No. 6.—*Born 24-3-1883 at 6 a.m. (L.M.T) at 13° N, 77 E 35.*

Lagna Sun	Ketu	Saturn	Jupit.		Mars	Mercury Rahu	Moon	
Mercury Mars								
	RASI					NAVAMSA		
Venus					Sat.			
	NH-48						Ketu Lagna Sun Jupiter	Venus
		Rahu	Moon					

Balance of the Moon Dasa at birth : 6 years.

The Seventh House : The seventh house is Virgo in Chart No. 6. It is a dual sign, occupied by benefic 5th lord the Moon and aspected by 2nd and 9th lord Mars from the 12th house

and by 6th lord the Sun. The 7th house is blemished except
for the Moon's presence.

The Seventh Lord :   Mercury, the 7th lord, is with Mars
in the 12th house aspected by Lagna lord Jupiter and 10th
and 11th lord Saturn.

Kalatrakaraka :   Venus is in the 11th house in a friendly
sign.

Considered from the Moon :   The 7th house is a dual sign
occupied by 12th lord the Sun. It is hemmed inbetween Mars
and Ketu. The 6th lord Jupiter is in the 10th in a common
sign.

Conclusion :   The presence of karaka Venus in the 11th
house, a common sign as the 7th house both from Lagna and
the Moon, and the 7th lord Jupiter in another dual sign
resulted in two marriages. Married life was unhappy.

Contrast this with Chart No. 1 where the 7th lord Jupiter
and Venus are in dual signs but where the native had only one
marriage. Jupiter is the 7th lord and Venus is the karaka.
Mutual aspects between the two planets have kept the
marriage going.

The Seventh House :   The Lagna being Taurus, Scorpio
is the 7th house in Chart No. 7. It is aspected by no planet
and is free ef affliction.

The Seventh Lord :   The lord of the 7th house Mars is in
a benefic sign with Ketu aspected by the Moon and Jupiter.

Kalatrakaraka :   Venus, the Kalatrakaraka, is in a dual
sign aspected by Yogakaraka Saturn. He is in the 8th house, a
dusthana.

Considered from the Moon :   The 7th house is Libra occupied by Moon-sign lord Mars and aspected by Jupiter. The 7th
lord Venus is in a dual sign in the 9th aspected by malefic
10th and 11th lord Saturn.

Chart No. 7.—*Born on 12-2-1856 at about 12-21 p.m. (L.M.T.) at 18 N, 84 E.*

	Moon Rahu	Lagna	Sat.		Lagna Jupiter	Rahu	
Sun Mercury Jupiter	RASI				NAVAMSA		
	NH-29						
Venus		Mars Ketu		Merc.	Ketu	Sun Saturn Venus Mars	Moon

Balance of Venus Dasa at birth : 12 years, 3 months and 9 days.

Conclusion : Due to the occupation of Venus as 7th lord and as Kalatrakaraka of common sign, the native married a second time after the death of the first. Both marriages were fairly happy. The 7th lord Mars' association with Ketu gives tiffs between partners and a touchy wife. Saturn in the 7th from Venus is not so harmful as he would ordinarily be because he is a Yogakaraka. Jupiter's aspect on the 7th lord Mars was also responsible for a fair degree for happiness in married life. The position of Mars, lord of the 7th and Ketu in the 6th (12th from the 7th) is also significant.

The Seventh House : Leo the 7th house is occupied by 3 planets, *viz.,* Mars, Mercury and Venus in Chart No. 8. The 7th house is fortified by 9th lord Venus and 5th and 8th lord Mercury. Mars blemishes it slightly.

The Seventh Lord : The lord of the 7th house the Sun is in the 6th, a dusthana, but aspected by Lagna lord Saturn and the 2nd and the 11th lord Vargottama Jupiter (Jupiter occupies the same sign in Rasi and Navamsa).

Kalatrakaraka : Venus is in the 7th house with Mars and Mercury.

Considered from the Moon : The 7th house Scorpio is occupied by Vargottama Jupiter and aspected by 7th lord

Chart No. 8.—*Born on 8-8-1912 at 7-35 p.m. (I.S.T.) at 13° N, 77 E 30.*

Rahu		Moon Saturn			Saturn	Venus	

Rasi chart:

Rahu		Moon Saturn	
Lagna	RASI		Sun
			Mars Mero. Venus
	Jupiter		Ketu

Navamsa chart:

	Saturn	Venus	
Sun Rahu	NAVAMSA		
			Mercury Moon Ketu
Lagna	Jupiter	Mars	

Balance of Mars Dasa: 6 years, 1 month and 6 days.

Mars and Yogakaraka Saturn. The 7th lord Mars is with the Moon-sign lord and benefic 5th lord Mercury. These factors fortify the 7th house.

Conclusion : The native is happily married to a devoted and chaste wife with religious propensities. Compare Chart No. 8 with Chart No. 7. Both have the 7th lord in the 6th aspected by a functional benefic Jupiter. In Chart No. 7, Kalatrakaraka and 7th lord from the Moon, Venus, is in a dual sign. In Chart No. 8, Kalatrakaraka Venus is in the 7th house with two other planets. Yet the native of Chart No. 8 has had only one marriage and a stable one. This is because, Venus, although, as karaka in the 7th, is not good, here in this case the stigma is countered by Venus being Yogakaraka. Further he is in a fixed sign indicating fixity of affections. The 7th lord is aspected by Lagna lord Saturn. From the Moon also, the combination of Moon-sign lord Venus and Mars in Leo is desirable. Mars as 7th lord aspecting the 7th house protects it.

Chart No. 9.—*Born on 3-11-1940 at 7-00 a.m. (E.S.T.) at 35 N 44, 81 W 21.*

Ketu	Jupiter Saturn			Sun	Venus Lagna		Rahu Moon
	RASI GII-54				NAVAMSA		
Moon	Mercury	Sun Lagna	Mars Venus Rahu	Ketu			Mars Mercury Saturn Jupiter

Balance of Ketu Dasa : 2 years, 7 months and 18 days.

The Seventh House : Aries is the seventh house in Chart No. 9 occupied by Yogakaraka but debilitated Saturn and 3rd and 6th lord Jupiter. The 7th lord Mars aspects the 7th from the 12th house. Debilitated Sun as 11th lord aspects the 7th house.

The Seventh Lord : Mars as the 7th lord is with Rahu and Lagna lord Venus is in the 12th house in a dual sign.

Kalatrakaraka : Venus is in the 12th house with Mars and Rahu.

Considered from the Moon : The 7th house Gemini is aspected by debilitated Saturn while the 7th lord himself is in the 12th from the Moon-sign. There are no benefic aspects on the 7th house.

Conclusion : The position of two natural enemies, the Sun and Saturn, across the Lagna and the 7th house leads to stiff opposition or conflicts between married partners. Venus and Mars, as Lagna and 7th lord, are together but with Rahu. This gives physical attraction between the couple but the malefic influences make harmony difficult. Jupiter although in the 7th is the 6th lord and not very helpful. From the Moon, the 1st and 7th lords are mutually adversely placed. This chart belongs to a woman who married in 1961 and separated from her husband in 1964. The marriage while it lasted was not at all happy.

Chart No. 10.—*Born 13-3-1948 at 10-30 a.m. (I.S.T.) at 11 N 06, 79 E 42.*

Sun Moon	Venus Rahu	Lagna		Lagna Mars Moon	Ketu Jupiter	
Mercury	RASI		Mars Sat.	Sat.	NAVAMSA	Sun
	GII-4					Venus
Jupiter		Ketu			Rahu Mercury	

Balance of Mercury Dasa : 3 years, 9 months and 27 days.

The Seventh House : Scorpio is the 7th house in Chart No. 10 aspected by no planet.

The Seventh Lord : Mars as lord of the 7th house is in the 3rd house in debilitation. He is with Yogakaraka Saturn.

Kalatrakaraka : Venus is in the 12th, a malefic house, with Rahu and aspected by Saturn, rendered malefic by association with debilitated Mars. Venus is aspected by 8th lord Jupiter.

Considered from the Moon : The 7th house is Virgo, aspected by 6th lord the Sun and a malefic Saturn. The 7th lord Mercury is in the 12th from the Moon aspected by a malefic Mars. There are no benefic influences on the 7th lord or 7th house.

Conclusion : The native was deserted by her husband three days after marriage. He was found to be a characterless cheat and debauchee. The association of 7th lord Mars with Yogakaraka Saturn gave a well-to-do and socially well-placed partner but the debility of Mars made him debased.

The Seventh House : Pisces being the 7th receives no aspects, benefic or malefic, in Chart No. 11.

The Seventh Lord : Jupiter, the 7th lord, is in the 9th house aspected by Mars, lord of the 3rd and the 8th.

Kalatrakaraka : Venus, Kalatrakaraka, is well placed in the 4th with Lagna lord Mercury and 12th lord Sun. Jupiter and Venus have exchanged signs (parivartana), mutually benefiting each other.

Considered from the Moon : The Moon being in Leo, the 7th house is Aquarius. Seventh lord Saturn is exalted in the 3rd with Yogakaraka Mars. The 7th house from the Moon is free from aspects, malefic or benefic.

Chart No. 11.—*Born 26-12-1953 at 11-47 p.m. (I.S.T) at 10 N 23, 78 E 55.*

		Jupiter			Mercury	Venus
			Ketu	Lagna Sat.		Ketu Sun
	RASI				NAVAMSA	
Rahu			Moon	Rahu Mars		
Sun Venus Mercury	G III-20	Mars Saturn	Lagna	Moon		Jupiter

Balance of Sun Dasa at birth : 5 years, 10 months and 9 days.

Conclusion : The strength of the 7th lord and Kalatra-karaka, Jupiter and Venus respectively, and the blemish-free 7th lords and 7th houses both from Lagna and the Moon have given a happy marriage. The aspect of Mars on Jupiter is toned down by the exaltation of Saturn in a benefic sign and has resulted only in a headstrong but generally pleasant married partner.

The Seventh House : Sagittarius, a benefic sign, rises on the 7th house in Chart No. 12. It is not occupied by any planet. The 7th lord Jupiter aspects it from the 11th house while the 6th and 11th lord Mars, and 5th and 12th lord Venus aspect it from the Lagna. The 7th house is quite fortified.

The Seventh Lord : Jupiter occupies the 11th house with 9th lord Saturn who is debilitated. Venus, the ruler of the sign where Saturn gets exalted, is in a quadrant so that he gets neechabhanga (cancellation of debility).

Chart No. 12.—*Born 21-5-1940 at 7-50 a.m. (I.S.T.) at 13° N, 77 E 30.*

Ketu	Jupiter Saturn	Sun Mercury	Lagna Mars Venus	Venus Merc. Sun			Jupiter
				Ketu			Moon
	RASI				NAVAMSA		Rahu Saturn
	GI-12			Mars			
	Moon		Rahu		Lagna		

Balance of Jupiter Dasa at birth: 1 year, 6 months and 22 days.

Kalatrakaraka : Venus occupies a friendly sign in association with Mars who, as 6th and 11th lord, is a malefic. Venus is aspected by 9th lord Saturn.

Considered from the Moon : The 7th house Taurus is occupied by 8th and 11th lord Mercury and 10th lord Sun. The 7th lord Venus in the 8th is with Moon-sign lord Mars. The 7th is fairly balanced.

Conclusion : There is a preponderance of benefic influences on the 7th house due to the aspect of two benefics, Jupiter and Venus, on it. Venus is not only a benefic lord but also the Kalatrakaraka and so his aspect on the 7th house becomes quite desirable. The aspect of Mars on the 7th is not so welcome since he happens to be the ruler of malefic Bhavas, but his maleficence is kept in check by the aspect of 9th lord neechabhanga Saturn. The native has a happy married life. The aspect of 7th lord Jupiter on the 7th and of Karaka Venus also on it have given the native a devoted wife.

The Seventh House : Cancer, the 7th house, is not occupied or aspected by any planets in Chart No. 13.

The Seventh Lord : The Moon is placed in the 2nd house aspected by Saturn, the Ascendant and 2nd lord, 3rd and 12th lord Jupiter, and 4th and 11th lord Mars afflicted by Rahu.

Chart No. 13.—*Born 16-10-1918 at 2 p.m. (L.M.T.) at 13° N, 77 E 35.*

	Ketu	Jupit.		Jupiter Saturn	
Moon	RASI		Rahu	NAVAMSA	Venus
Lagna		Sat.	Moon		Ketu
Mars Rahu	Sun Mercury	Venus	Mars	Sun Mercury	Lagna

Balance of Rahu Dasa at birth : 11 years, 8 months and 20 days.

Kalatrakaraka : Venus is debilitated in the 9th house. He obtains cancellation of debility by virtue of his sign-dispositor Mercury being in a quadrant from Lagna. He is in parivartana with the 9th lord Mercury. Venus is also subject to a *papakartari yoga.*

Considered from the Moon : The 7th house is occupied by Moon-sign lord Saturn The 7th lord Sun is debilitated in the 9th but obtains concellation of debility due to his exaltation sign-lord Mars being in the 10th from the Moon. The Sun is also Vargottama (occupies the same sign in Rasi and Navamsa) and forms a Budha-Aditya Yoga with Mercury, who as lord of 5th and 8th is Vargottama. The Sun is aspected by Moon-sign lord Saturn and 2nd and 11th lord Jupiter.

Conclusion : The 7th house both from Lagna and the Moon being free of malefic influences gives a happy married life. The *papakartari yoga* caused to Kalatrakaraka Venus is toned down by the Sun and Saturn being the significators of the 7th house (that is, the lords of Lagna and the 7th house from the Moon) and can have no adverse effect on the Bhava or karaka in question. The extremely powerful situation of the 7th lord, particularly from the Moon, has given the native a partner who is not only materially well placed but also held in great reverence for his character, integrity and learning. The Budha-Aditya Yoga relating to the 7th lord has given an intellectual husband while making the native also highly intelligent and learned in her own sphere of activity.

The Seventh House : Gemini being the 7th house is not occupied by any planets in Chart No. 14. It is aspected by the 6th and 11th lord Venus from Lagna.

The Seventh Lord : Mercury, the 7th lord, is in the 11th house with 9th lord the Sun and Rahu. The Lagna and 7th lords are in *dwirdwadasa* (2/12 positions).

Kalatrakaraka : Venus, the natural significator, is in the Lagna in a kendra aspected by 5th and 12th lord Mars.

Considered from the Moon : The 7th house is Leo aspected by Moon-sign lord Saturn, while the 7th lord Sun is debilitated with Mercury and Rahu in the 9th. The Sun gets cancellation of debilitation since his exaltation-sign lord Mars is in a quadrant from Lagna.

Chart No. 14.—*Born 3-11-1957 at 10-20 a.m. (I.S.T.) at 13° N, 77 E 30.*

	Ketu			Rahu Sun		Venus Mercury	Moon
Moon				Mars			
	RASI			———	NAVAMSA		Lagna Jupiter
	G-IV-158			Sat.			
Lagna Venus	Saturn	Sun Mercury Rahu	Mars Jupit.				Ketu

Balance of Jupiter Dasa at birth : 4 years, 4 months and 17 days.

Conclusion : Both from Lagna and Chandra Lagna, the 7th lords are afflicted by Rahu. Further from the Lagna, the 7th lord is in the 11th with Rahu. This results in a husband who was already married to another at the time of marriage with the native. The Sun as 9th lord with 7th lord Mercury gives a partner who is well-off but Rahu's presence makes him immoral. The aspect of Venus on the 7th house is not very helpful since he is a functional malefic for Sagittarius ascendant.

The Seventh House : Pisces, the seventh house, is occupied by 3rd and 8th lord Mars in Chart No. 15. It is not aspected by any planet.

The Seventh Lord : Jupiter, the 7th lord, is in the 9th house with Saturn, the 5th and 6th lord. He is aspected by Lagna lord Mercury and 12th lord, the Sun.

Chart No. 15.—*Born 8-12-1941 at 1-20 a.m. (I.S.T.) at 13° N, 77 E 35.*

Mars		Jupiter Saturn		Lagna	Venus	Ketu
Ketu	RASI		Moon	Mars Sun	NAVAMSA	
Venus	GII-240		Rahu	Sat.		Jupiter
	Sun Mercury		Lagna		Rahu Mercury	Moon

Balance of Saturn Dasa at birth : 13 years, 2 months and 22 days.

Kalatrakaraka : Venus is in the 5th house aspected by 11th lord, the Moon and 7th lord Jupiter.

Considered from the Moon : The 7th house is occupied by Venus, who as 4th and 11th lord, becomes a malefic for Cancer. The 7th house is aspected by Jupiter, the 6th and 9th lord. The 7th lord Saturn is in the 11th with Jupiter.

Conclusion : The 7th lord in the 9th gives a well-placed partner. Saturn's association as 5th and 6th lord gives the partner a rigid and conservative nature while the position of Mars as a malefic lord creates tension and quarrels in married life, largely due to temperamental differences. But the position of Venus and the benefic disposition of Jupiter rule out any major trouble such as separation or divorce in married life.

The Seventh House : The 7th house Leo in Chart No. 16 is aspected by 7th lord the Sun and 2nd and 11th lord Jupiter. The Sun is Vargottama.

Chart No. 16.—*Born 25-2-1953 at 6-54 a.m. (I.S.T.) at 8° N, 29, 76 E 59.*

Venus Mars Mercury	Jupiter		
Lagna Sun	RASI	Moon Ketu	
Rahu	G IV-16		
	Saturn		

Lagna Venus			Rahu
Sun	NAVAMSA		Mercury
Mars			Moon
Ketu	Saturn	Jupiter	

Balance of Saturn Dasa at birth : 18 years and 2 months.

The Seventh Lord : The Sun as 7th lord is strongly placed in a quadrant. He is not aspected by any planet.

Kalatrakaraka : Venus is exalted and Vargottama in the 2nd house. He is with 3rd and 10th lord Mars and 5th and 8th lord Mercury. Mercury is debilitated but gets cancellation of debility due to Jupiter occupying kendra from the Moon.

Considered from the Moon : The 7th house is occupied by Rahu, the 7th lord Saturn is exalted but aspected adversely by Mars, the Yogakaraka. The 7th lord Saturn is aspected also by 6th and 9th lord Jupiter.

Conclusion : The native has a generally happy married life but Rahu in the 7th, Mars aspecting Saturn adversely and associating with Kalatrakaraka Venus can give domestic bickerings.

The Seventh House : Scorpio is the 7th house occupied by the 8th and 11th lord Jupiter and debilitated Moon in Chart No. 17. The Moon does not get neechabhanga.

Chart No. 17.—*Born 13/14-8-1948 at 00-07 a.m. (I.S.T.) at 13° N, 77 E 35.*

Rahu	Lagna	Venus	Sun Ketu Jupit.	Mercury Saturn	
RASI G.IV-160		Sun	Lagna Venus	NAVAMSA	
		Merc. Sat.	Moon		Mars
Moon Jupiter	Ketu	Mars			Rahu

Balance of Mercury Dasa at birth : 9 years, 2 months and 5 days.

The Seventh Lord : Mars the 7th lord is in the 5th in a dual sign hemmed inbetween Saturn and Ketu and therefore subject to *papakartari yoga.*

Kalatrakaraka : Venus is in the 2nd house from Lagna in a dual sign.

Considered from the Moon : The 7th house Taurus is aspected by debilitated Moon and 2nd and 5th lord Jupiter. The 7th lord Venus is in the 8th in a dual sign.

Conclusion : The 7th lord Mars and Venus both as karaka and 7th lord from the Moon in dual signs gave the native two wives. The 8th lord and debilitated Moon in the 7th resulted in a clandestine marriage with another woman before the native's regular marriage took place. The *papakartari yoga* of the 7th lord Mars resulted in disharmony in married life when the wife left the husband on learning of his secret marriage.

Chart No. 18.—*Born 2–4–1947 at 7–02 a.m. (I.S.T.) at 26 N 23, 78 E 04.*

Sun Mars	Lagna	Rahu			Mercury	Lagna Rahu Moon	
Mercury Venus	**RASI**	Sat.		Venus	**NAVAMSA**		Mars
	G.IV-190	Moon					Jupiter
	Jupiter Ketu			Sun	Ketu	Saturn	

Balance of Ketu Dasa at birth : 4 years, 9 months and 7 days.

The Seventh House : The 7th house Libra is not occupied by any planet but is aspected adversely by Mars from the 12th house in Chart No. 18.

The Seventh Lord : The 7th lord from Lagna Venus is in the 11th house with 3rd and 6th lord Mercury. He is aspected by the 4th lord Moon.

Kalatrakaraka : Venus is in the 11th house with 3rd and 6th lord Mercury aspected by the Moon.

Considered from the Moon : The 7th house is occupied by 2nd and 11th lord Mercury and 3rd and 10th lord Venus.

Conclusion : The relationship between the 7th and 11th houses both from Lagna and Chandra Lagna has resulted in *dwikalatra yoga*. The native has two wives, both alive.

Chart No. 19.—*Born 16–3–1938 at 9–30 p.m. (I.S.T.) at 12 N 18, 76 E 42.*

Saturn Venus Mercuty Sun	Mars	Ketu	
Jupiter	RASI		
	G.IV-156		
Rahu	Lagna	Moon	

Moon Lagna Ketu			
	NAVAMSA		Mars
			Sun
Venus Saturn	Mercury	Jupiter Rahu	

Balance of Sun Dasa at birth: 0 year, 1 month and 29 days.

The Seventh House: Mars, is the 7th lord, occupies the 7th house in Chart No. 19. It is subject to *papakartari yoga* caused by Ketu and Saturn.

The Seventh Lord: Mars is the 7th lord and occupies his own sign in the 7th house. He is also subject to a *papakartari yoga* caused by Saturn and Ketu.

Kalatrakaraka: Venus is exalted in the 6th house with Yogakaraka Saturn, 11th lord, the Sun, and 9th and 12th lord Mercury in a dual sign.

Considered from the Moon: The 7th house is occupied by Saturn, Venus, Mercury and the Sun as 5th and 6th lord, 2nd and 9th lord, 1st and 10th lord and 12th lord respectively in a dual sign. The 7th lord Jupiter is in the 5th with cancellation of debility.

Conclusion : The presence of 4 planets in a common sign in the 7th house from the Moon in a dual sign, karaka Venus also in the 7th sign and the connexion between the 11th and 7th houses from the Moon gave the native two marriages, the second occurring after the death of the first husband.

Chart No. 20.—*Born 7–4–1893 at 9–31 a.m. (L.M.T.) at 20 N 56, 75 E 55.*

RASI (NH-62)

Sun Mercury Venus	Rahu Jupiter	Mars	Lagna
	RASI		Sun
	NH-62		Venus
Moon		Ketu	Sat.

NAVAMSA

	Moon	Mars	Saturn Rahu
Ketu	NAVAMSA		Jupiter
Venus			
Ketu	Mercury	Lagna	

Balance of Ketu Dasa at birth : 6 years, 4 months and 4 days.

The Seventh House : The 2nd lord Moon occupies the 7th house aspected by the 7th lord Jupiter and the 6th and 11th lord Mars in Chart No. 20.

The Seventh Lord : Jupiter is the 7th lord placed in the 11th house with Rahu.

Kalatrakaraka : Venus, the karaka, is in the 10th house exalted with 3rd lord the Sun and Lagna and 4th lord Mercury aspected by Saturn, the 8th and 9th lord but in a dual sign.

Considered from the Moon : The 7th house Gemini is a dual sign and aspected by the 8th lord Moon and the 2nd and 3rd lord Saturn. The 7th lord Mercury is in a dual sign with Venus and the Sun, the 6th and 11th lord and 9th lord respectively.

Conclusion : The 7th lord Jupiter in the 11th with Rahu, the 7th occupied by the Moon and aspected by Mars, Venus in a common sign in association with two planets aspected by Saturn lends credence to the rumour the native had 5 wives. Of the fact, he had at least two wives there is no doubt.

Loss of Husband or Wife

Just as in timing the event of marriage we should consider the periods and sub-periods that operate, in judging coverture (duration of married life), an assessment of the running Dasas and Bhuktis is necessary. Although the Bhava is the seventh, we must take into account the 8th and 9th houses also. The 8th house rules 'mangalya' or the strength of the

Chart No. 21.—*Born 7-10-1954 at 10 p.m. (I.S.T.) at 12 N 18, 76 E 42.*

	Lagna	Ketu	Merc. Ketu Sat.
	RASI	Jupit.	
Moon	GIII-32		
Mars Rahu	Venus	Mercury Saturn	Sun

			Sun Moon Venus
	NAVAMSA		Lagna Jupiter
Mars			Rahu

Balance of Moon's Dasa at birth : 1 year, 9 months and 13 days.

marital bond. The 9th house rules *sowbhagya* or good fortune. Good fortune covers not only material affluence but also a long-lived married partner.

The Seventh House : In Chart No. 21 the 7th house is Scorpio occupied by Venus, lord of Lagna and the 6th. It is hemmed in between malefics, exalted Saturn and Mars and Rahu. It is aspected by exalted Jupiter lord of the 8th and 11th.

The Seventh Lord : Mars is the 7th lord placed in the 8th house with Rahu and aspected by the exalted Yogakaraka Saturn.

Kalatrakaraka : Venus is in the 7th house subject to a malefic yoga caused by Mars and Rahu on one side and Saturn on the other side. Venus is aspected by exalted 8th and 11th lord Jupiter.

Considered from the Moon : The 7th house is Cancer occupied by exalted Jupiter lord of 3rd and 12th and aspected by exalted Saturn, lord of the Moon-sign. The 7th lord from the Moon is himself being aspected by Jupiter in exaltation.

Conclusion : The presence of the 7th lord Mars in the 8th and of Saturn's aspect on it together with Rahu's association indicates loss of husband or 'vaidhavya' during Mars and Rahu Dasa. The native married in August 1976. Her husband died in a drowning accident in June 1977, just 10 months after marriage. Both events occurred in Venus Bhukti of Rahu Dasa. Rahu is in the 8th afflicting the 8th house with Mars and Saturn. There is a classical dictum that "if Rahu combines with Mars and Saturn and occupies the 7th or 8th house, early widowhood is indicated". Venus is the Kalatrakaraka and Lagna lord but his presence in the 7th house only afflicts him by the *papakartari yoga* to which the Bhava is subject. Afflicted

Venus, therefore, deprived the girl's married life in his sub-period.

Chart No. 22.—*Born 22-11-1939 at 10-10 p.m. (I.S.T.) at 12 N 9, 77 E 9.*

Moon Jupiter	Saturn Ketu		Lagna
Mars	**RASI**		
	GII-38		
	Sun Mercury Venus	Rahu	

Venus		Saturn Ketu	
	NAVAMSA		
Merc. Mars			
Moon	Rahu		Lagna Sun Jupiter

Balance of Mercury Dasa at birth : 14 years, 8 months and 29 days.

The Seventh House : Capricorn the seventh house is not occupied by any planet in Chart No. 22. It is aspected by debilitated Saturn, lord of the 7th.

The Seventh Lord : Saturn is the 7th lord debilitated in the 10th house. He does not obtain cancellation of debility but is afflicted by Ketu.

Kalatrakaraka : Venus, the karaka, is in the 5th house in association with the Sun and Mercury, the 2nd and the 3rd and the 11th lords respectively aspected by Jupiter lord of the 6th and 9th from the 9th house.

Considered from the Moon : The 7th house is Virgo aspected by the Moon-sign lord Jupiter and the 2nd and 9th lord

Mars. The 7th lord Mercury is in the 9th with the 3rd and 8th lord Venus and the 6th lord Sun.

Conclusion : The 7th house is afflicted because although the 7th lord aspects it, the aspect is of a planet rendered malefic by debility and association with a node. The 8th house is occupied by Mars who though a Yogakaraka is not welcome here. He is particularly harmful in the 2nd, 4th, 7th, 8th and 12th houses from Lagna or Chandra Lagna. The debilitation and eclipse of the 7th lord Saturn and Mars in the 8th house resulted in the death of wife. The 9th house, though occupied by 9th lord, is subject to *papakartari yoga* caused by Mars and Saturn. The 9th lord Jupiter also suffers thereby and his aspect on Venus is not too effective. Moreover, the 8th and 10th lords have exchanged signs so that Saturn who is the 7th lord also is afflicted by this *parivartana*. The marriage took place in 1968

Chart No. 23.—*Born 16-3-1937 at 6-45 p.m. (I.S.T.) at 28 N 51, 78 E 49.*

Sun Saturn	Venus Moon	Ketu		Lagna Rahu		Mercury	
Mercury		RASI				NAVAMSA	Venus
Jupiter				Jupit.			Sun Saturn
	GIII-238						
	Rahu Mars		Lagna		Moon		Mars Ketu

Balance of Venus Dasa at birth : 2 years, 2 months and 3 days.

and wife died in 1970. Both events occurred in the sub-period of Rahu in the Dasa of Venus. Venus is the Kalatrakaraka with the 3rd and 12th lord Mercury. Rahu afflicts the 7th lord by his complement Ketu.

The Seventh House : Pisces, the 7th house, is occupied by 5th and 6th lord Saturn and 12th lord the Sun, both malefics in Chart No. 23. It is subject to a *subhakartari yoga* caused by Mercury on one side and Venus and the Moon on the other side.

The Seventh Lord : Jupiter the 7th lord is in debility in the 5th house. He obtains cancellation of debility since his sign dispositor Saturn is in a quadrant from the Lagna. He occupies the same sign in Navamsa being Vargottama and has exchanged signs with the 5th lord Saturn.

Kalatrakaraka : Venus is in the 8th with the 11th lord the Moon hemmed inbetween malefics the Sun and Saturn on one side and Ketu on the other.

Considered from the Moon : The 7th house is aspected by its own lord Venus. The 8th house has two malefics Mars and Rahu with no redeeming features.

Conclusion: Although the 7th lord Jupiter is strongly placed, his exchange of signs with 5th lord Saturn is not desirable as it can deny marriage or progeny. Further the affliction to the 8th house from the Moon is heavy resulting in a Vaidhavya Yoga. The native married in Ketu Bhukti of Rahu Dasa and was widowed in the same Bhukti, exactly a year later. The strength of the 7th lord gave a good husband and did not deny marriage. But the several afflictions to the 7th house and 7th lord, to Venus and particularly to the 8th lord from both Lagna and Chandra Lagna and the running Dasa being that of the afflicting planet Rahu resulted in death of

husband. The 9th lord Venus as lord of the house of good
fortune is in the 12th (house of loss) from the 9th house.

Chart No. 24.—*Born 2–11–1755 (N.S.) at about 8 p.m.
at 46 N 30, 30 E.*

Ketu			Mars Lagna		Sun Venus		Mars Jupiter
	RASI			Rahu Sat. Lagna	NAVAMSA		
Saturn	NH-22						Ketu
	Mercury	Sun Moon Venus	Jupit. Rahu		Mercury	Moon	

Balance of Mars Dasa at birth : 2 years, 5 months and
9 days.

The Seventh House : Sagittarius is the 7th house in Chart
No. 24 aspected by 6th and 11th lord Mars. Mars is Vargottama since he occupies the same sign in Navamsa.

The Seventh Lord : Jupiter as the 7th lord is with Rahu
in the 4th. He is aspected by 6th and 11th lord Mars.

Kalatrakaraka : Venus is in his own sign but with a
Vargottama 2nd lord, the Moon and 3rd lord, the Sun. He is
aspected by the 8th and 9th lord Saturn. Moreover, he is very
close to the Sun.

Considered from the Moon : The 7th lord Mars is in the
9th in a dual sign Vargottama. The 7th house is aspected by
Kalatrakaraka Venus, the 10th lord the Moon and 11th lord
the Sun.

Conclusion : The 7th lord afflicted by Rahu and Mars gave a disgusting husband who was at once stupid and stubborn. The 8th lord Saturn is in the 8th but afflicted by Mars and eclipsed 7th lord Jupiter. The 9th lord Saturn is in the house of loss or the 12th house from the 9th which resulted in widowhood in Saturn Dasa, Saturn Bhukti. Saturn is the 2nd lord and occupant from the 7th house, Sagittarius, and becomes a maraka to the husband.

Chart No. 25.—*Born 1/2–2–1953 at 0–43 a.m. (I.S.T.) at 12 N 18, 76 E 42.*

Venus Mars	Jupiter				Lagna
		Ketu			Mercury Sun Rahu
Sun Mercury Rahu	RASI G.IV-326	Moon	Ketu	NAVAMSA	Mars
	Saturn Lagna			Saturn Moon	Jupiter	Venus

Balance of Venus Dasa at birth : 4 years, 2 months and 12 days.

The Seventh House : Aries, the seventh house, is occupied by the 6th lord Jupiter and aspected by exalted Yogakaraka Saturn in Chart No. 25.

The Seventh Lord : Mars, the 7th lord, is in the 6th house having exchanged signs with the 6th lord Jupiter. He is conjoined with Lagna lord Venus.

Kalatrakaraka: Venus is in the 6th exalted conjoining the 7th lord Mars.

Considered from the Moon: The 7th house Aquarius is hemmed inbetween malefics, the Sun and Rahu on one side and Mars on the other side. The 7th lord Saturn is exalted in the 3rd aspected by 5th and 8th lord Jupiter.

Conclusion: The native's husband died in Venus Bhukti of Mars Dasa. Both Dasa and Bhukti lords are in the house of loss from the 7th house. The 8th house from the Moon is occupied by Mars. Mars, the 9th lord, is in the 12th house from the 9th in *parivartana* with 8th lord Jupiter. This weakens mangalyasthana. From the Lagna itself both karaka and 7th lord are in the 6th house which is the 12th house from the 7th house. Further the exchange of signs between the 6th and 7th lords from Lagna, namely, Jupiter and Mars respectively, only weakens the 7th house.

Mars and Venus in Marriage

An Indian scholar, noticing the high degree of stability and harmony in marriages in India, began collecting case-histories of married couples. He managed to get 603 cases for study. The age-group selected was 30 to 40. All the people concerned were born between 1931-40 and married between 1955-60. The economic background was mostly rural and agricultural though 22% of the case-histories concerned people who derived their livelihood from commercial and industrial occupations. In most cases, the informants were males. It was found that divorces and separations were about 6% and deaths of husbands or wives 10%. The scholar's findings were that 47% was positive, 42% neutral and 11% negative. By positive he means very successful marriages. By neutral he means a fair degree of harmony in domestic lives. And by negative he means disharmonious family lives. His conclusion was that these figures proved the efficacy of astrology in marital settlements. The system of matrimonial matching of horoscopes, invariably resorted to by parents prior to the settling of marriages, ensures to a certain extent their stability and harmony.

In our experience, apart from the other astrological considerations, the mutual dispositions of Mars and Venus are to be carefully studied. It cannot be a coincidence that divorce, separation and crimes of passion increase whenever there is a conjunction of Venus and Mars, especially when the constellations involved are those of malefic planets. Children born when there is a Venus–Mars conjunction should be brought up in a disciplined manner and taught to avoid dissipating habits of immediate pleasure. The adverse effects of conjunction should be made to express themselves through constructive channels if Jupiter aspects the combination or is in a quadrant therefrom.

Venus is associated with many fascinating aspects of life. He rules the wife, conveyance, sex-harmony and union, art, attachment, family happiness, marriage in general, vitality, fertility, physical beauty and friendliness. Mars abounds in energy, aggressiveness, fortitude, driving force and in association of Venus, a tendency to excess of sensual gratification. It is therefore necessary that in the horoscope of a couple, Mars–Venus conjunction or opposition should have the benefic steadying effect of a favourable disposition of Jupiter; or in the alternative the conjunction or opposition takes place in the constellations of Jupiter or Mercury or even Venus, Jupiter and Mercury being more preferable. Venus–Mars disposition is an important factor for physical attraction. But in the absence of

Jupiter's or even Saturn's benign influence real compatibility may be lacking. Venus–Mars conjunction makes one fond of pleasure. demonstrative and adds a zest to one's sensual life. When Venus and Mars are involved in adverse aspects, difficulty through excesses and trouble through marriage follow as a matter of consequence. Venus in a good sign or constellation can temper the roughness of Mars, but if Rahu is also involved, it makes one lascivious, lewd and wicked. Ketu-Venus–Mars association (or even mutual aspect) is not desirable unless the constellation involved belongs to Jupiter or Mercury or even benefic Moon, though the last circumstance may render the native's thinking highly sensual irrespective of the chart being of a boy or of a girl. Ketu-Venus–Mars (or Saturn) denotes danger of scandal in marriage But if the 10th or house of Karma is well disposed, the affliction is somewhat tempered.

Let us take the example of a person having Venus–Mars conjunction in Taurus, the Lagna being Scorpio. Venus, Kalatrakaraka, in the 7th is not generally favoured by ancient writers on the theory of *karako-bhavanasaya* as the indications of the 7th house are said to be inhibited. Experience has however revealed that this textual dictum is not quite valid. In fact Venus in the 7th is one of the finest combinations for a fairly happy marriage, denoting affection between the couple. When, in the case under reference, Venus is in Krittika ruled by the Sun and Mars is in Mrigasira, the 7th house gains considerable strength and the married life will be happy though crossed by frequent emotional clashes. If such a native is married to one who has Taurus rising with Venus and Mars in Scorpio, each will constantly try to appease the dictates of the others' emotions and over-indulge in sensual pleasures to the utter detri-

ment of their health.   Venus in Taurus is good but in a fiery
constellation (Krittika) it gives rise to stubbornness.   In Rohini
on the other hand, the finer qualities of Venus find expression.
It is always better to look for trinal or quadrangular disposition
of Mars from the Lagna or the Moon, no matter even if they
conjoin provided they are in different constellations.   A similar
disposition in the partner's horoscope is desirable though not
essential.

In selecting partners for marriage, more than Kuta agreement, it is the basic structure of the horoscopes that is important. One may possess outer charm but may have a stony heart,
acute selfishness and seek only self-aggrandisement. Generally
those who have a conjunction of the Sun, Mars and Mercury
in the ascendant will be disposed as above unless there are
relieving features such as the aspect of Jupiter. We have with
us a number of horoscopes in which the Moon occupies a
martian constellation with the Sun and Saturn in the 12th therefrom.   Many of them have confirmed that their lives have been
beds of thorns.   When the lord of the 7th is in the 6th with
Venus in the constellation of Rahu, one will be frigid, though
attractive.   The need for assessing the structure of the horoscope can never be overemphasized.

The method of comparing the horoscopes for purposes of
marriage has been fully discussed in my book *Muhurta* or
Electional Astrology.

The Seventh House : Gemini, a dual sign, is the 7th
house. It is occupied by Rahu aspected adversely by Mars, 5th
and 12th lord and malefic Saturn in Chart No. 26.

The Seventh Lord : Mercury, the 7th lord, is exalted in
the 10th house in a common sign with 9th lord the Sun

Chart No. 26.—*Born on 10-10-1871 at 2 p.m. (L.M.T.) at 51 N 27, 2 W 35.*

			Rahu		Mercury	Ketu	Moon Mandi
			Jupit.	Venus			
	RASI				NAVAMSA		
			Moon				Saturn Sun
Lagna Ketu Saturn Mandi	Mars		Sun Merc. Venus	Mars	Lagna Rahu		Jupiter

Balance of Rahu Dasa at birth :   13 years, 8 months and 13 days.

and 6th and 11th lord Venus debilitated. This combination of planets is afflicted by Saturn's aspect.

Kalatrakaraka : Venus is in the 10th debilitated with the Sun and Mercury in a dual sign aspected by Saturn.

Considered from the Moon : The 7th house is aspected by 7th lord Saturn and Yogakaraka Mars. The 7th lord Saturn is in a common sign with Ketu.

Conclusion : The 10th house occupied by lords of the 10th, 2nd and the 7th leads to Jara Yoga which results in the native having extra-marital relations with many women. The native was a glutton for sexual experiences and could never adapt himself to the restraints of marriage. The 7th lord Mercury in the 10th with Venus and the Sun aspected by Saturn, all in common signs, with Rahu in the 7th made the native's wife too a social cock who carried on affairs with all sorts of men. The couple had agreed between themselves that each should have his or her own way in so far as their private lives were consideled.

Chart No. 27.—*Born on 6-4-1886 at about 6-30 p.m. (L.M.T.) at 17 N 30, 78 E 30.*

Sun	Moon Mercury		Sat.	Jupit.	Mercury	Ketu
Ketu Venus				Sun		
	RASI				NAVAMSA	
			Rahu Mars	Sat. Venus		Mars
	THC-110					
	Lagna Mandi		Jupit.	Mandi	Rahu	Lagna	Moon

Balance of Venus Dasa at birth : 11 years, 9 months and 9 days.

The Seventh House : Aries is the 7th house occupied by 10th lord the Moon and 9th lord Mercury in Chart No. 27. There is no aspect on the 7th.

The Seventh Lord : Mars, the 7th lord, is in the 11th with Rahu aspected by Saturn and Venus.

The Kalatrakaraka : Venus is in the 5th with Ketu aspected by Mars.

Considered from the Moon : The 7th house is aspected by 3rd and 6th lord Mercury and 4th lord the Moon. The 7th lord Venus is the 11th with Ketu aspected by Mars.

Conclusion : The 7th lord Mars is in the 11th in combination with Rahu both in the constellations of Venus and aspected by Saturn from the constellation of Mrigasira. The Kalatrakaraka Venus is, in turn, afflicted by association with Ketu situated in the constellation of Rahu aspected by Mars. Both the lord of the 7th and Venus have been much afflicted. The native disliked his wife and was a profligate. All the attempts of the wife to wean him away from his evil ways failed. Out of sheer disgust the lady returned to her parents' house. The sensual life led by the native resulted in his contracting dreadful venereal complaints.

Some General Observations

When Venus, Mars and Jupiter in one horoscope are situated in the other horoscope in a trine or 3 and 11 positions, that is, if in the boy's horoscope Venus is in Taurus and in the girl's horoscope, in Cancer or Virgo, it is a favourable position. When the Sun and the Moon have similar harmonious positions, except 2 and 12 (*dwirdwadasa*), there is usually a strong attachment. Here again if the husband's Sun is in Cancer and the wife's is in Virgo, the needed harmony exists. When the Sun and the Moon are disposed as suggested above but Mars in one case is in a sign, which happens to be the 12th from Venus in the other horoscope, attachment exists, but there cannot be normal happiness in their private lives. If Venus in one horoscope is in a sign occupied by Saturn in the other a serious and industrious partner is indicated. Mars in the 7th, unaspected by benefics, indicates frequent quarrels leading to misunderstandings. Saturn in the 8th aspected by Mars (especially 4th or 8th house aspect) is not conducive to mutual understanding. Saturn in the 7th confers stability in the marriage but the husband or wife manifests coldness and not warmth.

A strong malefic in the 4th affects married happiness unless neutralised by a benefic aspect. If the Janma Rasi (Moon sign) of the wife (or husband) happens to be the Lagna of the husband (or wife), or if the Lagna of the wife (or husband) happens to be the 7th from the position of the lord of the 7th (in the other) the married life will be stable and built on mutual understanding and affection.

If certain afflictions are present in one horoscope, it is said they can be mitigated by looking for a partner whose horoscope has similar afflictions.

One of the most misunderstood and misapplied astrological dicta is the one relating to the so-called evil of Mars (Kuja Dosha).

"If Mars is in the 2nd, 12th, 4th, 7th or 8th house (either from the Ascendant or the Moon or Venus) in the horoscope of the female, the death of the husband will occur; a similar situation of Mars in the husband's horoscope causes the death of the wife." It should be noted that the strength of the dosha in 2, 12, 4, 7 and 8 is in ascending order. In assessing the quantum of dosha, Bhavas and not Rasis must be taken into account. The dosha of Mars is said to get neutralised or minimised in the following circumstances.

Mars in the 2nd is bad provided such 2nd house happens to be any sign other than Gemini and Virgo. Mars in the 12th causes dosha in all signs except Taurus and Libra. Mars in the 4th house causes affliction in signs other than Aries and Scorpio; when the 7th is other than Capricorn and Cancer, the dosha is given rise to. Mars becomes evil in the 8th in all signs except Sagittarius and Pisces. Mars produces no dosha whatever in Leo and Aquarius. The dosha is countered by the conjunction of Mars and Jupiter or Mars and the Moon.

The Dosha is not absolute. Its intensity can vary not only according to the exceptions given above but also according to the sign—friendly, exalted, own, inimical etc.—involved. We can therefore rate the afflictions as follows, taking Mars as the worst malefic, Saturn, Rahu and Ketu as less malefic and the Sun, least malefic, the maleficence being the highest in debilitation and lowest in exaltation.

| | 8th and 7th | | | 4th, 12th and 2nd | | |
	Mars	Saturn Rahu Ketu	Sun	Mars	Saturn Rahu Ketu	Sun
Debility	100	75	50	50	37.50	25
Inimical	90	67.50	45	45	33.75	22.50
Neutral	80	60.00	40	40	30.00	20.00
Friendly	70	52.50	35	35	26.25	17.50
Own	60	45.00	30	30	22.50	15.00
Exaltation	50	37.50	25	25	18.75	12.50

The table helps make an assessment of the total dosha in a chart so that if the dosha units in both charts are equal or nearly so, the matching can be said to be good. If the dosha in the male horoscope exceeds the dosha in the female horoscope by 25%, it is passable. If the dosha in the male horoscope exceeds this percentage or if the female chart has more dosha, then the charts cannot be matched.

Unconventional Marriages

The younger generation seeking to act on its own has set in a wave of unconventional marriages. The term unconventional here is used in the sense of so-called love, inter-caste or otherwise not traditionally and generally approved marriages.

Chart No. 28. —*Born   23-6-1894 at 10 p.m. (L.M.T.) at 0 W 5, 51 N 30.*

Mars Rahu		Jupiter Venus	Sun		Lagna	Ketu
Moon			Merc.			
	RASI			NAVAMSA		
Lagna				Sun Moon Venus		Mercury
	NH-64		Sat. Ketu		Rahu	Saturn Mars Jupiter

Balance of Rahu Dasa at birth : 9 years, 5 months and 12 days.

The Seventh House : Cancer the 7th house, in Chart No. 28 is not aspected by any planet but occupied by 6th and 9th lord Mercury.

The Seventh Lord : The Moon as the 7th lord is not afflicted by aspect or association.

Kalatrakaraka : Venus is in his own sign with Jupiter, the 3rd and 12th lord.

Considered from the Moon : The 7th house Leo has no afflictions but the 7th lord Sun is in the 5th aspected by an afflicted Mars and an equally afflicted Lagna-lord Saturn. The 8th house from Chandra Lagna is heavily afflicted by the concentrated influences of Mars, Rahu, Ketu and Saturn.

Conclusion : The rative, a duke of the British royalty married a common woman who was a divorcee. The proposed

5

marriage created a furore in the country but the native married
the woman of his choice for whom he had to abdicate the
throne. The 8th house signifying the martial bond is afflicted
in Navamsa also being occupied by Rahu and aspected by
Saturn.

Chart No. 29.—*Born 10-9-1938 at 9-00 a.m. (I.S.T.) at
13° N, 77 E 35.*

Saturn	Ketu					Mars Rahu Moon Mercury
Moon Jupiter			Sat.			
	RASI		---	NAVAMSA		
		Mars Merc Sun	Venus			
	RP 42/37					
	Lagna Venus Rahu		Lagna Ketu	Sun	Jupiter	

Balance of Saturn Dasa at birth : 5 years.

The Seventh House :   Aries being the 7th house, it is
occupied by Ketu and aspected by Lagna-lord Venus and Rahu
in Chart No. 29.

The Seventh Lord :   Mars, the 7th lord, is in the 11th with
the 11th lord the Sun and the 9th and 12th lord Mercury
aspected by 10th lord the Moon and 3rd and 6th lord Jupiter.

Kalatrakaraka :   Venus is in his own sign with Rahu
aspected by 3rd and 6th lord Jupiter.

Considered from the Moon :   The seventh house Leo is
occupied by Mars, Mercury and the Sun and aspected by

Jupiter. The 8th house is hemmed in between malefics Mars and the Sun on one side and Rahu on the other side at the same time being aspected by Saturn.

Conclusion: The presence of Ketu in the 7th, Rahu's affliction to Venus coupled with the *papakartari yoga* to the 8th house from the Moon resulted in the native, a Hindu, marrying a Christian colleague. The 7th house and the 8th lord the Moon in Navamsa are both heavily afflicted by the nodes, Mercury and Mars.

Chart No. 30.—*Born 23-1-1897 at about 12-00 noon (L.M.T.) at 5 E 44, 20 N 38.*

	Lagna	Mars	Moon Merc.	Sun		Venus Lagna
Venus			Ketu			Mars
	RASI			NAVAMSA		
Sun Rahu Mercury	NH-68		Jupit.			Rahu
	Saturn	Moon				Jupiter Saturn

Balance of Sun Dasa at birth : 0 year, 4 months and 15 days.

The Seventh House : The seventh house Libra in Chart No. 30 is neither occupied nor aspected by any planet.

The Seventh Lord : Venus, the 7th lord, is placed in the 11th house aspected by 9th and 12th lord Jupiter.

Kalatrakaraka : Venus is well placed in the 11th house aspected by Jupiter.

Considered from the Moon : The 7th house Pisces is neither occupied nor aspected by any planet. The 7th lord Jupiter is in the 12th aspected by Venus, Mars and Saturn.

Conclusion : The 7th lord from the Moon is afflicted by the malefic aspects of Mars and Saturn. The 8th house from Lagna is occupied by Saturn and aspected by Mars. The 8th lord from the Moon, namely, Mars, is afflicted by Saturn's aspect. In Navamsa, the 8th is afflicted by debilitated Mars and afflicted Jupiter. The influence of Jupiter, as 9th lord in Rasi, on karaka and 7th lord Venus, 8th lord Mars (from the Moon) in the 9th and affliction to the 8th house (from Lagna both in Rasi and Navamsa) by malefics in watery signs led the native to marry a foreigner.

Chart No. 31.— *Born 22/23-11-1902 at 5-16 a.m. (L.M.T.) at 23 N 6, 72 E 40.*

	Ketu			Ketu	Lagna	Mercury
						Jupiter
Saturn Jupiter	RASI NH-70		Moon Mars	Sat.	NAVAMSA	
	Venus Sun	Mercury Rahu Lagna			Mars	Rahu	Moon Sun Venus

Balance of Venus Dasa at birth : 13 years, 11 months and 12 days.

The Seventh House :   Aries, the 7th house, is occupied by Vargottama Ketu and aspected by an afflicted 9th and 12th lord Mercury in Chart No. 31.

The Seventh Lord :   Mars, the 7th lord, is in the 11th receiving no aspects, good or bad, but with the 10th lord the Moon.

Kalatrakaraka :   Venus is in the 2nd house aspected by 2nd lord Mars and conjoining 11th lord the Sun.

Considered from the Moon :   The 7th house Aquarius is aspected by 4th and 9th lord Mars. The 7th lord Saturn is in his own sign but in the 6th house with debilitated Jupiter.

Conclusion :   The 8th house is aspected by 8th lord Venus who, in turn, is aspected by Mars. From the Moon, the 8th lord Jupiter is in the 6th with Saturn. The 8th house from the Moon is aspected by Saturn and Mars. The 7th house from Lagna is occupied by Ketu in Rasi. In Navamsa, the 8th house is hemmed between Mars and Saturn coming under a *papakartari yoga*. The native, a high-caste Hindu, married a Parsee widow with children, a marriage that shocked the people of his times. Afflictions to the 8th house and the 8th lord by Rahu, Ketu, Mars and Saturn in Rasi and Navamsa usually result in marriages that are socially not accepted or welcomed.

The Seventh House :   Aries is the 7th house free of both aspects and occupation in Chart No. 32.

The Seventh Lord :   Mars, the seventh lord, is in the 10th debilitated but with cancellation of debility as his exaltation sign lord Saturn occupies a quadrant from the Moon. Mars is with the 11th lord Sun, 9th and 12th lord Mercury and Ketu.

Kalatrakaraka :   Venus occupies his own sign Taurus with 3rd and 6th lord Jupiter.

Considered from the Moon :   The 7th lord Mercury is in the 8th with 9th lord Sun, Ketu and 5th and 12th lord Mars.

Chart No. 32.—*Born 24-7-1953 at 1-30 p.m. (I.S.T.) at 13 N 5, 80 E 15.*

		Venus Jupiter			Rahu		Lagna
			Sun Mars Merc. Ketu				Moon
	RASI				NAVAMSA		
Rahu							Venus Jupiter Mars
	RP 49/35						
Moon		Lagna	Sat.			Mercury Ketu	Saturn Sun

Balance of Ketu Dasa at birth :   0 year, 11 months and 10 days.

The 7th house is aspected by Saturn, lord of the 2nd and 3rd from the Moon.

Conclusion :   The presence of all malefics in the 8th and Saturn's aspect on the 7th house from the Moon led the native, a Brahmin, to marry a Christian youth. In Navamsa, the 7th lord Jupiter is with Mars and the 8th lord Saturn is combust.

XII

Concerning the Eighth House

The Eighth House deals with longevity, legacies, gifts and unearned wealth, nature of death, disgrace, degradation and details pertaining to death.

The following factors are important while judging the 8th house significations, namely, (a) The House, (b) Its Lord, (c) Its Occupants and (d) The Karaka or Indicator. The yogas formed in the 8th house will produce their own effects. The same considerations must be judged from the Navamsa chart also. Although there are several significations to the eighth house, we will focus our attention on the source and nature, time and place of death.

Results of the Lord of the Eighth House being situated in Different Houses

In the First House : - Penury and heavy debts will befall the native who has the 8th lord placed in the Ascendant with the Ascendant lord. Misfortune will follow him at every step. If the 8th lord is weak or placed in the 6th, 8th or 12th from Navamsa Lagna, the intensity of misfortune is reduced. If the 8th lord is severely afflicted the native will suffer bodily complaints such as disease and disfiguration. His constitution will be weak and he will have no bodily comforts. He will be the target of the displeasure of his superiors and higher-ups. Trouble from Government will cause him worries.

In the Second House :—The lord of the 8th house in conjunction with the 2nd lord in the 2nd house brings in troubles and problems of all sorts. The native suffers from eye and tooth troubles. He will have to eat unhealthy and tasteless or putrid foods. His domestic life will be filled with discontent and quarrels. His wife will not understand him. This may lead to estrangement and even separation. If longevity is good, he may suffer some severe illness. If the 8th lord is in the 6th, 8th or 12th from Navamsa Lagna, the intensity of the results will be reduced in degree.

In the Third House : If the lord of the 8th house combines with the lord of the 3rd in the 3rd, the third house significations suffer. The native's ears may cause problems or he may go deaf. Misunderstandings will crop up with brothers and sisters leading to quarrels. The native will be beset by all sorts of fears and mental anguish. He may imagine things and suffer from hallucinations. He may involve himself in debts and get into trouble thereby. If malefics afflict the 8th lord in the 3rd with the 3rd lord, the sufferings of the native will be unbearable. But if the 8th lord combines with the 6th or 12th lords, benefic results may come by. He may get a monetary windfall through writing or through the agency of a coborn.

In the Fourth House : - If the lord of the 8th house joins the 4th lord in the 4th house, the native's mental peace will be shattered. Domestic bickerings, financial and other problems will increase. Mother's health may suffer and cause great concern. The native may be beset with problems regarding his house, land and conveyance. If the affliction is heavy his land and immovable property may slip from his hands due to circumstances beyond his control. His conveyances may get lost or be destroyed. His pets may contract diseases and die. Malefics furthering the affliction may force him to seek his fortune abroad where he will meet with all sorts of troubles and losses. Reverses in profession and the displeasure of superiors are also likely.

In the Fifth House : -If the lord of the 8th is in the 5th with the 5th lord, the children of the native may get into trouble. They may commit some crime and invite situations that could affect the native's reputation. Or the native and his father may develop misunderstandings. The native's child may fall sick and suffer thereby. If the affliction is heavy, a child may die as soon as it is born or cause much grief to the native due to some incurable physical affliction or mental retardation. The native may also suffer much bodily ill-health. If the 8th lord is in the 6th, 12th or 8th from Navama Lagna, the evil results are greatly mitigated. But if fortified in a kendra (quadrant) or trikona (trine), the evil results are intensified. Since the 5th house is the *buddhisthana*, the native may also suffer nervous debility or breakdown or mental aberration.

When the 9th lord conjoins the 8th lord in the 5th house and the Lagna lord is debilitated, the native has neither knowledge nor wealth ; he is hostile, lustful and ill-temprered. He tends to be crafty, reviles God and pious men and is himself treated with contempt by his wife and children.

In the Sixth House :—If the lord of the 8th house joins the 6th lord in the 6th house, a Rajayoga results. Material affluence, fame and acquisition of objects desired are the good results. But because the 6th house is the house of disease the native may suffer ill-health. If afflicted, the native suffers loss of money through theft and trouble through courts and the police. The evil is intensified if the 8th lord is in a kendra or trikona. The native's maternal uncle may suffer much trouble. If the 6th lord is fortified, he is able to overcome all his troubles and emerge victor. No attempts made by his ill-wishers and enemies to harm him will succeed.

In the Seventh House : The lord of the 8th house placed in the 7th house with the 7th lord curtails longevity. The native's wife may suffer ill-health. If afflicted, the native will also suffer from disease. He may go abroad where he will meet with ill-health and problems. If the 7th and 8th lords are strong, the native will undertake foreign journeys on diplomatic missions and distinguish himself.

In the Eighth House : – If the lord of the 8th house occupies the 8th house in strength, the native lives long enjoying happiness. He will acquire lands, conveyance, power and position through the merit acquired in former lives. If the 8th lord is weak, he may have no serious troubles but may not also enjoy any luck or good fortune of significance. The father of the native may die or pass through some crisis. If the 8th lord is afflicted, the native will fail in his undertakings. He will be prompted to do the wrong things and thereby suffer loss.

In the Ninth House : – If the lord of the 8th house joins the 9th lord in the 9th house with malefics, the native may lose his father's property. Misunderstandings with father may arise. If the Sun, the natural significator of father is afflicted, father may die during the period of the 9th lord. If conjoined with benefics, the native acquires his father's property. Relations with father will be harmonious. If the 9th lord is weak, the native suffers all kinds of hardships, misery and unhappiness. His friends and kinsmen may desert him while his superiors will find fault with him. If the 8th lord is in the 6th, 8th or 12th from Navamsa Lagna, the evil results will be greatly reduced.

In the Tenth House : If the lord of the 8th house is in the 10th house with the 10th lord, the native has slow advancement in career. He faces obstacles and impediments in his activities. In the appropriate period he may be superseded by his subordinates and his merit may go unnoticed. He may resort to deceit and unrighteous means to gain his ends. His thinking will be clouded and his actions will invite the wrath of the government or the law. He may suffer poverty. If the 2nd lord is also afflicted and joins the 8th lord, his reputation may suffer due to involvement in huge debts and inability to repay them. If the 8th lord is placed in the 6th, 8th or 12th from Navamsa Lagna, the intensity of the evil is greatly reduced. The 8th lord in the 10th may also confer unexpected gains due to the death of the superiors or elders.

In the Eleventh House : - If the lord of the 8th house combines with the 11th lord in the 11th house, there may be trouble to close friends. Elder brother may pass through a difficult time. Relations with him will be strained and troubled. Or the elder brother may cause anguish to the native and his family by his unscrupulous behaviour and conduct. Business may suffer losses and run into debts. If benefic planets influence the combinations there will be troubles but the native gets help from friends and elder brother to overcome them. Afflictions will aggravate the malefic results.

In the Twelfth House :—The position of the 8th lord in the 12th house with the 12th lord gives rise to a Rajayoga. If benefics join the 8th lord, unfavourable results may be expected. Treachery of friends will result in many problems and grief. Unexpected expenditure will arise and there may be pecuniary losses. If the 8th lord is in the 12th house and the 12th lord is favourably placed in a trine or quadrant, the native will gain in religious learning and piety.   Some post or seat of authority may be thrust on him with all its attendant paraphernalia. If afflicted by malefics, the native may resort to vicious acts clandestinely. Such acts would include rape, adultery, conterfeiting of money (the 12th house is the house of secrecy and deceit. The 8th house signifies sudden gains of money) and smuggling activities.

These results are general. They must be modified on the strength of the Ascendant, the Moon and Dasas in operation. Where results pertain to criminal acts or unrighteous acts, the predictians must be made only after taking into account the strength of the Ascendant, the Moon and the 10th house (Karmasthana). If these factors are favuorably disposed, the native may be tempted to act in a certain manner but he will overcome the temptation and control himself. The act may be nipped at the state of mind and not allowed to manifest itself in action in such a case.

Other Important Combinations

If the 8th house is occupied by malefics, the native dies an unnatural death such as suicide, murder or accident. If benefics influence the 8th house, death will be natural, that is, through disease or old age. If the 6th and 8th lords are related, death follows ill-health. If the 6th house and 8th house in this case are severely afflicted, death comes after prolonged suffering as in the case of a chronic disease.

Longevity (length of life) can be divided into 4 groups:
1. Balarishta or Early Death   upto 8 years
2. Alpayu or Short Life— 8 years to 32 years

3. Madhyayu or Medium Life—32 years to 75 years
4. Purnayu or Full Life 75 years to 120 years.

The following combinations pertaining to the divisions of life-span have been called from ancient, authoritive classical works.

Balarishta

The following combinations indicate Balarishta.

(1) If the Moon occupies the 8th, 12th or the 6th house and is aspected by malefic Rahu, the child dies early.

(2) If the Moon conjoins with Saturn, the Sun is in the 12th house and Mars is in the 4th house, both the child and mother die.

(3) If the Moon in Lagna with no benefic aspects, and if both be hemmed inbetween malefic planets, both the mother and child will die.

(4) When the 6th, 8th and 12th houses are occupied by malefics with no benefic associations and Venus or Jupiter is between malefics, both the mother and child die.

(5) If malefics occupy the 1st, 6th, 7th and 8th houses from Lagna, both the mother and child die.

(6) If the eclipsed Moon joins Saturn in Lagna and Mars occupies the 8th house, both the mother and child will die.

(7) If malefics occupy the 6th and 12th houses from Lagna, the child dies soon after birth.

(8) If the waning Moon occupies Lagna and a malefic planet occupies a kendra or the 8th house from Lagna, the child dies soon.

(9) If benefic planets aspected by malefic planets occupy the 6th or the 8th house from Lagna, the child dies in a month.

(10)   If the Sun, Mars and Saturn conjoin the 6th or the 8th house from Lagna with no benefic conjunctions or aspects, the child dies quickly.

(11)   If the Sun, Mars and Saturn occupy the 5th house from Lagna, death of the child occurs.

(12)   If the Langa lord is debilitated and Saturn occupies the 7th or the 8th house from Lagna, the child suffers much and dies quickly.

(13)   If the Lagna lord conjoins the Sun and the 8th lord is depressed, the child dies early.

(14)   If the Moon occupies a malefic sign or Navamsa with no benefic aspects and malefics occupy the 5th or the 9th house, the child dies early.

(15)   If the Lagna, the 8th, the 9th and the 12th houses are occupied by the Moon, Mars, Sun and Saturn respectivel the child dies quickly.

(16)   The Moon conjoined with malefics in the 5th, 9th 12th, 7th and the Lagna causes the death of the child unless aspected or conjoined with a benefic.

(17)   When the Moon occupies the Lagna or 6th, 8th or the 12th houses from the Lagna aspected by a malefic without any benefic aspects and there are no benefics in the kendras, the child dies soon.

(18)   When Lagna is a watery sign with the Moon in it and Saturn occupies it or the 7th house with benefic planets in kendras, the child dies early.

(19)   If malefics occupy the Lagna and the 7th house and the Moon conjoined with a malefic is not aspected by any benefic planet, the child dies early.

(20)   If the waning Moon occupies the 12th house, the malefics are all in the 8th house and there are no benefics in the kendras, the child dies quickly.

(21)   When the Moon and Rahu conjoin with a malefic and Mars occupies the 8th house, the child dies early. If the Sun occupies Lagna in this case, an operation will be the cause of death.

(22)   If a retrograde planet occupies the 6th or 8th house or a kendra in a sign ruled by Mars and also aspected by Mars, the child lives for 3 years.

(23)   If the Moon and Mars occupy the Lagna in Cancer and there are no planets in the 4th, 7th, 8th and 10th houses the child dies in 3 years.

(24)   If the 6th or 8th house is Cancer occupied by Mercury and aspected by the Moon, the child dies in the 4th year.

(25)   If the Lagna is occupied by Rahu and aspected or occupied by only malefics, the child dies in the 5th year.

(26)   If Venus be in Leo or Cancer in the 6th, 8th or the 12th house aspected by a malefic, the child dies in the 6th year.

(27)   If the Lagna is afflicted by Mars or Saturn and the 7th house is occupied by the waning Moon, the child dies in the 6th or 7th year.

(28)   If Saturn, Mars and Venus are in Lagna without Jupiter's aspect and the waning Moon is in the 7th house, the child dies in the 7th year.

(29)   If the 6th and 8th houses are occupied by benefics and malefics are in the 5th and the 9th houses, the death of the child takes place in the 8th year.

Antidotes for Balarishta

Certain dispositions of benefic planets and the Moon can ward off death in childhood. The following are some standard combinations :

If the Moon is full or occupies exaltation, a benefic sign or Navamsa, the danger of childhood death is averted. When the Ascendant lord is strong in a kendra in association with or aspected by a benefic and is free of malefic aspects, any Balarishta Yoga is nullified. If Jupiter, Venus or Mercury occupy a quadrant free of malefic aspects, then also the child lives long in spite of other afflictions to the chart. Rahu in the 3rd, 6th or the 11th house from Lagna counteracrs other combinations for early death. Jupiter strong in a kendra protects a child from death in infancy. If the birth occurs during night in the bright half of the lunar month (Sukla Paksha) or during the day in the dark half of the lunar month (Krishna Paksha), the child lives long even if the Moon is in the 6th or 8th house aspected by both malefic and benefic planets. The Moon in exaltation aspected by Venus or the ruler of the sign occupied by the Moon in the Lagna aspected by benefic planets protects the infant from death. If 3 planets at birth occupy exaltation or own signs, it helps the child tide over other malefic planetary yogas harmful to longevity. The Ascendant lord, strongly placed in a quadrant or trine, neutralises other afflictions. Rahu in Lagna in Aries, Taurus or Cancer aspected by benefic planets protects the child.

Alpayu

Alpayu is the span of life that falls between 8 and 32 years

The following are some of the combinations for Alpayu :

(1)   The Sun, the Moon and Mars in the 5th house from Lagna may cause death in the 9th year.

(2)   If the Lagna lord is a malefic and occupies the 12th place from the Moon and is also aspected by malefic planets, death occurs in the 9th year.

(3)   If the Moon be in Leo, the Sun and Saturn be in the 8th from Lagna and Venus in the 2nd, the child dies in the 12th year.

(4)   If the Sun occupies Taurus Navamsa and Saturn Scorpio Navamsa, life ends at 12 years.

(5)   When Saturn in Leo in Navamsa is aspected by Rahu, the child can have a violent end at 15 years age.

(6)   If the lord of Lagna is exalted but not aspected by any benefic planet ; and Saturn in Navamsa, occupies Pisces or Sagittarius and is aspected by Rahu, the native's term of life is 19 years.

(7)   When the Moon occupies the 6th or the 8th from Lagna and malefic planets in kendras do not receive any benefic aspects, death comes in the 20th year.

(8)   If Mars and Jupiter are in Lagna, the Moon is in the 7th, and 8th house is occupied by a benefic or malefic, life ends at 22 years.

(9)   If the Lagna lord is in Lagna, the 8th lord is in the 9th and the planet in the 8th house is aspected by a malefic, the native lives for 24 years.

(10)   If the 8th and 12th lords are devoid of strength and Saturn occupies Lagna in a common sign, death occurs at 25 years.

(11)   If Mars is in Lagna and the Sun and Saturn occupy quadrants, life ends at 20 years.

(12)   If the 8th lord from Lagna or the Moon be in the 12th or a kendra, the native lives for 28 years.

(13)   If Saturn occupies the Lagna in an inimical sign and benefics are in the 3rd, 6th, 9th or 12th houses, the native lives for 26 or 27 years.

(14)   When the Sun, the Moon and Saturn conjoin in the 8th house, the native lives for 29 years.

(15)   When the 8th lord is in a kendra and Lagna lord is weak, the native lives for 32 years.

(16)   If Mercury in strength occupies a kendra and the 8th house be free of occupation by any planet, the native dies in his 30th year.

(17)   If the Lagna lord and the Moon be weak and occupy Apoklimas (3, 6, 9, 12) and be aspected by malefics, the native lives for 32 years.

(18)   If the Lagna be occupied by the Sun and hemmed in on either side by malefics, the native lives upto 31 years.

(19)   When there are no benefics in kendras and the 8th house is occupied by a planet, the native lives for 30 years.

(20)   When the 8th lord being Saturn, or a malefic in conjunction with another malefic planet occupies an evil shashtyamsa, the native is short-lived.

(21)   When the Lagna is occupied by malefics and the Moon also is with malefics with no benefics aspects, Alpayu is the result.

Madhyayu

Madhyayu extends from 32 to 75 years.

The following combinations denote medium life :

(1)   If Jupiter as Lagna lord is weak and malefics occupy the 6th, 8th or 12th houses, quadrants and trines, the native will have Madhyayu.

(2)   If a malefic is in the 8th, Saturn is in the 6th, and a benefic is in a trine or quadrant, Madhyayu is indicated.

(3)   If malefics occupy the 2nd, 3rd, 4th, 5th, 8th, and 11th, the native will have the medium term of life.

(4) If the Lagna lord is weak, malefics occupy 6th, 8th or 12th houses, Jupiter is in a trine or quadrant and malefic joins the Lagna, the native has Madhyayu.

(5) Benefics in kendras, the Moon in exaltation and the Lagna lord strong confer a longevity of 60 years.

(6) If a benefic occupies kendras, Jupiter is in Lagna and the 8th house from the Moon or the Lagna is free from the aspect or association of malefics, one lives for 70 years

(7) If Mercury occupies a kendra in strength, the 8th house is not occupied by any planet but aspected by a benefic, the native lives for 40 years.

(8) If a benefic planet occupies the 7th and the Moon is in Lagna or in Cancer, the native lives for 60 years.

(9) If Jupiter is in a kendra, the Lagna and the Moon are free from malefic aspects or associations, the 8th house is vacant and a benefic is in a kendra, medium life is the result.

(10) If the 8th lord be in kendra, and the Sun and Saturn occupy the 3rd or 6th which should be Capricorn, the native lives for 44 years.

(11) If the 8th lord is in Lagna and the 8th house is not occupied by any benefic, the native lives for 40 years.

(12) If the Moon be in the Lagna or the 8th or the 12th house, if Mercury be in the 4th or the 10th house and if Venus and Jupiter join in any house, the native lives for 50 years.

(13) If the Lagna lord joins the Moon in the 6th, 8th or 12th houses but is otherwise strong (in vargas) and the Lagna lord occupies Capricorn or Aquarius in Navamsa, the native lives for 58 years.

(14) If all the planets are in the 5th house, the native lives for 60 years.

(15) If benefics occupy their own Rasis and the Moon is exalted in Lagna, the native lives for 60 years.

Purnayu

Long life or Purnayu (75 to 120 years) is indicated if benefics occupy kendras and the Lagna lord is with benefics or aspected by Jupiter. When 3 planets are in the 8th house occupying respectively an exaltation sign, a friendly sign and own sign, long life is the result. If Saturn or the 8th lord is conjoined with an exalted planet, Purnayu results. In the following cases, the span of life is long :

(1) If the Sun, Saturn and Mars occupy movable Navamsa, Jupiter and Venus occupy fixed Navamsas and the Moon and Mercury are in dual Navamsas, the native lives upto 100 years.

(2) If the Ascendant lord is in a quadrant and malefics occupy the 12th and the 6th houses, the person born lives very long.

(3) If the 10th lord is exalted and the 8th house has malefic planets, it gives the native long life.

(4) If malefics occupy the 3rd, 6th and 11th and the benefics are grouped in the 6th, the 7th or the 8th from Lagna, the native lives long.

(5) When the Ascendant lord conjoins or receives the aspect of Venus and Jupiter and is himself in a kendra (quadrant), the native will be long-lived.

(6) If the Lagna and 8th lords are in the 8th or the 11th, the native is long lived.

(7) If Saturn joins the 1st, the 10th and 8th lords in a kendra, long life is indicated.

(8) If the 8th lord occupies his own sign or Saturn is in the 8th house, the native lives long.

(9) If Jupiter is exalted, benefics occupy their Moolatrikona Rasis and the Ascendant lord is powerful, the person concerned lives for 80 years.

(10) If benefics occupy the 5th and 9th houses and the Lagna is a Keeta Rasi with Jupiter in it, the native will have a lease of 80 years of life.

(11) If all the planets occupy the 9th houses, the native will have Purnayu.

(12) If all the planets are in kendras and in malefic Navamsas, the native lives for 80 years.

(13) If malefics occupy Upachayas (3, 6, 10, 11) in benefic Navamsas in depression and benefics occupy kendras, the native gets Purnayu.

(14) If the latter half of Dhanus (Sagittarius) be rising, all the planets be in their exaltation and Mercury occupies 24° of Taurus, the native lives the full period of life.

(15) If Saturn occupies the 1st or the 9th and the Moon occupies the 12th or the 9th house, the native enjoys Purnayu.

The life of a native may be fixed as long, medium or short according as the Lagna lord and all the benefic planets are in kendras (1, 4, 7, 10), Panaparas (2, 5, 8, 11) and Apoklimas (3, 6, 9, 12) respectively. If the 8th lord and malefic occupy kendras, Panaparas or Apoklimas, the span of life is respectively short, medium or long

Just because a chart contains the planetary positions given above, a conclusion on the longevity cannot be made at once. The relative strengths of the planets must be balanced before a correct assessment of longevity can be made.

Planets in the Eighth House

The Sun :— If the Sun occupies the 8th house in exaltation, the native lives long. He will be charming and an eloquent speaker. If the Sun is afflicted, he will be troubled with sores, in the face and head and be disgruntled in life. His eyes will be weak. He will suffer penury and an uneventful life. If associated with the 8th or 11th lord he may gain monetary benefits all of a sudden through speculation. He will have limited progeny, mostly male. If the Sun is in the 8th, the Moon or Rahu is in the 12th and Saturn is in a trine, the native suffers from dental problems.

The Moon :—The native with the Moon in the 8th is subject to mental aberration. He is apprehensive and suffers from psychological complexes. He will be capricious and unhealthy. The native may lose his mother in infancy or boyhood. His built will be slender and eyesight will be weak. He acquires possessions easily through legacies or inheritance. He will be fond of fighting and amusement and be large-hearted. The native suffers from excessive perspiration. If Mars and Saturn conjoin and the Moon is in the 8th house, the native's eyesight will be afflicted.

Mars :— The native will be short-lived unless there are other alleviating factors, and he may suffer the loss of wife (or husband). He will have very few children. He may seek to gratify his passions by resorting to extra-marital life. He will hate his relatives. His domestic life will be marred by quarrels and he suffers from bloodly complaints like piles. He will rule over many people.

If Mars is in the 8th, the Lagna is a fixed sign, Venus is in the 9th, the Moon is in the 7th and Jupiter is the 2nd lord, the native will be condemned to lead a life of servitude.

Mercury :—When Mercury is in the 8th, the native will possess many good qualities. He will be known for his breeding and courteous disposition. He will inherit as well as earn much wealth. He will be learned and famous for his scholarship in many subjects. He will live long but have a weak constitution.

Jupiter :—The native will be unhappy but generous hearted. He will live long. He will have difficulty in speech. He may do ignoble deeds but pretend to be noble. He may have liaisons with widows. He will have dirty habits and suffer from colitis. He will have a painless death. If Jupiter is debilitated and the Moon is in the 4th house from Lagna, the native will be a menial, being always ordered about.

Venus :—The position of Venus in the 8th gives many blessings. The native will come by much wealth. He will live a life of comfort and possess all the conveniences for such life. The native's mother may suffer danger. The native himself may meet with emotional disappointments early in life. As a consequence he may resort to a life of piety in later life. If exalted in the 8th, the native gains much wealth. If Venus in the 8th is debilitated in Rasi or occupies a saturnine Navamsa and is aspected by Saturn, the native suffers subordination and leads a life of drudgery along with his mother.

Saturn :—Saturn in the 8th house gives good longevity but many responsibilites in life. The native will discharge his duties through sheer perseverance against odds which will be many. He will have defective eyes. He will have very few children. He will have a paunch and be inclined to seek the company of women outside his caste. He may be predisposed to suffer from asthma, consumption and lung disorders. If afflicted by malefic planets, his children will cause him pain and grief. The native will be dishonest and cruel. When Saturn is in the 8th with Mars, Rahu is in Lagna and Gulika occupies a trine, the native suffers disease in his generative organs. If the Moon joins Saturn in the 8th, the result is flatulence and spleen troubles.

Rahu :—The native will suffer from public censure and humiliation. He will be troubled by many ailments. He will be vicious, quarrelsome and unscrupulous. If the Moon conjoins with a malefic planet and Rahu is in the 8th, 12th or 5th house, the native will suffer from mental disorders.

Ketu :—If Ketu in the 8th is aspected by a benefic, the native will enjoy much wealth and live long. If Ketu is afflicted, the native covets others' wealth and women. He will suffer from diseases due to disorders in the excretory system and also those due to a life of profligacy and excesses.

The 8th house rules suffering and afflictions here cause chronic or incurable bodily or mental diseases.

Saturn in the 8th with a malefic planet or Rahu in the Lagna causes stomach complaints. If the Lagna is aspected by a malefic planet, the 8th lord is weak and the 8th house is aspected or occupied by Saturn, it results in a disease that will prevent the intake of food. Depending upon the exact nature of affliction, the disease may take the form of minor ailments like severe colds or mumps or be something serious like cancer.

Nature of Death

Planets and afflictions to the 7th house indicate the nature of death. If a benefic planet occupies the 7th house from Mandi in Navamsa, death will be happy. Malefics in the same position give a painful death. If Saturn occupies the 7th house from the sign occupied by Mandi in Navamsa, death comes through snakes or thieves or supernatural beings. If Mars occupies this sign, the native is killed in a fight or battle. If either of the luminaries occupy this sign, the native may suffer a sentence of death passed by the courts or a political death. The Moon, in particular, could cause death by being mauled by an aquatic animal.

If the 8th house is occupied by one or more malefics, death is painful due to a grave disease or violent happening such as accident, murder or suicide etc. But if there is a benefic planet in the 8th house, the native has a natural and peaceful end.

If the Moon occupies the 8th together with Mars, Saturn or Rahu, death may be caused by epilepsy. Waning Moon in any house afflicted by malefics also causes the same kind of death. If the Moon in the 8th is aspected by a strong Saturn, surgery or some ailment of the anus or the eye may be the cause of death. If waning Moon in conjunction with Mars, Saturn or Rahu occupies the 8th death may occur by possession or drowning or fire or a weapon. If the Moon, the Sun, Mars and Saturn occupy the 8th or the 5th or the 9th, death is caused by fall from elevated place, drowning or thunderstorm or lightning. If the Moon is in the 8th, Mars is in the 9th, the Sun is in Lagna and Saturn is in the 5th, death may result by a thunderbolt or fall of a tree. When the waning Moon is in the 6th or 8th and the 4th and the 10th are occupied by malefic planets, death is brought about through the scheming of an enemy.

If the Sun is in the 8th, the Moon is in Lagna, Jupiter is in the 12th and a malefic planet occupies the 4th, the person may die as a result of falling from a cot. When the Lagna lord occupies the 64th Navamsa from Lagna or is combust or occupies the 6th, death occurs due to starvation. If the Sun is in the 4th, the Moon is in the 10th and Saturn is in the 8th, the native may be hit accidentally by a log of wood and die. If the Sun, the Moon and Mercury occupy the 7th, Saturn occupies the 1st, and Mars the 12th, the end comes about peacefully in tranquil surroundings outside the country of birth.

If the Sun and the Moon occupy the 8th or the 6th, the native is killed by a ferocious animal.

If Mercury and Venus occupy the 8th, the native dies while asleep. If Mercury and Saturn occupy this house, the native will be sentenced to the gallows. If the Moon and Mercury join the 6th or the 8th, poison will be the cause of death.

If the Moon, Mars and Saturn are in the 8th, death occurs by a weapon. Mars in the 12th and Saturn in the 8th cause a similar end. If Mars is in the 6th, the native is killed by a weapon. Rahu in the 6th with the 4th lord causes death by violence involving robbery or theft. Ketu gives similar results. The native dies through burns or a weapon if the Moon occupies Aries or Scorpio and is hemmed inbetween malefics. If the Moon is in the 8th, Mars is in the 10th, Saturn is in the 4th and the Sun is in Lagna, death is due to a blunt object like a club ; and if Mars is in the 7th and the Moon and Saturn occupy Lagna, one is tortured to death.

If Mars and the Sun exchange signs and are in kendras to the 8th lord, the native may be sentenced to death by the government. If the Lagna and 8th lords are weak and Mars is in conjunction with the 6th lord, the native may be killed in war. When Saturn occupies Lagna, Rahu is in the 7th with the waning Moon and Venus is debilitated, the person will suffer amputation of the hands and feet. When the Lagna ruled by Mars (if the Navamsa is ruled by Mars) is occupied by the Sun and Rahu, Mercury and the waning Moon occupy Leo, the native dies as a result of his belly being ripped. When Saturn is in Lagna with no benefic aspects and the Sun, Rahu and waning Moon combine, the native is either stabbed or shot dead.

As a general rule, the Moon in a dusthana aspected by the Lagna lord in conjunction with Saturn, Mandi and Rahu, causes an unnatural death.

If the lord of the 10th from Navamsa Lagna is with Saturn or occupies the 6th, 8th or 12th, the native dies through poisoning. When the same lord is with Rahu or Ketu he may end his life by hanging. When the 5th or the 9th sign from the Moon is aspected or occupied by a malefic planet and when a Sarpa (serpent), Nigada (fetters), Pasa (noose) or Ayudha (weapon), drekkana rises in the 8th Bhava, i.e., the 22nd drekkana, the death is brought about by suicide by hanging. When malefics occupy the 4th and the 10th or the trines and when the 8th lord combines with Mars in Lagna, the native kills himself hanging.

The 22nd drekkana is reckoned from the Lagna drekkana. If the Lagna is 27° Aquarius, Lagna drekkana is the 3rd drekkana of Aquarius. The 22nd drekkana from this is the 1st drekkana of Libra.

(For details of different kinds of drekkanas that can indicate unnatural death such as suicide, murder, assassination, accident etc., see Table of Drekkanas.)

If Venus is in Aries, the Sun is in the Lagna and the Moon conjoins a malefic planet in the 7th house, a woman is the cause of death. If the Sun, the Moon and a malefic planet are in Pisces which happens to be Lagna and if the 8th is occupied by a malefic, death is due to a wicked mistress. If the Moon and Saturn occupy the 8th, and Mars is in the 4th or the Sun is in the 7th ; or the Moon and Mercury are in the 6th, the native dies through food poisoning.

When the Lagna lord or the 7th lord conjoins the 2nd and 4th lords, death results through indigestion. When the Moon occupies the 8th in a watery sign, consumption leads to death.

When Mercury in Leo is aspected by a malefic planet, death is caused by fever. When Venus occupies the 8th house and is aspected by a malefic, death is from consumption, rheumatism or diabetes. When Jupiter occupies the 8th house in a watery sign, affection of the lungs brings about death. If Rahu is in the 8th house aspected by a malefic, death follows an attack of small-pox, boils, snake-bite, fall or biliousness. Diarrhoea is the cause of death when Mars in the 6th house is aspected by the Sun. If Mars and Saturn occupy the 8th house, death is caused by affliction to the aorta. Mercury and Venus in the 9th house also cause death by heart disease. The Moon in Virgo hemmed in between malefics causes death through anaemia. When these particular yogas are absent in a horoscope, classical works refer to the lord of the 22nd drekkana to find out the cause of death. It may also be determined from the decanate occupied by the planet in the 8th house.

The 22nd drekkana falling in different signs gives a clue to the cause of death :

Aries :
First decanate (ruled by Mars)   spleen and bilious complaints or poisoning.
Second decanate (ruled by Sun) —watery diseases.
Third decanate (ruled by Jupiter)— drowning in water.

Taurus :
First decanate (ruled by Venus) asses, horses, mules.
Second decanate (ruled by Mercury)—bilious complaints, fire or murder.
Third decanate (ruled by Saturn)—fall from a horse or building.

Gemini :
First decanate (ruled by Mercury)—cough, lung infections, bronchitis.

Second decanate (ruled by Venus)—typhoid.

Third decanate (ruled by Saturn)—fall from a conveyance, height.

Cancer :

First decanate (ruled by Moon)—drinks, thorns.

Second decanate (ruled by Mars)—poison.

Third decanate (ruled by Jupiter)—tumour, hallucinations, syncope.

Leo :

First decanate (ruled by Sun)—drinking contaminated water.

Second decanate (ruled by Jupiter)—water in the lungs, dropsy.

Third decanate (ruled by Mars)—travel-sickness, surgery.

Virgo :

First decanate (ruled by Mercury)—headache, wind disease.

Second decanate (ruled by Saturn)—fall from a height.

Third decanate (ruled by Venus)—explosion, glass, drowning.

Libra :

First decanate (ruled by Venus)—woman, fall, animal.

Second decanate (ruled by Saturn)—indigestion, gastritis.

Third decanate (ruled by Mercury)—water, snakes.

Scorpio :

First decanate (ruled by Mars)—poison, weapons.

Second decanate (ruled by Jupiter)—prostrate trouble, carrying heavy weights, complaints in hip.

Third decanate (ruled by Moon)—earth (mines), stones.

Sagittarius :

First decanate (ruled by Jupiter)—anal and colon complaints.

Second decanate (ruled by Mars)—poison, arrows, sharp instruments.

Third decanate (ruled by Sun)—abdominal complaints, water, or aquatic animals.

Capricorn :

First decanate (ruled by Saturn)—mauling by lion or wild animal, scorpion sting.

Second decanate (ruled by Venus) snake-bite.

Third decanate (ruled by Mercury) - thieves, gun shot, fever.

Aquarius :

First decanate (ruled by Saturn)—woman, pelvic disorder, venereal complaints.

Second decanate (ruled by Mercury)—disease in internal organs of generative system.

Third decanate (ruled by Venus)— infection.

Pisces :

First decanate (ruled by Jupiter) dysentery, ascitis, oesophagitis.

Second decanate (ruled by Moon) – dropsy, oesophagitis.

Third decanate (ruled by Mars) — distension of the stomach.

Table of Drekkanas

	Ayudha (weapon)	Pasa (noose)	Nigala (fetters)	Pakshi (bird)	Sarpa (serpent)	Chatushpada (quadruped)
(Drekkanas)	3rd of Leo	2nd of Scorpio	1st of Capricorn	1st of Leo	1st of Scorpio	1st of Cancer
	3rd of Aries			1st of Aquarius	3rd of Cancer	2nd of Aries
	3rd of Sagittarius			3rd of Taurus	3rd of Pisces	2nd of Taurus
	3rd of Libra			2nd of Libra		1st of Leo
						3rd of Scorpio
Decanates	3rd of Gemini					
	1st of Sagittarius					
	1st of Aries					
	2nd of Virgo					
	2nd of Gemini					

If there are planets influencing the 8th house by aspect or occupation, they cause ailments or wounds in the part of the body represented by the sign ruling the house. If more than one planet aspects or occupies the 8th house, death may come about as a result of two or more diseases.

If the 8th house is occupied by a malefic, death is painful whether natural or violent. But if the 8th house is beneficially disposed, the native has a sudden and quick end.

Thus where the 8th house is neither occupied nor aspected by any planet, the lord of 22nd drekkana gives the clue to the cause of death. Planets occupying or aspecting the 8th house indicate the cause of death. The Sun influencing the 8th house causes death through fire, the Moon through water, Mars by weapons, Mercury through fever, Jupiter through causes that cannot be diagnosed, Venus through excesses and Saturn through starvation, malnutrition, etc.

The place of death is indicated by the sign occupied by the lord of Navamsa Lagna, or the sign occupied by the planet aspecting the lord of Navamsa Lagna, or the lord of the sign in Navamsa occupied by the lord of the Navamsa Lagna. These places indicated by the signs give a general idea of the place of death.

If the 8th house is a movable sign, the native dies in a foreign country or in a place far away from his birth-place. When it happens to be a fixed sign, death occurs in his place of birth. When this is the case and planets are also so placed as to indicate death at birth-place, no matter where the native is settled or pursuing his occupation, he may be drawn to visit his birth-place at the time of death. If the 8th house falls in a common sign, the native dies while travelling or when commuting from one place to another.

Time and Fructification of the Results of the Eighth Bhava Determining Longevity

The longevity of a native can be determined by different methods. But according to most classical works, it is not possible to determine the span of life before twelve years after birth. This is because the life of the new-born baby is regulated by the actions (karma) of its parents. If the baby dies within the first four years after birth, it is said to be due to the mother's bad karma. Death between four and eight years is attributed to the bad actions of the father. If the child dies between eight and twelve years, it is because of its own sins from previous lives.

The correct determination of longevity has always been a hard nut to crack. There are several methods in vogue, both astrological and astrologico-mathematical. The *maraka vichara* (inquiry into death) on the basis of Vimshottari Dasa has, at least in our humble experience, proved quite satisfactory as it enables one to judge fairly correctly, the probable length of one's life on this planet. Of the mathematical systems, Pindayurdaya and Amsayurdaya, especially the latter, seems to have received considerable attention from several well-known ancient writers. Varahamihira says that Satyacharya's view that the longevity conferred by a planet depends upon its Navamsa position is in conformity with the views of the majority of astrological writers. The purely mathematical methods of longevity must be applied to thousands of horoscopes before a conclusion can be arrived at as to their workability. One should not reject these methods basing the conclusions on a small number of instances. We have been testing these various methods and find some of them, particularly the Amsayurdaya, yield fairly approximate results.

The Pindayu Method

Pindayu is also called Grahadattayurdaya as it is the total of the terms of life granted by all the planets when in a state of deep exaltation.

Each planet is supposed to give a certain term of life when it occupies its deep exaltation point and half the period when it occupies its deep debilitation point. At intermediate positions it gives the period equal to half the term plus the period proportionate to the planet's distance from its debilitation point.

The term of life given by each of the planets in its deep exaltation is as follows : –

Sun—19 years
Moon—25 years
Mars—15 years
Mercury—12 years
Jupiter—15 years
Venus—21 years
Saturn—20 years

The same planets in debilitation give the following terms : –

Sun—9 years 6 months
Moon—12 years 6 months
Mars—7 years 6 months
Mercury—6 years
Jupiter—7 years 6 months
Venus—10 years 6 months
Saturn—10 years

These are the terms of life each planet gives to the native, provided, the planets are not affected otherwise, either by the conjunction or by the aspect of malefics. But it is very rare that we come across horoscopes, not affected in anyway by adverse planetary positions. Out of these terms certain deductions are to be made to substitute for the evil aspects and other malefic influences. For this what is called Harana or reduction is employed. There are various kinds of Haranas which require careful application and which depend upon the intensity of the evils in any particular horoscope.

Four kinds of Haranas of reductions should be applied. They are :

1. Chakrapatha Harana,
2. Satruksehtra Harana,
3. Astangata Harana, and
4. Krurodaya Harana.

Chakrapatha Harana

The Lagna is the Ascendant. The 7th house from it or the 180th degree is the Descendant. The Descendant is the horizon. The westward direction from the Ascendant to the horizon covers the 12th, 11th, 10th, 9th, 8th and 7th Bhavas. Planets found within 180° west of the Ascendant undergo this reduction, while planets which at birth are below the horizon, *i.e.*, occupying the first six Bhavas are exempt from this reduction. Those that are nearest to the Lagna in its western direction lose a great part of their terms of life, while planets at the farthest distance from the Ascendant are not subjected to so much loss. This reduction or Harana varies also with the nature of the planet. In the case of benefics, the amount of Harana is half of what it is in the case of malefics. The Moon, Jupiter, Venus and well-associated Mercury are benefics while the Sun, Mars, Saturn and badly afflicted Mercury are malefics.

Chakrapatha Harana
To the West of Ascendant.

Planet	12th Bhava	11th Bhava	10th Bhava	9th Bhava	8th Bhava	7th Bhava
Malefic	1	1/2	1/3	1/4	1/5	1/6
Benefic	1/2	1/4	1/6	1/8	1/10	1/12

If there are two or more planets in any of these six houses, the reduction must be applied only to the strongest planet in each of the houses.

Satrukshetra Harana

After the Chakrapatha Harana is made, Satrukshetra Harana must be applied. This is based on the position of planets in their inimical houses. When a planet occupies an inimical sign, one-third of the term obtained after Chakrapatha Harana must be deducted. This reduction should not be made if the planet is retrograde or vakra. Some authors say that Mars is exempted from Satrukshetra Harana, while others claim only vakra planets must be considered. The Sanskrit word used is *vakra*. By this is meant both Mars and retrogression. But for all practical purposes, both planets in retrogression and Mars are not subjected to Satrukshetra Harana.

Astangata Harana

Asta means combustion. When a planet is very close to the Sun it seems to lose all its vitalising influences by being absorbed by the Sun's intense power, so much so that it becomes practically useless. Therefore when a planet is within certain degrees from the Sun, it is said to be in combustion and one-half of the term left after the Chakrapatha and Satrukshetra Haranas are carried out must be deducted. When the

Moon is 12° forwards or backwards of the Sun, he is Astangata. If Mars, Mercury, Jupiter, Venus and Saturn are 17°, 14°, 11°, 10° and 5° respectively either backwards or forwards of the Sun, they get combust. Mercury and Venus, if retrograde, get combust only when 12° and 8° forwards or backwards respectively of the Sun. But it must be noted that Venus and Saturn are exempt from Astangata Harana even when combust as almost all authorities agree on this point.

Krurodaya Harana

When one or more malefics occupy the Lagna, reduction due to their presence must be made in the term already obtained after the reductions due to Chakrapatha. Satrukshetra and Astangata Haranas have been made.

This is done by multiplying the number of Amsas that Lagna has passed by the total of the planetary terms. The product is divided by 108. The quotient so obtained is deducted from the total term of life. The remainder is converted into months, days, etc., and added on to the quotient which represents years.

If malefic in the Ascendant is aspected by a benefic, the Harana fraction so obtained is half of what it would otherwise be. If two or more planets occupy the Lagna, the planet nearest to the Lagna—degree must be taken into account. Thus if Lagna is 15° of a sign and Mars is 20° and Saturn 25° of the same sign, preference is given to the nearest planet, namely, Mars.

The method of Pindayu is best explained by an illustration :
Chart No. 33.—*Born 8–8–1912 at 7–35 p.m. (I.S.T.) at Bangalore.*

Longitudes of planets at birth

Planet	Degrees	Minutes
Sun	114	26
Moon	55	03
Mars	141	49
Mercury	135	25
Jupiter	224	25
Venus	123	42
Saturn	41	36
Rahu	354	15
Ketu	174	15

Rahu		Saturn Moon			Saturn	Venus	
Lagna	RASI		Sun	Rahu Sun	NAVAMSA		
			Venus Merc. Mars				Mercury Moon Ketu
	Jupiter		Ketu	Lagna	Jupiter	Mars	

Balance of Mars Dasa at birth : 6 years, 1 month and 6 days.

The Nirayana longitudes of planets are given for Chart No. 33.

The arc of longevity is obtained by deducting the longitude of exaltation point from the longitude of the planet. If the difference is more than 180°, keep it as it is. If the difference is less than 180°, rectify it by subtracting it from 360°. This gives the Arc of Longevity.

A planet when in deep exaltation gives the full term of life ascribed to it. If its position is otherwise, then the number of years it gives is determined by the rule of three.

The period contributed by a planet

$$= \frac{\text{planet's full term of life} \times \text{arc of longevity}}{360°}$$

We shall now determine the Arcs of Longevity of the different planets.

Planet	Its Longitude	Its Deep Exaltation
Sun	114° 26′	10°
Moon	55° 3′	33°
Mars	141° 49′	298°
Mercury	135° 25′	165°
Jupiter	224° 25′	95°
Venus	123° 42′	357°
Saturn	41° 36′	200°

The following Arcs of Longevity obtain in the chart :

Planet	Arc of Longevity	
	Degrees	Minutes
Sun	255	34
Moon	337	57
Mars	203	49
Mercury	330	25
Jupiter	230	35
Venus	233	34
Saturn	201	36

Sphuta Ayurvarsha (period contributed by each planet's longitude)

Sun $\quad \dfrac{255° \ 34′ \times 19}{360°} = $ 13 years 5 months 26 days

Moon $\dfrac{337° \ 57' \times 25}{360°}$ = 23 years 5 months 19 days

Mars $\dfrac{203° \ 49' \times 15}{360°}$ = 8 years 5 months 26 days

Mercury $\dfrac{330' \ 25' \times 12}{360°}$ = 11 years 0 months 0 days

Jupiter $\dfrac{230° \ 35' \times 15}{360°}$ = 9 years 7 months 9 days

Venus $\dfrac{233° \ 18' \times 21}{360°}$ = 13 years 7 months 9 days

Saturn $\dfrac{201° \ 36' \times 20}{360°}$ = 11 years 2 months 12 days

Applying the Haranas or reductions to the terms of life obtained so far, we get the following results :

Planet	Sphutavarsha			Chakrapatha	Satrukshetra	Astangata
	y.	m.	d.			
Sun	13	5	26	—	—	—
Moon	23	5	19	—	—	—
Mars	8	5	26	1/6	—	—
Mercury	11	0	0	—	—	—
Jupiter	9	7	9	1/6	—	—
Venus	13	7	9	—	1/3	—
Saturn	11	2	8	—	—	—

Of Mars, Mercury and Venus in the 7th house, Mars as the strongest suffers reduction. No Krurodaya Harana is necessary since there are no malefics in Lagna.

The following terms are obtained after applying all the reductions :

Planet	Graha Ayurdaya		
	y.	m.	d.
Sun	13	5	26
Moon	23	5	19

Planet	Graha Ayurdaya		
	y.	m.	d.
Mars	7	0	26
Mercury	11	0	00
Jupiter	8	0	3
Venus	9	0	26
Saturn	11	2	12

Total period granted by the planets   83 y. 3 m. 22 d.

We must still determine the terms of life granted by the Lagna which is Aquaruis 9° 42'. It has passed 2 Navamsas (6° 40') which gives 2 years and the balance of 3° 2' converted into time gives 10 months 28 days. Lagna therefore gives 2 years 10 months 28 days. The total longevity would be 83 years 3 months 22 days + 2 years 10 months 28 days = 86 years 2 months 20 days.

Longevity = 86 years 2 months 20 days.

The Amsayu Method

The Amsayu (longevity due to Navamsa) is held by Bhattotpala to be the only correct method. *Manitha* and *Saravali* suggest that Amsayu should be applied only when the Lagna lord is more powerful than the Sun and the Moon. Whatever the divergent views held in regard to the circumstances under which the different methods of longevity determination are to be applied, it seems to be clear that Varahamihira and his illustrious commentator Bhattotpala have approved the Amsayu Method as of much importance.

Sreepathi has dealt with Amsayu in his Paddhati but as usual, the average reader finds it difficult to understand the method, not to mention of its practical application because the language and terminology employed are too tough.

According to Satyacharya, the longitude (sphuta) of a planet is first converted into minutes (kalas). This is divided by 200. The quotient denotes the total number of Navamsas passed by a planet from the first point of Aries. The quotient is again divided by 12 to obtain the number of Navamsas passed in the sign considered. This number denotes the years. The remainder will give the fraction of a year granted by the particular planet.

The longitude of the Lagna is also subjected to the same calculations to get period of life it grants.

The period so granted by a planet is subject to both Bharana (increase) and Harana (reduction) in the following manner :

(a) A planet when exalted or retrograde gives thrice the number of years obtained by the above calculations.

(b) A planet when vargottama or occupying own Navamsa or own Rasi or own Drekkana gives twice the number of years.

(c) Where a planet is to be multiplied twice or thrice due to its situation according to both (a) and (b), the multiplication is to be done only once by the strongest factor.

The reductions are the same as in the Pindayu Method.

(d) *Chakrapatha Harana* : The reductions in respect o Chakrapatha are as per details given on page 99 for Pindayu.

(e) *Satrukshetra Harana* : Every planet in an inimical house loses one-third the term of life left after Chakrapatha reduction. This reduction, however, does not apply to Mars and retrograde planets.

(f) *Astangata Harana* : Planets when combust in the Sun lose one-half of their period remaining after reduction due to Chakrapatha and Satrukshetra occupation. Mars, Mercury,

Jupiter, Venus and Saturn are combust when within 17°, 14°, 11°, 10° and 5° respectively backwards or forwards of the Sun. Venus and Saturn are exempt from this reduction.

(g) *Krurodaya Harana* : Even if evil planets occupy the Ascendant, no reduction is to be made unlike in Pindayurdaya.

The method is best illustrated by an example.

Chart No. 34.—*Born 29/30-12-1879 at 1 a.m. (L.M.T.) at 9 N 50, 78 E 15.*

Saturn	Mars		Ketu Moon	Jupit.		Ketu	Moon
Jupiter				Merc.			Venus
	RASI				NAVAMSA		
	NH-46						
Rahu Sun	Mercury Venus	Lagna		Sat.	Rahu Mars	Lagna	Sun

Balance of Jupiter Dasa at birth : 4 years, 1 month and 20 days.

Planet	Longitude	Longitude in Minutes
Sun	257° 4'	15424
Moon	89° 58'	5398
Mars	23° 26'	1406
Mercury	234° 36'	14076
Jupiter	317° 57'	19077
Venus	211° 57'	12717
Saturn	348° 32'	20912
Lagna	182° 19'	10938

In order to get the Navamsas passed in a sign (which denote the number of years granted by each planet in whole numbers), divide the longitude of a planet in minutes by 200.

$$\text{Sun} = \frac{15424}{200} = 77\,\frac{24}{200}$$

Dividing again the quotient 77 by 12, we get a remainder of 5 which is the number of Navamsas passed by the Sun from the first point of Aries. In other words, the Sun contributes 5 whole years and 24/200 of a year, *i.e.*, 5 years 1 month 13 days. Similarly find out the term granted by each of the planets.

Planet	Term granted		
	y.	m.	d.
Sun	5	1	13
Moon	2	11	26
Mars	7	0	10
Mercury	10	4	17
Jupiter	11	4	19
Venus	3	7	2
Saturn	8	6	21
Lagna	6	8	8

Bharanas and Haranas

Bharanas: The Moon is vargottama, Mars occupies his own sign in Rasi and Navamsa and Jupiter occupies his own sign in Navamsa. Therefore, their periods are doubled.

	y.	m.	d.					y.	m.	d.
Moon =	2	11	26	×	2	=		5	11	22
Mars =	7	0	10	×	2	=		14	0	20
Jupiter =	11	4	19	×	2	=		22	9	08

Haranas

Chakrapatha :   Mars, a malefic, is in the 7th house and suffers reduction by 1/6th his term got after Bharana.

The Moon, a benefic, is in the 9th house and suffers reduction by 1/8th the term he gets after Bharana.

After the Chakrapatha reduction, we have

Mars   =   11 years 8 months 17 days
Moon   =   5 years 2 months 23 days

Satrukshetra :   The Moon and Mercury occupy inimical signs and suffer reduction by 1/3rd of their respective terms. The Moon's term after Chakrapatha Harana = 5y. 2m. 23d. The Moon's term after 1/3 reduction = 3y. 5m. 25d. Mercury's term = 10y. 4m. 17d. Mercury's term after 1/3 reduction = 6y. 11m. 1d.

Astangata Harana

No planet is combust.

Adding up the terms granted by all the planets :

Planet	Term of life		
	y.	m.	d.
Sun	5	1	13
Moon	3	5	25
Mars	11	8	17
Mercury	6	11	1
Jupiter	22	9	08
Venus	3	7	1
Saturn	8	6	22
Lagna	6	8	8
Total	68y.	10m.	5d.

The native of Chart No. 34 died on 15-4-1950, that is, at the age of 70 years 3 months 15 days which is quite close to the term obtained on the basis of Amsayurdaya.

Other Methods

There are several other mathematical methods of determining longevity like Jeevasarmayu, etc., but we feel that their exposition in these pages is not necessary. The most reliable mathematical method, in our humble view, is that of Jaimini. This has been elaborately dealt with, with examples, in our book *Studies in Jaimini Astrology*, to which readers may refer, in case they are interested in learning the Jaimini method.

Ashtakavarga method is equally important. But, it does not seem to be quite reliable. The Ashtakavarga method of longevity determination has been explained in detail in our book *Ashtakavarga System of Prediction*.

Yet another method given in classical texts which seems, in our experience, to be over-simplified is to add the longitudes of Saturn, Jupiter, the Sun and the Moon. This gives a point in the zodiac after expunging multiples of 12°. In the case of short, middle and long life, death occurs when Saturn transits over this point in his first, second and third cycles respectively.

Although Jaimini's method, Pindayurdaya and Amsayurdaya yield fairly accurate results, it is wise to determine longevity on the basis of the strength of the chart and the Dasas and Bhuktis. The first step would be to see if a given chart belongs to Balarishta, Alpayu, Madhyayu or Poornayu, on the basis of the combinations given earlier. Then, longevity can be fixed by determining the most powerful marakas or death-inflicting planets.

Determining the Period of Death

In the I Volume of this work, we have discussed in brief under the caption "Determination of Longevity", the principles for determining the killer-planets. In this chapter we propose to deal with the same subject in somewhat greater detail, even at the risk of repetition, so that the reader can understand the subject more thoroughly.

Death dealing or maraka planets can be divided into 3 groups :

(*a*) Primary Determinants of Death,

(*b*) Secondary Determinants of Death, and

(*c*) Tertiary Determinants of Death.

Primary Determinants of Death : The 3rd and the 8th house are the houses of life. The 12th houses from these two, namely, the 2nd and the 7th are the houses of death.

(*a*) The 2nd and 7th lords cause death.

(*b*) The occupants, particularly malefics, of the 2nd and 7th houses.

(*c*) The planets, especially malefics, associating with the 2nd and 7th lords.

Of these, the planets in conjunction with the 2nd and 7th lords are the most powerful in causing death.

Secondary Determinants of Death :

(*a*) Benefic planets in association with the 2nd and 7th lords are less powerful in causing death than malefic planets.

(*b*) Lords of the 3rd and the 8th.

(*c*) The lord of the 3rd or 8th house associating with the 2nd or the 7th lord.

Tertiary Determinants of Death :

(*a*) Saturn in conjunction, aspect or association with

any of the primary or secondary determinants of death.

(b)   The lord of the 6th or the 8th house.

(c)   The weakest planet in the horoscope.

The following planets are called *chidra-grahas* and the strongest of them can cause death in his period :

(a)   the lord of the 8th house

(b)   the planet occupying the 8th house

(c)   the planet aspecting the 8th house

(d)   the lord of the 22nd Drekkana

(e)   the planet in association with the 8th lord

(f)   the lord of the 64th Navamsa occupied by the Moon

(g)   the bitter enemy of the 8th lord.

The 8th house is the house of life and if afflicted terminates life. If the 8th lord is in the 6th, 8th or the 12th house, death of the person can occur,

(1)   in the Dasa and Bhukti of the 8th lord, or

(2)   in the Dasa of the lord of the sign occupied by Saturn in the sub-period of the 8th lord, or

(3)   in the Dasa of the 8th lord and Bhukti of the 9th lord.

The planets most afflicted by maraka properties by aspect, association or occupation will cause death.

If the Lagna lord is in the 6th, 8th or the 12th houses with Rahu or Ketu, death takes place in the Dasa of the planet associating with Lagna lord or in that of the 8th lord. If Lagna lord is not associated with any planet, the ruler of the sign occupied by Lagna lord or the 8th lord will be fatal. When Rahu Dasa operates at the appropriate time (when life has been determined to be short, medium or long), it can be a killer. If out of Saturn, the lords of Lagna, the 8th or the 10th

house, the weakest planet is associated with Rahu, this planet
can cause death in its period, according to *Jataka Parijatha*. If
the 8th lord is strong, the lord of Lagna can kill in his period.
If the Lagna lord is strong, the 8th lord can kill in his Dasa. If
the Lagna and 8th lords occupy a quadrant or trine with
another planet, death occurs in the Dasa of the planet in the
8th house. If the 8th house is not occupied by any planet,
death takes place in the Dasa of Lagna lord when Saturn
transits Lagna or the 8th house.

If Lagna is a Seershodaya sign (Gemini, Leo, Virgo, Libra,
Scorpio and Aquarius), death takes place in the periods of the
lord of the 2nd or Lagna or of Rahu according as Lagna is a
movable, fixed or common sign. If the Lagna is a Prushtodaya
sign (Aries, Taurus, Cancer, Sagittarius and Capricorn), death
may come about in the periods of the lord of the Lagna
Drekkana, the planet aspected by the lord of Lagna Drekkana
and the planet in conjunction with the lord of the Lagna
Drekkana respectively if the rising sign is movable, fixed or
common.

Death-inflicting Transits

Standard classical works on astrology give several methods
based on transits of certain planets by which the period of
death may be gauged with a fair degree of accuracy. Death
indicated on the basis of transits can happen only when the
directional influences in the birth charts warrant. Otherwise
misfortunes such as ill-health, loss of money, misunderstanings
with kith and kin and separations, may happen. Readers must
clearly bear this in mind when interpreting the following
combinations bearing on transits.

Saturn, the Ayushkaraka, is also the Mrutyukaraka. When

Saturn passes through the houses occupied by the 8th lord or the 12th lord from Lagna, death occurs. Passage of Saturn through these houses or their trines with reference to any other house in the horoscope results in the destruction of that house.

Saturn's transit of the sign (or its trines) occupied by the lord of the 22nd Drekkana or Mandi brings about death.

When Saturn passes through the sign (Rasi and Navamsa) denoted by the difference obtained by subtracting the longitude of Saturn from that of Mandi, death is likely. Add up the longitudes of the 8th, 12th and 6th lords. Saturn passing through the sign (or its trines) indicated by the sum indicates death. Saturn's transit of the sign as far removed from Mandi as Mandi is from the 8th lord is also a fateful transit.

Jupiter also indicates death when he arrives at a sign that is triangular to the one occupied by the 8th lord. His transit through the Rasi (or its trines) resulting from the sum of the longitudes of the Lagna, the Sun and Mandi causes death. When Jupiter crosses the Rasi indicated by the sum of the longitudes of Jupiter and Rahu or through its trines, death can be expected.

When the Sun transits the Dwadasamsa he occupies in Rasi, or the Navamsa occupied by the 8th lord or the Navamsa occupied by Lagna lord or the trines of any one of these signs, death may be apprehended. When the Sun passes through the 6th, 7th or the 12th house from Venus, then also death is possible.

When the Moon crosses the Rasi or Navamsa occupied by the 8th lord or the Sun or their trines, death is likely. Add together the longitudes of Mandi and the Moon. The sign indicated by the sum can also cause death when the Moon

8

passes through it.   Death is possible when the Moon crosses the sign occupied by the lord of the 22nd Drekkana reckoned from the Moon or through the trines of these houses.   The transit of the Moon through the Lagna, the 8th or the 12th house also causes death.

Find out the Navamsa, Dwadasamsa and the Drekkana occupied by Mandi.   The transits of Jupiter through the sign indicated by the Navamsa, of Saturn through that of Dwadasamsa and the Sun through the one (or its trines) indicated by the Drekkana indicates death.   The Lagna denoted by the sum of the Lagna, the Moon and Mandi indicates the time of death.

Chart No. 35.—*Born 30/31-1-1896 at 4–30 a.m. (L.M.T.) at 22 N, 73 E 16.*

RASI chart:

		Mandi	
Mercury Rahu	RASI	Moon Jupit.	
Sun	RP. 3-112	Ketu	
Lagna Mars Venus	Saturn		

NAVAMSA chart:

		Sun Saturn Venus
Moon	NAVAMSA	Mars Ketu
Rahu		
Mercury	Jupiter	Lagna

Balance of Mercury Dasa at birth : 5 years, 1 month and 6 days.

As earlier cautioned these transits must be looked into only after determining the maraka Dasas and Bhuktis on the strength of the Ascendant, the Moon and other planets. Transits are always secondary in importance. They are like catalytic agents. All conclusions must be primarily drawn on the basis of Dasa-vichara (analysis of Dasa).

The 8th House : Cancer as 8th house is occupied by 8th lord Moon in association with exalted Jupiter in Chart No. 35. It is aspected by 5th and 12th lord Mars, exalted karaka and 3rd lord Saturn and 9th lord Sun.

The 8th Lord : The 8th lord Moon occupies his own sign Cancer in association with exalted Lagna lord Jupiter. Further the 8th lord is full and very powerful. He is aspected by an exalted 3rd lord Saturn and 5th and 12th lord Mars.

The 3rd house and lord : Saturn is the 3rd lord exalted in an upachaya, the 11th house. He is also the *ayushkaraka* and powerfully placed. The 3rd house is occupied by 7th lord Mercury and afflicted by Rahu. Considered from the Moon, the 8th house Aquarius is occupied by afflicted Mercury, the 3rd and 12th lord. The 8th lord Saturn is exalted in the 4th. The 3rd lord Mercury is in Ayusthana with Rahu.

Conclusion : The strong disposition of the Lagna lord, the 8th houses and 3rd house and their respective lords both from Lagna and Moon-sign would place the native in the Poornayu group.

Timing Death : In Chart No. 35, the Lagna is Sagittarius. The 3rd lord Saturn is in the 11th exalted. The 8th lord Moon is in own house with exalted Jupiter. The 2nd lord is again Saturn exalted in the 11th while the 7th lord is in the 3rd (2nd Bhava) with Rahu. From the Moon, the 2nd lord is the Sun and he is in the 7th while the 3rd lord Mercury is in the 8th with Rahu. The 7th and 8th lord from the Moon is Saturn. Rahu is a malefic associated with 7th lord from Lagna.

Coming to Navamsa, the 2nd and 3rd lords are Venus and Mars respectively, while the 7th and 8th lords are Jupiter and

Mars respectively. From the Moon, the 2nd and 3rd are ruled by Jupiter and Mars respectively. The malefic associate with the 2nd lord is Saturn. We give below a table showing the units of maraka power that each planet gets by virtue of ownership, occupation and association. Students of astrology will be able to appreciate the whole procedure better.

| Planet | Power of marakas obtained by | | | No. of Units |
	Ownership	Location	Association	
Sun	2nd lord from Moon 7th lord from Moon in Amsa	2nd from Lagna 7th from Moon	With 2nd lord in Amsa	5
Moon	8th lord	8th from Lagna	—	2
Mars	8th lord in Amsa	—	—	3
	3rd lord in Amsa	—	—	
	3rd lord from Moon in Amsa	—	—	
Mercury	7th lord	3rd from Lagna	—	
	3rd lord from Moon	8th from Moon	—	
	8th lord from Moon in Amsa	3rd from Lagna in Amsa	—	6
Jupiter	7th lord in Amsa	2nd from Lagna in Amsa	With 8th lord from Lagna	4
	2nd lord from Moon in Amsa	—	—	

| Planet | Power of marakas obtained by | | | No. of Units |
	Ownership	Location	Association	
Venus	2nd lord in Amsa	—	With 7th lord from Moon in Amsa	2
Saturn	2nd lord	—	With 2nd lord in Amsa	6
	3rd lord	—	With 7th lord from Moon in Amsa	
	8th lord from Moon			
	7th lord from Moon			
Rahu	—	3rd from Lagna	Malefic associate of 7th lord	3
		8th from Moon		
Ketu	—	2nd from Moon	With 8th lord in Amsa	4
			With 3rd lord in Amsa	
			With 3rd lord from Moon in Amsa	

Out of a total of 35 units of maraka, Saturn and Mercury each get 6 units while the Sun gets the next highest number of 5 units. As the lord of the 9th and powerfully aspected by

Jupiter, the Sun loses the maraka power in his Dasa, but would produce the same in the Bhukti within the Dasa of another malefic. Mercury Dasa comes very late in life (being also Dasa at birth) so that possibility of death in his Dasa is out of question. Saturn Dasa will come in the native's 90th year, which is far too late. Saturn by virtue of his inherent affinity with Rahu *(Sanivad Rahu)* delegates his maraka or killing power to Rahu.

Rahu, it will be seen, occupies the 3rd house and is in association with Mercury, lord of the 7th from Lagna and who owns the 8th from the Moon in Navamsa. As Rahu happens to be a malefic associate of the 7th lord he has every qualification to inflict death in his Dasa. As we have already noticed, Saturn has the largest number of units for killing next to Mercury who cannot do his job ; and as Saturn himself cannot cause death, he must naturally delegate his power on the planet occupying his sign. Such a planet would be Rahu.

Rahu is in the 8th from the Moon. Hence Rahu gets the power to kill in his Dasa. Mercury Dasa rules at birth with a balance of 5 years 1 month 6 days. Then the Dasas of Ketu, Venus, Sun, Moon and Mars last for 50 years bringing the total to 55 years 1 month 6 days from birth. This will be upto about 7-3-1951. Then Rahu Dasa commences. When will he kill ? His Dasa extends for 18 years. Will Rahu spare the native all the 18 years ? Ketu is a likely candidate. Ketu should partake of the characteristics of the Sun but as the Sun himself has 5 units, Ketu has only 4 units of maraka power so that he would rather assume the responsibility himself than allow Ketu to do it.

Gochara influences must also synchronise with the time of death. The sub periods of Rahu, Jupiter, Saturn, Mercury,

Ketu and Venus in the Dasa of Rahu last for 14 years 6 months 18 days. This will bring the age to about 69 years 7 months 24 days. Venus Bhukti in Rahu Dasa ends by about 25-9-1965 from which date Sun Bhukti commences. The Sun as we have already seen owns the 2nd from the Moon Lagna and occupies the 7th maraka from the Moon while he is placed in the 2nd from Lagna. In the Navamsa again he owns the 7th from the Moon and is associated with the 2nd lord from Lagna. Moreover he is a bitter enemy of Rahu and in Rasi the major and sub-lords are in *dwirdwadasa* (2/12) while in Amsa, they are in *shashtashtaka* (6,8). Thus the Sun is fully empowered to kill in his Bhukti which runs between 25-9-1965 and 19-8-1966.

When maraka Dasa is operating the momentum of the last signal for death is given by Ayushkaraka Saturn in his transits. Death occurs when Saturn in his transit passes through the Rasi and Amsa occupied by him at birth or its trines. Saturn occupies Libra in Rasi and Gemini in Navamsa. Aquarius is in trine to both these signs. Saturn enters Aquarius by February 1964. He will occupy Aquarius Rasi and Gemini Navamsa by February–March 1966.

The native died on 7–2–1966.

Balarishta

Predictions regarding the longevity of children are generally not advisable. A chart with severe afflictions may give a sickly childhood or make one prone to recurring accidents. But the question of death itself is best left untouched. Anyway we give here some charts illustrating death in childhood.

In Chart No. 36 the Moon is in the 8th house with Rahu and is aspected by a malefic planet Saturn. Lagna is aspected by Mars adversely. Jupiter, no doubt, aspects Lagna but as 8th

Chart No. 36.—*Born on 16-12-1950 at 10-30 p.m. (I.S.T.) at 22 N 34, 88 E 24.*

Moon Rahu				Mars	Saturn Sun	
Jupiter	RASI				NAVAMSA	Venus Rahu
Mars	GD-55		Lagna	Ketu Jupit.		
Mercury Venus Sun			Sat. Ketu		Mercury	Moon Lagna

Balance of Saturn Dasa at birth :   12 years,   4 months and 6 days.

lord his presence in the 7th is not welcome (the 7th is the 12th from the 8th house). Afflictions to the Moon and Lagna generally cause death in infancy or childhood. The child died at the age of 2½ years.

In Chart No. 37 the Moon is afflicted by Rahu and Saturn. He does not receive any benefic aspects. Both Rahu and the Moon move into the twelfth Bhava. The child died in its 3rd year.

In Chart No. 38 the Moon is in a malefic sign afflicted by Mars and Saturn. There is a particular yoga by which 'if the Moon occupies a malefic sign or Navamsa with no benefic aspects and malefics occupy the 5th or the 9th house, the child dies early'. Here the Moon is not only in a malefic sign as well as Navamsa but is also severely afflicted by two powerful natural as well as functional malefics, Mars and Saturn. The

Chart No. 37.—*Born 2-2-1871 at 5-21 p.m. (L.M.T.) at 54 N 56, 1 W 25.*

		Jupiter	Moon Rahu	Moon Rahu	Lagna	Mars	
Venus							Sun
	RASI		----		NAVAMSA		Jupiter Saturn
Sun	GD-7		Lagna				
Mercury Saturn Ketu			Mars	Merc.	Venus		Ketu

Balance of Rahu Dasa at birth :   0 years, 2 months and 29 days.

Chart No. 38.—*Born 7-8-1873 at 9-05 a.m. at 54 N 56, 1 W 25*

	Rahu		Venus	Lagna Sat.	Mercury Mars	Ketu
			Sun	Moon Sun		
	RASI		----		NAVAMSA	Jupiter
Saturn Moon	GD-13		Merc. Jupit.	Venus		
		Ketu Mars	Lagna	Rahu		

Balance of Sun Dasa at birth : 1 year, 6 months and 27 days.

5th house is occupied by a malefic planet Saturn. The child died on 14–8–1873, hardly a week after birth.

Chart No. 39.—*Born 22-10-1960 at 2-32 a.m. (L.M.T.) at 38 N 17, 88 W 55.*

			Mars		Ketu		Jupiter
Ketu							Moon Mercury
	RASI				NAVAMSA		
	GD-91		Lagna Rahu				
Saturn Jupiter	Moon Mercury Venus	Sun		Sun	Lagna Saturn Rahu Mars	Venus	

Balance of Jupiter Dasa at birth : 2 years, 7 months and 13 days.

'Malefics in the Lagna and the 7th house and the Moon with a malefic, if not aspected by benefic planets, causes early death of the child.' In Chart No. 39 Rahu occupies the exact Lagna degree and Ketu is in the 7th aspected by Mars. The Moon is in the 4th with benefics but hemmed between malefics Saturn and the Sun. He receives no benefic aspects. The child died in Saturn Dasa, Ketu Bhukti. The Balarishta Yoga applying in Chart No. 38 applies here also. The Moon occupies a malefic sign in Rasi and is not aspected by any benefic planet. Saturn, a malefic, aspected by another malefic Mars, occupies the 5th house.

Chart No. 40.—*Born 14-4-1920 at 9 p.m. (E.S.T.) at 14 E 31, 51 N.*

Venus Mercury	Sun Ketu				Sun	Lagna Rahu	
Moon			Jupit.				
	RASI			Mars Moon	NAVAMSA		Mercury Saturn
			Sat.				
	GD-109						
		Mars Lagna Rahu			Ketu	Moon Venus	Jupiter

Balance of Rahu Dasa at birth :   12 years, 2 months and 2 days.

In Chart No. 40 the Lagna and 7th house are occupied by Mars–Rahu and Sun–Ketu respectively. The Moon is in Aquarius aspected by malefic Saturn and does not receive any beneficial aspects. The Lagna is hemmed between Mars and Rahu degreewise though all three occupy the same sign. The girl died in April 1929 just at the end of the Balarishta span.

In Chart No. 41 the Moon is not afflicted much and is aspected by Jupiter who is combust. But powerful debilitated malefics occupy the main quadrants, namely, Saturn occupies the 7th and Mars, the 10th house, both aspecting the Ascendant. According to classical works 'if the Lagna lord is debilitated and Saturn occupies the 7th or the 8th house from Lagna, the child suffers much and dies quickly'. Venus is the Lagna lord and he is not only debilitated but also eclipsed by Ketu and

Chart No. 41.—*Born 1–9–1968 at 10–30 a.m. at 13° N, 77 E 35.*

	RASI GD-115				NAVAMSA		
Rahu	Saturn			Merc. Lagna Venus	Saturn Moon		Ketu
			Mars	Mars			
			Sun Jupit.				
Moon		Lagna	Merc. Venus Ketu	Rahu		Jupiter	Sun

Balance of Ketu Dasa at birth : 5 years, 4 months and 14 days.

in the 12th house. Debilitated Saturn occupies the 7th house. The boy died in September 1975 in his 8th year.

In Chart No. 42 the Moon is in a dusthana afflicted by Ketu. Malefics in the 6th and 12th houses with no benefic aspects cause Balarishta. Here Ketu is in the 6th and Rahu is aspected by Saturn and Mars is in the 12th. The boy died in March 1929.

Alpayu

In most cases of Alpayu, the Ascendant and 8th house and their lords are weak either due to occupation, aspect or other affliction. Benefics may also be weak while malefics may be strong in kendras.

The Eighth House (Chart No. 43) : Capricorn is the 8th house free of aspects or occupation. It is hemmed between malefics Saturn and Ketu.

Chart No. 42.—*Born 21–2–1925 at 5–15 p.m. (C.E.T.) at 14 E 31, 51 N.*

	Mars			Saturn	
Sun Mercury		Rahu			Moon Lagna Ketu
Venus Moon Ketu	RASI GD-119	Lagna	Rahu Sun	NAVAMSA	Venus
Jupiter	Saturn				Mercury Jupiter	Mars

Balance of Moon Dasa at birth : 1 year, 0 month and 0 days.

Chart No. 43.—*Born 19-10-1959 at 11-45 p.m. (I.S.T.) at 20° N, 56', 77 E 48.*

Ketu	Moon		Moon	Rahu Saturn	
		Lagna			Lagna
Saturn	RASI GD-83	Venus		NAVAMSA	Mercury
	Jupiter	Sun Mars	Rahu Merc.	Venus Mars	Sun	Ketu Jupiter	

Balance of Sun Dasa at birth : 0 years, 10 months and 21 days.

The Eighth Lord :   Saturn is in the 7th in a kendra but in the 12th house from the 8th house. He is aspected by a combust Mars.

Ayushkaraka :   Saturn is in his own sign but in a marakasthana and aspected by a malefic Mars.

Considered from the Moon :   The 8th lord is in the 12th from the 8th.

Conclusions :   The Lagna is fairly strong being Vargottama and Lagna lord is exalted but in an asterism of the 2nd lord Sun. Strong malefics occupy kendras. Mars, who is combust, aspects the Lagna adversely The 3rd house and 3rd lord are both afflicted by Rahu. The native died at 16 years in Ketu Bhukti, Mars Dasa.

Within the span of Alpayu, the Sun, the Moon, Mars and Rahu (part) Dasas operate. Mars is the 7th lord from the Moon

Chart No. 44. *—Born 4-4-1948 at 6 a.m. (I.S.T.) at 26 N 18, 73 E 04.*

Sun Lagna Mercury	Rahu	Venus		Venus		Ketu	Jupiter
	RASI		Mars Sat.	Mars Sat.	NAVAMSA		Mercury Moon
Moon				Sun			
	GD-85						
Jupiter		Ketu			Rahu	Lagna	

Balance of Moon Dasa at birth : 1 year, 11 months and 7 days.

and is with the 2nd lord from Lagna, namely the Sun. He is aspected by 7th lord Saturn. Ketu should give the results of Mars and Jupiter. Jupiter is the 8th lord from the Moon and placed in the 7th from there becoming a maraka.

The Eighth House (Chart No. 44) : Libra is occupied by a malefic Ketu and aspected by a debilitated Mars.

The Eighth Lord : Venus is well placed in his own sign Taurus but in the constellation of 6th lord the Sun.

Ayushkaraka : Saturn is in the 5th house aspected by 5th lord the Moon but in very close conjunction with debilitated Mars. He occupies the constellation of 7th lord Mercury.

Considered from the Moon : The 8th house is aspected by 3rd and 12th lord Jupiter from a nodal* asterism. The 8th lord is in the 3rd with Mercury, 6th and 8th lord. Two powerful malefics afflict the Moon.

Conclusion : Lagna is occupied by a malefic 6th lord Sun and a maraka, Mercury. Lagna lord Jupiter is in a kendra but in the asterism of a node who occupies the 8th house in affliction.

Either in the I Volume or in the II Volume of this work we have not so far touched the significance of asrerisms or constellations as it forms a distinct subject by itself. The significance of constellational lords is highlighted by Satyacharya and hence its importance cannot be under-rated. The lordships of planets assigned to constellations are on the basis of the Vimshottari Dasa lords. (Krittika, Uttara and Uttarashadha—the Sun ; Rohini, Hasta and Sravana—the Moon ; Mrigasira, Chitta and Dhanishta—Mars ; Aridra, Swati and Satabhisha —Rahu ; Punarvasu, Visakha and Poorvabhadra—Jupiter ; Pushyami, Anuradha and Uttarabhadra—Saturn ; Aslesha, Jyeshta and Revati— Mercury ; Makha, Moola and Aswini—Ketu ; and Pubba, Poorvashadha and Bharani—Venus.)

Thus in this chart Jupiter who is in the 3rd house is in the constellation of Moola ruled by Ketu, one of the nodes.

Longevity must come within Alpayu due to the malefic nature of the asterisms occupied by Lagna lord, 8th lord and 3rd lord and the severe affliction to the Moon.

Death occurred in Saturn Bhukti, Rahu Dasa. Rahu in the 2nd house in a sign of Mars is a powerful maraka. His sign-dipositor Mars is the 2nd lord and in the 7th from the Moon with 2nd lord Saturn. Saturn, the Bhukti lord, is also a maraka, particularly from the Moon both in Rasi and Navamsa.

Chart No. 45.—Born 26-5-1950 at 6-30 a.m. (I.S.T.) at 82 E 13, 16 N 52.

Venus Rahu	Mercury	Lagna Sun			Venus	Sun Ketu		Lagna
Jupiter	RASI				Mars Jupit.	NAVAMSA		
	GD-51		Sat Moon					
					Mars Ketu	Moon Mercury	Rahu	Saturn

Balance of Venus Dasa at birth : 2 years 1 month and 15 days.

The Eighth House : The 8th house is Sagittarius aspected by 7th lord eclipsed Mars.

The Eighth Lord : Jupiter, the 8th lord, is in a kendra aspected by Moon and Saturn. Jupiter is in an asterism of Rahu who though in the 11th is aspected by 7th lord Mars.

Ayushkaraka : Saturn occupies his inimical sign Leo with 3rd lord Moon and is aspected by 8th lord Jupiter.

Considered from the Moon : The 7th lord Saturn occupies the Moon-sign while the 8th house is occupied by exalted Vargottama but eclipsed Venus and aspected by an afflicted Mars. The 8th lord Jupiter is in a kendra in the 12th from the 7th house.

Conclusion : Both from Lagna and the Moon, the 8th lords are well placed. But Lagna lord Venus though exalted is afflicted by Rahu and Mars in the constellation of Mercury, the 2nd lord, a maraka, placed in the 12th house. This would make the 8th lord stronger than Lagna lord causing Alpayu. The native died in Venus Bhukti of Moon Dasa. Venus occupies Pisces with Rahu aspected by Mars and is in the asterism of 2nd lord Mercury. The Moon occupies the 4th with karaka Saturn (the 7th lord from Moon) and is aspected by 8th lord Jupiter proving maraka there by.

Chart No. 46.—*Born 29-1-1955 at 10 p.m. (I.S.T.) at 9 N 58, 76 E 17.*

Moon Mars		Ketu	Moon
Mercury	RASI	Jupit.	
Sun	GD-59		Ketu
Rahu Venus	Saturn	Lagna	Mars

Lagna Venus		Sun Saturn	
		NAVAMSA	Rahu Jupiter
Mercury			

Balance of Mercury Dasa at birth : 3 years, 5 months and 9 days.

9

The Eighth House : It is aspected by an exalted ayush-karaka Saturn who is in the asterism of the 7th lord.

The Eighth Lord : In Chart No. 46 Mars is in the 7th house (in the 12th from the 8th) with 11th lord Moon aspected by 7th lord exalted Jupiter.

Ayushkaraka : Saturn is exalted in the 2nd and is aspected adversely by 8th lord Mars.

Considered from the Moon : The eighth house is occupied by exalted Saturn and aspected by 2nd lord Mars. The 8th lord is in the 10th eclipsed and aspected by Saturn.

Conclusion : The 8th lord is in a kendra while Lagna lord is weakly placed in the 6th house subject to a *papakartari* caused by Sun and Mars. Further he occupies the constellation of the 8th lord.

Venus Dasa, Jupiter Bhukti killed the native. Venus is the 2nd lord from Lagna, the 2nd and 7th lord from Navamsa Lagna and in the 2nd from the Moon in Navamsa. Jupiter as 7th lord from Lagna becomes a powerful maraka, more so being aspected by 2nd occupant Saturn.

The Eighth House : In Chart No. 47 Taurus is aspected by 3rd and 6th lord Jupiter.

The Eighth Lord : Venus is debillitated in the 12th house with 12th lord Mercury.

Ayushkaraka : Saturn occupies his moolatrikona sign Aquarius but in a nodal constellation.

Considered from the Moon : The 8th house is adversely aspected by an afflicted Mars and Moon-sign lord Jupiter. Jupiter is in parivartana with 12th lord Mars and is aspected by 2nd and 3rd lord Saturn. The 8th lord is the Moon himself afflicted by Mars and Rahu.

Chart No. 47.—*Born 2-11-1935 at 5-40 a.m. (I.S.T.) at 13° N 28', 77 E 32.*

			Ketu		Sun		Ketu
Saturn	RASI				NAVAMSA		Mars
			Venus Sat.				
	G. 1-6						
Rahu Moon Mars	Jupiter	Sun Lagna	Venus Merc.	Lagna	Rahu	Moon	Jupiter Mercury

Balance of Venus Dasa at birth : 6 years, 1 month and 24 days.

Conclusion : The Lagna and 8th lord Venus is debilitated in the 12th house. The Lagna is occupied by a malefic, debilitated Sun. The Moon is also severely afflicted by malefics. The chart therefore comes within Alpayu.

Death took place in Venus Bhukti of Mars Dasa. Venus is with Mercury who is the 7th lord from the Moon. He is in the 2nd from Navamsa Lagna with 2nd lord Saturn. He is also the afflicted 8th lord. Mars, the Dasa lord, is the 2nd and 7th lord from Lagna and from the Moon in Navamsa. He is debilitated in Navamsa and aspected by 2nd and 3rd lord Saturn which renders him a first-rate maraka.

The Eighth House : In Chart No. 48 Scorpio is the 8th house aspected by an exalted 4th lord Moon.

The Eighth Lord: Mars is in the 12th in exact conjunction with 2nd and 7th lord Venus and is also combust. He is with 3rd and 6th lord Mercury.

Chart No. 48.—*Born 3-4-1949 at 8 a.m. (I.S.T.) at 13° N, 77 E 35.*

Sun Mars Venus Mercury	Lagna Rahu	Moon		Jupit.	Moon	Rahu	Saturn
	RASI				NAVAMSA		
Jupiter	G II-50		Sat.	Sun			
		Ketu		Mars Venus	Ketu	Mercury	Lagna

Balance of Moon Dasa at birth : 9 years, 6 months and 23 days.

Ayushkaraka : Saturn is in the 5th in an inimical sign in the constellation of Ketu who occupies marakasthana, the 7th heuse.

Considered from the Moon : The 8th house has no aspects and is not occupied by any planet either. The eighth lord Jupiter is in the 9th debilitated.

Conclusion : Lagna is occupied by Rahu and Lagna lord is in the 12th in exact conjunction with a maraka Venus in a constellation ruled by Mercury who is the 3rd and 6th lord and placed in the 12th. Further both Lagna and 8th lords are in combustion. The Moon is exalted but is aspected by malefic Saturn and debilitated Jupiter indicating a short life.

The native died in Venus Bhukti, Rahu Dasa. Rahu is in Lagna in a martian sign. Mars is in the 7th, from the Moon. Rahu should give results similar to Saturn who is the natural significator of death in an asterism ruled by Ketu, a maraka. Rahu occupies the second from Navamsa Moon. Venus, the Bhukti lord, is a maraka from Lagna, from Navamsa Lagna and also from the Moon in Navamsa, being lord of the 2nd and 7th from all these points.

Chart No. 49.—*Born 24-8-1944 at 5–15 a.m. (W.T.) at 41 N 28, 81 W 40.*

		Sat.				Sun
	RASI	Rahu Lagna	Sat. Ketu Mars	**NAVAMSA**		
Ketu		Sun Jupit. Venus	Lagna Merc.		Rahu Jupiter	
	GD-81					
	Moon	Merc. Mars	Moon	Venus		

Balance of Rahu Dasa at birth :   13 years,   7 months and 27 days.

The Eighth House : Capricorn is the 8th house aspected by 2nd lord Sun, 6th and 9th lord Jupiter and 4th and 10th lord Venus.

The Eighth Lord : Saturn is the 8th lord placed in the 12th house.

Ayushkaraka : Saturn is the 7th and 8th lord as well placed in a dusthana, the 12th house.

Considered from the Moon : The 8th house is Taurus and receives no aspects while the 8th lord Venus is in the 11th house hemmed between Mars and Rahu.

The Lagna is occupied by a node and Lagna lord is in a kendra. But Lagna lord is the Moon himself placed in a nodal constellation. There are no other planets in kendras. The 3rd lord Mercury is also afflicted being in a cusp and with malefic Mars. The lord of longevity, Saturn, is in the house of loss, the 12th house. The chart therefore cannot give much longevity.

Death took place in Saturn Dasa, Saturn Bhukti. Saturn is a first-rate maraka being the 7th and 8th lord. He is also the 2nd lord from both Navamsa Lagna and the Moon in Navamsa and occupies a marakasthana in Navamsa.

Madhyayu

Chart No. 50.—*Born 25–12–1917 at 11–55 p.m. (G M.T) at 0 W 05, 51 N 31.*

		Moon Jupiter	Ketu			Lagna Moon Jupiter	
	RASI		Sat.		Mars	NAVAMSA	Rahu Sun
Venus	GD-79				Sat. Ketu		
Mercury Sun Rahu		Mars Lagna			Merc.		Venus

Balance of Moon Dasa at birth : 7 years, 7 months and 6 days.

The Eighth House : The 8th house is Aries aspected adversely by the 8th lord Mars and Saturn, the 5th and 6th lord in Chart No. 50.

The Eighth Lord :   Mars the 8th lord is placed in Lagna Kendra and aspected by 7th lord Jupiter and Saturn.

Ayushkaraka :   Saturn is placed in the 11th house aspected by 2nd and 9th lord Venus.

Considered from the Moon :   The 8th house is Sagittarius occupied by 2nd and 5th lord Mercury, 4th lord Sun and Rahu and aspected by 7th lord Mars.   The 8th lord Jupiter is in the Moon-sign itself, a quadrant.

Conclusion : Lagna lord is in a kendra afflicted and eclipsed. The 8th lord too is in a kendra aspected by 7th lord Jupiter. But Jupiter occupies the asterism of a benefic Moon. So also Saturn occupies the constellation of Lagna lord. Here both malefics and benefics occupy trines and quadrants indicating medium life.   Also, there is a yoga 'if the 8th lord is in a kendra and the 8th house is not occupied by any planet, the native lives for 40 years'.

Death took place in Mercury Bhukti, Jupiter Dasa. Jupiter is the 7th lord from Lagna and hence a killer.   Mercury though Lagna lord is heavily afflicted and becomes a maraka.

The Eighth House :   In Chart No. 51 Aries is aspected by 6th lord Saturn and 7th lord Jupiter.

The Eighth Lord: Mars is afflicted by Rahu and Saturn.

Ayushkaraka :   Saturn occupies his moolatrikona sign but is subject to affliction by Rahu and Mars.

Considered from the Moon :   The 8th house is occupied by malefics, Mars, Saturn and Rahu while the 8th lord being Saturn is also heavily afflicted.

Conclusion :   If Lagna lord is weak, malefics occupy the 6th, 8th or 12th houses, Jupiter occupies a trine or quadrant and malefic occupies Lagna, Madhyayu is caused according to *Jataka Parijatha*. Here Lagna lord is in a quadrant in own

Chart No. 51.—*Born 12–7–1877 at 10 a.m. (L.M.T.) at 46 N 13, 6 E 07.*

			Merc. Sun		Mercury	Jupiter Mars	Sun Saturn
Saturn Mars Rahu	RASI		Moon Venus		NAVAMSA		Ketu
			Ketu	Lagna Rahu Moon			
	GD-73						
Jupiter			Lagna	Venus			

Balance of Mercury Dasa at birth : 12 years, 5 months and 28 days.

sign while being with 12th lord Sun and aspected by 7th lord Jupiter weakens him.   Malefics Mars, Rahu and Saturn are in the 6th and Ketu is in the 12th.   Jupiter occupies the 4th house, a quadrant and malefic Mars aspects Lagna adversely. The yoga is literally fulfilled except for occupation of Lagna by a malefic. Instead, there is malefic aspect on Lagna from Mars, Otherwise too, Lagna lord in a quadrant and 8th lord is afflicted and weak so that medium life can be expected.

Death occurred in Venus Bhukti, Sun Dasa.   The Sun is the 12th lord aspected by 7th lord Jupiter.   He is also the 2nd lord from the Moon in the 12th from him with 3rd and 12th lord Mercury.   In Navamsa, he is the 8th lord both from Lagna and Moon and is with the 2nd lord Saturn.   Venus is not only an apparent maraka but being in the constellation of Mercury who, in turn, is influenced by 2 marakas Sun and Jupiter gets maraka power.

Chart No. 52.— *Born 17-10-1867 at 2–30 p.m. (L.M.T.) at 46 N 13, 6 E 07.*

	Moon			Ketu Mercury	Mars	
Ketu Jupiter	RASI		Rahu	NAVAMSA		Lagna Saturn
Lagna	GD-75					Moon
	Saturn	Sun Venus Mercury Mars		Jupit. Venus	Sun Rahu	

Balance of Mars Dasa at birth : 5 years and 7 months.

The Eighth House : Rahu occupies the 8th house and is aspected by 3rd and 12th lord Jupiter and Lagna lord Saturn.

The Eighth Lord : The Sun is in a kendra and with 4th and 11th lord, Mars, 6th and 9th lord Mercury and 5th and 10th lord Venus.

Ayushkaraka : Saturn occupies an Upachaya, the 11th house.

Considered from the Moon : The 8th house is Sagittarius whose lord Jupiter is in the 10th with Ketu.

Conclusion : Both Lagna and 8th lords are fairly strong but the 8th lord Sun is stronger than Lagna lord both by placement and association. The 8th house is afflicted by Rahu but also aspected by Lagna lord Saturn. Both benefics and malefics occupy trines and quadrants indicating Madhyayu.

The native died in Rahu Bhukti of Saturn Dasa. Dasa lord Saturn is a powerful killer being the 2nd lord from Lagna, 7th

occupant from the Moon and 7th lord from both Lagna and
Moon in Navamsa. Rahu in a sign ruled by 8th lord Sun should
additionally give saturnine results and becomes a strong
maraka.

Chart No. 53.—*Born 29-5-1917 at 3-00 p.m. (E.S.T.)
at 718 W, 42 N 05.*

	Mercury Mars	Jupiter Sun Venus	Ketu			Ketu	Sun	
			Sat.			NAVAMSA		
	RASI							Lagna Venus Saturn
	GD-99		Moon	Jupit.				
Rahu			Lagna	Mars Merc.		Moon	Rahu	

Balance of Venus Dasa at birth : 1 year, 0 months and
0 days.

The Eighth House : The eighth house is occupied by own
lord Mars and Lagna lord Mercury. It is aspected by 5th and
6th lord Saturn.

The Eighth Lord : Mars is the 8th lord and occupies his
moolatrikona sign Aries with Lagna lord Mercury and is aspected by Saturn.

Ayushkaraka : Saturn is in the 11th house in his own
asterism aspected by 8th lord Mars.

Considered from the Moon : The 8th house is Pisces free
of any afflictions by aspect or occupation. The 8th lord Jupiter
occupies the 10th house with Moon-sign lord Sun and 10th

lord Venus. He is subject to a *papakartari yoga* caused by Mars and Ketu.

Conclusion : The Lagna and 8th lord are together and afflicted by Saturn. The Moon is also in the 12th house but two benefics Jupiter and Venus occupy a trine. Jupiter aspects Lagna. These planetary positions indicate Madhyayu.

The native died in Saturn Bhukti, Jupiter Dasa. The Lagna being Virgo, Jupiter becomes a powerful maraka. Saturn is the 7th lord both from the Moon in Rasi and from Navamsa Lagna and therefore empowered to kill in his period.

Chart No. 54 —*Born 12–1–1863 at 6–33 p.m. (L.M.T.) at 22 N 40, 88 E 30.*

	Mars	Ketu	
Mercury Sun Venus	RASI		
	NH-36		
Lagna	Rahu	Jupiter	Moon Sat

Venus	Mercury	Saturn	Moon Mars
Rahu	NAVAMSA		
Sun			Ketu
Lagna	Jupiter		

Balance of Moon Dasa at birth : 3 years, 3 months and 27 days.

The Eighth House : In Chart No. 54 Cancer is aspected by 9th lord Sun, 6th and 11th lord Venus and 7th and 10th lord Mercury.

The Eighth Lord : The Moon is 8th lord in the 10th with 2nd and 3rd lord Saturn.

Ayushkaraka :   Saturn occupies the 10th with 8th lord Moon. He has exchanged signs with 7th and 10th lord Mercury,

Considered from the Moon :   The 8th house is occupied by 8th lord Mars and aspected by 7th lord Jupiter. The 8th lord being Mars himself is in his own sign in the 8th house.

Conclusion :   The Lagna lord Jupiter is powerful in the 11th house but subject to a *papakartari yoga* caused by Rahu and Saturn, while the 8th lord Moon occupies a kendra. The Lagna lord and all the benefics are in Panaparas (2, 5, 8, 11) or succeedent houses indicating Madhyayu.

Death came about in Sun Bhukti, Jupiter Dasa. Jupiter is a strong maraka because he owns the 7th from the Moon, occupies the 2nd from the Moon and is subject to a *papakartari yoga*. In Navamsa, he owns the 7th from the Moon. The Sun, Bhukti lord, occupies the 2nd house with 7th lord Mercury.   In Navamsa also, he is in the 2nd house.

Chart No. 55.—*Born 24–3–1883 at 6 a.m. (L.M.T.) at 13° N, 77 E 35.*

Lagna Sun	Ketu	Saturn	Jupit.		Mars	Mercury Rahu	Moon	
Mercury Mars ——— Venus	RASI NH-48					NAVAMSA		
					Sat.			
		Rahu	Moon				Ketu Lagna Sun Jupiter	Venus

Balance of Moon Dasa at birth :   6 years.

The Eighth House :   It is occupied by Rahu and aspected by Lagna and 10th lord Jupiter (see Chart No. 55).

The Eighth Lord :   Venus is well placed as 8th lord in the 11th house.

Ayushkaraka :   Saturn is in the 3rd house aspected by 2nd and 9th lord Mars and has exchanged signs with 3rd lord Venus.

Considered from the Moon :   The 8th house is occupied by Ketu and subject to *papakartari yoga* caused by the Sun and Saturn. The Moon-sign lord Mercury and 8th lord Mars conjoin in the 6th house aspected by 7th lord Jupiter.

Conclusion :   The Lagna lord Jupiter is strong in a kendra, the 8th lord Venus is also favourably disposed in the 11th and Ayushkaraka Saturn is beneficially situated in the 3rd house, which factors favour long span of life. But Lagna is hemmed between malefics Mars and Ketu. So also is the 8th house

Chart No. 56.—*Born 9–3–1894 at 3–00 a.m. (C.E.T.) at 13 E 42, 51 N.*

Rahu Moon Mercury	Jupiter			Lagna Sun
Sun	RASI GD-107	Jupit.	NAVAMSA	Ketu
Venus		Rahu		
Lagna Mars	Saturn	Ketu	Moon Mars / Saturn	Mercury Venus

Balance of Saturn Dasa at birth : 1 year, 9 months and 19 days.

from the Moon while the Sun, a malefic, occupies Lagna indicating medium span of life.

Death took place in Saturn Dasa, Mars Bhukti. Saturn occupies the 3rd house aspected by 2nd lord Mars. Bhukti lord Mars is a malefic being the 2nd lord and having joined 7th lord Mercury. Mars is therefore a maraka.

The Eighth House : In Chart No. 56 Cancer is the 8th aspected adversely by 5th and 12th lord Mars. It is powerfully aspected by 2nd and 3rd lord and karaka exalted, Vargottama Saturn. Venus, the 6th and 11th lord, also aspects the 8th house.

The Eighth Lord : The Moon occupies a quadrant with 7th lord Mercury and Rahu. He is aspected by Mars.

Ayushkaraka : Saturn is very powerfully placed in the 11th house in Vargottama exaltation.

Considered from the Moon : The 8th house Libra is occupied by a powerful karaka. The 8th lord Venus is in the 11th house in exchange of signs with Saturn. He is aspected by Moon-sign lord Jupiter from the 3rd house.

Conclusion : The Ascendant, the 8th lord, and the Moon are severely afflicted by malefics. The Lagna lord occupies a malefic house, the 6th house. The 8th house from the Moon is slightly better. This should have caused even Balarishta or Alpayu but the strength of karaka Saturn pushes longevity into the Madhyayu group.

Death took place in Venus Dasa, Ketu Bhukti. Venus occupies the 2nd house and has exchanged signs with 2nd lord Saturn. Ketu is in a mercurial sign. Mercury is a powerful maraka both from Lagna and the Moon as the 7th lord and passes on his killing powers to Ketu. Ketu becomes fatal in Bhukti.

Purnayu

Chart No. 57. – *Born 12–2–1880 at 0–40 a.m. (L.M.T.) t 41 N 2, 93 W 25.*

Saturn		Mars	Ketu		Mars	Ketu	Moon	Lagna Jupiter
Jupiter Moon Sun Mercury	RASI					NAVAMSA		
	GD-97				Sat.			
Venus Rahu		Lagna				Venus	Sun Rahu Mercury	

Balance of Jupiter Dasa at birth : 9 years, 10 months and 17 days.

The Eighth House : Taurus is aspected by yogakaraka Saturn and occupied by 2nd and 7th lord Mars.

The Eighth Lord : Venus is also the Lagna lord and occupies the 3rd house with Rahu. He is aspected by the 4th and 5th lord Saturn and adversely by 7th lord Mars.

Ayushkaraka : Saturn is in the 6th house but has exchanged signs with 6th lord Jupiter gaining strength thereby. Also he occupies his own sign in Navamsa.

Considered from the Moon : The eighth house is aspected by Moon-sign lord Saturn while the 8th lord is in the Moon-sign with 2nd lord Jupiter, 7th lord Sun and the 6th lord Moon.

Conclusion : Venus, the Lagna and 8th lord, would seem afflicted by Rahu but both planets occupy a Venusian constellation which is ruled by Lagna lord. As such the disposition of Lagna and 8th lords in own constellation aspected by an equally beneficially disposed ayushkaraka Saturn has conferred the full span of life.

The native died in June 1969 in Rahu Bhukti, Mars Dasa in his ninetieth year. Generally the 8th lord in own sign or Saturn in the 8th, free of afflictions, give Purnayu. Mars the Dasa lord, is a maraka being the 2nd and 7th lord and placed in the 8th house. He is the 3rd lord from the Moon in Rasi and the 7th lord in Navamsa and a first-rate killer. Rahu is with Venus in the 3rd house aspected by Saturn and Mars. Rahu gives the results of Venus (the planet with whom he associates), Jupiter (his sign-dispositor) and Saturn (*Sanivad Rahu*). Venus is the 8th lord in the 7th from the Moon in Navamsa, Jupiter is the 3rd lord from Lagna, 2nd lord from the Moon in Rasi, the 7th lord from Navamsa Lagna and in the 2nd from Navamsa Moon, while Saturn is the natural death-dealer. Therefore, Rahu becomes maraka.

Chart No. 58.—*Born 24–5–1819 at 4–04 a.m. (L.M.T.) at 51 N 30, 0 W 5.*

Rahu Mars Saturn	Mercury Venus	Sun Lagna Moon		Mars Rahu	Sun Lagna	Moon	Venus
Jupiter	RASI NH-27				NAVAMSA		
		Ketu					Ketu Mercury Jupiter Saturn

Balance of Moon Dasa at birth: 7 years and 3 months.

The Eighth House : Sagittarius rises in the 8th house aspected by 9th and 10th lord Saturn.

The Eighth Lord : Jupiter is in the 9th debilitated but has exchanged signs with 9th lord Saturn.

Ayushkaraka : Saturn is in the 11th in mutual exchange of signs with 11th lord Jupiter in his own constellation gaining strength thereby. He is with 7th lord Mars and Rahu, both Vargottama.

Considered from the Moon : The Moon being in Lagna, we find the same planetary situations recur.

Conclusion : Lagna lord Venus is in the 12th in an asterism ruled by 5th occupant Ketu who is Vargottama and who, in turn, is in a constellation ruled by 4th lord Sun. The Sun occupies a kendra and is exalted in Navamsa which indirectly strengthens Lagna lord Venus. The Lagna itself is very powerfully situated occupied by the Sun and exalted Vargottama Moon, all in a lunar constellation. (This constellation is particularly strong since its lord, the Moon, is very strongly disposed.) The Lagna is aspected by 8th and 11th lord Jupiter who primarily gives the results of a strong Saturn. Saturn also aspects Lagna and he is strong for two reasons : (1) occupation of own constellation and (2) exchange of signs with 11th lord Jupiter. This extraordinary strength of the Lagna places the chart in the Purnayu group.

The native died in 1903 in Mercury Dasa, Saturn Bhukti. Mercury is the 2nd lord placed in the 12th. He is the 3rd lord from Navamsa Lagna and the 2nd lord from Navamsa Moon. His Dasa becomes fatal. The Bhukti lord Saturn is with maraka Mars in Rasi and aspected by the same maraka in Navamsa becoming a maraka himself.

10

Chart No. 59.— *Born 7–5–1861 at 2–51 a m. (L.M.T.) at 88 E 30.*

Moon Lagna	Venus Sun Mercury		Ketu Mars	Jupit.		Ketu	Mercury
		Jupit				Saturn
	RASI				NAVAMSA	
		Sat.	Moon			Lagna
	NH-35					
Rahu				Rahu Sun Venus	Mars	

Balance of Mercury Dasa at birth : 10 years, 2 months and 20 days.

The Eighth House : Libra is the eighth house aspected by 8th lord Venus, 6th lord Sun and 7th lord Mercury. Saturn also aspects it.

The Eighth Lord : The eighth lord Venus occupies the 2nd house with 6th lord Sun and 7th lord Mercury.

Ayushkaraka : Saturn is in the 6th house in an inimical sign.

Considered from the Moon : The same situation obtains, the Moon being in Lagna.

Conclusion : Superficially, the chart does not, by the disposition of 8th lord, 8th house and Saturn indicate Purnayu. But a closer look will reveal 8th lord Venus occupies his own constellation, so does the 6th lord with whom he associates closely. The Lagna is occupied by 5th lord Moon and Lagna lord aspects both Lagna and the Moon in exaltation. According to a classical dictum, 'if the 10th lord is exalted and the 8th house has malefic planets, the native will be long-lived'. Here the Lagna and 10th lord Jupiter is exalted and the 8th house, through vacant, is aspected by malefics Sun and Saturn. According to another dictum 'if Jupiter is exalted, benefics occupy their moolatrikona signs and the Lagna lord is powerful, the person concerned lives for 80 years'. Jupiter is exalted. The natural benefic Venus occupies own constellation. Functional benefic 2nd and 9th lord Mars also occupies his own asterism while the 5th lord Moon is very beneficially disposed aspected by exalted Jupiter from the former's moolatrikona sign. The conditions of the yoga are fulfilled for all practical purposes.

The native died in Jupiter Dasa, Jupiter Bhukti. Jupiter as Lagna lord would not have ordinarily conferred maraka results but here he occupies the constellation of Mercury, a

Chart No. 60.—*Born 26-7-1856 at about midnight at 53 N 2, 6 W 16.*

Rahu Jupiter		Moon Lagna	Merc. Sat.	Rahu Sat.		Lagna Moon	Mercury
			Sun Venus				
	RASI				NAVAMSA		
	NH-31						
		Mars	Ketu	Jupit.	Sun Venus Mars		Ketu

Balance of Moon Dasa at birth: 6 years, 6 months and 18 days.

powerful maraka, both by ownership and occupation. Hence, Jupiter gets the power to kill.

The Eighth House : In Chart No. 60 Sagittarius is the eighth house aspected by 2nd lord Vargottama (occupies the same sign in Navamsa) Mercury and Saturn, the 9th and 10th lord.

The Eighth Lord : Jupiter is in the 11th house in his own sign with Vargottama Rahu aspected by Saturn.

Ayushkaraka : Saturn occupies the 2nd house with Mercury but in the constellation of Rahu. Rahu, in turn, is well placed in the 11th house in Vargottama with 8th lord Jupiter.

Considered from the Moon : The same planetary positions obtain since the Moon occupies Lagna.

Conclusion : Lagna is Vargottama and occupied by exalted and Vargottama 3rd lord Moon. The Moon, moreover, has exchanged signs with Lagna lord thereby strengthening both Lagna and the 3rd house. The 8th house is aspected by a strong well-placed karaka who also aspects the 8th lord Jupiter. Jupiter is powerful having gained his moolatrikona Navamsa and being with Rahu in Rasi. Rahu is Vargottama in the 11th. All these dispositions favour Purnayu.

The death of the native took place in Venus Dasa, Venus Bhukti. Venus is in the 3rd in a constellation of Mercury and is aspected by 8th lord Jupiter. In Navamsa, Venus is in the 7th house with the 7th lord both from Lagna and the Moon.

The Eighth House : In Chart No. 61 Sagittarius is the 8th house occupied by Lagna lord Venus and aspected by 9th and 10th lord Saturn.

The Eighth Lord : Jupiter, the 8th lord, is in a quadrant in the 10th house with 2nd and 5th lord Mercury and 4th lord Sun.

Chart No. 61.—*Born 12–2–1856 at 12–21 p.m. (L.M.T.) t 18 N, 84 E.*

Moon Rahu	Lagna	Sat		Lagna Jupiter	Rahu	
Sun Mercury Jupiter	RASI			NAVAMSA		
	NH-29					
Venus	Mars Ketu		Merc.	Ketu	Sun Saturn Venus Mars	Moon

Balance of Venus Dasa at birth : 12 years, 3 months and days.

Ayushkaraka : Saturn is in the 2nd house aspected by Lagna lord and 8th lord Jupiter.

Considered from the Moon : The eighth house is Scorpio and is neither occupied nor aspected by any planet. The eighth ord Mars is with a malefic Ketu in the 7th which is the 12th rom the 8th house aspected by 9th and 12th lord Jupiter.

Conclusion : The Lagna lord Venus in a dusthana, in the th house, the 8th lord Jupiter in a quadrant, the 8th lord from he Moon afflicted and weak in the 12th from the 7th house hould have given Alpayu but actually the chart is of a Purnayu ative. Venus, the Lagna lord, though in a dusthana occupies is own constellation in Rasi and his moolatrikona sign in Navamsa. The 8th lord Jupiter also occupies his own constellation in the 10th house. Mars is also in his own constellation nd Vargottama aspecting the Moon as Moon-sign lord. Ayush-

karaka Saturn is in the 2nd but in a strong martian conste
lation and aspected by a favourably disposed 8th lord. A
these factors promote longevity.

The death of the native occurred in Moon Bhukti of Satur
Dasa. Saturn is a maraka in his Dasa as he occupies the 2n
house from Lagna and the 3rd house from the Moon. Satur
is in the 7th house from Navamsa Lagna. The Moon is th
3rd lord placed in the 12th house and, therefore, capable c
killing in his Bhukti.

Chart No. 62.—*Born 15–8–1872 at 5–17 a.m. (L.M.T.*
at 22 N 30, 88 E 30.

		Rahu		Lagna	Sun		Rahu Moon Venus
	RASI		Lagna Mars Jupit.	Jupit.	NAVAMSA		
			Sun Venus Merc.				
	NH-43						
Moon Saturn	Ketu			Ketu	Mercury Saturn		Mars

Balance of Ketu Dasa at birth: 3 years, 2 months an
22 days.

The Eighth House : Aquarius is the 8th house aspected b
2nd lord Sun, 4th and 11th lord Venus and 3rd and 12th lor
Mercury. It is also aspected by debilitated Mars.

The Eighth Lord : Saturn, the eighth lord, is in the 6t
house with the Lagna lord Moon.

Ayushkaraka : Saturn is also the karaka besides being the 8th lord and occupies the 6th house with Lagna lord Moon.

Considered from the Moon : The 8th house is occupied by exalted Jupiter and debilitated Mars. The eighth lord is the Moon himself being placed with 2nd and 3rd lord Saturn.

Conclusion : The disposition of the 8th house from Lagna does not seem to indicate Purnayu but the association of Lagna and 8th lords, Moon and Saturn, is welcome. Their sign-dispositor Jupiter is exalted indirectly strengthening them. Jupiter is exalted in Lagna giving it strength. Mars is debilitated in Lagna but this is offset by his occupation of the asterism of the 8th lord. The presence of exalted Jupiter in Lagna and the strength gained by Lagna and 8th lords indirectly puts the chart in the Purnayu span of life.

Death took place in Jupiter Dasa, Rahu Bhukti. Jupiter, the Dasa lord, is in the constellation of Mercury who is in the 2nd house with the 2nd lord Sun. Mercury is also the 7th lord from the Moon. Rahu is in Taurus ruled by Venus who also is in the 2nd house with 2nd lord Sun. Rahu should also give the results of Saturn who, in turn, is also the 7th lord from Lagna and the 2nd and 3rd lord from the Moon. Rahu, therefore, gets the power to kill in his sub-period.

The Eighth House : In Chart No. 63 Taurus is the 8th house aspected by Lagna and 8th lord Venus and 11th lord Sun. It is also aspected by a debilitated Jupiter.

The Eighth Lord : Venus occupies the 2nd house aspected by the 2nd lord Mars.

Ayushkaraka : Saturn occupies the 4th house, a quadrant, his own sign Capricorn in Vargottama. He is with debilitated 3rd and 6th lord Jupiter.

Chart No. 63.—*Born 23–11–1902 at 5–16 a.m. (L.M.T.) at 23 N 6, 72 E 40.*

	Ketu			Ketu	Lagna	Mercury
						Jupiter
Saturn Jupiter	RASI NH-70		Moon Mars	Sat.	NAVAMSA	
	Venus Sun	Mercury Lagna Rahu		Mars	Rahu	Moon Sun Venus

Balance of Venus Dasa at birth : 13 years, 11 months and 12 days.

Considered from the Moon : The 8th lord Jupiter is in the 6th house with a powerful Ayushkaraka. Mars, the 4th and 9th lord and Ayushkaraka Saturn aspect the 8th house.

Conclusion: The Lagna is occupied by 9th and 12th lord Mercury and Vargottama Rahu. Ayushkaraka Saturn, who is strongly placed, aspects Lagna. Lagna lord Venus is in a saturnine asterism and aspected by his sign-lord. The strength of the 8th house from both Lagna and the Moon, of Ayushkaraka and the Lagna indicate Purnayu. The native died in Mercury Bhukti of Saturn Dasa. Saturn is a powerful maraka from the Moon. From the Lagna, he is with the 3rd lord Jupiter and becomes a killer. The Bhukti lord Mercury is the 12th lord and is placed in the 2nd house from Lagna. Mercury is also the 2nd lord from the Moon.

Unnatural Death

Rules handed down to us from the ancient writers are not unworkable. Many of them are applicable with suitable modifications. Unnatural deaths are those which occur due to external agents. They may be sudden and unexpected as in the case of accidents by fire, drowning, traffic accidents or even murder. They may also be pre-meditated as in the case of suicide. Nevertheless they are not caused by disease or old age although it is quite possible a sick man may by run over by a car or an old woman commits suicide by jumping down from a height. The cause of death is what differentiates whether the death is unnatural. In most cases unnatural deaths are invariably violent.

It will be seen that in the majority of cases, apart from the influence of the 8th house, 22nd drekkana, etc·, Mars,

Chart No. 64. –*Born 4-4-1948 at 6 a.m. (I.S.T.) at 73 E 04, 26 N 18.*

Lagna Sun	Rahu	Venus		Venus		Ketu	Jupiter Mercury
Mercury			Mars Sat.	Sat Mars			Moon
	RASI				NAVAMSA		
Moon	GD-85			Sun			
Jupiter Mandy		Ketu			Rahu Mandi	Lagna	

Balance of Moon Dasa at birth : 2 years, 11 months and 7 days.

Rahu and Saturn have a sinister role to play. The constellations also play an important role in judging both span of life and nature of death.

The Eighth House : In Chart No. 64 Libra, the 8th house, is occupied by Ketu and aspected by 2nd and 9th lord neechabhanga Mars.

The Eighth Lord : Venus is in his own sign in Rasi in the 3rd house and exalted in the Navamsa.

Ayushkaraka : Saturn is placed in a trine but with Mars aspected by 5th lord Moon.

Considered from the Moon : The 8th house is aspected by 3rd and 12th lord Jupiter while the 8th lord Sun is in the 3rd house.

Conclusion : The lord of Lagna is in the 10th house but in the asterism of Ketu who is in the 8th house. The 8th lord Venus is well placed apparently but occupies the asterism of the 6th lord Sun. The Moon is afflicted by two malefics, Saturn and Mars, both being very closely placed without any beneficial aspects. The native died on 5-10-1964 in Rahu Dasa, Saturn Bhukti. Rahu occupies the 2nd house and is in a martian sign. Mars is a maraka as 2nd lord from Lagna and the 7th occupant from the Moon with Saturn, the 2nd lord therefrom. Further Rahu is aspected by afflicted Saturn. Rahu occupies Bharani, ruled by 8th lord. Saturn is in a constellation ruled by 7th lord Mercury and is a maraka being conjoined with 2nd lord Mars, as 2nd lord from the Moon in the 7th therefrom. In Navamsa also, both Rahu and Saturn possess strong maraka powers by occupation and rulership.

The girl died in a bus accident. The 8th house is aspected by Mars and occupied by Ketu. The major lord is in Aries (second house indicates face) in a Venusian constellation indicating vehicles. The face was crushed and death was instantaneous.

Chart No. 65.—*Born 15–7–1942 at 2–30 p.m. (I.S.T.) at 77 E 29, 8 N 11.*

		Lagna Saturn Venus	Jupit. Merc.	Mars	Mandi	Saturn	
Ketu			Sun Moon Mars	Ketu Jupit.			Sun
	RASI				NAVAMSA		
Mandi			Rahu	Lagna Merc.			Rahu
	AM-65-782					Moon	Venus

Balance of Saturn Dasa at birth : 2 years, 2 months and 0 days.

The Eighth House : Sagittarius, a fiery sign, is the 8th house and is aspected by 8th lord Jupiter and 2nd and 5th lord Mercury.

The Eighth Lord : Jupiter occupies the 2nd house with 2nd lord Mercury.

Ayushkaraka : Saturn is in Lagna Kendra with Lagna lord Venus aspected by no other planet.

Considered from the Moon : The 8th house Aquarius is occupied by Ketu and aspected by neechabhanga 5th and 10th lord Mars and 6th and 9th lord Jupiter.

Conclusion : All the angles (kendras) are afflicted by malefics. Saturn afflicts Lagna, Rahu, the 4th house, Mars, Saturn and Ketu the 10th house and Saturn, the 7th house. Though Lagna lord occupies the Ascendant, in Navamsa, he is debilitated. He occupies an asterism ruled by Mars in Rasi. The 8th house falls in Ayudha Drekkana.

The native's clothes caught fire on 16–12–1964 and death occurred on 19–12–1964. This was in Rahu Bhukti of Ketu Dasa. Rahu occupies a maraka place from the Moon and a constellation of Venus who as Lagna lord is in the 2nd Bhava. The Dasa lord Ketu is in the 8th from the Moon aspected by Mars and Saturn. Ketu according to the dictum *Kujavad Ketu* is like Mars and hence, death by burns.

Chart No. 66.—*Born 3–4–1949 at 8 a.m. (I.S.T.) at 77 E 35, 13° N.*

Sun Mars Venus Mercury	Lagna Rahu	Moon			Jupit.	Moon	Rahu	Sat. (R)
	RASI G. II-50		Sat. (R)		Sun	NAVAMSA		
Jupiter								
		Ketu			Venus Mars	Ketu	Mercury	Lagna

Balance of Moon Dasa at birth : 9 years, 6 months and 23 days.

The Eighth House : Scorpio is aspected by 4th lord Moon.

The Eighth Lord : Mars as 8th lord is in the 12th house combust in the Sun with 2nd and 7th lord Venus and 3rd and 6th lord Mercury.

Ayushkaraka : Saturn is in an inimical sign in the 5th house aspecting the Moon.

Considered from the Moon : The 8th lord Jupiter is in the 9th with neechabhanga while the 8th house does not receive any aspects.

Conclusion : The Lagna and 8th lord being in the 12th house, weak by combustion and association with marakas does not indicate good longevity. The Moon though exalted is aspected very closely by malefic Saturn. Jupiter is also aspecting the Moon. The 8th house falls in the 2nd Drekkana of Scorpio which goes by the name of Nigada (fetters) Drekkana.

The native died on 2–12–1977 after a month as a result of serious injuries in a motor bike accident. This was in Rahu Dasa, Venus Bhukti. Rahu is in Aries ruled by Mars who is in the 12th with marakas Venus and Mercury. Mars is a maraka from the Moon. Venus, the Bhukti lord, is a first-rate maraka being the 2nd and 7th lord from Lagna. The 7th house is afflicted by the 8th house aspect of Mars and occupation by Ketu. Ketu gives results similar to Mars and Mars is the 8th lord in the 12th in exact degree association with Vahanakaraka Venus. The sign being a common sign, the accident occurred on a road.

Chart No. 67.—*Born 26–11–1959 at 4–30 p.m. (I.S.T.) at 79 E 33, 29 N 23.*

Ketu	Lagna		Rahu		Moon
					Mars
	RASI			NAVAMSA	
			Lagna		Saturn Venus
	AM-79-247				
Saturn	Sun Mars Merc. (R) Jupiter	Moon Venus Rahu	Jupit.	Sun	Merc. (R) Ketu

Balance of Moon Dasa at birth: 4 years, 5 months and 7 days.

The Eighth House : In Chart No. 67 Sagittarius is occupied by 9th and 10th lord Saturn.

The Eighth Lord : Jupiter is in the 7th house in the 12th from the 8th house with 7th lord Mars, 4th lord Sun and 2nd and 5th lord Mercury all afflicted.

Ayushkaraka : Saturn is in the 8th house whose lord Jupiter is in the 12th therefrom.

Considered from the Moon : The 8th house is Aries free of aspects but the 8th lord is in the 3rd in own sign with 12th lord Sun, 4th and 7th lord Jupiter and Moon-sign lord Mercury.

Conclusion : The Lagna is aspected by malefics. Jupiter is a benefic but his presence as 8th lord in the 7th weakens him. Lagna lord Venus is weakened by Rahu and Saturn's aspect. The Moon is also eclipsed and afflicted by Saturn's aspect.

The girl was crushed to death under a speeding truck on 19-12-1978, in Saturn Bhukti, Rahu Dasa. The 8th house is occupied by a malefic while the 8th lord is with malefics Mars and Sun in a Nigada (fetters) Drekkana. Lagna lord Venus is with Rahu aspected by Saturn indicating a violent end.

Dasa lord Rahu is in the 5th in a mercurial sign. Mercury whose results, he reflects, is the 2nd lord in the 7th house with 7th lord Mars. Rahu becomes a powerful killer. Saturn, the Bhukti lord, is in the 8th and the natural significator of death. Dasa lord Rahu occupies a common sign with Venus, ruler of vehicles. Saturn too is in a dual sign indicating death while commuting. Going a little further, Rahu is with the Moon indicating public transport being involved in the death.

The Eighth House : In Chart No. 68 Taurus is occupied by 2nd and 7th lord Mars, 3rd and 6th lord Jupiter, 11th lord Sun and 10th lord Moon.

Chart No. 68.—*Born 24–5–1906 at 4 p.m. at 0 W 05, 51 N 30.*

	Mercury	Sun Jupiter Moon Mars	Venus			Saturn Sun		
Saturn			Rahu		Rahu			
	RASI					NAVAMSA		Moon Ketu Jupiter
Ketu								
	GD-3							
		Lagna				Venus Mercury	Lagna	Mars

Balance of Mars Dasa at birth : 5 years, 7 months and 3 days.

The Eighth Lord : Venus is in the 9th house hemmed between Mars and Rahu.

Ayushkaraka : Saturn occupies his own sign Aquarius in the 5th house.

Considered from the Moon : The 8th house is aspected adversely by Mars and Moon-sign lord Venus while the 8th lord Jupiter is in the 1st with Mars and Sun, both malefics.

Conclusion : The 8th house is occupied by the New Moon, 6th lord Jupiter and malefics Sun and Mars. The 8th lord is subject to a *papakartari yoga.* There are no benefics save afflicted Mercury in the quadrants.

The native died by drowning in a boat accident in May 1926 in Venus Bhukti of Rahu Dasa. Rahu is in the 10th in Cancer whose lord Moon is a maraka being placed with 2nd and 7th lord Mars. Rahu is in the 3rd from the Moon. Bhukti lord is subject to a heavy hemming in by malefics and occupies the 2nd house from the Moon in Rasi and from Lagna in Navamsa. The New Moon, Mars and Sun in the 8th house cause death through water or other natural elements. Here Dasa lord is in a watery sign and Bhukti lord Venus is between afflicted watery Moon on one side and Rahu in a watery sign on the other side indicating a watery grave.

Chart No. 69.—*Born 10–11–1897 at 1–15 a.m. (L.M.T.) at 45 N, 93 W.*

		Moon	
	RASI		Ketu
Rahu	GD-43		Lagna
	Mars Saturn	Venus Sun Mercury	Jupit.

Moon	Jupiter		Mercury Sun
	NAVAMSA		Mars Ketu
Rahu			
	Venus	Lagna Saturn	

Balance of Sun Dasa at birth : 1 year, 3 months and 17 days.

The Eighth House : The Lagna being Leo, the 8th house is Pisces aspected by own lord Jupiter.

The Eighth Lord : Jupiter is in the 2nd house with no aspects or associations.

Ayushkaraka : Saturn occupies a martian watery sign with Mars in the 7th from the Moon. In Navamsa, though exalted and aspected by Jupiter, he is aspected by an afflicted debilitated Mars.

Considered from the Moon: The 8th house is subject to
a *papakartari yoga* caused by Rahu on one side and Mars and
Saturn on the other side. The 8th lord is again Jupiter not
afflicted by aspect or association in Rasi but aspected by
Saturn in Navamsa.

Conclusion: The 7th house from the Moon is afflicted
by malefics Mars and Saturn while the 8th house from the
Moon is hemmed between malefics, one set of them being in
a watery sign and the other being Rahu who should give
Saturn's results being placed in Capricorn. Saturn, in turn, is
s in Scorpio. Waning Moon associated with Mars, Saturn
or Rahu causes death by possession, drowning or fire.
Here Mars and Saturn afflict the Moon from a watery sign. The
native, a sailor, died on 25-9-1925 in the ramming of his ship.

Mercury Bhukti of Rahu Dasa was on during this period.
Mercury is the 2nd lord placed in the 3rd house in the constellation of the 8th lord. From the Moon, he is the 2nd lord in Rasi
and the 7th lord in Navamsa. The Dasa lord is Rahu. He should
give the results of Saturn the ruler of the sign he occupies and
also because of the dictum 'Sanivad Rahu'. Saturn is the 7th
lord from Lagna and in the 7th from the Moon with Mars, the
7th lord from Chandra Lagna. The end was violent. The 22nd
Drekkana is the 3rd decanate of Pisces and is a Sarpa (serpent)
Drekkana.

The Eighth House : In Chart No. 70 Aquarius is the 8th
house occupied by 6th and 9th lord Jupiter.

The Eighth Lord : Saturn is the 8th lord in the 3rd house
with 5th and 10th lord Mars and 3rd and 12th lord Mercury. He
is aspected by Lagna lord Moon.

Ayushkaraka : Saturn occupies the 3rd house from Lagna
and the 7th house from the Moon in association with Mars and
Mercury. In Navamsa, he occupies his own sign with Mars.

11

Chart No. 70.—*Born 15–10–1891 at 10–30 p.m. (G.M.T.)*
at 53 N 12, 0 W 30.

			Rahu Jupit.			
Moon	Rahu					
Jupiter		Lagna	Sat. Mars			Mercury
	RASI			NAVAMSA		
	GD-45					
Ketu	Sun Venus	Mars Sat. Merc.	Venus		Sun	Moon Lagna Ketu

Balance of Jupiter Dasa at birth: 12 years, 2 months and 16 days.

Considered from the Moon: The 8th house is occupied by 6th lord debilitated Sun and Venus. It is hemmed between malefics, Ketu on one side and Mars, Saturn and Mercury on the other side. Jupiter aspects the 8th house from the 12th house from the Moon.

Conclusion: The 7th house from the Moon is affflicted by Mars and Saturn while the 8th house is occupied by fiery Sun who also afflicts the 8th lord Venus. 'If the Sun is in the 8th house, Moon is in the 10th house and Saturn is in the 8th house, the native may be hit accidentally by a log of wood and die.' In this case, the Sun is in the 4th, the Moon though in the 9th is aspected by 10th lord fiery Mars and Saturn is the 8th lord so that the conditions are fulfilled indirectly. The native was accidentally shot and died on 2-1-1930. The preponderance of martian influences and the *papakartari* to the 8th house from

Moon by Ketu (*Kujavad Ketu*) and Mars and Saturn caused
death by a fire-arm. Saturn alone could have caused death
through a blunt object such as a log of wood as indicated in the
particular yoga. Death occurred in Sun Bhukti of Mercury Dasa.
The Sun is the 2nd lord from Lagna in the 8th from the Moon. He
associates with the 8th lord Venus and occupies a martian constellation. Mars, in turn, is in the 7th from the Moon, The Dasa
lord Mercury is in the 3rd and 12th lord conjoining 7th lord
Saturn in the 7th from the Moon.

Chart No. 71.—*Born 25–10–1904 at 8–57 p.m. (G.M.T.)
at 15 N 30, 0 W 05.*

	Jupiter Moon		Lagna		Jupiter	Lagna Ketu
Ketu	RASI			NAVAMSA		Saturn
Saturn	GD-49		Mars Rahu	Sun		
	Venus	Mercury Sun		Moon Merc.	Rahu Mars	Venus

Balance of Sun's Dasa at birth : 5 years, 10 months and
3 days.

The Eighth House : Capricorn is occupied by its own lord
Saturn. It is not influenced by any other planet.

The Eighth Lord : Saturn occupies his own sign.

Ayushkaraka : Saturn occupies the 8th house in his own
sign.

Considered from the Moon : Scorpio is occupied by 2nd and 7th lord Venus and aspected by Mars from a fiery sign. Mars is with Rahu and his aspect is therefore highly maleficent.

Conclusion : There are no heavy afflictions to the 8th house from the Lagna or the Moon-sign. But the 5th house from the Moon is afficted by Mars and Rahu. Saturn, a malefic occupies the 8th house While the 8th house from the Moon has Venus afflicted by Mars. The 7th house from Navamsa Lagna is also afflicted by Mars and Rahu. Death occurred in a motor accident and the native died on 29-6-1927 in Moon Bhukti of Mars Dasa.

The Moon is the 2nd lord, in Rasi, the 3rd lord in Navnmsa and placed in the 8th from Navamsa Lagna. Mars occupies the 3rd from Lagna and is with Rahu. Rahu gives results similar to the Sun, his sign-dispositor, and Saturn. The Sun is the 3rd lord in the 7th from the Moon and Saturn is the 8th lord from Lagna and 2nd lord from the Moon in Navamsa.

The Eighth House : In Chart No. 72, the 8th is occupied by 8th lord Saturn and aspected adversely by Mars, the 6th and 11th lord, and an afflicted 7th lord Jupiter.

The Eighth Lord : Saturn, the 8th lord, occupies his own sign and is aspectsd by Mars and Jupiter.

Ayushkaraka : Saturn is also the karaka and is aspected by 7th lord, afflicted Jupiter, and 6th and 11th lord Mars.

Considered from the Moon: The 8th house is Taurus aspected by 3rd and 6th lord Jupiter. The 8th lord is in the Moon-sign with debilitated Sun and aspected by Saturn from Capricorn.

Conclusion : Death takes place in captivity when the 22nd Drekkana happens to be either Nigala, Sarpa or Pasa. In this case the 22nd Drekkana is the first of Capricorn and hence a

Chart No. 72.—*Born 2–11–1755 at about 8 p.m. at 46 N 30, 30 E.*

		Mars Lagna		Sun Venus		Mars Jupiter
Ketu			Rahu Sat. Lagna			
	RASI			NAVAMSA		
Saturn	NH-22					Ketu
	Mercury	Sun Moon Venus	Jupit. Rahu	Merc	Moon	

Balance of Mars Dasa at birth : 2 years, 5 months and 9 days.

Nigala one. Death occurred in captivity as the native, the heroine of the French revolution of 1791, was guillotined. Mars aspects the 8th house and Saturn as Ayushkaraka is also in a Nigala Drekkana. 'When the 5th or the 9th sign from the Moon is aspected or occupied by a malefic planet and when a Sarpa, Nigala or Pasa Drekkana rises in the 8th Bhava, death is brought about by hanging' is literally fulfilled in this case. Mars is in the 9th from the Moon and 8th house rises in a Nigala Drekkana.

Death occurred in Saturn Dasa, Saturn Bhukti. Saturn is the 8th lord from Lagna in the 8th and in Navamsa, powerfully aspects the 7th house in association with Rahu.

The Eighth House : In Chart No. 73 Virgo rises in the 8th Bhava aspected by Jupiter and exalted Venus.

Chart No. 73.—*Born   12-2-1809 at   7-32   a.m. (L.M.T.) at 35 N, 89 E.*

Jupiter Venus	Ketu			Rahu			
Sun Lagna Mercury	RASI			Moon Lagna	NAVAMSA		Jupiter
Moon	NH-24			Merc.			
	Saturn	Rahu Mars		Venus	Sun Mars	Saturn	Ketu

Balance of Sun Dasa at birth : 2 years, 1 month and 6 days.

The Eighth Lord : Mercury is well placed in the Ascendant with the 7th lord Sun.

Ayushkaraka : Saturn occupies Scorpio in the 10th house aspected by Jupiter in own sign.

Considerd from the Moon : The 8th house is aspected by Saturn while the 8th lord Sun occupies the 2nd house with Mercury.

Conclusion : The 22nd Drekkana is an Ayudha Drekkana, being the 2nd of Virgo. The 8th lord Mercury, is in a constellation of Rahu who, in turn, is in association with the planet of violence, Mars.

The native was assassinated on 14-4-1865. A combination in *Goutama Samhita* says that if the lord of the 8th is in the Ascendant and the waning Moon is aspected by Mars, death will be due to a weapon. The 8th lord Mercury is in the Ascendant and the waning Moon in the 12th house is aspected by Mars.

According to *Jataka Tatwa* and other classical works when Saturn, Sun and Mars are in the 10th, 7th and 4th respectively death is by assassination. Here we find Saturn is in the 10th, Mars aspects the 4th and the Sun aspects the 7th.

The native was shot to death in Saturn Dasa, Mercury Bhukti. The Dasa lord Saturn as an occupant of the 10th house causes Mrityu Yoga and becomes a maraka. Also he is the 2nd lord from the Moon and is aspected by 2nd lord Jupiter. Mercury, the Bhukti lord, is in the 2nd from the Moon in Rasi, and is the 8th lord from both Rasi and Navamsa Lagna.

Chart No. 74.— *Born 2–10–1869 at 7–45 a.m. (L.M.T.) at 21 N 37, 69 E 49.*

	Jupiter			Moon Ketu	Venus	Sun Mars
		Rahu				
Ketu	RASI	Moon		NAVAMSA		
	NH-41		Jupit. Lagna Merc.			
Saturn	Mars Mercury Venus Lagna	Sun	Sat.		Rahu	

Balance of Ketu Dasa at birth: 6 years 10 months and 28 days.

The Eighth House : It is occupied by 3rd and 6th lord Jupiter and aspected by Saturn and Mars.

The Eighth Lord : Venus, the 8th lord, occupies his own sign but is with Mars and hemmed between malefics, Saturn and Sun.

Ayushkaraka : Saturn is in Scorpio aspected by 3rd and 6th lord Jupiter.

Considered from the Moon : The eighth house is aspected by the Sun and the 8th lord Jupiter, by Mars and Saturn.

Conclusion : Jupiter though in the 8th house is in Krittika ruled by the Sun. He is aspected by Mars and Saturn. According to a classical yoga found in *Gautama Samhita*, Mars in the Lagna unaspected by benefics and the waning Moon in the 11th cause the native to die by being wounded above the naval region by a weapon. The native, an apostle of non-violence, was assassinated by a fanatic communalist.

The assassination occurred in Sun Bhukti, Jupiter Dasa. Jupiter is in the 8th aspected powerfully by Mars, the 2nd and 7th lord. The Sun is in the 2nd from the Moon and in the 12th from Lagna.

The Eighth House : In Chart No. 75 A fiery sign Aries rises on the 8th Bhava and is occupied by Lagna and 10th lord Mercury and 3rd and 8th lord Mars and aspected by Saturn, the 5th and 6th Lord.

The Eighth Lord : Mars occupies his own sign in the 8th house with Mercury and is aspected by Saturn.

Ayushkaraka : Saturn occupies the 11th house and is aspected by 8th lord Mars from the 8th house.

Considered from the Moon : The 8th house is Pisces free of aspects or associations but the 8th lord Jupiter is with Venus and the Sun and subject to a *papakartari yoga* caused by Mars and Ketu.

Conclusion : The native was a President of the United States of America and was shot dead on 22–11–1963. The 8th house, 8th lords both from Lagna and Moon are considerably afflicted by malefics. Mars in the 8th house causes sudden

Chart No. 75.—*Born 29–5–1917 at 3–00 p.m. (E.S.T.) at 71 W 8, 42 N 05.*

	Mercury Mars	Jupiter Sun Venus	Ketu			Ketu	Sun	
			Sat.					
	RASI				NAVAMSA			Lagna Venus Saturn
	GD-99		Moon	Jupit.				
Rahu			Lagna	Mars Merc.	Moon	Rahu		

Balance of Venus Dasa at birth : 1 year.

death. He died in Saturn Bhukti, Jupiter Dasa. Jupiter is the 7th lord while Saturn is the 7th lord both from Moon and Navamsa Lagna.

The Eighth House : In Chart No. 76 Aries is the 8th house here also aspected by the 8th lord Mars, exalted Saturn and 7th lord Jupiter.

The Eighth Lord : Mars is with exalted Saturn in the 2nd house aspecting his own sign.

Ayushkaraka : Saturn occupies the 2nd house in exaltation with 3rd and 8th lord Mars.

Considered from the Moon : The 8th house is aspected by Saturn and occupied by Rahu. The 8th lord, the Moon himself, is well placed in Vargottama with Vargottama Moonsign lord Jupiter and 6th and 11th lord Venus. He is aspected by Saturn afflicted by Mars. The Moon is subject to a *papakartari* caused by the Sun and Ketu.

Chart No. 76.—*Born 20–11–1925 at 1–00 p.m. (E.S.T.) at 71 W 8, 42 N 05.*

				Ketu Merc.	Mars	Lagna	Saturn
			Rahu				
	RASI				NAVAMSA		
Ketu							Sun
	AM. 68-719						
Jupiter Moon Venus	Sun Mercury	Mars Saturn	Lagna	Jupit Moon			Rahu

Balance of Sun Dasa at birth: 4 years, 9 months and 7 days.

Conclusion : The native was also shot to death on 4–6–1968 for political reasons. The 8th house and 8th lord from Lagna and Moon are heavily afflicted by malefics. Death occurred in Saturn Bhukti, Jupiter Dasa both being first rate marakas. Jupiter is the 7th lord and Saturn occupies the 2nd house with 3rd and 8th lord Mars.

The Eighth House : In Chart No. 77 Jupiter, the 2nd and 5th lord, occupies the 8th house.

The Eighth Lord : Mercury is in the 9th house with 7th lord Venus and 10th lord Sun and aspected by malefic Mars.

Ayushkaraka : Saturn occupies the 7th house with Mars and exalted Moon.

Considered from the Moon : The 8th house Sagittarius is aspected by own lord Jupiter and 7th and 12th lord Mars.

Conclusion : The native suffered a violent end in Saturn Dasa, Jupiter Bhukti. Two malefics in the 7th from Lagna and

Chart No. 77.—*Born 29-7-1883 at 2 P.m. (L.M.T.) at 41 N, 16 E.*

Ketu	Moon Saturn Mars	Jupit.				Moon Saturn Jupiter
		Sun Merc. Venus	Rahu			Mars Lagna Venus
	RASI			NAVAMSA		Ketu
	NH-50					
	Lagna	Rahu			Mercury Sun	

Balance of Moon Dasa at birth : 3 years, 8 months and 26 days.

the 8th house from the Moon aspected by Jupiter resulted in a tragic death. Saturn rules the 3rd house from Lagna and is in the 7th from it, a maraka house. In Navamsa, he is the 7th lord from Navamsa Lagna and joins the 2nd lord Moon. The sub-lord Jupiter owns the 2nd from Lagna and occupies the 8th house. In Navamsa, he is with a maraka Saturn and is the 7th lord from the Moon.

The Eighth House : In Chart No. 78 Taurus is the 8th house subject to a *papakartari yoga* caused by Rahu and Mars.

The Eighth Lord : Venus is in a fiery sign Aries with Mars, Sun and Mercury aspected by Saturn.

Ayushkaraka : Saturn is in the 10th aspected by a powerful Mars.

Considered from the Moon : The 8th house is occupied by Saturn and aspected by Mars. The 8th lord Moon, though with Jupiter, is with Ketu also.

Chart No. 78.—*Born 20-4-1889 at 6-30 p.m. (L.M.T.) at 48° N, 13° E.*

	Sun Mars Mercury Venus		Rahu				Mercury Rahu	Sun
			Sat					
	RASI				Sat.	NAVAMSA		Moon
	NH-58							
Moon Jupiter Ketu		Lagna			Mars Venus Lagna Ketu			Jupiter

Balance of Venus Dasa at birth :   16 years, 4 months and 6 days.

Conclusion : The 8th houses and 8th lords both from Lagna and the Moon are heavily afflicted by Saturn-Mars influences. It is believed the native committed suicide which is borne out by the afflictions to the 8th house and the Moon's affliction by Ketu. Death occurred in Rahu Dasa, Moon Bhukti. Rahu is in the 7th from the Moon in a mercurial sign and in the 7th from Navamsa Lagna. His sign dispositor Mercury whose results he must reflect is in the 7th from Lagna and is the 7th lord from the Moon. The Moon, the Bhukti lord, occupies the 3rd from Lagna and is in the 7th from the major lord.

The Eighth House : In Chart No. 79 Cancer is occupied by Ketu, Venus and Saturn.

The Eighth Lord : The Moon is in the 9th house hemmed between Saturn and Sun.

Chart No. 79.—*Born 25–9–1916 at 1–58 p.m. (L.M.T.) at 27 N 28, 77 E 41.*

	Jupiter			Mars Sun			
			Venus Ketu Sat.	Venus			Jupiter Ketu
	RASI			Rahu	NAVAMSA		Moon Saturn
Rahu	AM. 68-917		Moon				
Lagna		Mars	Sun Merc.	Lagna			Mercury

Balance of Venus Dasa at birth : 17 years, 3 months and 27 days.

Ayushkaraka : Saturn is in the 8th house afflicted by Ketu and associating with Venus.

Considered from the Moon : The 8th house Pisces is aspected by Sun and Mercury while the 8th lord Jupiter is in a fiery sign aspected by malefics Mars and an afflicted Saturn.

Conclusion : The native, the leader of a national political party, was killed and the body thrown on the rails, according to reports. Mars, Saturn and Ketu influences on the 8th house and 8th lord indicate a violent end.

The death occurred on 10/11–2–1968 in Rahu Dasa, Ketu Bhukti. Both are marakas by virtue of the houses they occupy. Rahu is aspected by Mars and Ketu is with Saturn. In Navamsa also, they occupy maraka houses.

The Eighth House : In Chart No. 80 Cancer rising gives Aquarius as the 8th house. It is aspected by debilitated Mars.

Chart No. 80.— *Born 6–10–1885 at 1–36 a.m. (L.M.T.) at 20 N 30, 72 E 58.*

Ketu			Sat.	Sat.	Mercury
	RASI		Lagna Mars	Rahu	Sun Venus
			Moon	Mars Lagna Jupit.	NAVAMSA	Ketu
	NH-54				
	Venus		Rahu Sun Jupit. Merc.		Moon

Balance of Venus Dasa at birth : 9 years, 9 months and 9 days.

The Eighth Lord : Saturn is the 8th lord and occupies the 12th house.

Ayushkaraka : Saturn occupies a friendly sign in the 12th house.

Considered from the Moon : The 8th house is occupied by Ketu and aspected by as many as 5 planets—Sun, Rahu, Jupiter, Mercury and Saturn. The 8th lord Jupiter is in the 2nd with Rahu, Mercury and Sun. The closeness of the 8th lord Jupiter to Rahu is to be especially noted.

Conclusion : This is also a case of unnatural death but different from the previous ones in that it is one of self-infliction. The native threw himself before a running train and ended his life.

The nature of death is signified by Lagna lord Moon occupying an Ayudha Drekkana, Ketu being in a Sarpa Drekkana and the 7th and 8th lord Saturn also being in an Ayudha Drekkana. Suicide is always preceded by frustration and disoppointment n life which means the karakas for the mind, body and soul (Moon and Sun) must be afflicted. Here the Moon occupies a malefic Drekkana and is aspected by 8th lord Saturn. The Sun s eclipsed.

The death occurred in Jupifer Dasa, Ketu Bhukti. The major lord Jupiter is in the 3rd with a maraka planet, namely, the 2nd lord Sun, Rahu and 3rd lord Mercury. He is in the 2nd from the Moon. The sub-lord Ketu is in the 8th from the Moon in the constellation of a powerful maraka Saturn.

The Eighth House : In Chart No. 81 Pisces is occupied by the Moon and aspected by Mars and Venus.

Chart No. 81.—*Born 21–10–1953 at 2 a.m. (I.S.T.) at 18 N 31, 73 E 55.*

Moon			Jupit.	Rahu	Lagna Venus	Mercury
	RASI		Ketu		NAVAMSA	
Rahu	GD-57		Lagna	Mars		
	Sun Mercury Saturn	Venus Mars		Sat.	Moon Sun Jupiter	Ketu

Balance of Saturn Dasa at birth : 1 year, 2 months and 16 days.

The Eighth Lord : Jupiter is in the 11th house free of any afflictions.

Ayushkaraka : Saturn is exalted in the 3rd house but is combust and with 2nd lord Mercury. He is aspected by 8th lord Jupiter.

Considered from the Moon : The 8th house is occupied by malefics, Sun and Saturn, but aspected by Moon-sign lord Jupiter. The 8th lord Venus is with Mars.

Conclusion : The native died on 4–4–1972 after consuming poison. The 8th house is aspected by Mars who is also in the 7th from the Moon. Malefics are present in the 8th from the Moon as well. The Moon, ruler of the mind, is in a *dusthana* aspected by malefic Mars and debilitated Venus. The Sun is not only debilitated and associating with his bitter enemy Saturn but also in a nodal constellation.

The native died in Ketu Dasa, Ketu Bhukti. Ketu occupies the 12th house. He should give the results of the lord of the sign he is in and also of Mars (*Kujavad Ketu*). The Moon, his sign-dispositor, is in the 8th house both in Rasi and Navamsa. Mars is in the 2nd house from Lagna, and in the 7th from the Moon as 2nd lord thereby becoming a powerful maraka.

The Eighth House : In Chart No. 82 it is not occupied by any planet but is aspected by an afflicted 6th lord Saturn and 7th lord Jupiter.

The Eighth Lord : The 8th lord Mars is in the 6th with 6th lord Saturn and Rahu.

Ayushkaraka : Saturn is afflicted by Rahu and Mars in the 6th house.

Considered from the Moon : The 8th house is occupied by a heavily afflicted 7th and 8th lord Saturn, Mars and Rahu. The 8th lord is also Saturn and is with malefics Mars and Rahu.

Conclusion : The presence of malefics in the 8th from the Moon and the afflictions to the 8th lords both from Lagna and

Chart No. 82.—*Born 12-7-1877 at 10 a.m. (L.M.T.) at 46 N 13, 6 E 07.*

		Merc. Sun		Mercury	Jupiter Mars	Sun Saturn
Saturn Mars Rahu	RASI	Venus Moon		NAVAMSA		Ketu
		Ketu	Lagna Moon Rahu			
	GD-73					
Jupiter		Lagna				

Balance of Mercury Dasa at birth : 12 years, 5 months and 28 days.

Moon resulted in the native consuming poison and killing himself. The Moon is subject to a *papakartari yoga* caused by the Sun and Ketu. Death occurred on 30-6-1922 in Venus Bhukti of Sun Dasa. The Sun is the 12th lord from Lagna. He is the 2nd lord from the Moon and the 8th lord from Navamsa Lagna. Bhukti lord Venus is the 2nd lord from Lagna and in the 12th from the Navamsa Lagna.

The Eighth House : In Chart No. 83 Leo is the 8th house occupied by Rahu and aspected by an afflicted 3rd and 12th lord Jupiter and Lagna and 2nd lord Saturn.

The Eighth Lord : The Sun, ruler of the eighth house, is in the 10th in debility with Mars, Mercury and Venus. He is aspected by an eclipsed Jupiter.

Ayushkaraka : Saturn occupies the 11th house aspected by 7th lord Moon.

12

Chart No. 83.—*Born 17–10–1867 at 2–30 p.m. (L.M.T.) at 46 N 13, 6 E 07.*

		Moon			Mercury Ketu	Mars	
Jupiter Ketu	RASI				NAVAMSA		Lagna Saturn
Lagna	GD-75		Rahu				Moon
	Saturn	Sun Venus Mercury Mars		Jupit. Venus		Rahu Sun	

Balance of Mars Dasa at birth : 5 years and 7 months.

Considered from the Moon : The 8th house is Sagittarius free of aspect or association but the 8th lord Jupiter is in the 10th with Ketu.

Conclusion : Saturn occupies the 7th from the Moon, the Moon is afflicted by malefics Saturn and Mars, the 8th house is occupied by Rahu while the 8th lord from the Moon is eclipsed by Ketu. The native committed suicide on 7–7–1922 by consuming poison. This was in Rahu Bhukti, Saturn Dasa. Rahu is in the 8th from the Lagna and gives results similar to Saturn (*Sanivad Rahu*). Saturn is a first rate maraka. He is the 2nd lord from Lagna, occupies the 7th house from the Moon, and owns the 7th houses both from Navamsa Lagna and Navamsa Moon.

The Eighth House : In Chart No. 84 Aries, a malefic sign, rises on the 8th Bhava. It is aspected adversely by Mars and malefic Saturn.

Chart No. 84.—*Born 25–12–1917 at 11–55 p.m. (G.M.T.) at 0 W 05, 51 N 31.*

	Jupiter Moon	Ketu		Lagna Moon Jupiter		
		Sat.	Mars			Rahu Sun
	RASI			NAVAMSA		
Venus	GD-79		Ketu Sat.			
Mercury Sun Rahu		Mars Lagna	Merc.			Venus

Balance of Moon Dasa at birth : 7 years, 7 months and 6 days.

The Eighth Lord : Mars, the 8th lord, is in the Ascendant aspected by malefic Saturn.

Ayushkaraka : Saturn is in the 11th house aspected by 2nd and 9th lord Venus.

Considered from the Moon : The 8th house is Sagittarius occupied by 2nd and 5th lord Mercury, 4th lord malefic Sun and Rahu and aspected by 7th and 12th lord malefic Mars. The 8th lord Jupiter is placed in the Moon-sign Taurus.

Conclusion : Malefics either aspect or occupy the 8th house from Lagna and the Moon. Rahu, in addition, eclipses the 8th house from the Moon. The native died from an overdose of sleeping pills on 20–1–1957 in Mercury Bhukti, Jupiter Dasa. Jupiter is the 7th lord from Lagna and the 8th lord from the Moon. Mercury is the 2nd lord from the Moon and is in the 8th therefrom becoming a maraka.

XIII

Concerning the Ninth House

The ninth house signifies father, righteousness, preceptor, grand-children, intuition, religion, sympathy, fame, charities, leadership, long journeys and communication with spirits.

In judging the events ruled by the ninth house, the following factors must be taken into account, *viz.*, (*a*) The House, (*b*) Its Lord, (*c*) Its Occupants and (*d*) The Karaka or significator. The Sun is the karaka for father. Yogas formed in the 9th house or involving the 9th lord produce their own results. These considerations must be judged from the Navamsa chart also. The ninth house, although it denotes several significations, is primarily concerned with father and long distance travel.

Results of the Lord of the Ninth House being situated in Different Houses

In the First House: When the ninth lord is placed in the first house, the native becomes a self-made man. He earns much money through his own efforts. If the 9th lord combines with the Lagna lord in the first house and associates with or is aspected by a benefic planet, the native is fortunate with riches and happiness.

In the Second House : When the ninth lord is placed in the 2nd house beneficially, the native's father is a rich and influential man. The native acquires wealth from the father. Malefics influencing the ninth lord in the 2nd house ruin or destroy paternal property.

In the Third House : If the lord of the ninth is placed in the 3rd, the native makes his fortune through writing, speeches and oratorial abilities. The native's father will be a man of moderate means while the native advances his fortune through his co-borns. If malefics afflict the ninth lord in the 3rd house, the native may land in trouble through his writings which may be irrational and even obscene depending upon the nature of affliction. He may be forced to sell his paternal property because of troubles occurring through his writings.

In the Fourth House : The ninth lord in the 4th house gives vast landed properties and beautiful bungalows. Or the native may earn through estate and land dealings. His mother will be a rich and fortunate woman. He will inherit his father's immovable properties. If the ninth lord is afflicted in the 4th house, the native may not have any domestic unhappiness. His early life will be crossed by miseries due to a hard-hearted father or disharmony between parents. If Rahu afflicts, mother may be a divorcee or living separately from his father.

In the Fifth House : The ninth lord in the fifth house gives a prosperous and famous father. The native's sons may also be very fortunate in life and enjoy success and distinction.

In the Sixth House : The ninth lord in the sixth house gives a sickly father afflicted with chronic diseases. If benefics flank such a sixth house, the native may gain wealth through successful termination of father's legal problems, and by way

of compensation, costs, etc. If malefics afflict the ninth lord
in the sixth house, the native's attempts to make his fortune
may be frustrated through litigation involving his father or
debts contracted by him.

In the Seventh House : The native may go abroad and
prosper there. His father may also prosper in foreign lands.
He will get a noble and lucky wife. If ascetic yogas are present
in the chart, the native may seek spiritual guidance and fulfilment abroad. If *asubhayogas* spoil the ninth lord, the father
may meet with his death abroad.

In the Eighth House : The native may lose his father
early in life. If malefics afflict the eighth house in such a case,
he may suffer severe poverty and heavy responsibility due to
father's death If benefics influence the ninth lord, the native
may inherit substantial paternal property. Afflictions may cause
the native to abandon traditions or damage religious institutions and trusts set up by the family.

In the Ninth House : The ninth lord in the ninth house
gives a long-lived and prosperous father. The native will be
religiously inclined and be charitable. He will travel abroad
and earn money and distinction thereby. If afflicted by malefics
or if the 9th lord occupies the 6th, 8th or 12th from Navamsa
Lagna, the native's father will die early.

In the Tenth House : If the ninth lord is in the tenth
house, the native will become very famous and powerful. He
will be generous and occupy posts of authority. He will earn
much wealth and acquire every kind of comfort and luxury.
His means of livelihood will be righteous and he will be a law
abiding citizen.

In the Eleventh House : The native will be exceedingly
rich. He will have powerful and influential friends. His father

will be a well-known and well-placed man· If afflicted, un-
faithful friends will destroy the native's wealth through selfish
scheming and fraud.

In the Twelfth House : The position of the lord of the
ninth house in the twelfth house gives a poor background. The
native will suffer much and will have to work very hard in life.
Even then success may not come to him. He will be religious
and noble but always in want. Father may die early leaving
the native penniless.

These combinations are very general and cannot be applied
without taking into account the concerned karaka and the other
planetary dispositions in the chart. If the ninth lord is very
powerful, he becomes capable of conferring fortune even if
placed in a malefic house. If the ninth lord is afflicted but the
ninth house is beneficially disposed, the intensity of the malefic results will be greatly reduced. Great skill is required in
interpreting the *bhava* and in no case is a literal application of
the results mentioned above desirable.

Other Important Combinations

The following are some of the yogas culled from ancient
sources :—

When the Sun occupies the 9th, 8th, 11th or 12th house
which should be a fixed sign and the Lagna is not aspected by
the Moon, the father will not be present at the time of the
birth of the child. He may be in his own town. When the Sun in
such a position occupies a movable sign, the father will be
away in a foreign country at the birth of the child. If the Sun,
Mars and Saturn combine in the 4th or the 10th house, the
birth is of a posthumous child.

When the 5th or the 9th house from the Lagna be a malefic sign and is occupied by the Sun, the father of the child

will die soon. The Sun and malefics in the 10th house from the Moon also indicate early death of father. If Saturn and Mars conjoin in Aries, Leo or Aquarius which should be the 5th, 7th or the 9th house from the Sun, the father of the child will be in some sort of captivity at the time of its birth. When the Sun is afflicted by conjunction with malefics, the child's father's life will be adversely influenced. If the Moon, Mars, Mercury and Saturn be together, the native will have two fathers and two mothers. That is, in other words, he may be taken in adoption. The Sun aspecting the Ascendant indicates the native may inherit wealth from his father. If the 9th house be a movable sign or the 9th lord be in a movable sign either in conjunction with or aspected by Saturn and the 12th lord is strong, the native will be adopted by another.

If the 4th lord conjoins the 9th lord in the 6th house, the native's father will be a profligate. When the 5th lord is a benefic and the Sun is also beneficially disposed, the native will give happiness to the father. If the 5th lord or the Sun is afflicted by Saturn, Rahu or Mandi, the native will be a source of misery to the father. If the Ascendant of the native happens to be the same sign as that rising in the 10th house of the father, the native will be a dutiful son. If Jupiter in the 9th house occupies his own Navamsa, the native will be endowed with a high sense of filial duty. If the Ascendants of the native and his father are mutually in the 6th and 8th, the pair will always be at variance. If the Sun is in an inimical sign, the native will studiously cause pain to his father. If the Sun and Moon be in trine to Mars and Saturn, the child will be abandoned by both parents. Saturn, Mars and Rahu in the 11th or the 9th house from the Lagna cause father's death. If the Sun or the Moon occupy a kendra in a movable sign, the native will not perform the last rites of the father.

If the 9th house is occupied by a benefic, the native is lucky. If the 9th lord is aspected by a malefic, inimical or debilitated planet and is in the 6th house, the person suffers in every respect. If the 9th lord be in a malefic *shashtyamsa* or occupy a debilitated sign or Navamsa or be weak or if malefics occupy the 9th house, the native is unfortunate in life.

If a malefic, eclipsed or debilitated planet occupy the 9th house, the native will be luckless, poor or unprincipled. But if the malefic in the 9th be exalted, in own or a friendly sign, the opposite results are produced.

If the 11th lord is in the 9th influenced by the 10th lord, the native is lucky wherever he may go. The same result is indicated if the 9th lord is in the 2nd aspected by the 10th lord. If the 2nd lord is in the 11th, the 11th lord is in the 9th and the 9th lord is in the 2nd, one becomes extremely fortunate and earns well. If the 3rd and 9th lords join together or be aspected by benefics or are placed in benefic signs or Navamsas, the native's fortune is advanced through a brother. If the 5th and 9th lords combine or are beneficially disposed by aspect or association, the native's children bring him prosperity. Venus or Jupiter in the 9th or aspecting the 9th lord indicate a fortunate life. Mutual exchange of houses between the Lagna lord and the 9th lord gives every kind of fortune.

If the 9th lord is aspected by a benefic and is in a watery sign in a quadrant, the native goes on a pilgrimage and has dips in a sacred river. Jupiter aspecting the 9th house or the combination of the 9th and 10th lords gives travels to many holy spots and religious centres. If the 9th house from the Moon be beneficially aspected and occupied by a benefic also, the native will go on a long pilgrimage. If Jupiter is in the

9th and the Moon, Jupiter and Ascendant are aspected by Saturn, the person becomes the founder of a system of philosophical thought. If Jupiter, the Sun and Mercury occupy the 9th, one will be highly learned and wealthy.

If the Lagna lord is in the 12th and the Moon and Mars conjoin in the 10th which should be a malefic sign, the person will go abroad but good fortune will evade him. If the Sun, the Moon and Saturn are in the same sign, the person will be wicked and deceitful and try to travel abroad. If the lord of the 12th from the sign occupied by the Lagna lord is a watery sign, the native becomes prosperous in foreign lands. Planets in the 9th if not associated with Mercury and Jupiter make one diseased, forlorn and face captivity and misery.

Planets in the Ninth House

The Sun : The native may change his faith if the Sun is afflicted. He displays hostile feelings towards his father, lacking respect for elders and spiritual preceptors. But if the Son is not afflicted, the person will be a dutiful son having regard for spiritual pursuits. The Moon combining with the Sun here causes eye troubles. Venus with the Sun gives sickness and ailments. The health will be ordinary and the native gets little patrimony. He will be ambitious and enterprising.

The Moon: The native will be fortunate and prosperous. He will have many sons, friends and kinsmen. He will be principled and generous-minded. If Saturn, Mars and Mercury aspect the Moon, the native will become a ruler. If the Moon combines with Mars, he may cause a fatal injury to his mother. If Venus conjoins the Moon in the 9th, the person may lead an immoral life. He will act in league with his step-mother. Saturn

here causes one to suffer much. The native may build charitable institutions. He will acquire good immovable property
and also visit foreign countries.

Mars : The native will wield authority and be affluent.
He will have children and be happy. He will not be a dutiful
son but otherwise generous and famous for his good qualities.
If either Jupiter or Mercury conjoin Mars, the native will be
learned in religion and spiritual lore. Venus here gives two
wives and foreign residence. It also gives the native proficiency
in law. Saturn with Mars in the 9th indicates addiction to
other women and a wicked nature. He will be self-seeking,
stubborn and impetuous.

Mercury : The native will acquire much education and
wealth. He will be a great scholar. He will be interested in
theosophy and metaphysics. He will have a scientific mind,
and fond of music and pleasure if Venus joins Mercury. Jupiter
with Mercury in the 9th confers wit and wisdom. He may
travel abroad on invitations and be invited to lecture in educational institutions. Relations with father will be friendly and
happy.

Jupiter : The native may become an exponent of law,
philosophy, etc. If Jupiter is aspected by benefic planets he
acquires much immovable property. He will be fond of his
brothers. If the Moon and Mars influence Jupiter he will
become a great military leader or commander. If the Sun and
Venus join Jupiter, the native becomes characterless. Jupiter
beneficially aspected by Saturn makes the native live a life of
austerity and strive for divine communion. He may visit foreign
lands as a lecturer, preacher, etc. He will be conservative and
principled.

Venus : The native is born fortunate and endowed with fame, learning, children, wife and generally every kind of happiness. The Sun with Venus makes one sauve and polished in speech but one may suffer from many physical complaints. Venus with Saturn makes the person a diplomat or otherwise engaged in similar work under a king or government. He will be well known for his balanced views on men and matters. Venus with the Sun and Moon may involve the person in quarrels with women resulting in loss of money. The Sun and Saturn with Venus give criminal tendencies, and other combinations warranting, the person may face conviction. He can also be notorious as a libertine.

Saturn : The native will lead a lonely life and may not marry. He will be well known for his valour on the battle field. The Sun with Saturn causes serious conflicts with the father and also with his own children. He may suffer from growths or lumps in the stomach. Mercury with Saturn makes the native untruthful and deceitful although he may be wealthy. Thrifty in domestic life, somewhat irreligious, he may become a founder of charitable institutions.

Rahu : The native will have a nagging and domineering wife. He will be impolite and miserly, suffering from emaciation and generally inclined to be of loose morals. He will hate his father and revile God and religion. But he may become famous and acquire much wealth.

Ketu : The native will be short-tempered and may get upset over trifles. He will be eloquent but employ this ability to scandalise others. Fond of pomp and show, haughty and arrogant, he will, however, be valorous. Often treating his parents badly and generally hostile towards them, he will be short-sighted but save much money through frugal living. He will have a good wife and children.

Times of Fructification of the Results of the Ninth House

The following factors must be considered in timing events relating to the ninth house :—

(*a*) Lord of the 9th house, (*b*) Planet or planets aspecting the 9th house, (*c*) Planet or planets occupying the 9th house, (*d*) Planets aspecting the lord of the 9th house, (*e*) Planet or planets in association with the lord of the 9th house, (*f*) The 9th lord from the Moon, and (*g*) the Sun who is the karaka for father.

These planets may influence the ninth house as either the lords of the main periods or as lords of the sub-periods. (1) The sub-periods of planets capable of influencing the 9th house in the major periods of those who are also capable of influencing the 9th house produce results relating to the 9th house *par excellence.* (2) The sub-periods of planets associated with the 9th house in the major periods of planets who are not associated with the ninth house produce results pertaining to the ninth house only to a limited extent. (3) The sub-periods of planets not associated with the 9th house in the main periods of planets who are associated with the 9th house produce results relating to the 9th house to a very small extent.

(*a*) Lord of the 9th house— Mars, (*b*) planets aspecting the 9th house—Saturn, (*c*) planets in the 9th house —none, (*d*) planets aspecting the 9th lord--Jupiter, (*e*) planets in association with 9th lord—Mercury, (*f*) lord of the 9th house from the Moon---Venus, and (*g*) the Sun.

Chart No. 85.- *Born 24–3–1883 at 6 a.m. (L.M.T) at 13 N, 77 E 35.*

Lagna Sun	Ketu	Saturn	Jupit.		Mars	Mercury Rahu	Moon	
Mercury Mars					Sat.			
Venus	RASI					NAVAMSA		
	NH-48							
		Rahu	Moon				Ketu Lagna Sun Jupiter	Venus

Balance of Moon Dasa at birth :   6 years.

Mars, Saturn, Jupiter, Mercury Venus and the Sun can influence the 9th house in their Dasas or Bhuktis. Saturn and Mars can, more than the other planets, influence 9th house results during either their Bhuktis or Dasas. Ketu being in a martian sign and also according to the dictum *Kujavad Ketu* can also influence the 9th house equally strongly in his sub-period or main period.

The sub-period of Ketu in the major period of Saturn was important in the native's life in relation to the 9th house significations. He lost his father, his guardian angel, during this period.

The 9th house has mainly to do with father, prosperity or fortune and long distance travel. The results relating to the 9th house may manifest during the Dasa of the lord of the 9th house. If this Dasa does not operate during the life-time of the native, planets influencing the 9th house by aspect, occu-

pation or in association with the lord of the 9th house give
rise to the 9th house significations.

Nature of Results

Subject to the general principles enumerated so far, the
following results relating to the ninth house are likely during
the Dasas and Bhuktis of the several planets :—

The Sun : Progress in religious education and spiritual
pursuits. Happiness from sons and acquisition of property
through self-exertion. Illness due to glandular irregularities.
Income through agriculture. *The Moon :* Access to reading
and higher education. Participation in projects of humanitarian
and social significance. Travels both within and outside the
country of birth and residence. Fame and success. *Mars :*
Inclination to be harsh and rude. Father suffers sickness.
Agricultural ventures fail but success comes in trade and business. Life of despondency due to circumstances. Ill-will with
brothers and death of one of them. *Mercury :* Gains knowledge in many subjects and succeeds in learning music. Gets
children. Interest in literature grows. Fame through scientific
inventions and discoveries. Becomes popular. *Jupiter :* Takes
interest in religious and similar institutions. Performs many
ceremonies. Gives much happiness to father. Gives away
much money in charity. *Venus :* Becomes selfish but religious
and learns much under spiritual preceptors. Fame through
poetry and arts. *Saturn :* Becomes a successful lawyer and
founds charitable institutions. Builds up a big bank-account
through miserly habits. Shows ungratefulness to parents and
becomes irreligious. *Rahu :* Domestic unhappiness. Indulges
in adultery and other vices. Becomes stingy and rude. If Rahu
is in dignity, the native makes fast progress in spiritual evolu-

tion. If badly placed. causes much suffering to parents. *Ketu* Suffers from eye trouble, gets many children and enjoys domestic harmony. But becomes untruthful and irreligious.

The following results are likely during the Dasa of the lord of the ninth house :—

If the lord of the ninth house occupies the Lagna in conjunction with the Lagna lord, the native acquires every kind of comfort. If benefics aspect the 9th lord, his Dasa brings in conveyances. The native gets a position of authority and power. He acquires wealth and riches and leads a happy life. He may work in the top levels of government service and occupy a post equivalent to a king or minister. He inherits paternal property and builds it up through his own efforts as well. Many relatives will depend upon his hospitability for their living and shelter. The native becomes famous both for his generous instincts and his achievements in career. If the 9th lord is weak, debilitated or eclipsed or in malefic Navamsas, that is, the 6th, 8th or 12th from Navamsa Lagna, the results will be quite contrary. The native suffers penury and instead of maintaining others will be forced to seek food from others. If Rahu and the 9th lord combine in strength, the native may serve foreign powers. If it is Mars, he will hold top rank in the armed or police forces. If Saturn or Mercury be the 9th lords, the native may become a law-officer such as a judge or a banker respectively.

If the 9th lord occupies the 2nd house with the 2nd lord, his Dasa will bring in unlimited wealth through family business or property. He will eat very good food and enjoy a luxurious life. He will have many relatives who will hold him in regard and affection. His face gets a radiant hue and his speech becomes eloquent. If malefics combine with the 9th lord, the native's resources and inheritance dwindle on account of family squabbles and litigation. If the 9th lord combines with the 2nd lord and the 8th lord, the native suffers disgrace and humilia-tion. He may even be thrown to the streets and suffer un-imaginable poverty. If the period is a maraka one, the native may die through the sources indicated by the 9th lord. If the 9th lord occupies the 6th, 8th or 12th Navamsa, then also the degree of beneficial results will be greatly modified.

If the 9th lord joins the lord of the 3rd in the third house, brothers will prosper. The native will show an inclination for writing on religion and spirituality. The native will earn through music and musical instruments. He will make many trips abroad as well as to holy spots and pilgrim-centres. If, however, the 9th lord occupies the 6th, 8th or 12th Navamsas, the native's fortune will be only mediocre. If the lord of the 9th house joins the 4th house with the 4th lord, the native becomes very happy and learned. If Venus and Jupiter also join, the native acquires many conveyances and lands. If the 9th lord is exalted in this position, the native may become a President or ruler of a country in the Dasa of the 9th lord. Saturn combining with the 9th lord in the 3rd house takes the native to foreign lands where he will serve the government or ruler. If fortified Mercury joins the 9th lord and the 4th lord in the 4th house, the native becomes the head of a center of learning or research. If the 9th lord occupies the 6th, 8th or 12th Navamsa from Lagna, the same results will be experienced on a lesser scale.

If the lord of the 9th house joins the 5th lord in the 5th house, the native experiences great clarity of thought and con-sequent tranquility. His father will help him with money and in other ways also to advance his career and interests. His children will distinguish themselves in academics and bring much happiness to the native. A son may become very famous and earn governmental patronage. The native's son will also prosper very well and enjoy all kinds of luxuries.

If the 9th lord and the 6th lord occupy the 6th house, the Dasa will generally be good. If benefics aspect, the native will earn well and advance in his career. His father's health will improve during this period. If malefics aspect the 9th lord, the native's father will die during this period. He may contract huge debts and be drawn into endless litigation. If well-placed by aspect the Dasa of the 9th lord will give the native the post of a judicial or similar officer. He will have many servants and men at his beck and call. If Mars be there, the native inherits landed property. If Mercury also influences the 9th lord, his Dasa will bring profits through royalty on books through legal bequests. If Jupiter be there, the native acquires immense wealth through his own learning.

If the lord of the ninth house occupy the 7th house with the 7th lord, the native will earn wealth in foreign lands. He will be sent abroad on diplomatic and similar assignments. His birth is in a prosperous family and he will enjoy all sorts of luxuries and comforts. Women will flock round him and he gets every kind of sensual enjoyment. Mars with the 9th lord gives the native landed property abroad while he will earn through women if Venus is involved. Fortune booms after marriage and the wife will be a noble and rich woman hailing from a respectable family. If the 9th lord be placed in the 6th, 8th or 12th from Navamsa Lagna, the results will be greatly modified. The wife will be sickly although gracious and gentle. The native, though earning well, may during the period of the

9th lord have to defray expenses on account of liabilities and litigation. If the lord of the ninth house occupy the eighth house with the eighth lord and is aspected by benefic planets, the native's father will die leaving the native a large inheritance. The native may also lose his married partner by death or divorce and obtain much money in the form of a bequest or alimony. If badly afflicted by malefics, the native will not only suffer bereavements but also lose his wealth and lands. He may wander aimlessly from place to place and suffer hunger and thirst.

If the ninth lord is in the ninth house, the period proves very lucky to the native. He will marry a very eligible and good natured partner and travel abroad. He will invest wisely in father's business and expand it beyond expectations. He will earn great wealth. If the Sun combines with the 9th lord and is aspected by benefic planets, the native wins elections and becomes a great politician. He will be well known for his states- manship and political acumen. If Rahu joins the 9th house the native's father becomes very famous in foreign lands. If male- fics like Saturn and Mars afflict the ninth house and lord, the native becomes a leccher and indulges in vile acts. If only Saturn aspects the 9th house, the native, though prosperous, suffers stomach complaints. If the afflicting planets be the Sun, the Moon and Mars, the native loses both his parents and also a limb. If Jupiter aspects the ninth house, he becomes pious and dutiful towards his parents during the period of the ninth lord.

If the lord of the 9th house is in the 10th house with the 10th lord beneficially disposed, the native becomes renowned for his learning. He gets settled in his career and leads a very successful life. He will have every kind of luxury and comfort at his command. He will do charitable deeds such as building rest houses and hospitals. He will earn much wealth through service to the Government. He will be honoured many times. If the 9th lord is afflicted by malefics, the results will be quite contrary. The native will lose his job. If in a profession, he will earn the wrath of people and be forced to close down his practice. He will lead an unrighteous life and seek to earn through illegal and shady means. He will lose his property and may suffer punishment by the ruler. If the 9th lord in the 10th house is well placed but the 9th lord occupies the 6th, 8th or 12th Navamsas, results will be good but their degree will be only middling.

If the lord of the ninth house occupies the eleventh house with the eleventh lord, the native prospers in the family business. If the Moon is also there in a watery sign, the, business relates to products of the sea such as fish, sharks, pearls and the like. If Jupiter or Mercury aspect the ninth lord in the eleventh house or if the eleventh lord be one of these planets gains will be through the newspaper, publication of books or educational institutions. If Venus be the planet, the native earns through hotels, cinema, restaurants but if Venus is afflicted by Rahu, Saturn, Mandi and Ketu, it will be through prostitution. If malefics afflict the 9th lord, the native's friends will turn against him and deprive him of all his wealth. He will be forced to beg for mere survival. If the 9th lord occupies the 6th, 8th or 12th houses in Navamsa, the native earns moderate wealth and will be fairly well-off.

If the lord of the ninth house occupies the twelfth house with the twelfth lord, the native will be spiritually inclined and will spend all his wealth in charity. He will lead a pure and honest life. He will lose his father during the Dasa of the 9th lord or may live far away from him. If the 9th lord in the twelfth house is afflicted, the native will lose money through foolishly investing it. He may be robbed of his valuables by thieves or in a dacoity if Mars adversely aspects or influences the ninth lord. If the 6th or 8th lord combines with the 9th lord in the 12th house, the native will lose his ancestral lands and money. If the 12th house is represented by a biped or quadruped sign and the 9th lord is afflicted by malefics and is himself debilitated or eclipsed, the native will lose his cattle, pets, horses and also his servants and workers in the Dasa of the ninth lord.

In predicting results, the strengths of the karaka Sun, 9th lord and other planets influencing him by aspect and association, the running Dasas and Bhuktis must be judiciously assessed first. Conclusions must be drawn only after the entire chart is analysed. No planet, by itself, if afflicted or beneficially disposed, can entirely influence the significance of the ninth Bhava without being itself affected by the other relevant factors.

Father

The longevity of father is judged on the strength of the 9th house and the position of the natural significator, the Sun. The 7th and 8th houses from the 9th house and other maraka houses and planets from it help in estimating the span of life of the father. Sometimes maraka planets with reference to the karaka Sun can also be used to judge death of father. Afflictions to the Sun or his occupation of malefic houses results in early death of father. If the 9th lord is in a kendra or the 11th house or aspects the 9th house or is otherwise fortified, the native's father lives long.

Chart No. 86.—*Born 14–4–1857 at 1–45 p.m. (L.M.T.) at 51 N 30, 0 W 05.*

Rahu	Jupiter Sun Mercury	Venus Mars	Sat.		Sat. Venus	Jupiter Moon	Sun Ketu	Lagna Mercury Mars
	RASI					NAVAMSA		
			Lagna					
	GD-123							
Moon			Ketu			Rahu		

Balance of Ketu Dasa at birth :   6 years, 8 months and 7 days.

The Ninth House :   Aries is the ninth house occupied by the exalted Lagna lord Sun, Vargottama 5th and 8th lord Jupiter and 2nd and 11th lord Mercury. It is between malefics Rahu and Mars.

The Ninth Lord :   Mars is in the 10th house with 10th lord Venus.

Pitrukaraka :   The Sun is exalted in the 9th house with Jupiter and Mercury. He is hemmed in between malefics Rahu and Mars.

Considered from the Moon :   The ninth house is Leo aspected by Moon-sign lord Jupiter, 2nd lord Saturn and 5th and 12th lord Mars.   The ninth lord is the Sun who is exalted but between malefics Rahu and Mars.   The ninth house and the ninth lord are considerably afflicted.

Conclusion : The ninth house and lord are both quite afflicted. The presence of karaka Sun in the 9th house with 8th lord Jupiter is not conducive to longevity of father.

The following planets can give the results of the 9th house with reference to father.

1. Sun—as pitrukaraka
2. Jupiter—being in association with the Sun
3. Mercury—being in association with the Sun
4. Mars—being the 9th lord
5. Venus—being placed with 9th lord Mars.

The Sun in exaltation with Vargottama Jupiter in the 9th house and the 9th lord in a kendra gave an exalted father—the native was born to royal parents. But the *papakartari* to the 9th house (from Rahu and Mars), the 9th lord (from Saturn and Sun) and the karaka (from Rahu and Mars) together with the presence of the karaka in the relevant house deprived the native of his father very early in life. Since the planets capable of influencing the 9th house are all well placed, the native's father could enjoy Rajayoga results but his longevity was curtailed. He died in February 1861 in Jupiter Bhukti, Ketu Dasa. The Bhukti lord, Jupiter, is the 12th lord from the 9th house The Dasa lord Ketu is in a mercurial sign. Mercury is the 3rd lord from the 9th associating with the 12th lord Jupiter. Ketu should give results similar to Mars according to the dictum 'Kujavad Ketu'. Mars in the 2nd from the 9th house with the 2nd and 7th lord therefrom, namely, Venus and therefore, becomes a powerful maraka.

A noteworthy feature of the chart is the Moon's occupation of the constellation Moola. This constellation occurring at the junction of Jyeshta and Moola is called *gandantha* and is capable of causing the death of father.

Chart No. 87.—*Born 23–4–1877 at 10–25 p.m. (L.M.T.) at 54 W 56, 1 W 25.*

	Sun Venus	Mercury		Rahu		Sarurn Mars	Venus
Saturn Rahu							Sun Jupiter
	RASI				NAVAMSA		
Mars		Ketu Moon	Merc.				
	GD-125						
Jupiter	Lagna				Lagna Moon		Ketu

Balance of Venus Dasa at birth : 3 years, 5 months and 12 days.

The Ninth House: Cancer is the ninth house aspected by exalted Lagna and 6th lord Mars.

The Ninth Lord : The Moon occupies the 10th house aspected by a malefic Saturn, Mars as Lagna and 6th lord and Jupiter as 2nd lord and is closely associated with Ketu. The 9th lord is heavily afflicted.

Pitrukaraka : The Sun though exalted is in the 6th house, a *dusthana*, with 7th and 12th lord Venus and is aspected by exalted Mars and an afflicted Saturn.

Considered from the Moon : Karaka Sun occupies the 9th house in exaltation but he is aspected by Mars, Saturn and Jupiter.

Conclusion : The presence of karaka Sun in a *dusthana* and his association with a maraka planet Venus and the affliction to the 9th lord Moon, especially by the nodes, resulted in the early death of father in September 1877. This was in Mercury Bhukti, Venus Dasa. Mercury occupies the 2nd house from the Sun. The Dasa lord Venus is the 2nd and 7th lord from the Pitrukaraka.

Chart No. 88. — *Born 6-10-1950 at 2-18 p.m. (I.S.T.) at 27 N 42, 75 E 33.*

				Lagna	Venus		
Rahu							
Jupiter	RASI		Moon	Sat. Ketu Merc.	NAVAMSA		Sun
Lagna	G.III-122						Rahu
	Mars		Saturn Merc Ketu Venus Sun		Jupiter Moon Mars		

Balance of Saturn Dasa at birth : 3 years, 7 months and 27 days.

The Ninth House : The ninth house is occupied by as many as 5 planets. Lagna and Saturn, 9th lord Mercury, Ketu, 5th and 10th lord Venus and 8th lord Sun occupy it.

The Ninth Lord : Mercury is the 9th lord exalted in the 9th house in close association with Saturn and Ketu, Venus and the Sun.

Pitrukaraka : The Sun occupies the 9th house with the 9th lord Mercury, Ketu, Venus and Saturn.

Considered from the Moon : The ninth house has Rahu in it and is aspected by several planets—2nd lord Sun, 3rd and 12th lord Mercury, 7th and 6th lord Saturn and 4th and

11th lord Venus. The 9th lord Jupiter is in the 12th from the
9th aspected by Mars.

Conclusion : The 9th lord Mercury is exalted but he is
eclipsed. Further he occupies the constellation of the 8th lord.
The presence of the karaka Sun in the 9th is not at all
desirable. The Rahu–Ketu axis is spread across the 9th house
both from the Moon and the Ascendant. The native was in her
second year when her father died in Saturn Dasa, Jupiter
Bhukti. The Dasa lord Saturn is with the 2nd and 12th lords
from the 9th house, Venus and the Sun respectively, in the 9th
house. He is also in the 7th, from the 9th house from the
Moon. The Bhukti lord Jupiter is a maraka from the 9th house.

Chart No. 89.—*Born 2–5–1947 at 7–20 p.m. (I.S.T.)
at 23 N 21, 82 E 21.*

RASI					NAVAMSA		
Mars Venus	Mercury Sun	Rahu			Rahu	Mercury	Moon
	RASI		Sat.	Mars	NAVAMSA		Lagna Jupiter
	G. IV-166			Venus			
	Lagna Ketu Jupiter	Moon				Saturn Ketu	Sun

Balance of Moon Dasa at birth : 3 years, 6 months and
23 days.

The Ninth House : Scorpio being the Ascendant, Cancer
is the 9th house. It is occupied by 3rd and 4th lord, malefic
Saturn and aspected by 2nd and 5th lord Jupiter.

The Ninth Lord : The Moon as 9th lord is in the 11th house aspected by malefic Saturn, Lagna lord Mars and 7th and 12th lord Venus.

Pitrukaraka : The Sun is exalted but with the 8th and 11th lord Mercury in the 6th house, a *dusthana.* He is subject to a *papakartari yoga* caused by Mars on one side and Rahu on the other side. Further, he is aspected by malefic Saturn.

Considered from the Moon : The 9th house is occupied by Rahu while the 9th lord Venus though exalted is in the 7th with 3rd and 8th lord Mars. Karaka Sun is in the 8th, a *dusthana,* from the Moon, as well.

Conclusion : Severe afflictions to the Sun deprive one of father early in life. The ninth house and the ninth lord as well as pitrukaraka are quite heavily afflicted. The father died in Mercury Bhukti, Mars Dasa. Planets capable of influencing the 9th house are its lord Moon, its occupant Saturn, Mars and Venus as planets aspecting 9th lord Moon, the same lords from the Moon, karaka Sun and Mercury who is with the Sun. The father died in Mars Dasa, Mercury Bhukti. Mars occupies the 12th house from karaka Sun who is himself in a *dusthana.* From the Moon, Dasa lord Mars is a maraka with reference to the 9th house Mercury, the Bhukti lord becomes the 2nd lord from the 9th house and is the 2nd lord and in the 12th house from the 9th lord causing death of father. In Navamsa also, the 9th lord Moon is in the 12th from powerfully by Lagna indicating early death of father.

The Ninth House : In chart No. 90 Virgo is occupied by the 7th lord Moon and Lagna lord Saturn. It is aspected powerfully by the 3rd and 12th lord Jupiter.

The Ninth Lord : Mercury is the 9th lord placed in the 10th house with the 8th lord, debilitated Sun. The Sun does not get cancellation of debility.

Chart No. 90.—*Born 29-10-1951 at 12-48 noon (I.S.T.) at 23 N 23, 85 E 23.*

Jupiter			
Rahu	RASI		
Lagna	G.II-188		Ketu Mars Venus
		Sun Mercury	Sat Moon

	Mercury		Saturn Lagna
Rahu	NAVAMSA		
Sun			Ketu
Venus	Jupiter	Mars	Moon

Balance of Mars Dasa at birth : 5 years and 3 months.

Pitrukaraka : The Sun is in a quadrant but quite weak by debilitation. In addition, he afflicts the 9th lord Mercury.

Considered from the Moon : The 9th house is Taurus, neither occupied nor aspected by any planet. The 9th lord Venus occupies an inimical sign in the 12th house with Ketu and the 8th lord Mars.

Conclusion : Although the 9th house from Lagna is relatively free of affliction, the pitrukaraka is in debility in the constellation of Rahu. From the Moon, the 9th lord is heavily afflicted. The father of the native died in March 1962 In Saturn Bhukti of Rahu Dasa. The Bhukti lord Saturn occupies the 2nd house from Venus (the 9th lord from the Moon) and is also the 7th lord therefrom. Rahu who is the lord of the Dasa is in the 7th from Venus and in a saturnine constellation gaining thereby strong maraka powers.

Chart No. 91.—*Born 1–8–1949 at 12–42 noon (I.S.T.) at 22 N 18, 70 E 56.*

		Mars	Rahu			
Rahu			Lagna Moon Mars Jupit.			
	RASI	Sun Merc.		NAVAMSA		
Jupiter		Sat Venus	Merc.			Saturn Venus
	G.IV-260					
	Lagna Moon	Ketu	Sun			Ketu

Balance of Saturn Dasa at birth : 8 years, 3 months and 3 days.

The Ninth House : Mars, the 2nd and 7th lord, occupies the 9th house.

The Ninth Lord : The lord of the 9th house, Mercury. occupies the 10th house, a kendra with pitrukaraka Sun. He is hemmed between malefics Mars and Saturn and aspected by 3rd and 6th lord Jupiter.

Pitrukaraka : The Sun occupies the 10th house in Cancer with 9th lord Mercury. He is also subject to a *papakartari yoga* caused by Mars on one side and Saturn on the other and aspected by Jupiter.

Considered from the Moon : The same picture obtains since the Moon occupies Lagna.

Conclusion : The 9th lord is in a kendra, so also the karaka Sun but both are quite afflicted. But 9th lord Mercury is strengthened by his occupation of his own constellation.

The native's father died in January 1973 in Jupiter Dasa, Rahu Bhukti. Since the 9th lord is afflicted together with the Sun, the father cannot live very long. But the position of the 9th lord in a kendra in a beneficial constellation cannot deprive the native of her father very early in life either. Saturn is one of the afflictors to the 9th lord as the constituent of the *papakartari yoga* which means his Dasa must take away the father, who died just before the commencement of the Dasa. Dasa lord Jupiter is a maraka both by lordship and occupation from the 9th house and pitrukaraka and the 9th lord respectively. The Bhukti lord Rahu is in a jupiterian sign and thereby becomes a maraka in his Bhukti.

Afflictions to the pitrukaraka by association, aspect, placement or otherwise are very important in depriving a native of his father. In Chart No. 86. the karaka Sun though exalted is in the 9th afflicted by *papakartari yoga* and occupying a nodal constellation, killing the father, when the native was about $4\frac{1}{2}$ years old. In Chart No. 87, pitrukaraka is again exalted but in a *dusthana* from Lagna, in the 9th from the Moon, afflicted by malefic aspects and in a nodal constellation ruled by Ketu killing the father within 6 months after the native's birth. In Chart No. 88, the Sun (pitrukaraka) is afflicted and is in the 9th afflicted by the nodes. The father died in the 2nd year of the native. In Chart No. 89, the Sun is again exalted but in a *dusthana* both from Lagna and Chandra Lagna, subject to a *papakartari yoga* and afflicted by Saturn's malefic aspects with the result the father died when the native was about 7 years old. In Chart No. 90, the pitrukaraka is in a nodal constellation in debility without cancellation of debility, depriving the native of her father quite early in life. In Chart No. 91, the karaka Sun is afflicted by *papakartari yoga* but is in a kendra with the 9th lord. The native of Chart No 90 lost her father when about 11 years while the father of the native of Chart No. 91 lived until the native was 24 years. In both cases the karaka Sun and 9th lord Mercury are in the 10th. In Chart No. 90, the Sun is debilitated with no relief and in a nodal constellation with the node Rahu being in a maraka house with 9th lord Mercury who is in Visakha, ruled by the 3rd and 12th lord Jupiter. In Chart No. 91, the Sun is in a friendly sign in the constellation of the 9th lord Mercury who in his turn is in the 10th itself in his own constellation. In Chart No. 90, the Sun occupies the 2nd house from the Moon while in Chart No. 91, he occupies the 10th from the Moon as well. We see karaka Sun, though afflicted by *papakartari yoga* in Chart No. 91, is comparatively much stronger than in Chart No. 90.

Chart No. 92. — *Born 31–1–1938 at 0–23 a.m. (I.S.T.) at 8 N 44, 77 E 44.*

Mars Saturn	Ketu		Lagna Moon	Ketu		Sun Venus Jupiter
Sun Jupiter Venus Moon	RASI G.IV-90			NAVAMSA		
Mercury	Rahu	Lagna		Mercury	Rahu	Saturn Mars

Balance of Sun's Dasa at birth : 0 year, 1 month and 2 days.

The Ninth House : In Chart No. 92 the 9th house is aspected by own lord Mercury, and 2nd and 7th lord Mars.

The Ninth Lord : Mercury, the 9th lord, occupies the 3rd house and is aspected by 4th and 5th lord Saturn.

Pitrukaraka : The Sun occupies the 4th house, a quadrant, with 10th lord Moon, Lagna lord Venus and 3rd and 6th lord Jupiter. He is not aspected by any planet.

Considered from the Moon : The 9th house is aspected by two malefics, Mars and Saturn, as well as Jupiter (who gets cancellation of debility) and the 9th lord Mercury is in the 12th house, while the karaka Sun is in a kendra.

Conclusion : The 9th house from Lagna, the 9th lord Mercury and karaka Sun are well placed with slight afflictions. The 9th lord occupying the constellation of the Lagna lord and aspecting the 9th house are important factors conducive to the long life of the father. The native's father died in the former's 41st year in Mercury Bhukti of Jupiter Dasa. Mercury occupies the 7th from the 9th and the 12th from the Sun. Jupiter, the Dasa lord, is the 7th lord from the 9th house and is in the 8th therefrom gaining maraka strength.

The Ninth House : In chart No. 93 the lord of the 9th house Venus occupies the 7th house with 3rd and 10th lord Mars and 5th and 8th lord Mercury.

The Ninth Lord : Venus as the lord of the 9th house is in an inimical sign Leo with Mars and Mercury and hemmed between malefics Sun and Ketu.

Pitrukaraka : The Sun occupies a friendly sign in the 6th house aspected by 2nd and 11th lord Jupiter who is Vargottama (as he occupies Scorpio in Navamsa also) and Lagna lord Saturn.

Chart No. 93.—*Born 8–8–1912 at 7–35 p.m. (I.S.T.) at 33° N, 77° 35′.*

	Saturn Moon			Saturn	Venus	
Rahu						
Lagna	RASI	Sun	Rahu Sun	NAVAMSA		Mercury Moon Ketu
		Venus Merc. Mars				
	Jupiter	Ketu	Lagna	Jupiter	Mars	

Balance of Mars Dasa at birth : 6 years, 1 month and 6 days.

Considered from the Moon : The 9th house is Capricorn aspected by karaka Sun. The 9th lord Saturn is in Chandra-kendra with the exalted 3rd lord Moon and is aspected by Vargottama 8th and 11th lord Jupiter.

Conclusion : The 9th lord occupies a kendra. The 9th house from the Moon is fortified while the 9th house from Lagna has no afflictions. Only the 9th lord is afflicted by Mars and the karaka Sun occupies a *dusthana* afflicted by Saturn. But Saturn does not afflict in the strict sense of the term being the Lagna lord. The native's father died when the former was about 32 years in Jupiter Dasa, Ketu Bhukti. Jupiter, the Dasa lord, who is also the lord of the 3rd from 9th, is in the 2nd (a marakasthana) from the 9th. Ketu, the sub-lord, occupies the 12th house from the 9th and the 2nd house from the 9th lord Venus.

Chart No. 94.—*Born 24-10-1949 at 3-33 p.m. (I.S.T.) at 13° N, 77 E 35.*

Rahu					Lagna Mars
Lagna Jupiter	RASI		Mars Sat.	Venus Rahu ———— Jupit.	NAVAMSA	Mercury Ketu
Moon Venus	Sun	Merc. Ketu	Sun	Saturn Moon	

Balance of Saturn Dasa at birth : 3 years, 3 months and 18 days.

The Ninth House : In this case also, Libra is the ninth house and is occupied by debilitated pitrukaraka and 7th lord Sun. The Sun gets neechabhanga (cancellation of debility due to his sign-depositor Venus being in a quadrant from Lagna). The 9th house is hemmed between benefics Moon and Venus on one side and Mercury on the other side. It is also aspected by Lagna lord Saturn.

The Ninth Lord : Venus as the 9th lord occupies a powerful kendra, the 10th house, in the company of debilitated Moon (who also gets cancellation of debility due to his sign-dispositor Mars being in a quadrant from Lagna). He is aspected by the sign-lord Mars.

Pitrukaraka : The Sun is in the 9th house itself with cancellation of debility. He is aspected by Lagna lord Saturn and is subject to a *subhakartari yoga* caused by Mercury and Moon–Venus.

Considered from the Moon : The 9th house is Cancer and is aspected by Jupiter. It is not occupied by any planet. The 9th lord Moon is in the 1st house with his debility cancelled aspected by sign lord Mars.

Conclusion : The 9th lord is strongly fortified. The aspect of Mars, even if malefic, is not really so harmful as being the lord of the sign occupied by 9th lord it only strengthens the 9th lord. The presence of karaka Sun in the 9th is not very welcome but there is the protecting *subhakartari yoga.* The 9th house is quite strong save the Sun's presence there.

The native's father must therefore live fairly long.

Compare this chart with Chart No. 93. The father of the native of Chart No. 93 had no career as such nor any earnings. He was dependent on his father (native's grand-father) until the latter's death after which he was taken care of with great love and affection by his son (native of Chart No. 93). In Chart No. 93, the 9th lord Venus occupies Makha whose lord Ketu is in the 8th house, the worst *dusthana.* Mercury ruler of the 8th is in the 12th therefrom. Venus is in Leo whose lord Sun is again in the 12th therefrom.

In Chart No. 94, the 9th lord Venus occupies Jyeshta ruled by Mercury who is also in the 8th house but in exaltation in the 8th itself. Venus is in Scorpio whose lord Mars is not only in a kendra but also aspects Venus powerfully. The father of Chart No. 94 is a man of international renown and the leading authority in his field well established in life. The asterism occupied by a planet is very important in judging

its significations. The native of Chart No. 93 is the father of
the native of Chart No. 94.

Incidentally note the artrological hereditary factors in the
two charts. Both have Aquarius ascending aspected by Saturn
from a kendra, Rahu in the 2nd, Mars in the 7th and Ketu
in the 8th. One has pitrukaraka Sun in the 6th house, a
dusthana and the other in the 9th house (the relevant Bhava).
Both have a Vargottama planet in the 10th, Jupiter in Chart
No. 93 and the Moon in Chart No. 94. Chart No. 94 has 6th
lord Moon neechabhanga in the 10th house while Chart No. 93
has the 6th lord exalted and aspecting the 10th house. In
both, the Lagna lord Saturn aspects the Sun. In Chart No. 94,
9th lord Venus is in the 10th, a kendra aspected by 10th
lord Mars from the 7th. In Chart No. 93, 9th lord Venus
occupies the 7th, also a kendra, in association with 10th lord
Mars. In Chart No. 93, Mercury is powerful being Vargottama
while in Chart No. 94, he is in his sign of exaltation. In
Chart No. 93, 2nd and 11th lord Jupiter is Vargottama while
in Chart No. 94, Jupiter who has the same lordship is also
Vargottama but neecha with neechabhanga caused by his sign-
dispositor Saturn occupying a quadrant from Lagna.

The Ninth House : In Chart No. 95 Capricorn is occupied
by Jupiter, the 8th and 11th lord. He is debilitated but obtains
cancellation of debility since Mars who gets exalted in Capricorn is in a quardrant from the Moon. Ketu is also in the 9th
house and is aspected by 7th and 12th lord Mars.

The Ninth Lord : Saturn is in the 6th house but exalted
and aspected by the karaka exalted Sun and 2nd and 5th lord
Mercury.

Pitrukaraka : The Sun is exalted but in the 12th house
with 2nd and 5th lord Mercury. He is aspected by exalted
6th lord Saturn.

Chart No. 95.—*Born 12–5–1925 at 7–30 a.m. (I.S.T.) at 13 N 04, 80 E 17.*

	Mercury Sun	Venus Lagna	Mars	Sat.		Mercury	Ketu
			Rahu	Venus			
	RASI				NAVAMSA		
Ketu Jupiter				Jupit. Mars			Lagna
	GD-127						
Moon		Saturn		Rahu Sun			Moon

Balance of Venus Dasa at birth :   13 years, 9 months and 9 days.

Considered from the Moon : The 9th house is Leo. The 9th lord Sun who is also the Pitrukaraka is exalted in the 5th house with 7th and 10th lord Mercury aspected by exalted 2nd and 3rd lord Saturn.

Conclusion : The ninth house is quite strong except for some affliction from Mars. The 9th lord is quite powerful being exalted and in a constellation ruled by Rahu, the nodal axis in turn being spread across the 3rd and 9th houses. Rahu is in turn aspected by exalted Saturn, the 9th lord. The Sun though in the 12th is fortified by his occupation of his own constellation. The native's father is a big business magnate and still actively alive at 75 years. The karaka and the 9th lord, both in exaltation, are in favourable constellations. They mutually aspect each other gaining strength thereby. Rahu Dasa Saturn Bhukti could see the death of the native's father. Saturn is the 2nd lord from Pitrusthana (9th) and is in the 7th from Pitrukaraka. The Dasa lord Rahu is in the 7th from the 9th house. Rahu should give the results of Saturn as well who is a maraka from the 9th.

The Ninth House : In Chart No. 96 the Langa lord Moon occupies the 9th house and is not aspected by any planet.

The Ninth Lord : Jupiter is the 9th lord and occupies the 4th house in Vargottama with Rahu. He is aspected by 5th and 10th lord Mars.

Pitrukaraka : The Sun occupies Lagna and is aspected by 10th lord Mars.

Considered from the Moon : The 9th house Scorpio is occupied by 11th and 12th lord Saturn and aspected by 2nd and 9th lord Mars but by his 8th house aspect.

Chart No. 96. *Born 4–8–1958 at 6–40 a.m. (I.S.T.) at 9 N 55, 78 E 7.*

Moon	Ketu Mars		Venus	Sat.	Ketu Venus	
	RASI		Sun Lagna	Lagna	NAVAMSA	
			Merc.			Mars Mercury
	RP. 23/46					
	Saturn	Jupiter Rahu		Sun	Rahu	Jupiter	Moon

Balance of Saturn Dasa at birth : 10 years, 7 months and 25 days.

Conclusion : The 9th house and the karaka are free of afflictions but the 9th lord is blemished by association with Rahu and the aspect of Mars. Jupiter is no doubt Vargottama but occupies a martian constellation. Mars is a powerful maraka from the 9th house both by ownership and occupation. He is afflicted by Ketu as well. Jupiter associates with Rahu but Rahu is also in Chitta. The native's father died in April 1979 in Rahu Bhukti of Mercury Dasa. Dasa lord Mercury is the 7th lord from the 9th house and occupies the 2nd from Pitrukaraka. Rahu who rules the Bhukti is in the 8th from the 9th house.

The Ninth House : In Chart No. 97 Leo is aspected by 5th and 12th lord Mars.

The Ninth Lord : The Sun is the 9th lord as well as Pitru-karaka and occupies the 12th house with 7th and 10th lord Mercury. He is aspected by Lagna lord exalted Jupiter. He is afflicted by the *papakartari yoga* caused by Rahu and Saturn.

Considered from the Moon : The 9th house Aquarius is occupied by 6th and 11th lord Mars while the 9th lord is exalted in the 5th with the 5th lord.

Conclusion : The karaka and 9th lord Sun are in a *dusthana* while the 9th house is aspected by Mars. The 9th lord Sun occupies the constellation of Mercury who as the 2nd lord is a maraka from the 9th house. Saturn, the 9th lord from the Moon, is also in a constellation ruled by Jupiter, 2nd lord from the 9th from the Moon. These weaken the 9th house to some extent. The father of the native died in Rahu Bhukti of Saturn Dasa. Saturn is the 7th lord from the 9th house and in the 12th from the Sun. Rahu, the Bhukti lord, is in the 2nd from the Sun. The Dasa and Bhukti lords are the consti-tuents of the *papakartari yoga* afflicting the 9th lord.

Chart No. 97.—*Born 12–12–1954 at 7–30 a.m.   (I.S.T.) at 13 N 04, 80 E 17.*

			Ketu Moon	Sun		Saturn Moon Venus	
Mars			Jupit.	Mars Ketu			
	RASI			———	NAVAMSA		Rahu
	RP. 23/45			Merc.			
Lagna Rahu	Mercury Sun	Venus Saturn				Lagna	Jupiter

Balance of Jupiter Dasa at birth : 8 years, 5 months and 23 days.

In Charts No. 96 and 97, the 9th houses do not seem to be strongly afflicted. In Chart No. 96, the Lagna lord occupies the 9th house and the 9th lord is Vargottama. In Chart No. 97, the 9th lord is aspected by exalted Lagna lord Jupiter. Nevertheless, in both charts the 9th lords occupy constellations of maraka planets from the 9th house which diminishes the vitality of the 9th Bhava. If in Chart No. 96, Jupiter had occupied Visakha, the father would have lived longer. In Chart No. 97 also, the Sun in Visakha (whose lord Jupiter would be exalted in the 8th) or Anuradha (whose lord Saturn would be exalted in the 11th with the 11th iord) would have prevented the father from dying in Saturn Dasa.

Fortune and Long-Distance Travel

Long-distance travel in modern times can be interpreted as travel abroad. The ninth house and its lord are important in

finding out if a chart holds prospects for such travel. Common
and movable signs are more capable of giving foreign journeys
than fixed signs. Watery signs are also to be taken into account
since in ancient times going abroad invariably meant crossing
the seas and travel by ship. The Lagna lord and its position
must also be considered since foreign travel may be just a
journey and back to one's homeland or it could also end in
settling there for good. Alternately residence may be extended
for many years before returning to the homeland.

Ancient texts have not mentioned any planet as karaka or
natural significator of travel. Sahams employed in *Varshaphal charts can be tried but how far they can be effectively
made use of can be determined by an earnest student only
after he has studied a number of charts.

There are two *sahams* mentioned namely, *paradesa* (foreign
country) saham and *jalapathana* (voyage) saham, which could
be considered for predicting foreign travel.

Paradesa Saham :   9th house – 9th lord + Ascendant.
$$\qquad\qquad\qquad\quad\ (a)\qquad\qquad(b)$$
Jalapathana Saham :   Cancer 15° – Saturn + Ascendant.
$$\qquad\qquad\qquad\quad\ (a)\qquad\qquad\quad(b)$$

If the Ascendant does not lie between the two values (*a*
and *b*), 30° must be added to the value obtained above in order
to get the required Saham.

If the Saham or its lord is not related to the Ascendant
or the 9th house or otherwise well placed, then the event of
the Saham may not materialise fully, The Saham aspected by
the 7th, 9th or 12th lord who in turn is related to any of

---

* For calculation and interpretation of Sahams, read *Varshaphal* or
The Hindu Progressed Horoscope by Dr. B. V. Raman.

these houses indicates foreign travel in the periods of appropriate planets.

When the planet occupying the 12th house from that of the lord of the Lagna is well placed in an exalted or friendly house or is aspected by a friendly or exalted planet, the native will prosper in his homeland. If there is no planet in the 12th house, the lord of the house can be considered instead.

If the 12th lord from the sign occupied by the Lagna lord is in an inimical or debilitated state or is otherwise weak, the native goes abroad. If the 12th lord from the sign occupied by the lord of Lagna is in a quadrant or trine or in the Ascendant and in a friendly, own or exaltation sign and is well placed, the native goes abroad to countries that are prosperous. If the Lagna lord is in a movable sign aspected by planets in movable signs, then also there will be foreign travel and the native prospers abroad. The Dasas of planets in the 9th house or aspecting the 9th house, the 9th lord and 12th house are very important in predicting foreign travel or residence.

Besides the all-important 9th house ruling long journeys, the 3rd house governs short journeys, the 7th house rules foreign travel and the 12th house, long journeys and residence in distant lands.

We have found in our experience the karakatwa or lordship or Bhava occupation of planets that indicate foreign travel gives a clue to the reasons for travel abroad. For instance, if the 4th and 9th lords are related, one may go abroad for higher studies or on a teaching mission. If the 9th and 10th lords are related it may be for reasons of career and professional advancement. If the 6th lord is also involved, the native may visit a foreign country on an official assignment sponsored by his employer. If Mercury is the planet, education, research, learning, writing or similar reasons may take one abroad. If it is Jupiter, then the native may travel in foreign lands either as a visiting professor, for lecturing on some subjects, or on religious, spiritual or cultural missions. If the 11th lord is involved, travel abroad will be mostly connected with gains; if on a political mission, to secure loans and financial and other assistance; if on business, to expand or market products and so on. If the 7th lord and/or the Sun is thrown in with planets causing foreign travel, a native may go abroad as a diplomat or delegate. If Venus and the 7th lord are associated with long-distance yoga causing planets, the native may go abroad following marriage. If Venus and Saturn, the 11th and 10th lords are related art-shows or some talent in fine arts may take the native abroad. If these planets are powerfully placed, film-shooting and similar assignments could take the native abroad.

If Lagna lord is weak and the 6th house or lord is involved travel abroad may take place for medical reasons, *viz.*, treatment or surgery. If the 9th and 12th lords are afflicted by malefics, the native may go abroad in connection with nefarious activity such as smuggling, trading in flesh, espionage and so on. If the 6th or 8th lords and houses are related to planets causing foreign travel, the native may flee abroad for political or criminal reasons.

If Saturn, Jupiter and the 12th lords are favourably disposed the native may go abroad to set up an ashram or on a religious or spiritual mission.

In Chart No. 98 the Lagna lord occupies the 6th house in exaltation. There being no planets in the 12th, its lord is Saturn and he is placed in his own sign. The native, owner of a national daily and many other businesses, has made his fortune in the country of his birth.

Chart No. 98.—*Born   18–4–1904 at 5–57 p.m. (L.M.T.) at 25 N 18, 3 E 0.*

Jupiter Venus Ketu	Sun Mars Mercury	Moon		Moon			Sun
	RASI			Rahu	NAVAMSA		
Saturn				Jupit.			Ketu
	GD-129						
		Lagna	Rahu		Venus Mercury		Mars Saturn

Balance of Sun Dasas at birth : 1 year, 0 month and 13 days.

Chart No. 99.—*Born 12–5–1925 at 7–30 a.m. (I.S.T.) at 13° N 04, 80 E 17.*

	Mercury Sun	Venus Lagna	Mars	Sat.		Mercury	Ketu
			Rahu	Venus			
	RASI				NAVAMSA		
Ketu Jupiter				Jupit. Mars			Lagna
	GD-127						
Moon		Saturn		Rahu Sun			Moon

Balance of Venus Dasa at birth : 13 years, 9 months and 9 days.

In Chart No. 99 the Lagna lord occupies Lagna itself. The Sun and Mercury occupy the 12th house from Venus. The Sun is exalted. The native, an heir to a large estate, being the son of a newspaper-magnate, and himself involved in it, his fortune too bloomed in the country of his birth.

Note in both charts the Dasas of planets in the 8th house or of the 8th lord have not operated so far. In Chart No. 98, the native was born in the Sun's Dasa followed so far by the Moon, Mars, Rahu, Jupiter and Saturn Dasas. Although there has been foreign travel in relevant Bhuktis, the Dasa lords not having a direct bearing on the 9th house, have not given residence abroad so far. In Chart No. 99, the native was born in the Dasa of Venus. He has so far gone through the Dasas of the Sun, the Moon, Mars and Rahu. Here also the Dasa lords are not directly involved with the 8th house and have only given foreign journeys. Foreign residence is unlikely since Lagna lord occupies Lagna in a fixed sign. Unless the placement of the Ascendant and other planets warrants residence abroad, the Dasas by themselves cannot give these results.

The native of Chart No. 100 sailed for England in 1905 in Rahu Bhukti, Ketu Dasa. The Dasa lord Ketu is with the 9th lord Jupiter aspected by Yogakaraka Mars. The Bhukti lord Rahu is in the 12th house in a mercurial sign which also rules foreign journeys. The 9th house is Pisces a watery sign and the 9th lord occupies a common sign. During Rahu Dasa also, the native went abroad several times representing his country. Rahu is in the 12th house and aspected by a powerful 9th lord Jupiter. Jupiter is in a constellation ruled by Venus, the 4th lord, and is aspected by 5th and 10th lord Mars. This Jupiter influences Ketu and Rahu, the lords of the Dasas which gave him much foreign travel. Jupiter's occupation of the constellation

Chart No. 100.—*Born 14–11–1889 at 11–03 p.m. (L.M.T.) at 25 N 25, 82 E.*

		Rahu		Merc.	Mars	
		Lagna Moon		Rahu Lagna		Sun Saturn
	RASI				**NAVAMSA**	
		Sat				Ketu Jupiter
	NH-59					
Jupiter Ketu	Sun	Mercury Venus	Mars	Venus Moon		

Balance of Mercury Dasa at birth : 13 years, 7 months and 6 days.

Chart No. 101.—*Born 22/23-11-1902 at 5-16 a.m. (L.M.T.) at 23 N 6, 72 E 40.*

	Ketu				Ketu	Lagna	Mercury
							Jupiter
	RASI		Moon Mars	Sat.	**NAVAMSA**		
Saturn Jupiter	NH-70						
	Venus Sun	Mercury Lagna Rahu			Mars	Rahu	Moon Sun Venus

Balance of Venus Dasa at birth :   13 years, 11 months and 12 days.

of 4th lord took the native abroad in Ketu Dasa for reasons of education. In Rahu Dasa, the influence of Mars as 10th lord on the 9th lord made itself felt and travel abroad was mainly because of the native's political career.

We see the 12th lord Mercury occupies Libra associating with Venus in his moolatrikona sign. The narive was a very popular political figure in the country of his bitth.

The first and most important happening in the life of the native of Chart No. 101 was his trip to England for education. This was in the Sun's Dasa, Jupiter's Bhukti. The Sun is in a watery sign in Scorpio aspected by the 7th lord Mars. From the Moon the Sun occupies the 4th house governing education. Lagna lord Venus is in Scorpio, and the 9th and 12th lord Mercury occupies Lagna with Rahu who is Vargottama. The personality of the native must therefore necessarily be influenced by a foreign background and this was possible because his education was abroad. Jupiter, the Bhukti lord, is in the 3rd and occupies a movable sign. In the Moon Dasa he came back to his own country where he distinguished himself in scientific circles. The 12th lord Mercury is in Lagna aspected by Saturn from his own sign indicating prosperity and success in the country of his birth. Rahu Dasa conferred on the native great name and fame as a scientist of international reputation and gave wide travelling all over the world. Rahu is in Lagna in a movable sign with Mercury. Mercury is the 9th and 12th lord and Venus the sign-dispositor of Rahu is in Scorpio allowing extensive travel. Rahu is with Mercury, the karaka for intellectual learning and it was because of his scientific knowledge and eminence that he went abroad.

The native of Chart No. 102 went abroad twice, both times on a spiritual mission. This was in Jupiter Dasa and

Chart No. 102.—*Born 12–1–1863 at 6–33 p.m. (L.M.T.) at 22 N 40, 88 E 30.*

	Mars	Ketu		Venus	Mercury	Saturn	Moon Mars
	RASI			Rahu	NAVAMSA		
Mercury Sun Venus	NH-36			Sun			Ketu
Lagna	Rahu	Jupiter	Moon Sat.	Lagna	Jupiter		

Balance of Moon Dasa at birth : 3 years, 3 months and 27 days.

Chart No. 103.—*Born 16–10–1918 at 2 p.m. (L.M.T.) at 13° N, 77 E 35.*

		Ketu	Jupit.			Saturn Jupiter	
Moon	RASI			Rahu	NAVAMSA		Venus
Lagna			Sat.	Moon			Ketu
	Mars Rahu	Sun Mercury	Venus	Mars		Sun Mercury	Lagna

Balance of Rahu Dasa at birth : 11 years, 8 months and 20 days.

Jupiter Bhukti when he was invited to address the Parliament of Religions in Chicago. Jupiter the Dasa lord is in the 11th house in a movable sign aspected by the 12th lord Mars. Jupiter is also in a martian constellation. The influence of Dasa lord Jupiter gave a spiritual colouring to the native's journey abroad. It was to fulfil a spiritual mission started by his mentor. The second time, the native went abroad was in Venus Bhukti. Venus is a movable sign with the 9th lord Sun and 10th lord Mercury.

The Ascendant lord Saturn occupies the 8th house. The 9th lord Mercury occupies the 10th house in a movable sign and the 9th house has Venus, the 10th lord in it. Since the Lagna lord occupies a *dusthana* in a fixed sign, subject to appropriate Dasas and Bhuktis the native may go abroad. In

Chart No. 104.—*Born 8–8–1912 at 7–35 p.m. (I.S.T.) at 13° N, 77 E 30.*

Rahu	Moon Saturn			Saturn	Venus	
Lagna	RASI	Sun	San Rahu	NAVAMSA		Mercury Moon Ketu
		Mars Merc. Venus				
Jupiter		Ketu	Lagna	Jupiter	Mars	

Balance of Mars Dasa at birth : 6 years, 1 month and 6 days.

Mercury Dasa, Venus Bhukti, she went on a world tour. Both Bhukti and Dasa lords are directly related to the 9th house, one as occupant and the other as its lord.

The native of chart No. 104 first went abroad in Venus Bhukti, Saturn Dasa. Saturn, although the Lagna lord, is also the 12th lord. Venus, the Bhukti lord, is the 9th lord placed in the 7th house with the 3rd lord Mars. He went abroad a second and third time in the same Dasa, Jupiter Bhukti. Jupiter occupies a watery sign Scorpio and is aspected by the 12th lord Saturn. Mercury Dasa, Mercury Bhukti also took him abroad. Mercury though the 5th and 8th lord is in the 7th house with the 9th lord Venus. Because of the powerful disposition of Lagna lord Saturn in the 4th house in a fixed sign, relevant Dasas and Bhuktis during his lifetime can only give foreign travel but not residence.

Chart No. 105.—*Born 3-8-1942 at 7-23 a.m. (I.S.T.) at 13° N, 77 E 35.*

	Moon	Saturn	Jupit Venus		Jupiter Venus	Lagna	Mars Moon Saturn
Ketu			Sun Merc.	Ketu			
	RASI				NAVAMSA		
			Lagna Mars Rahu				Rahu
	G.I-16						
				Merc. Sun			

Balance of Ketu Dasa at birth : 2 years and 7 months.

The native of Chart No. 105 first went abroad in the Sun's Dasa, Jupiter's Bhukti. The Sun is the Lagna lord and is placed in the 12th house in Cancer in a watery sign aspected by 7th lord Saturn. The next Dasa was of the Moon, the 12th lord placed in the 9th house and foreign residence continues. The Lagna is occupied by 9th lord Mars with Vargottama Rahu. The Lagna lord occupies the 12th house in a watery, movable sign indicating residence abroad in the appropriate Dasas.

Chart No. 106. *Born 17-9-1941 at 10 a.m. (I.S.T.) at 22 N 34, 88 E 24.*

Ketu	Mars Saturn	Jupiter		Lagna Mars		
	RASI	Moon		NAVAMSA		Ketu
			Sun Venus Rahu			Mercury
	GI-36	Lagna Venus	Sun Merc. Rahu	Saturn	Moon	Jupiter

Balance of Saturn Dasa at birth : 3 years, 0 month and 27 days.

In spite of every effort to come back to India, the native has been forced to stay back in a foregin country. The native went abroad in Mercury Dasa. Mercury is the 9th and 12th lord exalted in the 12th house and aspected by the 3rd lord Jupiter. The Lagna is a movable sign occupied by its own lord and aspected by a powerful 7th lord Mars. From the Moon also, Mercury as 3rd and 12th lord is in the 3rd aspected by the 9th lord Jupiter. Ketu Dasa was also lived abroad. Ketu is in Pisces, a watery sign aspected by 9th and 12th lord Mercury. From the Moon, Ketu is in the 9th house. Venus Dasa now running has given no possibilities of his return home. Venus occupies Libra aspected by the 7th lord Mars.

In Chart No. 107 the Lagna lord Venus occupies Aquarius but in the 9th Bhava. He is with the 3rd lord Moon. The 9th lord Saturn is well placed in his own sign in a movable sign with exalted 7th and 12th lord Mars. He is aspected by exalted 8th and 11th lord Jupiter from the 3rd house. The native went abroad in Saturn Dasa. His efforts at coming back have been in vain and he has been forced to reside there.

Chart No. 107.—*Born 12–1–1932 at 2–30 p.m. (I.S.T.) at 32 N 10, 74 E 14.*

Rahu		Lagna		Ketu	Moon	Lagna Mercury	
Moon Venus			Jupit.	Mars Sat.			
	RASI				NAVAMSA		
Mars Saturn	GI-38						
Sun Mercury			Ketu	Sun		Venus	Rahu

Balance of Jupiter Dasa at birth : 10 years, 5 months and 23 days.

The native of Chart No. 108 went abroad in the beginning of the Sun's Dasa to start a new life there. The Sun, though the 4th lord, is with the 3rd lord Moon and in a watery

sign Pisces.   The Lagna lord Venus is in the 12th aspected by
9th lord Saturn from a watery sign Cancer in the 3rd house.
This is a case of residence abroad.

Let us apply the test of Sahams defined earlier.

Foreign or Paradesha Saham = 9th house — 9th lord + Lagna lord

$$= \text{9th house} - \text{Saturn} + \text{Venus}$$
$$= (279°\ 7' - 115°\ 08') + 13°\ 56$$
$$= 177°\ 55'.$$

Adding 30° because Lagna is not between the 9th house and
9th lord.

Paradesha Saham = 207° 55' or Libra 27° 5'.

Chart No. 108.— *Born 13-3-1948 at 10-30 a.m. (I.S.T.)*
at 11 N 06, 79 E 42.

Moon Sun	Venus Rahu	Lagna		Lagna Moon Mars		Ketu Jupiter	
Mercury			Sat Mars	Sat			Sun
	RASI				NAVAMSA		
	G. III-4						Venus
Jupiter		Ketu		Rahu Mercury			

Balance of Mercury Dasa at birth : 3 years, 9 months and
27 days.

The Saham is aspected by its lord Venus who is in the 12th
house. Venus as the Saham lord is also aspected by the 9th
lord Saturn.

Voyage Jalapathana Saham = Cancer 15°—Saturn + Lagna
$$= (105° - 115° 8') + 39° 7'$$
$$= 28° 59'.$$

Adding 30° because Lagna is not between Cancer 15° and Saturn, we get Jalapathana Saham = 58° 59' or Taurus 28° 59'. In this case also, the Saham lord is Venus aspected by 9th lord Saturn and in the 12th house.

In Chart No. 109, the Lagna lord is in the 9th house and the 9th lord is exalted in the 5th house in a movable sign.

Chart No. 109.— *Born 28-4-1945 at 11-39 p.m. (I.S.T.) at 11 N 15, 75 E 49.*

Venus Mercury Mars	Sun		Sat. Rahu	Venus	Rahu		
	RASI			Merc. Sat.	NAVAMSA		Mars Moon Sun
	G III-6		Jupit.				
Lagna Ketu	Moon				Lagna Jupiter	Ketu	

Balance of Saturn Dasa at birth : 17 years, 6 months and 10 days.

The native went abroad in Mercury Dasa. Mercury is the 7th lord placed in a watery sign with 12th lord Mars and aspected by 3rd lord Saturn. The Lagna itself is aspected by Jupiter from the 9th house and the 3rd lord Saturn from the 7th house. Saturn in turn is aspected by 12th lord Mars justifying the native's status as an immigrant-resident abroad.

Foreign or Paradesha Saham = 9th house − 9th lord + Lagna lord

= 9th house − Sun + Jupiter

= 145° 52' − 16° 25' + 146° 16'

= 275° 43'.

Adding 30° because the Ascendant is not between the 9th house and the 9th lord, Paradesha Saham = 305° 43' or Aquarius 5° 43' ruled by Saturn. Saturn is in the 7th house from Lagna in a common sign aspected by 12th lord Mars and in 3/11 position from 9th lord Sun.

Voyage or Jalapathana Saham = Cancer 15° − Saturn + Lagna

= 105° − 74° 34' + 265° 52'

= 296° 18'.

Adding 30° because Lagna is not between Cancer and Saturn, Jalapathana Saham = 326° 18' or Aquarius 26° 18' ruled by Saturn. Saturn as already seen, is so placed as to indicate foreign travel.

Chart No. 110.—*Born 31-8-1944 at 4-30 a.m. (I.S.T.) at 10 N 50, 78 E 42.*

		Sat.	Mars		
		Rahu Lagna	Ketu Venus Sat. Moon	NAVAMSA	
Moon Ketu	RASI G.III-180	Sun Jupit. Merc.	Lagna		Sun Rahu Jupiter
		Mars Venus	Merc.		

Balance of Sun Dasa at birth : 2 years, 2 months and 16 days.

In Chart No. 110 the Lagna lord Moon occupies the 7th house, a movable sign. The 7th lord Saturn occupies the 12th a common sign aspecting the 9th lord Jupiter and the 3rd and 12th lord Mercury placed in the 2nd house. These factors indicate residence abroad. The native left India in Rahu Dasa. Rahu is in Lagna but in a watery sign Cancer. Its lord Moon, whose results he should give, is in the 7th house. Rahu must give the results of Saturn according to the dictum 'Sanivad Rahu' and Saturn is not only the 7th lord but also in the 12th house. The next Dasa is of Jupiter, the 9th lord, and after that of Saturn, the 7th lord indicating continuance of residence abroad.

Applying the Saham test :

Foreign or Paradesha Saham = 9th house—9th lord + Lagna lord

$$= 352° 58' - \text{Jubiter} + \text{Moon}$$
$$= 352° 58 - 136° + 275° 5'$$
$$= 132° 3'.$$

There is no need to add 30° because Lagna is between the 9th house and 9th lord,

Paradesha Saham = 132° 3' or Leo 12° 3 ruled by the Sun. The Sun is in the 2nd house but in close conjunction with 9th lord Jupiter and 3rd and 12th lord Mercury, and aspected by the 7th lord Saturn from the 12th house.

Voyage or Jalapathana Saham = Cancer 15°— Saturn + Lagna

$$= 105° - 76° 39' + 102° 58'$$
$$= 141° 19'.$$

The Lagna is not between Cancer 15° and Saturn. Adding, therefore, 30°, Jalapathana Saham = 171° 19' or Virgo 21° 19' ruled by Mercury. Mercury is not only the 3rd and 12th lord but is with 9th lord Jupiter aspected by the 7th lord Saturn from the 12th house, indicative of foreign journey.

In Chart No. 111, the 9th lord Mercury occupies a movable watery sign Cancer in the 7th house. The Lagna lord Saturn

powerlul and exalted in Libra (movable sign) in the 10th
house aspected by 3rd and 12th lord Jupiter from a common
sign.   Saturn in turn aspects the 9th lord Mercury.   The native
left India in Mercury Bhukti of Jupiter Dasa. The Bhukti lord
Mercury is the 9th lord and Jupiter is the 12th lord both indicating foreign travel. Mercury's position in the 7th in his constellation and conjoining Yogakaraka, Venus and 4th and 11th
lord Mars is a powerful combinatition for success and
prosperity abroad.

Chart No. 111.—*Born 24–8–1953 at 4–10 p.m.   (I.S.T.)
at 13 N 13, 79 E 08.*

		Jupit.	Rahu			Sun
Moon	RASI	Venus Ketu Mars Merc.	Merc Mars	NAVAMSA		Venus
Rahu Lagna	G.IV-92	Sun	Lagna			
	Saturn			Moon	Jupiter Saturn	Ketu

Balance of Mars Dasa at birth : 1 year, 8 months and
11 days.

Foreign or Paradesha Saham = 9th house — 9th lord + Lagna lord

$$= 152° \ 42' - \text{Mercury} + \text{Saturn}$$
$$= 152° \ 42' - 115° \ 44' + 181 \ 43'$$
$$= 218° \ 41' \text{ plus } 30°.$$

since Lagna is not between the 9th house and the 9th lord.

∴ Paradesha Saham = 248° 41' or Sagittarius 8° 4' ruled
by Jupiter who is the 12th lord and aspects the 12th house
and exalted Lagna lord Saturn in the 10th house.

Voyage or Jalapathana Saham = Cancer 15° − Saturn + Lagna

$$= 105° − 181° 43' + 272 42'$$
$$= 195° 59' \text{ plus } 30°$$
$$= 225° 59' \text{ or Scorpio } 15° 59'$$

since Lagna does not lie between Cancer 15° and Saturn ruled by Mars who occupies the 7th house, a watery sign, with 9th lord Mercury and is in mutual aspect with Lagna lord Saturn.

Chart No. 112.—*Born 29-9-1946 at 11-58 a.m. (I.S.T.) 13° N, 77 E 35.*

		Rahu				Lagna Sun	Venus Moon
			Sat.	Ketu			
	RASI				NAVAMSA		
				Mars			Mercury Rahu
	G. 1-20						
Lagna	Ketu	Jupiter Mars Venus Moon	Sun Merc.	Jupit.	Saturn		

Balance of Jupiter Dasa at birth : 5 years, 5 months and 1 day.

The 9th lord Sun joins the exalted 7th lord Mercury in Virgo in a common sign aspected by 3rd lord Saturn. The Lagna lord occupies a movable sign in the 11th house with 12th lord Mars As soon as Mercury Dasa began, the native went abroad for study and later continued his stay there for his career. Mercury, the Dasa lord, is also the 9th lord from the Moon placed in the 12th house indicating that the Dasa will be spent abroad.

Foreign or Paradesha Saham = 9th house – 9th lord + Lagna lord

$$= 125° – Sun + Jupiter$$
$$= 125° – 163° \ 50' + 189° \ 8'$$
$$= 150° \ 18' \ plus \ 30°$$

because the Lagna is not between the 9th house and 9th lord.

∴ Paradesha Saham = 180° 18' or Libra 0° 18' occupied by Lagna lord Jupiter, Saham lord Venus, 8th lord Moon and the 12th lord Mars.

Voyage or Jalapathana Saham = Cancer 15° – Saturn + Lagna

$$= 105° – 104° \ 47' + 245°$$
$$= 245° \ 13' \ plus \ 30°$$

since Lagna is not between Cancer 15° and Saturn.

∴ Jalapathana Saham = 275° 13' or Capricorn 5° 13' ruled by Saturn who is in a movable sign as the 3rd lord in Cancer a watery sign.

Pilgrimages

From times immemorial the Hindus have attached great importance to bathing in sacred rivers and pilgrimages. This is shown by separate chapters and yogas being devoted to the question of *yatra* and *gangasnana*. A careful study reveals that pilgrimages to which religious touch was given were undertaken as part of education. Pilgrimages form the final phase of education and have their own moral, intellectual and social values. The waters of the Ganga and several other sacred rivers are full of medicinal virtue and a dip in these rivers is held so sacred that it washes away not only the physical dirt but the mental impurities as well. Even now the majority of the Hindus or for that matter people of all faiths yearn to undertake pilgrimages so that their existence on the earth may find fulfilment.

Some relevant combinations culled from ancient works are given below.

Jupiter, if combined with or aspected by the 10th lord, leads one to acts of piety. If the 7th, 5th, 9th, 10th lords and Jupiter combine in a watery sign, the native has dips in the rivers as sacred as the Ganges in Jupiter Dasa.

The Dasas of lords of the 5th and 7th houses do not give pilgrimages but prompt the native to devote his time to study of sacred lore, particularly the stories of Maha Vishnu. The Dasa of the 4th lord gives pilgrimages to many holy spots. If malefics occupy the 10th and 4th houses from Lagna, the native dies during his pilgrimage to a sacred shrine. If the lords of the 9th and 10th houses combine, the native goes on a long pilgrimage. Jupiter's aspect on the 9th house gives the native the good fortune of bathing in the Ganges. If benefics

Chart No. 113.—*Born 8-8-1912 at 7-35 p.m. (I.S.T.) at 13° N, 77 E 35.*

Rahu		Saturn Moon			Saturn	Venus	
Lagna		RASI	Sun	Rahu Sun	NAVAMSA		Mercury Moon Ketu
			Venus Merc. Mars				
	Jupiter		Ketu		Jupiter	Mars	

Balance of Mars Dasa at birth: 6 years, 1 month and 6 days.

aspect the 9th house and 9th lord occupies a trine or quadrant or the 11th house the native goes on a big pilgrimage. If the 9th lord from the Moon is in a kendra, then also the native goes to many holy spots.

In Chart No. 113 Jupiter is in the 10th aspected by the 10th lord Mars. In Jupiter Dasa, Jupiter Bhukti, the native not only had dips in the Ganges but also in many other sacred rivers and visited a number of holy places.

XIV

Concerning the Tenth House

The most difficult and at the same time the most importan-
part in the analysis of a horoscope is the determination or occut
pation or profession. In fact, the number of avocations today
is so vast and varied that it is nearly impossible to ascertain
with any degree of accuracy the exact nature of profession.
There are several difficulties that present themselves before an
astrologer in his task of adapting ancient astrological principles
to suit current professions. In former times occupations were
few and the differentiation between one occupation and another
was clearly marked. But proper and judicious investigation
into all the relevant factors will reveal which vocation and the
degree of success one may achieve in it.

The tenth house refers to occupation, profession, temporal
honours, foreign travels, self-respect, knowledge and dignity
and means of livelihood.

Primary Considerations

Before analysing the tenth Bhava, one must study the
general strength of the (a) the house, (b) its lord, (c) its
occupants and (d) the Karaka or indicator or natural significator
of the 10th house. Different yogas in the horoscope bearing
on the 10th house, its lord and Karaka also influence the 10th
house. The Navamsa chart must also be taken into account.

Results of the Lord of the Tenth House being situated in Different Houses

In the First House : When the lord of the tenth house occupies the Ascendant, the native rises in life by sheer dint of perseverance. He will be self-employed or pursue a profession of independence. When the Lagna and 10th lord combine in the first house the native becomes very famous and a pioneer in his field of work. He founds a public institution and engages himself in social projects.

In the Second House : The 10th lord in the second house makes the native fortunate. He rises well in life and makes a lot of money. He may engage himself in the family trade and develop it. If malefics afflict the 10th house he will suffer losses and be responsible for winding up the family business. He will prosper in catering and restaurant businesses.

In the Third House : The native may have to travel constantly on short-journeys. He will be a speaker or writer of celebrity if the 10th lord is well-placed. His brothers may be instrumental to some extent in advancing his career. If 10th lord is in the 6th, 8th or 12th from Navamsa Lagna or in an unfriendly constellation in the 3rd house, the native's rise in life is slow and beset with obstacles. If the 3rd lord is also afflicted, rivalry between brothers may lead to reversals, obstacles, etc., in the native's career.

In the Fourth House : The native will be a lucky man and highly learned in various subjects. He will be famous both for his learning and generosity. If the 10th lord is strong, the native is respected wherever he goes and he receives royal favour. He may engage in agricultural pursuits or in dealings with immovable properties. If the 4th lord, the 9th lord and the 10th are beneficially disposed and related to one another, the native wields great political authority as a president or head of a government. If the 10th lord is depressed, eclipsed, in an inimical sign or afflicted by malefic planets, the native will lose his lands and be forced to take to a life of servitude. The same result obtains if the 10th lord conjoins the 8th lord in the 4th house in a malefic shashtyamsa.

In the Fifth House : The native shines well as a broker and engages in speculation and similar business. If benefics join the lord of the 10th in the 5th house, the native leads a simple and pious life engaging himself in prayers and pious activities. He may become the head of an orphanage or remand home if the 10th lord occupies the 6th, 8th or 12th Navamsa.

In the Sixth House : The person will have an occupation bearing on judiciary, prisons or hospitals. If Saturn aspects the 10th lord, he may have to work all his life in a low-paying job with not much prospects. If benefics aspect the 10th lord, he holds a post of authority and will be held in high esteem for his character. If Rahu or afflicted malefics are with the 10th lord, he may suffer disgrace in his career. He may be exposed to criminal action and face imprisonment.

In the Seventh House : The 10th lord placed in the 7th house gives a mature wife who will assist the native in his work. He will travel abroad on diplomatic missions. He will be well known for his skill in talking and achieving objectives. He will make profits through partnerships and co-operative ventures. If malefics afflict the 10th lord, the native will be debased in his sexual habits and indulge in every kind of vice.

In the Eighth House : The native has many breaks in career. If the 10th lord is fortified, he will occupy a high office in his field but only for a short time. If a malefic planet afflicts the 10th lord the person has criminal propensities and commits

offences. If Jupiter influences the 10th lord by aspect or association in the 8th house, he will become a mystic or spiritual
teacher. Saturn here makes the person an undertaker or otherwise employed in burning ghats, graveyards, etc.

In the Ninth House : The 10th lord in the 9th house
makes the native a spiritual stalwart. He will be a beacon light
to spiritual seekers if Jupiter aspects the 10th lord. If both
benefics and malefics aspect the 10th lord, the native is
generally fortunate and well-to-do. He follows a hereditary
profession or that of a preacher, teacher or healer. The father
of the native has a great influence on him. He will be a dutiful
son and do many charitable deeds.

In the Tenth House : If the 10th lord is strongly disposed
in the 10th, the native can be highly successful in his profession and command respect and honour. If the lord is weak
and afflicted, he will have no self-respect, cringing for favours.
He will also be a dependent all his life. He will be fickle-minded. If the 10th lord occupies the 6th, 8th or 12th houses
from Navamsa, the native's career will be routine and ordinary.
If three other planets conjoin the 10th lord in the 10th house,
the native becomes an ascetic.

In the Eleventh House : The person earns immense riches.
Fortunate in every respect he will engage himself in meritorious
deeds. He will give employment to hundreds of persons and
will be endowed with a high sense of honour. He will have
many friends. If the eleventh house comes under affliction,
his friends will turn enemies and cause him every sort of hard-
ship and worry.

In the Twelfth House : If the 10th lord occupies the
twelfth house, the native will have to work in a far-off place.

He will lack comforts and face many difficulties in life. If
beneficially disposed, the native becomes a spiritual seeker.
He will be separated from his family and wander about without
success if malefics afflict the 10th lord. He will indulge in
smuggling and other nefarious activities. Rahu afflicting the
10th lord makes the native a cheat and a criminal. He causes
sorrow to his family and relatives.

Other Important Considerations

Astrology is a science of tendencies and predictions do not
imply fatalism or absolute predetermination. Consequently,
it is only one's natural aptitudes or leanings for specific occupations that can be known from the horoscope. Therefore, no
definite astrological factors can be fixed for each vocation.

Before judging the profession it is necessary to ascertain
the mental, intellectual and physical abilities of the native by a
careful examination of the strength or weakness of the Sun, the
Moon and the Lagna respectively. The position of Mercury is
equally important. For, though classical astrology has assigned
the mental outlook of a person to the position of the Moon,
yet our observations go to show that as the planet Mercury
rules *buddhi* or intelligence, his auspicious disposition is
equally important in order to measure one's mental make-up.
When either the Moon or Mercury receives a series of evil
aspects particularly those of Rahu and Saturn, one lacks the
strength of mind needed to faca critical situations and would
be unfit for professions involving responsibility and the ability
to meet critical situations.

It would, in our experience, be reasonable to expect a
planet in the tenth or ruling the 10th house to have more influence over the vocation than a planet of general prominence in

any other part of the chart. This however is different from
implying that the ruler of the 10th or a planet in the 10th house
can be considered a fixed factor for any of the professions. A
statistical study of over 50 charts has revealed that it is only in
15 charts that the 10th lord and the 10th Bhava were definite
factors in determining the native's profession. But the most
powerful planet in the chart will also have a bearing on
profession.

Going back to the ability to meet situations, a planet in the
10th house receiving a powerful aspect from a benefic denotes
that the individual is not lacking in the ability of the nature of
the aspecting planet that he could make a success of it. If the
Sun and Rahu are in the 10th house aspected by Jupiter, the
native may preside over political meetings and take interest in
political activities ; but politics will not be the native's profession. If the Sun and Mars are in the 10th house with Mars
fortified and in dignity, the native may be a medical man but
would be interested in politics and even involved in it.

For purposes of study, we may classify the various occupations into six broad groups or categories, viz., (1) Intellectual
avocations, (2) economic avocations, (3) aesthetic activities,
(4) routine works, (5) mechanical professions and (6) trades.

This classification is too general because it is impossible
to draw a line of distinction between the different categories.
An author, whose main work is intellectual, may spend a part
of his time in composing and printing or insurance business.
In his occupation, therefore, both the intellectual and economic
aspects come in. There are instances when people suddenly
change their careers from teaching to business. This is
explained by the fact that there is a special stimulus to certain

qualities at certain ages, probably depending upon the nature of the directional influences (Dasas and Bhuktis) operating then.

Taking the first group—Intellectual avocations—historians, mathematicians, scientists, philosophers, doctors, astronomers, astrologers, psychologists, psycho-analysts, judges, lawyers, etc., come under this group. To the economic group may be assigned politicians, bank workers, insurance workers, actuaries, industrialists, mill-owners and manufacturers. Musicians, actors, singers, dancers, dramatists, cinema stars, artistes belong to the Aesthetic group. Routine workers include the large number of clerks, shop assistants, waitors and the general staff in offices, government and business organisations. Labourers, agriculturists, carpenters, artisans, mechanics, compositors, mill-workers, etc., belong to the fifth group. The sixth, *viz.*. traders include the rank and file of merchants, booksellers, publishers, stationers, grocers, printers, journalists, manufacturing representatives, etc.

Each one of these avocations can be divided into a number of divisions. For instance, an artist may be a sculptor, photographer or etcher ; a musician may be a violinist, vocalist, composer or flutist. An engineer may be an inventor, designer or a mechanic and so on. Hence it would be impossible to make an entire catalogue of professions and group them to suit astrological factors.

Generally speaking Jupiter and Mercury refer to intellectual avocations, Venus to aesthetic professions, the Sun, the Moon and Mars to economic occupations, Mercury to traders, Saturn to hard working jobs and Rahu and Ketu to routine workers.

In a chart there may be blends of different planetary influences. A philosopher and a scientist are both intellectual
workers : but in the former case Jupiter will be prominent and
in the latter, Mercury. If these influences are further affected
by those of the Sun or Mars, then service under the State is
indicated.

Mercury is a very important planet for creative or fictional
writing. Jupiter end Venus influencing Mercury in the 10th
house may give rise to a poet. Mercury and Jupiter may make
one shine as an author or spiritual, literary and religious
subjects. Mercury's situation in the 10th is the best gift for an
author. In the absence of such a combination, Mercury should
occupy a quadrant, preferably the 7th house.

Chart No. 114.—*Born 14–11–1889 at 11–03 p.m.
(L.M.T.) at 25 N 25, 82 E.*

			Rahu	Merc.	Mars		
			Moon Lagna	Rahu Lagna			Sun Saturn
	RASI				NAVAMSA		
			Sat.				Ketu Jupiter
	NH-59						
Jupiter Ketu	Sun	Venus Mercury	Mars	Venus Moon			

Balance of Mercury Dasa at birth :   13 years, 7 months
and 6 days.

Mercury is powerfully placed in the 4th house in Libra
(Chart No. 114). Mercury combines with 4th lord Venus who

is also the generator of Malavya Yoga. Mercury as the intellectual planet is between the Sun and Mars revealing the native's political doctrines. His intellectual output in prison was prodiguous.

Three instances draw our attention in the matter of deciding profession. They are :—

(1) When the 10th house is not occupied by any planet

(2) When the 10th house is occupied by a planet

(3) When the 10th house is occupied by more than one planet.

Taking the first : When there is no planet in the 10th house, take the 10th lord as primary determinant and the lord of the Navamsa occupied by the 10th house as the secondary determinant. Between the two, the stronger planet generally indicates the nature of profession.

When the 10th house is occupied by a planet, then of the lord of the 10th house, its occupant and the lord of the Navamsa occupied by the 10th lord, the strongest planet becomes the primary determinant.

When the 10th house is occupied by more than one planet the most powerful planet becomes the prime determinant provided there is no conjunction. If there is a conjunction the stronger of the Navamsa lords of these two planets will give the clue. Or, when the different planets are more or less of equal strength, then there will be a blending of influences and more than one occupation may be indicated. These principles are very general and must be adapted suitably. The 10th house should be reckoned not only from Lagna but also from the Moon and the Sun. It is also common experience that the reckoning made from the strongest of these three centers gives good results in judging occupation.

Chart No. 115.—*Born 29–4–1901 at 10–10 p.m. (L.M.T.) at 35 N 40, 139 E 40.*

	Sun Mercury Venus	Ketu			Lagna Mercury	Mars	
					NAVAMSA		Rahu
	RASI RP-155/PN		Mars	Moon Ketu			
Lagna Saturn Jupiter			Moon		Saturn	Jupiter	Sun Venus

Balance of Sun Dasa at birth : 3 years, 9 months and 24 days.

The Lagna in Chart No. 115 is Sagittarius and is very powerful being occupied by own lord Jupiter. The 10th lord is Mercury and he occupies the Navamsa of Mars in great strength. He is Vargottama (occupies the same sign in Rasi and Navamsa). The chart belongs to a military emperor with aggressive tendencies. Mars as lord of the sign occupied by the 10th lord Mercury has given a militant profession.

From the Moon also, the 10th house is a sign ruled by Mercury who is in a martian Navamsa. From the Sun the 10th house being Capricorn its lord Saturn is in Scorpio Navamsa ruled by Mars again. Or consider the strongest of the Lagna, the Moon and the Sun. The Lagna is occupied by own lord Jupiter and 2nd and 3rd lord Saturn. The Sun sign is also strong, the Sun being exalted and with Mercury and Venus.

The Moon sign is Virgo aspected by Saturn.   The Lagna would emerge the strongest of the three and the 10th lord from here indicates a military profession.

In deciding the vocational determinant, another important factor is also to be considered, *viz.*, the planet whose shadvargas predominate in regard to the 10th lord and the 10th house.

In Chart No. 115, the Ascendant (10.2 rupas) is more powerfully than the Moon (8.8 rupas).   The 10th is occupied by the Moon. The 10th lord is Mercury and he is in the Navamsa of Mars.   Mercury occupies six vargas of Mars while Mars has 3 vargas of the Sun.   Though the Moon (occupant of the 10th house) is more important than Mercury (the ruler of the 10th house) yet as the Moon is in a *bhava-sandhi* (junction point), he is rendered incapable of giving the results of the 10th house. Therefore Mercury and his shadvarga strength, *viz.*, that of Mars, determine profession as being predominantly military.

Planets in the Tenth House

The Sun : The native is successful in all that he undertakes. He will be strong and happy. He will have sons, vehicles, fame, intelligence, money and power. He will be employed in government service.   He will acquire ancestral wealth. He will be fond of music and have personal magnetism.

If Mars associates with the Sun, the native becomes addicted to vices like drinking, etc.   If Mercury joins the Sun he acquires profound knowledge of the sciences. He will be fond of women and ornaments.   If Venus joins the Sun in the 10th house, the native gets a rich wife.   Saturn with the Sun generally causes sorrow and dejection.

The Moon :   The native will be religious, wealthy, intelligent and bold. He will succeed in all his evdeavours. He will

obtain corn, ornaments, women and will be skilled in the arts.
He will be of a helpful nature and virtuous. Jupiter with the
Moon makes the native learned in ancient subjects and skilled
in astrology. If Saturn aspects the Moon, the native will be
a dispassionate thinker but earning through printing and selling
books. He will have many friends and lead a comfortable and
long life. He will be the trustee of religious institutions.

Mars : Other combinations favouring the native may become a cruel ruler. He will be fond of praise and may take bold
steps in governing. He will be rash. He will earn much money.
If Mercury joins Mars, the person will be a skilled scientist or
technician patronised by the rulers. If Jupiter is with Mars, the
native becomes the head of low-class people. If with Venus, he
becomes a trader in foreign lands. If Saturn and Mars combine
in the 10th house, he will be daring but will have no progeny.

Mercury : He will be a happy and straightforward person. He will be a scholar in many subjects and engaged in
acquiring more knowledge and fame. He will be successful
in all his endeavours. He will have defective eyesight but
profound knowledge in astronomy and mathematics. If Venus
joins him, the native will have a charming wife and wealth.
If Jupiter, he will be unhappy, and childless but move in
prominent circles of the government. Saturn and Mercury
make the native toil in jobs like that of a copyist or proof-
reader and suffer penury.

Jupiter : The native will be a high official in the government. Rich, virtuous, steadfast in his spiritual or religious life,
wise and happy, he will be guided by high principles. If Jupiter
and Venus combine in the 10th house, the person is held in
esteem by the government and entrusted with the protection
of the Brahmins (learned people). If he is with Rahu, he

becomes a mischief-maker and will create trouble for others at every step. If Jupiter is aspected by Mars, the native heads research institutes, academics and educational institutions.

Venus : The native earns through houses and buildings. He will be highly influential and has many women working for him. He will be social, friendly and renowned. If Venus combines with Saturn, the native will profit from cosmetics and articles used by women. He will have healing powers and will be a skilled trader. His education will be disrupted. He will have respect for divine people.

Saturn : The native becomes a ruler or minister. He will be an agriculturist, brave, rich and famous. He will be dispassionate in nature and will work for the downtrodden masses. He will be judicious and work in the capacity of a judge. The native visits sacred rivers and shrines and in later life becomes an ascetic. His career will be marked by sudden elevations and depressions. If Saturn is associated with the 8th lord in a malefic Navamsa, the native suffers under a tyrannical superior officer. If the 10th lord joins Saturn together with the lord of the Navamsa occupied by the 10th lord and is influenced by aspect or conjunction with the 6th lord, the native will have more than one wife.

Rahu : There is a tendency to lusts after widows. He will be a skilled artist with a flair for poetry and literature. He travels widely and is learned. He will be famous and will engage himself in business. He will have limited issues. Bold and somewhat adventurous he commits many sins.

Ketu : The native will be strong, bold and well-known. He will commit vile deeds and be impure in his resolves. He will face many obstacles in all his undertakings. He will be very clever. If beneficially disposed, the native will be happy, religious, well read in the scriptures and visit many pilgrim centers and sacred rivers.

Time of Fructification of the Results of the Tenth House

The following factors are of significance in timing events connected with the tenth house :—

(*a*) Lord of the 10th house, (*b*) planet or planets aspecting the 10th house, (*c*) planet or planets posited in the 10th house, (*d*) planets aspecting the lord of the 10th house, (*e*) planet or planets in association with lord of the 10th house, and (*f*) the 10th lord from the Moon.

These factors may influence the 10th house either as lords of the main periods or as lords of the sub-periods. (1) The sub-periods of planets capable of influencing the 10th house in the major periods of planets which are also capable of influencing the 10th house produce results *par excellence* pertaining to the 10th house. (2) The sub-periods of planets associated with the 10th house in the major periods of planets which are not related to the 10th house produce results pertaining to the 10th house only to a limited extent. (3) Similarly the sub-periods of planets that are not related to the 10th house in the major periods of planets associated with the 10th house will produce effects pertaining to the 10th house only to a small extent.

In Chart No. 116, we note :—

(*a*)   Lord of the 10th house—Mercury
(*b*)   Planet aspecting the 10th house—Mars
(*c*)   Planets posited in the 10th house—nil
(*d*)   Planets aspecting the lord of the 10th house—nil

Chart No. 116.—*Born 26-2-1953 at 9-20 p.m.   (I.S.T.) at 13° N, 77 E 30.*

Venus Mars Mercury	Jupiter			Venus		Rahu
Sun			Ketu Moon	Sun		
Rahu	RASI			Moon Mars	NAVAMSA	Mercury
	GD-173					
		Saturn	Lagna	Ketu	Jupiter Saturn	Lagna

Balance of Mercury Dasa at birth : 7 years, 10 months and 26 days.

(*e*)   Planets in association with the 10th lord—Venus and Mars.

(*f*)   The 10th lord from the Moon—Mars.

Therefore Mercury, Mars and Venus can produce results of the 10th house in their Dasas and Bhuktis. The native graduated in engineering during Mars Bhukti, Venus Dasa both connected with the 10th house. He secured a lucrative job in a big Government undertaking in the same Bhukti and Dasa.

Going back to Chart No. 114, the beginning of Venus Dasa (Venus aspects the 10th house) saw the native settle down to the practice of Law (Mercury, Sun, Venus and Mars aspecting the 10th is a formidable combination). Ketu Bhukti in Venus Dasa saw the native President of the Indian National Congress—a great honour and also a great responsibility. Ketu is in the 6th with 9th lord Jupiter who aspects the 10th house and becomes capable of bringing distinction and authority in the native's career. The major and sub-lords, Venus and Ketu, are disposed in the 3rd and 11th from each other—an ideal combination for elevation in career. With the commencement of the Sun's Dasa, the native's popularity began to wax further. The Sun is a political planet and aspects the 10th. The Sun's Dasa was not eventful but the Sun being in a Keeta Rasi, a series of detentions took place. As soon as Mars Dasa began, the native became Vice-President of the Indian Interim Government. Mars is a yogakaraka. Rahu Bhukti made the native the first Prime Minister of India. Rahu is in a mercurial sign and is aspected by 9th lord Jupiter who, in turn, aspects the 10th house trinally forming a Rajayoga. The Dasa and Bhukti lords, Mars and Rahu, are in mutual quadrants.

Nature of Results

The lordship, aspects, location and the general strength of a planet capable of influencing the 10th house determine the nature of results the planet produces in its Dasa. In general, the following results, relating to the 10th house, are likely in the Dasas and Bhuktis of different planets.

The Sun : Acquisition of wealth and learning. Health gains vitality. Founds institutions and gets a high position. Domestic happiness and prosperity of sons. Succeeds in military career and political ambitions. *The Moon :* Becomes passionate and adulterous, suffers mental unrest and a trustee of some religious or social institution. Gives away money in charity. Gets many friends. Acquires health, wealth and comforts. If in unfriendly sign, death or illness to mother and danger from swindlers. *Mars :* Acquires wealth and fame.

Prospers in agriculture and gets good profits in business. Gets adoration of relations. Gains energy and clarity of thinking. If a Yogakaraka, happiness and success during the entire period. Gains through fine arts and increased income from lands. *Mercury :* Gains academic distinction and recognition. Enjoys fortune of a high order. Eye-sight deteriorates. Indulges in charity and noble deeds. Succeeds in trade, religious activity and spiritual evolution. *Jupiter :* Becomes virtuous. Acquires wealth and conveyances. Birth of issues. Prospers in agriculture *Venus :* Earns name, money and fame through law. Enjoys social life. Education suffers, Acts in accordance with scriptures doing his duty. *Saturn :* Goes on pilgrimages. Suffers from gastric complaints. Meets with success in a sensational way. Goes to foreign countries. If a malefic by lordship and occupation, a very bad period in life. *Rahu:* Involvement with undesirable women. Becomes a creative writer or artist. General prosperity. If Rahu is ill-disposed, mental derangement and affection. *Ketu :* Does highly intelligent work. Becomes spiritual and works for the poorer classes. Travels widely. Destruction of dear ones, properties and self-respect.

The following results can be generally expected to take place during the Dasa of the lord of the 10th house :—

Benefics with the 10th lord in the Ascendant with the Ascendant lord make the native renowned. He will occupy a top position in the Government and exercise much power and authority. He will be noble and engage himself in charitable deeds such as gifting away clothes, building hostels, orphanages, wells and hospitals. If the 10th lord is placed in the 6th, 8th or 12th in the Navamsa, the native will be a just and peace-loving man. He will be of moderate means with neither fame nor power.

If the 10th lord combines with malefics in the Ascendant, his Dasa brings in disgrace and humiliation. The native may live on gifts obtained at death and similar inauspicious ceremonies.

If the lord of the 10th house is placed in the 2nd with the 2nd lord, the native earns riches in the Dasa of the 10th lord. His fame for his riches spreads widely. His family will look to him for everything and will hold his opinions in high esteem. He will work for the government in an influential job with many servants at his beck and call. He will have many dependents. He will feed innumerable people. He will be magnanimous and always help orhers. If Rajayogas obtain in the chart, the native's power and authority will have no limit. If malefics combine in the 2nd house, the native suffers from eye-troubles and family misunderstandings. He will be beset with various kinds of troubles and lose his money. Poverty will stare him in the face. He will not get food and his speech assumes viciousness. He suffers ill-fame.

If the lord of the 10th house occupies the 3rd house with the 3rd lord, the native's prosperity booms in the Dasa of the 10th lord. He becomes famous as a bold writer during this period. He rises swifty in his career with frequent promotions. His brothers will prosper well. He acquires musical talent and becomes famous in this field. If the 10th lord in the 3rd is in the 6th, 8th or 12th Navamsa, the native has a mediocre period. He may work for newspapers or publishing houses. If the 3rd lord and karaka are afflicted, then misunderstandings will arise between brothers, and the native may suffer mental aberration. He will wander aimlessly during the 10th lord's Dasa.

If the lord of the 10th house occupies the 4th house with the 4th lord, the native enjoys mental happiness and gains fame through his immovable properties. His income will be through lands and buildings if the 4th lord is Mars or Mars associates with the 10th lord. He will also undertake agricul-tural pursuits. If Mercury or Jupiter is with the 10th lord, the native heads an educational or research organisation. His family will come to be known for its respectability. If male-fics afflict the 10th lord, the native suffers mental vacillation and takes wrong decisions which affect his reputation adver-sely.

If the 10th lord joins the 5th lord in the 5th house and benefics also aspect the combination, the native rises to the rank of a minister during this period. If powerful Rajayogas are present, the native may even become the ruler of a country. If a beneficially disposed 8th lord joins the combination, the native may become a ruler or prime-minister following the death of his predecessor. If Rahu or Saturn in strength is involved in the combination, the native is elected to office. His fame will spread widely and he will innovate many reforms helpful to society. If the 10th lord is in inimical signs or in the 6th, 8th or 12th from the Navamsa Lagna, the results will be greatly reduced and the native may be a mere member of the Assembly.

When the lord of the 10th house occupies the 6th house, the former's Dasa will make the native a court official. If powerful planets are involved, he becomes a High Court or Supreme Court Judge. If the 10th lord is of feeble strength, the native may work as a summons-bearer or bench-clerk or attendant in the courts. The native's maternal uncle will be an influential and prosperous man. If Mars, the Sun, Leo, Scorpio, Aries are the planets and signs involved, the native becomes a skilled surgeon or physician. If malefics afflict the 10th lord, the Dasa makes the native work for others at death and similar inauspicious ceremonies.

If the lord of the 10th house occupies the 7th with the 7th lord, the native works abroad where he gets distinction and recognition. He marries a wife from a good family. She will also work or otherwise boost his earnings by helping him in his work. He goes to many shrines, holy places and sacred rivers. If the Moon joins the 7th lord, his work will be connected with conveyances. If the combination takes place in an airy sign he may work as a pilot, in a fiery sign he may work for the railways and in earthy signs, he may work in automobile companies. If malefics afflict the 10th lord, he will follow a profession that may not fetch much money and as a consequence suffer penury. His wife will be a quarrelsome women coming from a low and uncultured family. If Mars afflicts the 7th house, she will leave him in the Dasa of the 10th lord.

If the lord of the 10th house is in the 8th with the 8th lord, the native may lose his job in humiliating circumstances in the Dasa of the 10th lord. If the 10th lord is fortified he will be only suspended and then reinstated. The native will hold low jobs or take to a career of crime if Rahu afflicts the Moon and the 10th lord. He will lose lands, and pests and other troubles will spoil his agricultural income. He will suffer breaks in education which may not be completed. He suffers losses through his vehicles and in every other manner.

If the lord of the 10th house is in the 9th with the 9th lord subject to beneficial aspects, the native leads a life of righteousness. He will earn through fair means and become well known for his sense of fairplay and justice. If Ketu joins the 10th lord, the person embarks on a life of spiritual sadhana. If the Sun influences powerfully the 10th lord, the native works for the Government or take up the medical profession. If the Moon be strong, he will work as an auditor or banker in the Government or in some big undertaking. If Mars aspects the 10th lord or associates with him, he will acquire immovable property from his father. If Mercury is powerfully disposed, he goes abroad for education and research in the Dasa of the 10th lord. The native will prosper along with his father if Jupiter associates with the 10th lord. Venus in the same position will confer on the native gold, precious stones, conveyances and all kinds of comforts in the 10th lord's Dasa. If Saturn is the influencing planet, the native will head an industrial or other concern employing labour. If Saturn and the 10th lord are both weakly disposed or if the 10th lord is in an inimical sign, eclipsed or debilitated or in the 6th, 8th or 12th in Navamsa, the native himself will be forced to work as a servant.

If the lord of the 10th house is placed in the 10th house with benefics, the native will become wealthy and fortunate. He achieves distinction in his profession but after a hard struggle. If Rajayogas are present, the native acquires power, status and eminence in the Dasa of the 10th lord. There will be many people working under him who will respect his word as law. The native enjoys good health and does many charitable deeds. He founds institutions relating to his field of activity. If afflicted by malefics, the native suffers poverty. He will have a step-mother who will ill-treat him and cause him hardships during the 10th lord's Dasa. He will lose his job and drift about in misery.

If the lord of the 10th house occupies the 11th house with the 11th lord, the native will become a rich and prosperous man. He will have many businesses and all his ventures will turn out successful. He will have powerful friends in the government and upper classes. His personality will acquire charm and he will be a popular figure in social circles. He will have many men at his command and get possession of many mansions. If the Moon is with the 10th lord, he earns through vehicles, trade in sea-products, milk, restaurants. If the Sun is with the 10th lord, his income comes from woollen-factories, match-industries, gold market and chemicals. If Mercury is with the 11th lord he earns distinction as a great intellectual and thinker and gets some fabulous cash award. If Jupiter, he will head many institutions of learning as a chairman or trustee. Or he may be a newspaper magnate or prosperous publisher. If the 10th lord is in a malefic Navamsa and the 11th house is also afflicted, these same sources will give the native losses. Or if the 10th lord is feeble in strength but not afflicted, his Dasa fetches the native moderate success and wealth.

If the ruler of the 10th house is placed in the 12th house with the 12th lord with benefics, the native may head a medical institution or a prison or a remand home in the 10th lord's Dasa. If the 10th lord is fortified, the native pursues his spiritual inclinations with zeal. If malefics afflict, the native suffers humiliation. He will lose his job and if in business, losses will accrue to him. He will have unconventional professions and people will revile at him. He wanders aimlessly with no domestic peace.

An examination of professional prospects would include the study of the 2nd house also as the source of income which must necessarily be through one's occupation. The ninth house is also of relevance since it rules luck or fortune and indirectly all distinction, fame, success and sudden gains as attributed to Bhagya. The 11th house rules gains and especially in professions that are in the nature of trade gives a clue to the calling in which the native would prosper.

The presence of powerful Rajayogas, Dhanayogas and Mahapurusha Yogas is of importance in assessing the general strength of the horoscope and the heights to which the native may rise.

If the 10th house is vacant, then the lord of the Navamsa occupied by the 10th lord gives a clue to the nature of the profession the native may follow. In this case also, the reckoning is to be made from the Lagna, the Moon or the Sun depending on whichever of the three is most powerful.

If the lord of the Navamsa occupied by the 10th lord is the Sun, the native earns through work connected with medicine, wool, grass, grain, gold, diplomacy and mediation and arbitration. If this planet be the Moon, the native will deal in ships, pearls, sea-products, agriculture, horticulture, humour (cartoonist), women and clothes. If Mars be the ruler of the Navamsa occupied by the 10th lord, the native makes his living through metals, minerals, buildings, occupations involving fire, thieving, feats of valour, military occupations, butchering, driving, chemist-shops and doctoring. If Mercury be the ruler, the native earns as a mathematician, poet, artist, sculptor, writer, journalist, astrologer, priest whose services can be engaged and similar callings. Jupiter gives the occupation of a judge, teacher, counsellor, lawyer, bankers, ministers, preachers, and similar callings. If Venus is the lord, the native earns as a dealer in gold, precious stones, cattle, apparel and textiles, beautician, perfumes, elephants, horses, cars and other conveyances, hoteliering, and through the show-business such as cinema, dancing, dramas and the like. Saturn makes one engage in humble professions such as craft, tilling,

factory and mill-workers, labour of every kind, jailors, war-
dens, shoe-maker, miner, practitioner of wichcraft, and
similar occupations.

The native of Chart No. 117 is a teacher in a college. The
Moon lord of the 10th house is in the 10th aspected by Mars
from a jupiterian sign and by exalted Saturn 4th and 5th lord.
The Moon indicates callings that relate to people. The 10th
lord occupies a jupiterian constellation as well which should
give a teaching job.

The nature of the sign in which the 10th house falls is
also of significance. Fiery signs on the 10th house indicate
engineering, steel and iron industries, combustion engines,
locomotives as describing the general nature of profession.
Mars in the 10th in Aries aspected by the Moon may give a

Chart No. 117.— *Born 10-4-1954 at 7-20 p.m. (I.S.T.)
at 12 N 18, 76 E 42.*

Sun Mercury	Venus	Jupiter	Ketu		Sun			Ketu Mars
			Moon		Sat.			Moon
	RASI					NAVAMSA		
					Lagna			Mercury Venus
	GD-177							
Mars Rahu		Lagna Saturn			Rahu			Jupiter

Balance of Jupiter Dasa at birth : 0 year, 4 months and
15 days.

job relating to automobiles. Mars and Mercury may make one a mechanical engineer. Airy signs denote intellectual professions philosophers, writers, thinkers, scientists and researchers. Libra on the 10th Bhava with Mercury and Rahu can make the native a scientist with an engineering back ground. Jupiter or Saturn could indicate legal profession while the Moon also there with Mercury may point to a writer on religion or fiction. Earthy signs rule professions that require practicality such as administration, economics and occupations such as construction of buildings, mining, agriculture, estate agencies and the like. Watery signs gives professions which are connected with liquids—chemistry, biology, dairy-farming, breweries, bottled drinks, laundries, shipping and water technology.

Movable signs endow the native with push, energy and enterprise so that such natives are best fitted for jobs requiring these qualities—salesmen, pioneering work, market executives. medical representatives, etc. Fixed signs give one the capacity to persevere against odds and a fixity of purpose. People with such signs on the 10th house will succeed as research workers. Common signs being mutable, if strong, give the capacity both for go-ahead jobs and those that require steady work depending upon the planets and signs involved.

Besides the 10th lord and house, the sign occupied by the 10th lord, other planets and sign or signs predominant in the chart as well as a fortified Lagna are some more factors that go to colour the occupation or vocation of the native. We give below some general guidelines on the nature of career the different signs and planets broadly indicate.

Aries : Natives born with Aries strong, fare well in careers that require enterprise, dynamism and energy. They are suited

for jobs requiring exploration and courage and do well as
soldiers, policemen, army workers, scientists, engineers,
dentists, surgeons, mechanics and metal and mineral tech-
nologists. Since Aries rules the head, as surgeons they exhibit
skill in brain surgery. Aries is the natural fighter. If Mercury
and Jupiter be strongly disposed, the native emerges as a
powerful writer, journalist or lawyer—fighting for a cause.
Venus strong makes Aries-natives dashing executives or salesmen. Mars strong gives industrial workers, hunters, explorers
and officers of law. If the Sun be strong, the native would
be an industrialist, politician or owner of a timber-yard or
lumber-yard. Saturn and Aries strong would give trade-
unionists.

Chart No. 118.—*Born 18-4-1904 at 5-57 p.m. (L.M.T.) at 25 N 18, 83 E 00.*

Jupiter Venus Ketu	Sun Mars Mercury	Moon		Moon			Sun
	RASI GD-129			Rahu	NAVAMSA		
Saturn				Jupit.			Ketu
		Lagna			Venus Mercury	Lagna	Saturn Mars

Balance of Sun's Dasa at birth : 1 year, 0 month and
13 days.

In Chart No. 118, Lagna is Vargottama, Lagna lord Venus
is exalted in the 6th house with 6th lord Jupiter, Mars is in

the 7th in his moolatrikona sign. Saturn, the Yogakaraka, occupies another kendra and both luminaries are exalted, lifting the chart well above average. The 10th lord Moon occupies Pisces Navamsa ruled by Jupiter. The 10th lord from the Moon, namely, Saturn occupies a Navamsa ruled by Mercury. The karaka Sun also occupies a Navamsa of Mercury. Mercury and Jupiter being dominant, the native's career is linked with communication (Mercury) and publishing (Jupiter). The native is a newspaper magnate. Aries is the most powerful sign in the chart because, being a quadarnt is occupied by exalted Sun, 9th lord Mercury and sign lord Mars. The native proved to be an independent and intrepid newspaperman even during the Indira Emergency when he was harrassed and bullied by the caucus in every conceivable manner.

Taurus : Natives with this sign strong are practical people with dogged determination and perseverance. Since it is the second sign of the zodiac, bankers, cashiers, capitalists, financiers and money-lenders are indicated. Cosmetics, jewellery, articles of fashion come under this sign. Taurus strong natives make good advertising and publicity agents. They can be good throat specialists and singers. Venus strong would make skilled instrumentalists and the Moon would give singers. Mercury–Moon–Venus would give composers, acousticians and audition experts. Mars and the Moon refer to agriculturists.

The native of Chart No. 119 is an accounts officer in a firm. The 10th house is aspected by the Moon and Jupiter. The 10th lord occupies a Navamsa of Mercury, the planet related to account-keeping, auditing, book-keeping and similar vocations. The Ascendant is Taurus, the second sign of the zodiac ruling finance and is occupied by the 10th lord Saturn.

Chart No. 119.—*Born 13–1–1944 at 1–49 p.m. (L.M.T.) at 22 N 35, 88 E 23.*

		Lagna Mars Saturn		Lagna	Mars Moon	Ketu Jupiter	
			Rahu				
	RASI				NAVAMSA		
Sun Ketu			Moon Jupit.	Sun Venus			
	RP-36/30						
Mercury	Venus				Rahu	Mercury	Saturn

Balance of Ketu Dasa at birth .   5 years, 11 months.

It is aspected by sign lord Venus and is powerful indicating a job connected with finances.

Gemini : Natives of Gemini make good workers in all areas of communication. They fare well as language experts, interpreters, sales agents, translators, reporters, writers and researchers. If the Sun be strong, they gain excellence in engineering branches and in analytical studies of law and education. Since Mercury is the planet of trade also, they do well as auditors, accountants and similar jobs. It also gives mathematicians and writers. If Mercury is predominant, fiction-writers and Jupiter strong would give drama-writers. Venus and Gemini would give poetic abilities. If Mercury and Jupiter are involved, there would be serious writing—history, biographies, essays ; Mercury, Mars and Jupiter with Gemini give proficiency in feature-writing, news-reporting and editing.

Chart No. 120.—*Born   29-6-1864 at about 3-55 a.m. (L.M.T.) at 22 N 35, 88 E.*

Mars Moon Ketu	Lagna Mercury	Sun Venus		Sun	Mars	Rahu	Jupiter
							Saturn
RASI				NAVAMSA			
		Venus					Moon
NH-39							
	Jupiter Rahu	Sat.			Ketu		Lagna Mercury

Balance of Venus Dasa at birth :   15 years, 6 months and 9 days.

Chart No. 120 is of a great educationist, mathematician and jurist.   The native had outstanding mental capacities with a distinct bent for mathematics. The Lagna is occupied by Mercury, the planet of intelligence.   He is in *parivartana* with Venus in Gemini.   Gemini is occupied by Lagna and 4th lords, Venus and Sun respectively, and aspected by Yogakaraka Saturn and Jupiter.   Gemini is the most powerful sign in the chart endowing the native with wide learning.

Cancer : Cancer strong in a chart indicates biology, botany, zoology, marine life, zoo-keeping, dairy-farming, bee-keeping and trade in honey, fish, etc.   Such natives make good house-keepers and can therefore work as matrons, housewives, hotel-superintendents and similar jobs.   They also make kind nurses and gentle doctors. Since Cancer is a domestic sign, if the Moon, Venus and Mars are involved, success is likely in hotel-running, snack–bars, bakery and confectionery business, ice-cream parlours, etc. If Cancer is afflicted, then the native's vocation will be connected with wines and breweries. They make good laundrymen and sailors since Cancer is a watery sign. If Saturn, Mercury or Jupiter is involved, the native tends to be good at archaeology, history, museum-work, teaching. The Moon and Jupiter would give teachers, social workers and institutional workers. The Sun and Cancer with Moon and Jupiter give philanthropists.

In Chart No. 121 Cancer, Ascendant, is occupied by its own lord the Moon, 10th lord Mars, 9th lord exalted Jupiter and Rahu. This is by far the most predominant Rasi in the chart. Mars as the 10th lord has given a technological background to the native but his expertise is in alcohol technology.

Chart No. 121.—*Born 28-5-1944 at 9-50 a.m. (I.S.T.) at 13 N, 77 E 35.*

	Mercury	Venus Sun	Sat.	Venus Jupit. Ketu		Sun	
			Lagna Moon Mars Rahu Jupit	Moon			
Ketu	RASI G IV-327				NAVAMSA		
					Saturn	Mercury Mars	Lagna Rahu

Balance of Mercury Dasa at birth : 6 years, 1 month and 28 days.

Cancer rules wines and breweries and Rahu afflicting the sign and planets in it has given the native the job of an alcohol technologist.

Leo : Leo being an utopion royal sign, Leo-strong natives fare well in jobs of authority and power. They make good executives, administrators and generally do well as the boss. They are fitted for jobs in administrative cadres and work well in the stock-exchange, investment business, jewellery and gold, circus-training, as forest officers, film and drama directors, foremen. Leo has a special propensity for the doctoring line, drugs and chemicals. The Sun and Mars predominant give political leaders and workers while the Sun and Venus give ambassadors, diplomats and foreign service jobs requiring polish and sophistication.

Chart No. 122. – *Born 12–5–1897 at 10–19 a.m. (L.M.T.) at 9 N 51, 78 E 37.*

	Venus	Sun Mercury				Mercury	Jupiter Rahu
			Ketu Lagna Mars				Venus
	RASI				NAVAMSA		Lagna Mars
Rahu			Jupit. Moon	Sun			
	NH-69						
	Saturn			Ketu Moon			Saturn

Balance of Sun Dasa at birth : 4 years, 6 months and 27 days.

The karaka for mind, Moon, in Leo in association with Jupiter, lord of the 9th and aspected by Saturn, lord of the 7th is the most important combination in Chart No. 122 around which the entire life of the native revolved. Besides causing Gajakesari Yoga, this combination gave the native a certain sensitiveness (lunar trait) that found expression in sublimal ways. Venus, the planet of poetry, who happens to be the lord of the 4th house is in the 10th in the house of practical Mars and aspected by *gnanakaraka* Jupiter from Chandra Lagna. This confers poetical talents of an extraordinary nature. The native was a great Tamil poet with skill in English and French versification also. The sign Leo in strength made the native essentially an ardent and a fiery nationalist.

Virgo : Virgo natives have an eye for detail. They make good teachers, manicurists, retail shop-keepers, clerks, receptionists, secretaries, postal employees, bus drivers and conductors, book-binders, stenographers, interpreters, translators, librarians, radio and television announcers, paper-dealers, handwriting and fingerprint experts, notaries public, computer operators, writers, editors, reporters, psychologists and psychiartrists, healers, doctors, explorers, detectives. They do well in jobs requiring intelligence and efficiency. Mercury and Virgo give book-keepers, statisticians, cashiers, bank-clerks. Saturn related to Virgo indicates typists, museum-curators and book-keepers while the Sun has to do with auditors, tax-officers and chartered accountants. Venus governs filing-clerks, sales girls or salesmen and librarians.

In Chart No. 123 the 10th house is Cancer occupied by the Moon indicating the job relates to the public. Mars and Jupiter aspect the 10th house and 10th lord indicating a post of authority. Chart No. 123 is of an income-tax official. The

Chart No. 123.—*Born 2-10-1926 at 8-5 a.m. (I.S T) at 16 N 13, 80 E 36.*

	Mars		Rahu		Rahu		Sun
			Moon	Lagna Moon Venus			Saturn
	RASI				NAVAMSA		Mercury Jupiter
Jupiter	GIV-228						
Ketu	Saturn	Lagna	Venus Sun Merc.	Mars		Ketu	

Balance of Mercury Dasa at birth : 7 years, 4 months and 22 days.

Chart No. 124.—*Born 9-5-1922 at 9-32 p.m. (I.S.T.) at 18 N 7, 83 E 27.*

Ketu	Sun	Mercury Venus			Saturn Mercury	Mars Rahu	Venus
	RASI				NAVAMSA		Lagna
	GIV-58						
Lagna Mars		Moon	Jupit. Sat. Rahu	Sun	Moon Ketu		Jupiter

Balance of Mars Dasa at birth : 0 year, 6 months and 6 days.

sign Virgo is strong, though in the 12th house, being occupied by exalted sign-lord Mercury, Venus and Sun and being aspected by Jupiter.

In Chart No. 124, the 10th house is Virgo which is also the most predominant sign in the chart. Saturn there indicates a job as a stenographer. Rahu in the 10th afflicts Virgo coming in the way of advancement.

Libra : Libra being the sign of the balance, natives with this sign strong make good management consultants, lawyers, judges, solicitors, logicians and officers of the law, diplomats and public relations officers. Since it is ruled by Venus, it gives singers, actors, beauticians, haber-dashers, fashion-models, interior decorators and furniture-makers, perfume-manufacturers, social workers, photographers, tea-shop and coffee-bar owners, snack and restaurant keepers and all similar trades Venus powerful with Rahu and the Moon would give artists, sculptors, cinema artistes and models. If Libra and Saturn and Venus figure in strength cartoonists, cameramen, tailors, dress-designers and make-up assistants would be the result. Mars, Rahu, Venus make the native work in cabaret shows, gambling casinos and similar haunts of sin and pleasure.

Note how Libra dominates in Chart No. 125. It is occupied by Lagna lord Venus, 9th and 12th lord Mercury and 11th lord the Sun *neechabhanga*. The native is a top executive in a management firm and a nutritional consultant.

Scorpio : Being a mystic sign, Scorpio produces mystics, philosophers, astrologers and occultists. Being secretive, detectives and clever criminals also come under this sign. Nurses, chemists, doctors, explorers, geographers, barbers, dentists, mechanics, men of the armed and police-forces, navigators, coffin-makers, undertakers, life-insurance agents

Chart No. 125.—*Born 20-10-1931 at 7-20 a.m. (I.S.T.) at 13 N 20, 74 E 45.*

			Lagna Jupit.	Ketu		
Rahu						
	RASI	Jupit.	Venus	NAVAMSA		Mars
Moon						
	GIV-28					Moon
Saturn	Mars	Lagna Sun Mercury Venus	Ketu	Sun Mercury Saturn	Rahu	

Balance of Mars Dasa at birth : 6 years, 10 months and 3 days.

and business and embalmers come under this sign. If Mars is strong, then railway and tram workers, police and army personnel, home guards, telephone operators and telegraphists are indicated. The Moon and Scorpio would give pearl-divers, dealers in sea-foods, corals, poisons, drugs and chemicals. The Sun strong would indicate an executive job in these callings.

Chart No. 126 is of an international figure in astrology whose predictions have been fulfilled to a remarkable degree. The mystic sign Scorpio is powerfully placed in the 10th house. It is aspected by exalted Moon and Lagna lord Saturn. It is occupied by Vargottama Jupiter and aspected by the 10th lord Mars. Four planets influence Scorpio in great strength.

Sagittarius : Sagittarius natives are bold and practical. They do well in sports, horse-training, as jockeys, stewards, preachers, freedom fighters, advocates for any cause, organisers, financiers, gamblers, leather-dealers and experts, shoe

Chart No. 126.—*Born 8-8-1912 at 7-35 p.m. (I.S.T.) at 13° N, 77 E 30.*

Rahu	Moon Saturn			Saturn	Venus
Lagna	RASI	Sun — Merc. Venus Mars	Sun Rahu	NAVAMSA	Moon Mercury Ketu
	Jupiter	Ketu	Lagna	Jupiter	Mars

Balance of Mars Dasa at birth : 6 years, 1 month and 6 days.

and footwear makers or dealers. Jupiter and Mercury strong would give rise to teachers, religious reformers, theologians. Saturn, Mercury and Jupiter would indicate lawyers, judges, magistrates and philosophers.

Chart No. 127 is that of a highly successful lawyer who later took part in the freedom movement and was the first President of the Indian Republic. The crux of the horoscope revolves round Sagittarius which is not only the Lagna but also the pivot of a powerful Rajayoga involving 5th lord Mars, Lagna lord Jupiter, 10th lord Mercury and Saturn. Mercury, Saturn and Jupiter (Vargottama) influence Sagittarius power-fully indicating the native's legal career.

Capricorn : This sign makes the native hard-working and able. Agriculture, mining, forest products, farming, horti-

Chart No. 127.—*Born 3–12–1884 at 8–45 a.m. (L.M T.) at 25 N 36. 95 E 10.*

Ketu		Moon	Sat			Mercury	Rahu Mars
	RASI			Venus	NAVAMSA		
	NH-54		Jupit.	Sun			Moon Jupiter
Mars Mercury Lagna	Sun	Venus	Rahu	Ketu		Lagna Saturn	

Balance of Mars Dasa at birth : 5 years, 10 months and 17 days.

Chart No. 128.—*Born 19-12-1952 at 11–16 p m. (I.S.T.) at 11 N 05, 77 E 20.*

	Jupiter				Moon	Sun	Venus
	RASI	Ketu	Sat.	Sat.	NAVAMSA		Rahu
Mars Rahu Venus Moon	GIII-146	Lagna	Ketu				
Sun	Mercury	Sat.		Mercury	Lagna	Mars Jupiter	

Balance of the Moon Dasa at birth : 9 years, 2 months and 3 days.

culture, mineralogy and geology, suit such natives well. They
have great organising capacities and make good conveners and
secretaries. Executive and political posts requiring patience
and plodding on come under Capricorn. Saturn strong makes
for bankers, merchants and agriculturists. Mars makes minera-
logists, geologists and forest officers.

Chart No. 128 is that of a businessman dealing in timber
in the forests of South India. Capricorn is the 6th house and
is occupied by the 10th lord Venus, exalted Yogakaraka Mars,
Moon and Rahu shifting emphasis to callings coming under
this sign.

Aquarius : Natives with Aquarius strong in the chart are
usually advisers of some sort-technical, legal, social or just
friendly. All innovative and unusual callings come under this
sign. Workers in electricity, atomic power, computer technology, automobile and aeroplane mechanics and television
technology come under Aquarius. Such natives are ingenious
and becomes inventors if Mercury is strong. They make good
astrologers, telepathists and hypnotists. Neurologists, X-ray
workers and dealers in medical appliance come under this sign.
They can also succeed in nature-cure therapy. Saturn strong
makes engineers and scientists. Aquarius strong produces
great philosophers also.

Mark the concentration of 3 planets—the Sun, Mercury
and Jupiter in Aquarius—a philosophical sign all in the 10th or
Karmasthana from Lagna in Chart No. 129. The native was a
real philosopher and Karmayogi. This combination of planets
also made the native an authority not only on astrology but also
in Indian sciences and history as well.

Pisces : Doctors, surgeons, nurses, monks, jailors and
prison-workers, sanatorium workers, convent-runners come

under this sign. Work requiring imagination suits such natives. Film-making, script-writing, composing, choreography, social work, work in orphanages, museum, library, club and similar bodies and group activity comes easily to natives with strong Pisces. They make good musicians, inspired poets and occult writers, travel agents, petrol and oil-dealers, sea-produce dealers, owners of amusement centres, anaesthetists, coast guards, private investigators and spirit mediums. Venus strong produces painters and actors.

Chart No. 129. *Born 12–2–1856 at about 2–21 p.m. (L.M.T.) at 18° N, 84 E.*

	Moon Rahu	Lagna	Sat.		Lagna Jupiter	Rahu	
Sun Mercury Jupiter							
	RASI				NAVAMSA		
	NH-29						
Venus		Mars Ketu		Merc.	Ketu	Sun Saturn Venus Mars	Moon

Balance of Venus Dasa at birth : 12 years, 3 months and 9 days.

The Lagna lord Moon in Chart No. 130 is in the 9th in Pisces in exact conjunction with Jupiter. Rahu (Vargottama) is also in Pisces aspected by Saturn. Pisces becomes the focal point of powerful planetary influences. The native was a man of various gifts — a great Sanskrit scholar, a powerful writer and poet and a strong, subtle lucid thinker.

Chart No. 130.—*Born 23–7–1856 at 6–24 a.m. (L.M.T.) at 18 N 32, 73 E 53.*

Moon Jupiter Rahu			Merc. Sat.	Sat. Rahu	Mercury		
	RASI NH-30		Lagna Sun Venus Lagna		NAVAMSA		
		Mars	Ketu	Moon Jupit.	Mars	Venus	Sun Ketu

Balance of Mercury's Dasa at birth : 13 years, 8 months and 14 days.

In addition the planets also signify a variety of professions, The Sun indicates those in authority, rulers, dignitaries, government, goldsmiths, jewellers, finaciers, occupations involving children, circus-trainers, theatre-owners and managers. The Moon governs travelling and all travelling requisites, sailors, nurses, liquor dealers, laundry-owners, gardeners, confectioners and bakers, house-keepers, dairy-owners, obstetricians, healing, plastics, catering, eating places and waiters. Mars signifies firemen, metallurgists, armament-factories, machine tools, soldiers, police, surgeons, dentists, barbers, cooks, hardware goods, locksmiths, boxers, butchers, chemists and druggists. Mercury rules documentation and recording and all jobs connected with such work, teaching, writing, clerks, accountants, book-keepers, postal men, bus drivers and train employees, architects, correspondents, stenographers, interpreters, messengers, reporters, radio and other communication media, stationeries, printing and telephone operators. Jupiter rules counsellors, lawyers, lecturers, publishers, writers, astrologers, travel-agents, priests and temple trustees and officials, cashiers, philosophers, literateurs, grocers and tobacconists. Venus refers to poets, artists, cinema artistes, dancers, singers, musicians, instrumentalists, hat and dress dealers and makers, silks and expensive textiles, perfumeries, cosmeticians, beauticians, entertainers of all kinds, dealers in furnishings, furniture-makers, coffee planters, tea estate owners, fancy articles, ladies' articles, objects of art and fashion, social secretaries, photography, engravers, cartoonists, flower sellers and embroiderers. Saturn indicates miners, coal and fuel of every kind, petrol, real estate business, craftsmen, plumbers, architects, cemetery, excavators, building contractors and masons, leather goods, hides, ice-making, time-pieces, coffin and tomb makers, farm and factory labour, watchmen, undertakers, priests, monks, nuns, renunciates and philosophers.

According to Jaimini, the planet that gets the largest number of degrees in a sign as his longitude becomes the Atmakaraka. The sign in which the Atmakaraka is situated in the Navamsa becomes what is called Karakamsa, a very important point in the horoscope. If the Sun is associated with Atmakaraka either in the Rasi or in the Navamsa, the native becomes a statesman or diplomat.

If the Sun as Atmakaraka is aspected by Jupiter, the native will be employed in a temple. If by Saturn, he will engage himself in vile occupation. If the Sun is aspected by Rahu, he will work for foreign concerns or foreign rulers. If with Venus, he will be engaged to serve outstanding women as companion, secretary or attendant. If the Sun is associated with Mars, he will head the local or district body. If with Mercury, he will be employed in the judiciary.

The Full Moon or Venus with Atmakaraka in Rasi or Navamsa makes one a journalist, writer, poet or a dramatist. If the Sun and Rahu join Karakamsa aspected by benefics, the native deals in 'poisonous medicines' implying a chemist, druggist, anaesthesian, etc. Electric, mechanical and allied jobs would come under Mars being in Karakamsa. Jupiter here would indicate avocations related to religious learning, priesthood, spirituality, etc.

Other Important Combinations

The 10th house rules Karma. It is not possible to find an English equivalent for this term but broadly interpreted Karma means what the native does in his life. The most important aspect of a person's existence is his activities and whether mundane or spiritual come under a study of the 10th house. Sanyasa Yogas are also signficant for in this case the native occupies himself or makes it his life's goal to seek the Divinity in and around him.

Below we give some combinations that comprehend the significations of the 10th house.

Jupiter, Mercury, the Sun and Saturn afficted in the 10th house prompt a person to indulge in vice. The afflicted Moon here makes the native a gambler and violent in disposition. If the 10th lord exalted but occupying the 6th, 8th or 12th house will never let the native finish any good work he under-takes. If the 9th or 10th houses are occupied by benefic planets and their lords and Jupiter are well-placed, the native will be a noble man of excellent deeds in conformity with customs and morality. If the planets in the 5th and the 10th houses and the lords of the Lagna, the 9th and 10th houses are strong in *shadbala*, the native will be very learned in the scriptures and Vedas. He will have intuitive knowledge as a result of initiation.

Three strong planets in the 10th house in own sign, exaltation or benefic vargas and the 10th lord also fortified make the native an ascetic. But if the 10th lord be weak and in the 7th house, the native will be of evil conduct. If the 2nd and 7th lords be two of the planets in the 10th house, the native will be lustful. Five planets including the 10th lord in a quadrant or trine give birth to a saint of great spirituality who will be a *jeevanmukta*. Four planets in the 10th house make one a renunciate. If the Sun be one of the planets in these two cases and causes combustion, the native though pious and spiritually inclined will not renounce the world.

If the Moon occupies a decanate of Saturn and is also aspected by Saturn or if the Moon is in the Navamsa of Saturn or Mars aspected by Saturn, the native leads a life of dispassion and renounces the world. If the Lagna lord is weak and free of planetary aspects but himself aspects Saturn, or if Saturn aspects the weak Lagna lord, then also the native will be a Sanyasi. If Saturn or the Lagna lord aspect the lord of the sign occupied by the Moon, the native becomes a member of a religious order. If the Moon is in a sign of Mars aspected by Saturn and in a decanate of Saturn, the yoga leads to asceticism.

If the Moon is in the 9th house free of aspects, the native becomes an ascetic. The presence of Rajayogas in the chart will not hinder the yoga for asceticism. If Aries, Scorpio, Aquarius, Capricorn, Pisces or Sagittarius be the Ascendant and Jupiter occupies the 9th house, the native becomes a holy man.

When all the four quadrants are occupied by benefics, the native is endowed with a very powerful intellect. He will possess many qualities of head and heart and earn oustanding fame, immense wealth and earn recognition. If the kendras are all occupied by malefics, the result is notoriety. Such natives resort to crime and hypocrisy, suffer poverty, possess women belonging to others, indulge in harmful occult rites and become dangerous to society. Benefics in the 10th from the Ascendant or the Moon make the native noble-minded while malefics make him addicted to evil deeds.

Then, there are special yogas. They do not indicate the nature of career a native is likely to take up but their presence enhances the degree of success in profession. More yogas in one chart indicate outstanding success, fame and distinction in life.

Chart No. 131.—*Born 11-12-1922 at 3-46 p.m. (L.M.T.) at 34 N 1, 71 E 34.*

Ketu	Lagna		Sun Jupit. Merc	Lagna
Mars			Rahu	
	RASI	Moon	Mars	NAVAMSA
	RP. 18/109			Venus Ketu
	Venus Mercury Sun	Jupiter	Rahu Sat.	Moon
				Saturn

Balance of Venus Dasa at birth : 3 years, 7 months and 6 days.

For details about such yogas and their interpretation, reference may be made to our book *Three Hundred Important Combinations.*

Actor : Chart No. 131 is of an actor who has been acclaimed as unparalleled in tragic roles. Lagna being Taurus, a Venusian sign, and the combination of versatile Mercury, talented Venus and the royal Sun aspecting Lagna have given the native acting histrionics. The aspect of Saturn on Venus is also responsible for his success as a cinema star. Lagna lord Venus aspecting the Lagna, Yogakaraka Saturn Vargottama in the 5th, the Sasi-Mangala Yoga in the 10th house, the Sankha Yoga caused by 5th lord Mercury, and 6th lord Venus in a kendra and the combination of the Sun and Mercury (kendra and kona lords) in a powerful kendra have resulted in an excellent Raja Yoga for fame, money and success. Mercury is

Chart No. 132.—*Born 12-3-1946 at 7-30 a.m. at 34 N 03, 118 W 17.*

Lagna Mercury Venus			Mars Rahu Sat Moon	Lagna		Mars Ketu Saturn	Sun Moon
Sun		RASI				NAVAMSA	
	GD-183						
		Jupiter		Merc.	Rahu Jupiter		Venus

Balance of Jupiter's Dasa at birth : 6 years, 8 months and 5 days.

the Atmakaraka and has given great skill in dramatics and voice modulation. His occupation of Pisces, an emotional sign, has given a flair for expressive acting.

Actress : The sign Pisces in Chart No. 132 is powerfully placed. Lagna is Vargottama with exalted Venus and *neechabhanga* Mercury and is aspected by Saturn. The powerful position of Venus has given success in Hollywood as a popular actress. The influence of Saturn gives a considerable fan-following. The 10th lord Jupiter is in Libra, a venusian sign indicative of a career in the show-world.

Chart No. 133. *Born 11–1–1894 at 4–55 p.m. (L.M.T.) at 13 N, 77 E 35.*

Rahu		Jupiter	Lagna	Moon Lagna		
Venus Moon		RASI		Rahu	NAVAMSA	
Sun				Jupit. Sun Venus		Ketu
		RP-111/4				
Mercury	Mars	Saturn	Ketu	Mars Saturn		Mercury

Balance of Rahu Dasa at birth : 1 year, 7 months and 21 days.

Archak (Temple Priest) : The 10th house is Pisces, a spiritual sign, occupied by Rahu in Chart No. 133. The 10th lord Jupiter is in Taurus aspected by Mars. In Navamsa, the 10th lord Jupiter occupies Capricorn with the Sun and Venus aspected by Saturn. The 10th lord in the 12th signifies a vocation connected with religion and rituals. The native is a priest in a temple. Aquarius is the strongest sign being occupied by the Moon and Venus and aspected by Mars. Aquarius is a philosophical sign which trait is brought out by its occupation of the 5th lord. Mars, the planet of action, aspects it which means, philosophy in ritual would be the native's calling.

Chart No. 134.—*Born 8–2–1857 at 8–30 a.m. (L.M.T.) at 42 N 39, 71 W 8.*

Rahu Jupiter Venus Lagna			Sat.	Sat.	Mercury		Mars Ketu
Mars		RASI	Moon	Moon	NAVAMSA		Lagna
Sun Mercury		RP. 23/15					
			Ketu	Rahu Jupit.	Venus		Sun

Balance of Mercury's Dasa at birth: 7 years, 3 months and 20 days.

Astrologer : The 10th house in Chart No. 134 is aspected by Saturn. The 10th lord Jupiter occupies his own sign Pisces with exalted Venus and Rahu. The Moon is in Cancer, in the 5th house, a spiritual and inspirational sign. The native of Chart No. 134 was a noted astrologer. Pisces, the sign of intuition, is powerfully placed and houses the 10th lord and Ascendant signifying the astrological potential of the native. The 2nd lord Mars is in the 12th house which is notvery good

for predictions but Jupiter's occupation of his own Navamsa
with Rahu enabled the native to produce many valuable books
on the subject. Further Jupiter and Venus form 2 of the
Pancha-Mahapurusha Yogas—Hamsa and Malavya.

Chart No. 135.—*Born 31–1–1887 at 11–1 p.m. (G.M.T.)
at 50 N 43, 2 W 25.*

	Moon		Sat.		Saturn	Mercury Rahu
Venus Ketu Mars			Jupit.			Sun
Sun Mercury	RASI RP. 17/15		Rahu	NAVAMSA		Lagna Moon
	Jupiter	Lagna	Ketu Mars	Venus		

Balance of Venus Dasa at birth : 15 years, 0 month and
27 days.

Astrologer : Chart No. 135 also belongs to an astrologer
who wrote many books on Western astrology. The 10th and
5th lords, Mercury and Saturn respectively, are in *parivartana*.
The 10th house is aspected by Jupiter from the 2nd house. The
5th lord in the 10th gives intuitive and psychic abilities while
Jupiter's presence in the 2nd house is important for giving
correct predictions. Jupiter's aspect on the 10th house and
the 10th lord Mercury in his own Navamsa made him a prolific
writer in his subject.

Banker : In Chart No. 136, the 10th house is Aries with
no planets in it. The 10th lord Mars aspects the 10th from a

mercurial sign and is with exalted Mercury. The 10th house is also aspected by Jupiter, the 5th lord and Dhanakaraka, who associates very closely with the 2nd lord Sun. The native is a rich and prosperous banker consistent with the influences of Mercury (money transactions) and Jupiter (from the 2nd house) on the 10th house.

Chart No. 136.—*Born 12/13-9-1897   at 2-51 a.m. (L.M.T.) at 26 N 17, 72 E 58.*

Moon			Lagna Ketu Venus	Rahu	Mercury
	RASI		Sun Jupit.	NAVAMSA	Mars
Rahu	RP–113/4			Venus	Saturn
Saturn		Merc. Mars	Moon Lagna Sun Jupit.	Ketu	

Balance of Mercury's Dasa at birth: 11 years and 9 months.

Body-Builder : Chart No. 137 is that of a body-builder of international renown. Note the predominant influence of Mars both on Lagna and Lagna lord. Saturn, the Lagna lord, occupies a martian sign Scorpio with Venus which gives unusual interest in one's physique and its development. Mars, the karaka for all physical fitness, aspects the Lagna. He is debilitated but gets *neechabhanga.* Jupiter in the 10th made the native an acknowledged authority on physical fitness and bodybuilding techniques. He has his own gymnasium in which he

Chart No. 137.—*Born 11-1-1899 at 8 a.m. (Madras Time) at 13 N 09, 78 E 11.*

			Ketu	Sat. Ketu		Mercury	
			Mars				Lagna
	RASI				NAVAMSA		
Lagna							
	RP-18/170						
Sun Moon Mercury Rahu	Venus Saturn	Jupiter		Venus Sun		Mars	Moon Rahu

Balance of Venus Dasa at birth :   13 years, 3 months and 0 days.

Chart No. 138.—*Born 8-7-1929 at 6-30 a.m. (I.S.T.) at 11 N 31, 79 E 52.*

	Rahu	Venus Jupiter	Merc. Sun	Venus		Saturn Jupiter Sun	Ketu
			Lagna Moon				Lagna Mars
	RASI				NAVAMSA		
	RP-18/119		Mars				
Saturn		Ketu		Rahu		Moon Mercury	

Balance of Saturn's Dasa at birth :   8 years, 6 months and 1 day.

trains students.   Jupiter in the 10th in Libra, therefore, made him a teacher as well as coach (adviser) to many.

Chemicals :   The native of Chart No. 138 is an employee in a firm of chemicals.   Cancer, the Ascendant, is occupied by the Moon.   Rahu ruling potions, poisons and chemicals is in the 10th.   This further indicated by 10th lord Mars in Leo which sign also refers to callings connected with chemicals. Rahu is also the Atmakaraka and signifies work related to chemicals and drugs.

Chart No. 139.– *Born 30-12-1907 at 9-55 p.m. (L.M.T.) at 13 N 45, 76 E 30.*

			Rahu		Moon		Rahu	Mercury Venus
Mars Saturn								
			Jupit.					Mars Saturn
	RASI					NAVAMSA		
Venus			Lagna		Jupit.			Lagna
	RP-203/6							
Sun Mercury Ketu		Moon				Ketu		Sun

Balance of Rahu Dasa at birth :   0 year, 3 months and 7 days.

Chief Justice :   Chart No. 139 is that of a very brilliant jurist who began his career as a lawyer, and came to occupy the highest judicial office in the State.   The 10th house is Taurus aspected by Saturn.   The 10th lord Venus is in the 6th house ruling the judiciary aspected by exalted Jupiter   The 10th house from the Moon is aspected by Moon-sign lord

Venus and occupied by exalted Jupiter. The chart gains
strength from the Lagna which is Vargottama. The Vipareeta
Rajayoga in both Rasi and Navamsa adds further vitality. In
Rasi, the 6th lord Saturn is in the 8th house, the 8th lord
Jupiter is in the 12th house and the 12th lord the Moon is in
the 3rd house. In Navamsa, the 6th lord Saturn is in the 12th
house, the 12th lord Moon is in the 8th house and the 8th
lord Jupiter is in the 6th house.

Chart No. 140.—*Born 24-2-1911 at 7-44 a.m. (L.M.T.)
at 20 N 28, 85 E 54.*

Lagna Venus	Saturn Rahu		Ketu	Jupiter
Sun				Saturn
Mercury	RASI RP-18/104	Sun	NAVAMSA	Venus Moon Mercury
Moon Mars	Jupiter Ketu		Moon Rahu	Lagna

Balance of Venus Dasa at birth : 17 years, 4 months and
16 days.

Craft and Woodworks' Dealer : In Chart No. 140 the
Lagna is occupied by exalted Venus which gives skill in fine
arts. The 10th house is occupied by the Moon and Mars who
as 5th, 2nd and 9th lord give financial success. The 10th lord
Jupiter is in Libra (ruled by Venus) aspected by Saturn indicating a business in craft. Mars in the 10th indicates woodwork.
The native of Chart No. 140 is a dealer in woodwork craft.

19

Chart No. 141.—*Born 4-8-1911 at 4-19 p.m. (L M T) at 13 N, 77 E*

	Rahu Saturn Mars						
			Sun	Ketu Jupit.	NAVAMSA		
	RASI			Venus			Rahu Mercury
			Merc.				
Lagna	Moon	Jupiter Ketu	Venus	Sat. Moon Sun		Mars	Lagna

RP-174/4

Balance of Mercury's Dasa at birth : 16 years, 7 months and 5 days.

Chart No. 142.—*Born 31-5-1918 at 12-22 p.m. (I.S.T.) at 13° N, 77 E 35.*

	Mercury Venus	Sun Jupiter	Ketu		Rahu	Venus	Sun
			Sat.		NAVAMSA		Moon
Moon	RASI		Lagna Mars				
Rahu				Sat. Mars	Mercury	Ketu	Jupiter Lagna

RP-163-A/4

Balance of the Moon's Dasa at birth : 0 year, 1 month and 28 days.

Coffee Merchant : In Chart No. 141 the 10th house Virgo is occupied by the 6th and 11th lord Venus. The 10th lord Mercury is in the 9th house in a constellation ruled by Venus. Venus governs all stimulants and occupies Virgo, an earthy sign. The native is a coffee merchant.

Captain (Army) : Chart No. 142 has a powerfully placed Aries being occupied by Mercury and Venus and aspected by Saturn. The Lagna is a fiery and royal sign Leo with Mars in it. Mars is the planet of war and the Lagna lord Sun who rules authority and power is in the 10th house. The native is a Captain in the Army.

Chart No. 143.—*Born 18-9-1940 at 7-23 p.m. (I.S.T.) at 8 N 48, 78 E 11.*

Lagna Moon Ketu	Jupiter Saturn			Mercury	
		Venus	Lagna Moon Sun		Rahu
	RASI	———	———	NAVAMSA	
		Mars	Ketu		
	GIV-286				
		Sun Merc. Rahu	Venus Mars	Jupiter	Saturn

Balance of Mercury's Dasa at birth : 6 years, 0 month and 28 days.

Cardiologist : In Chart No. 143 Pisces, being the Ascendant, gives a natural skill in healing and nursing. The Moon, 5th lord, is in Lagna. The 10th house is aspected by the 10th lord Jupiter who occupies Scorpio Navamsa ruled by Mars.

Mars refers to doctors, healers, surgeons, chemists and druggists. The combination of the Sun and Rahu is especially indicative of a medical career. The native is a cardiologist, cardiology being ruled by the Sun. The Sun placed strongly with an exalted Mercury gives an intelligent and research-oriented approach to his work in heart-surgery.

Chart No. 144.—*Born 16–3–1882 at 9–30 p.m. (L.M T.) at 32 N 19, 72 E 30.*

Sun Venus	Saturn	Jupiter Ketu	Mars	Lagna	Ketu		
Mercury				Mars			
	RASI				NAVAMSA		
Moon				Jupit.			Sun Moon
	RP-38/6						
	Rahu	Lagna		Merc.		Venus Rahu	Saturn

Balance of Mars Dasa at birth : 5 years, 10 months and 26 days.

Chief Medical Officer : In Chart No. 144 the 10th house Cancer is aspected by its lord the Moon. The 10th lord Moon is in Capricorn aspected by Mars and Saturn. The native retired as the State Inspector-General of Civil Hospitals. The relationship between the 10th house, Cancer, the Moon and Mars explains the native's medical profession. The 10th lord Moon in a kendra influenced by 3 planets gave him a post of authority.

Chart No. 145.-- *Born 8–5–1907 at 10–17 p.m· (L.M.T.) at 10 N 40, 76 E 30.*

Venus Moon Saturn	Mercury Sun		Jupit.	Jupit.		Mercury
			Rahu	Ketu		Saturn
Ketu	RASI			Venus	NAVAMSA	Rahu
Lagna Mars	RP-127/6				Sun Mars / Lagna Moon	

Balance of Saturn's Dasa at birth :   5 years, 0 month and 13 days.

Cloth Merchant : In Chart No. 145 the 10th house is aspected by exalted Venus, the Moon and Saturn. Consistent with the aspect of a powerful 11th lord Venus, the native is a prosperous businessman in textiles and garments. The association of the Moon, Venus and Saturn gives skill in dying, textiles and allied trades.

Dancer : In Chart No. 146 the Lagna is Gemini aspected by the Sun, Mars and Jupiter.   the 10th house is occupied by Rahu and aspected by the Moon and Mars.   Saturn and Venus are in *parivartana*. The native is a dancer. This is indicated by the Saturn-Venus relationship. Rahu in the 10th does not give a conventional calling. Pisces dominant rules the feet and Sagittarius occupied by 10th lord rules the legs referring to a career closely related to footwork such as dancing.

Chart No. 146.—*Born 31-12-1912 at 4-44 p.m. (L.M.T) at 13 N, 77 E 35.*

		Saturn	Lagna		Sat	Mars	Ketu	Jupiter
Rahu								
Venus	RASI				Merc.	NAVAMSA		
								Moon
	RP–161/6							
Sun Mars Jupiter	Mercury		Moon Ketu			Lagna Rahu	Venus	Sun

Balance of Mars Dasa at birth :   5 years, 4 months and 26 days.

Chart No. 147.—*Born 11-8-1921 at 8-18 p.m. (I.S.T.) at 13 N, 77 E 35.*

			Venus		Sun Moon Ketu		Lagna
Ketu							
Lagna	RASI		Sun Mars Merc.		Venus	NAVAMSA	
	RP. 162/6		Jupit.		Sat.		
		Moon	Sat. Rahu		Jupit.	Mars Mercury	Rahu

Balance of Rahu's Dasa at birth : 1 year, 2 months and 17 days.

Dancer : Chart No. 147 is also that of a dancer. Note the connection between Venus and Saturn which gives skill in art that is easily appealing to the masses. The 10th house is aspected by Saturn and the 10th lord Mars is with the 7th lord the Sun and Mercury. The native learnt dancing from her husband (10th lord with 7th lord) and pursued it as a career along with him.

Chart No. 148. — *Born 7/8-8-1894 at 5-30 a.m. (L.M.T)* *at 13 N 6, 78 E 7.*

Rahu	Mars		Jupit Venus	Moon	Ketu	Mars Venus	
			Sun Lagna Merc	Sun			
	RASI				NAVAMSA		Mercury
	RP-127/4						
		Moon	Sat. Ketu	Jupit. Lagna		Rahu	Saturn

Balance of Rahu's Dasa at birth : 0 year, 5 months and 4 days.

Superintendent of Police : In Chart No. 148 the Lagna being Cancer the 10th is the positive and fiery sign, Aries. It is occupied by Mars, an aggressive planet who also happens to be the 10th lord. The Lagna lord Moon aspects the 10th house and the 10th lord and, in turn, is aspected by Mars giving a strong, bold and spirited personality which is also firm and stable as indicated by the presence of the Lagna lord in the sign of the balance. The native was a high ranking police officer.

Chart No. 149.—*Born 5/6-10-1942 at 1-00 a.m. (W.T.) at 12 N 58, 77 E 34.*

		Saturn	Lagna		Moon Venus	Lagna		
Ketu			Jupit. Moon					Sun Mars Jupiter Saturn Rahu
	RASI					NAVAMSA		
			Rahu		Ketu			
	RP-36/38							
		Mercury	Venus Mars Sun				Mercury	

Balance of Mercury's Dasa at birth : 3 years, 8 months and 3 days.

Superintendent of Police : In Chart No. 149 the 10th house is Pisces fortified by the aspects of an exalted 10th lord Jupiter from the 2nd house (with the 2nd lord Moon) and the 6th and 11th lord Mars, 3rd lord Sun and 5th and 12th lord Venus. The influence of 4 planets on the 10th house is of significance especially that the 10th lord Jupiter is exalted and in *vargottama* position. The native is a dynamic police officer. Although Jupiter aspects the 10th, the aspects of Mars and the Sun are stronger, being to the exact degree of the 10th cusp, and determines the nature of work. The native occupies an enviable position in the hierarchy of the police force much in advance of many seniors in age. In Navamsa, the 10th lord Jupiter is exalted and is associated with Mars. Jupiter's aspect has given a smooth-sailing career with lots of luck, while Mars has been responsible for deciding the nature of career. Jupiter, though in the 2nd, moves into Lagna Bhava and his aspect on the 10th is therefore not total. Mars on the other hand occupies 20° 21′ of Virgo while Lagna being 21° 53′ of Gemini, the aspect is very strong taking the lead over the other influences.

Compare Chart No. 148 with Chart No. 149. The native of Chart No. 148 retired as a Superintendent starting his career as a police constable while the native of Chart No. 149 who has been but a few years in office has already reached the rank of Superintendent having thorough sheer merit.

In Chart No. 149, the 10th lord Jupiter is exalted and aspects the 10th house and is in turn aspected by the 9th lord Saturn. In Chart No. 148, the 10th lord Mars occupies his *moolatrikona* sign aspected by the Lagna lord Moon. In Chart No. 149, the Lagna lord Mercury is Vargottama in a trine in Libra while in Chart No. 148, the Lagna lord Moon occupies a kendra in Libra. Both charts have 4 planets in kendras. Chart No. 149, in addition, has 5th lord Venus in a kendra with *neechabhanga*. Chart No. 149 has the 9th and 10th lords related generating a powerful Raja Yoga while Chart No. 148 has no such yoga between the 9th and 10th lords. Mars Dasa yet to operate should see him occupy a very high position.

Director—Department of Geology: In Chart No. 150 the 10th house Aquarius is aspected by its lord Saturn from Leo. Saturn is also the 9th lord and his aspect gives a position of authority. The native was the director of the State geological department. Leo, the sign occupied by the 10th lord, rules hills and dales. The sign Capricorn also acquires importance being occupied by a powerful Vargottama Lagna lord Venus,

Chart No. 150.—*Born 7-12-1888 at about 5-30 p.m. (L.M T.) at 14 N 14, 76 E 26.*

		Lagna			Lagna Saturn	Moon Mars	
		Rahu		Sun Jupit.			Rahu
	RASI				NAVAMSA		
Mars Venus Moon Ketu		Sat.		Ketu Venus			
	Sun Jupiter Mercury					Mercury	

RP-4/4

Balance of Moon's Dasa at birth : 5 years, 0 month and 5 days.

Chart No. 151.—*Born 6-8-1906 at 12-38 p.m. (L.M.T.) at 17 N 46, 83 E 17.*

		Jupit.		Mercury Saturn		Lagna
Moon Saturn		Rahu Mars Sun	Moon Venus			Ketu
Ketu	RASI	Merc.	Jupit. Sun Rahu	NAVAMSA		
	Lagna	Venus		Mars		

RP-23/6

Balance of Rahu's Dasa at birth : 6 years, 11 months and 8 days.

the Moon and exalted Mars together with Ketu. Mars is the ruler of rocks, minerals and occupies an earthy sign which influences the 10th house signification indirectly since Mars aspects the 10th lord Saturn.

Doctor : Cancer, the sign of healing and nursing rises on the 10th house in Chart No. 151. It is occupied by Mars, the Sun and Rahu and flanked on both sides by Jupiter and Mercury, both benefics. The native was an eminent medical doctor with an international reputation. The Sun–Rahu conjunction in the appropriate signs, invariably produces outstanding medical men. The *subhakartari yoga,* to which the 10th house is subject, is also of significance ensuring a distinguished and successful career.

Chart No. 152.—*Born 23–5–1932 at 5–24 p.m. (I.S.T.) at 18 N 31, 73 E 52.*

Rahu	Mercury Mars	Sun	Venus	Lagna Venus	Sun Saturn		
			Jupit.	Jupit.			Rahu
	RASI				NAVAMSA		
Saturn				Ketu			
	RP-5/15						
Moon		Lagna	Ketu		Moon		Mars Mercury

Balance of Venus Dasa at birth : 1 year, 6 months and 18 days.

Doctor : The 10th house in Chart No. 152 is Cancer occupied by an exalted 6th lord Jupiter aspected by a powerful Mars. The native of Chart No. 152 is a doctor. The 10th house is aspected by Saturn from his own sign. Three planets in quadrants in their own and exaltation signs have given the native eminence and fame in his career.

Chart No. 153.— *Born 17–7–1896 at 5–45 a.m. (L.M.T.) at 31 N 39, 74 E 23.*

	Mars		Merc.	Merc.	Saturn	Ketu	
Rahu			Venus Sun Jupit. Lagna	Jupit.			
	RASI				NAVAMSA		Venus Sun Moon
	RP-217/6		Ketu				
		Saturn	Moon		Rahu	Lagna	Mars

Balance of Mars Dasa at birth: 6 years, 2 months and 20 days.

Doctor : The Lagna Cancer is occupied by exalted Jupiter, Venus and the Sun. The 10th lord Mars occupies his own sign Aries, a fiery sign, and from there aspects Cancer and the planetary group in Lagna. The emphasis shifts to Cancer and being the natural sign, ruling nursing, makes the native a skilled doctor.

Editor : Chart No. 154 is that of an editor of a newspaper of wide circulation. The Ascendant is Scorpio aspected by Mercury, the karaka for intellect, and exalted 2nd and 5th lord Jupiter. As 2nd lord, Jupiter in exaltation gives inspired expressive powers while as 5th lord gives lucidity and clarity of thought. The 10th lord the Sun occupies a mercurial sign in a martian constellation which made the native a dynamic and forceful newspaperman. The Atmakaraka is Mercury and occupies Leo, a powerful and fiery sign which tended to influence his editorials which were sharp and impactful. Contrast this with Chart No. 131. Both have Mercury as *atmakaraka* but in this case the influence of Mercury and Jupiter on Scorpio as ascendant gave rise to a writer while in the other, venusian sign and Venus influencing the ascendant resulted in a highly talented cinema actor.

Chart No. 154. — *Born 24-6-1896 at 4-58 p.m. (L.M.T.) at 13 N 4, 80 E 15.*

	Mars	Mercury	Sun Venus		Moon Saturn	Mars Ketu
Rahu	RASI		Jupit.		NAVAMSA	
				Lagna Sun		Mercury
	RP-18/116					
Moon	Lagna	Saturn	Jupit. Venus	Rahu		

Balance of Ketu Dasa at birth : 5 years, 10 months and 14 days.

In Chart No. 154, Mercury is aspected by Jupiter in Navamsa. Jupiter and Venus in the 5th from karaka gave prolific writing abilities. The Rasi Chart has 2 planets in exaltation and Mars, Lagna lord, in his moolatrikona sign rendering the chart highly potent.

Chart No. 155.—*Born 29–4–1948 at 9–48 a.m. (I.S.T.) at 12 N 52, 74 E 53.*

	Sun Mercury Rahu		Lagna Venus		Mars Ketu		Jupiter
			Sat.	Sat		NAVAMSA	
	RASI						
	G.IV-106		Mars	Lagna			
Moon Jupiter		Ketu			Moon	Venus Rahu	Sun Mercury

Balance of Venus Dasa at birth :   2 years, 10 months and 6 days.

Engineer : In Chart No. 155 the 10th lord Jupiter aspects the Ascendant Gemini powerfully with the Moon. Venus, a benefic, occupies Lagna. The Ascendant Gemini is a basically thinking sign and made powerful by the influence of 3 planets. Lagna lord Mercury is involved strong Budha-Aditya Yoga in Aries, a sign ruled by Saturn from Cancer.   The native consistent with the Lagna and strength of Mercury, is an engineer. The Sun–Rahu–Mercury conjunction occurs in a fiery sign and gives mechanical skills while Saturn's aspect could also give skill in building and similar areas of work. Saturn although in Cancer is in a mercurial constellation.   Cancer is the sign of the home, house and Mercury's asterism involved gives a flair for building-engineering or civil engineering. In Chart No. 152, Saturn aspects Virgo from a constellation of Jupiter who in turn is influenced by Mars giving doctoring abilities. In Chart

No. 155, karaka Sun occupies a mercurial sign with exalted Mercury. The 10th lord Jupiter is also in a Navamsa ruled by Mercury which planet would give a broad clue to the nature of native's work, *viz.,* engineering.

Chart No. 156.– *Born 8/9–7–1953 at   0 h. 03 m. a.m. (I.S.T.) at 22 N 34, 88 E 24.*

Lagna		Moon Jupiter Venus	Sun Mars	Venus	Rahu	Sun Mars	
	RASI		Merc. Ketu		NAVAMSA		Jupiter
Rahu				Lagna			
	G. 1-68		Sat.		Mercury	Ketu	Moon Saturn

Balance of Mars Dasa at birth : 5 years, 2 months and 14 days.

Engineer : The 10th house in Chart No. 156 is Sagittarius aspected by 6th lord Sun and 2nd and 9th lord Mars from a mercurial sign. The 10th lord Jupiter is with the Moon and Venus. Although there are no planets in the 10th house, there are planets aspecting it which must be taken into account for judging the nature of career. The native is an engineer. Mars and the Sun are in a sign of Mercury and are, in turn, aspected by Saturn. Saturn rules building contracts, Mars, earth, buildings and with the Sun indicates a career in engineering with contracts for civil construction from the Government. The 10th house from the Moon is not

occupied or aspected by any planet but the 10th lord Saturn
occupies a mercurial sign Virgo again indicative of engineering.

Chart No. 157.—*Born 10/11-2-1910 at 5-59 a.m.
(I.S.T.) at 10 N 51, 78 E 47.*

Saturn	Mars	Rahu		Sat.	Rahu		Lagna
Venus Sun Moon	RASI			Merc.	NAVAMSA		Jupiter
Lagna Mercury	RP-36/17			Moon			
	Ketu		Jupit			Sun Venus Ketu	Mars

Balance of Rahu's Dasa at birth : **9** years, 1 month and
2 days.

Film Studio Owner : Chart No. 157 belongs to a prosperous businessman. Libra, the sign of the balance, rises on
the 10th cusp aspected by a powerful 11th and 4th lord Mars.
The 10th lord Venus is in the 2nd house with the 7th and 8th
lords, the Moon and the Sun respectively. The native owns a
cinema studio which he rents out for very large sums to film-
shooting units. Mars, the planet aspecting the 10th house,
is the karaka for immovable property placed in the 4th house,
ruling buildings and similar structures. Mars occupies Bharani
ruled by Venus the 10th lord. Venus and Libra are rulers of
amusement centres, drama, entertainment and the show-world
in general which describe the general nature of property rented

out by the native. In Navamsa, the 10th lord Venus occupies his own sign.

Chart No. 158.—*Born 2-2-1942 at 6-54 p.m. (I.S.T.) at 18 N 58, 72 E 50.*

	Mars	Jupiter Saturn		Lagna		Moon Ketu	Jupiter
Ketu Mercury			Lagna				Sun Venus
	RASI				NAVAMSA		
Venus Sun	RP-36/83		Moon Rahu	Sat.			
					Mercury Rahu		Mars

Balance of Ketu Dasa at birth : 4 years, 1 month and 20 days.

Flight Lieutenant : The Lagna in Chart No. 158 being Cancer, the 10th house is in the sign of Aries which stands for aggressiveness and militancy. The 10th lord Mars occupies his own sign in great strength. The native is a flight lieutenant in the Air Force. Mars occupies a constellation ruled by Venus who is with the Sun indicating service under the 'king' or the country's forces in modern parlance.

Compare Chart No. 158 with Chart No. 160. Both natives work in the armed forces but the difference is in rank. In Chart No. 158, the 10th lord Mars forms a powerful Ruchaka Yoga in the 10th house, the most powerful quadrant. In Chart No. 160 the 10th lord Mercury occupies 3rd house in a friendly sign, the lord thereof being placed in the 12th, a *dusthana* explaining the native's relatively low cadre.

20

Chart No. 159.—*Born 13-1-1919 at 10–49 p.m. (L.M.T.) at 17 N 26, 78 E 27.*

		Moon Ketu	Jupit.	Lagna Jupit.		Saturn Venus	Mercury Ketu
	RASI				NAVAMSA		
Mars Sun Venus	RP-42/187		Sat.	Sun			
Mercury	Rahu		Lagna	Rahu			Moon Mars

Balance of Mars Dasa at birth : 4 years, 11 months and 10 days.

Governor (of State) : In Chart No. 159, the 10th house is occupied by Jupiter who has exchanged signs with the 10th lord Mercury. The Moon is exalted and the Sun is *vargottama.* The 3rd and 8th lord Mars is exalted in the 6th house while the 6th lord Saturn is in the 12th house generating a partial Vipareeta Raja Yoga. The 10th lord Mercury is in his own Navamsa while the 10th occupant Jupiter occupies own Navamsa. Mercury in the 8th from the Moon generates a partial Adhi Yoga. All the factors strengthen the chart greatly to confer high political offices on the native. He is now Chief Minister of a big state.

Group Subedar (Army) : The Lagna in Chart No. 160 is a fiery warrior sign Sagittarius with Mars and Venus in it. The Lagna lord Jupiter is in the 4th house aspected by Mars. Jupiter aspects the 10th house. The martian influence on

Chart No. 160.— *Born 4/5–2–1928 at 4–30 a.m. (I.S.T.) at 24 N 13, 75 E 30.*

Jupiter		Rahu				Lagna
Mercury	RASI		Moon	Sat. Ketu	NAVAMSA	
Sun				Merc.		Sun Rahu
	RP-36/82					
Venus Mars Lagna	Ketu Saturn				Mars Jupiter Moon	Venus

Balance of Saturn's Dasa at birth : 7 years, 2 months and 19 days.

Lagna and Lagna lord who is directly aspecting the 10th house must perforce give a fighting-spirit and a warrior's career. The native is in the armed forces. The 10th house from the Moon is again a militant sign Aries. The 10th house from the Sun is Libra but its lord is with the aggressive planet Mars.

Hotelier : In Chart No. 161 the Lagna is Pisces. The 10th house is Sagittarius which is not aspected or occupied by any planet. The Lagna gains predominance with 4 planets in it. Venus is exalted in Lagna in *parivartana* with Lagna and 10th lord Jupiter in Taurus. The native of Chart No. 161 is the owner of a restaurant. Taurus rules eating places, Venus rules places of pleasure and Pisces rules snack-bars, canteens, tea-shops, hotels and all similar businesses.

Industrialist : In Chart No. 162 the 10th house is occupied by Rahu and aspected by Mars. The 10th lord Saturn is in

Chart No. 161. *–Born 24–3–1906 at 6–53 a.m. (L.M.T.) at 13 N 30, 74 E 45.*

Lagna Moon Mercury Venus Sun	Mars	Jupiter		Sat. Merc. Rahu	Jupiter		
Saturn			Rahu	Lagna			Moon
	RASI				NAVAMSA		
Ketu				Venus			Mars
RP-25/6						Sun	Ketu

Balance of Jupiter Dasa's at birth : 2 years, 9 months and 11 days.

the 9th with the Moon aspected by 8th and 11th lord Jupiter. The native of Chart No. 162 is the owner of textile industries. Note the powerful combinations for financial prosperity caused by 2nd and 5th lord Mercury exalted and *vargottama* in the 5th house combining with 11th lord Jupiter. Jupiter in turn aspects the 9th and 10th lord Saturn. In the chart of an industrialist, the position of Saturn is always of significance since Saturn rules labour and industries are dependent mainly, if not entirely, on workers. Saturn is the 10th lord here and in the bhagyasthana.

Inspector of Police : Chart No. 163 is that of a police officer. Mars who gets *neechabhanga* aspects the 10th house in great strength. He is the Lagna lord as well, Lagna being Aries, a fiery sign. Lagna is further occupied by an exalted Vargottama Sun which makes the native regal in bearing and

Chart No. 162.—*Born 29–9–1933 at 10–15 a m. (I.S.T.) at 10 N 50, 78 E 42.*

		Lagna				Jupiter	Venus Sun Ketu	Saturn
Rahu		RASI		Ketu		NAVAMSA		Lagna Mars
Moon Saturn		RP-18/90						Moon
	Mars	Venus	Merc. Sun Jupit.			Rahu		Mercury

Balance of Mars Dasa at birth : 6 years, 5 months and 18 days.

Chart No. 163.—*Born 12–4–1899 at 7–30 a.m. (L.M.T.) at 13 N 15, 77 E 35.*

	Lagna Sun Mercury Moon		Ketu		Saturn Sun Mercury Venus		
Venus			Mars	Jupit.		NAVAMSA	Rahu
	RASI			Ketu			
	RP-81/2						
Saturn Rahu		Jupiter		Lagna	Moon		Mars

Balance of Venus Dasa at birth : 3 years and 9 months.

conduct and an imposing personality. The 10th lord Saturn occupies a martian Navamsa and the 10th from Navamsa Lagna is also occupied by Mars.

Chart No. 164—*Born 16-3-1929 at 11-15 p.m. (I.S.T.) 18 N 13, 73 E 52.*

Sun	Venus Jupitar	Rahu Moon	Mars			Moon	Saturn
Mercury							Ketu
	RASI			Rahu Mars	NAVAMSA		Venus Sun
	RP-18/20						
Saturn	Lagna Ketu			Merc.			Lagna Jupiter

Balance of Moon's Dasa at birth : 7 years, 4 months and 11 days.

Journalist : The native of Chart No. 169 is a correspondent of a national daily. The 10th house Leo is aspected by Mercury and Jupiter, both planets indicating intelligence and writing. The 10th lord Sun occupies a Jupiterian sign Pisces which gives an element of inspiration and intuition in the writings of the native. The Sun is subject to a *subhakartari yoga* being hemmed between benefics Mercury on one side and Jupiter and Venus on the other. The native works for a prestigious newspaper.

Judge : In Chart No. 165 the 10th house Taurus is aspected by Jupiter and the 10th lord Venus occupies a mercurial sign with Mercury and Lagna lord the Sun. The 10th house

Chart No. 165.—*Born 29-6-1924 at 11-18 a.m. (I S.T.) at 12 N 20, 76 E 38.*

	Moon	Merc. Sun Venus		Venus	Moon	Rahu	
Ketu Mars				Sun			
	RASI				NAVAMSA		
		Lagna Rahu		Mars Jupit.			
	RP-149/6						
	Jupiter	Saturn		Lagna Merc.	Saturn Ketu		

Balance of Moon's Dasa at birth : 7 years, 8 months and 12 days.

is aspected by yogakaraka Mars from a quadrant. The planet of justice is exalted in the 3rd house. Chart No. 165 is that of a judicial officer.

Judge : In Chart No. 166 the 10th house is Gemini. The 10th lord Mercury occupies Libra, the sign of the balance, with exalted Saturn, the planet of justice. The native of Chart No. 166 is a High Court Judge.

Judge : The 10th house Leo is aspected by Jupiter and Saturn indicating the native of Chart No. 167 to be a civil judge. The 10th lord Sun is in the Ascendant with Venus who rules counsellors.

Compare Chart No. 167 with Chart No. 166. Both natives belong to the judiciary but there is a difference in the ranks of the natives. Chart No. 166 has both Jupiter and Saturn ruling law and justice exalted, Mercury in Libra and the Moon in a

Chart No. 166.—*Born 4–10–1895 at 6–03 a.m. (L.M.T.) at 11 N, 76 E.*

Moon				Rahu	Sun
Rahu	RASI	Jupit.	Merc. Sat.	NAVAMSA	Lagna Mars
		Venus Ketu	Moon		
	RP-64/6				
	Mercury Saturn	Lagna Sun Mars	Venus	Jupiter	Ketu

Balance of Mercury's Dasa at birth : 11 years, 11 months and 9 days.

Chart No. 167.—*Born 21–11–1915 at 7-30 a.m. (I.S.T.) at 16 N 50, 75 E 40.*

	Moon		Sat.	Mars	Mercury	Saturn	Jupiter
Jupiter	RASI	Mars Ketu	Venus	NAVAMSA	Rahu
Rahu			Ketu		Sun
	RP-31/6				
	Venus Sun Lagna	Mercury	Lagna Moon		

Balance of the Sun's Dasa at birth : 4 years, 9 months and 29 days.

quadrant. Chart No. 167 is not so powerful since Jupiter and
Saturn have no particular dignity. Mercury occupies the same
sign Libra but the Moon is in a *dusthana* which does not
contribute to the strength of the chart.

Chart No. 168.—*Born 17–12–1893 at 8–02 a.m. (L.M.T.)
at 13 N, 77 E 35.*

Moon Rahu		Jupiter				Sun	Mars
		RASI		Rahu	NAVAMSA		Venus
Venus		RP-153/4		Jupit.			
Lagna Sun	Mercury	Mars Saturn	Ketu	Lagna	Mercury	Saturn Moon	

Balance of Saturn's Dasa at birth : 5 years, 5 months and
16 days.

Judge : The 10th house in Chart No. 168 is Virgo occupied by Ketu. It is aspected by Lagna lord Jupiter and the 8th
lord Moon. The 10th lord Mercury is in the 12th house
vargottama aspected by Jupiter from the 6th house. The planet
of law and justice Saturn is very strong being both exalted and
vargottama and aspects the Lagna giving the personality a
balanced judicious outlook. This outlook must influence the
native's career as well since Lagna lord occupies the house
signifying courts (the 6th house) from where he aspects both
the 10th house and 10th lord. This is the chart of a High Court
Judge.

Elevation to the High Court is indicated by the presence of Raja Yogas in the chart. The 9th lord Sun is in Lagna which is itself *vargottama*. Lagna is aspected by *vargottama* 2nd and 3rd lord Saturn who is exalted. The 10th lord Mercury is also *vargottama* and the relationship between Lagna lord and the 10th lord is always fortifying.

Chart No. 169.—*Born 16-3-1908 at 10-56 a.m. (L.M.T.) at 15 N 24, 75 E 39.*

Saturn Sun	Mars Venus	Lagna	Rahu	Rahu			
Mercury	RASI RP-64/4		Jupit. Moon		NAVAMSA		Moon
							Lagna Sun Venus
Ketu				Merc.	Mars	Jupiter	Saturn Ketu

Balance of Ketu's Dasa at birth : 0 year, 0 month and 13 days.

Landlord and Banker : In Chart No. 169 the 10th house Aquarius is occupied by the 2nd and 5th lord Mercury who is also the natural significator of commerce. As the 2nd lord ruling monies and the 5th ruling investments and aspected by the Moon (ruling public) as lord of the 3rd (neighbours, environment, surrounding regions), the native took up the business of banking giving loans to farmers and others in surrounding regions. The 10th lord Saturn is in the 11th

house with 4th lord Sun (immovable property) and aspected
by an exalted 11th lord Jupiter also gave him earnings from
his landed properties.

Chart No. 170—*Born 30/31–8–1913 at 4–52 a.m.(L.M.T.)
at 26 N 17, 72 E 56.*

	Mars Saturn			Mercury	Lagna Moon
Rahu		Venus	Ketu	NAVAMSA	
	RASI	Lagna Sun Merc. Moon			Sun Saturn Rahu
Jupiter	RP-190/6	Ketu			Mars Venus Jupiter

Balance of Ketu's Dasa at birth : 5 years, 1 month and
3 days.

Lawyer : The 10th house in Chart No. 170 is occupied
by Saturn and Mars. The 10th lord Venus is in Cancer aspected by Saturn. Saturn rules law. Jupiter aspects Lagna and
Mercury trinally giving an analytical intellect and a lawyer's
calling.

Lawyer : In Chart No. 171 the Lagna is a martian sign
with the Lagna lord occupying a dignified place in the 10th
house and free of afflictions. The 10th lord the Sun occupies
the 12th house in Libra with the intellectual Mercury. Chart
No. 171 belongs to a legal luminary of his times. Jupiter
occupies the 4th house as lord of Chandra Lagna and aspects
the 10th house from there which conferred on the native legal

Chart No. 171.—*Born 5-11-1870 at 6-49 a.m. (L.M.T.) at 22 N 40, 88 E 30.*

			Rahu Jupit.		Sun Rahu	Saturn	
Moon							
				Venus			Lagna Mars
	RASI				NAVAMSA		
			Mars	Merc.			
	NH-42						
Saturn Ketu	Lagna	Sun Mercury Venus			Moon Jupiter	Ketu	

Balance of Saturn Dasa at birth : 1 year, 3 months and 4 days.

Chart¹ No. 172.—*Born 10/11-7-1891 at 1-18 a.m. (L.M.T.) at 13 N, 77 E 35.*

	Lagna	Rahu	Sun Venus			Rahu		Sun Jupiter
Jupiter			Mars Merc.					Mercury
	RASI				NAVAMSA			
			Moon Sat.					Mars
	RP-4/70							
	Ketu			Venus	Lagna	Moon Saturn Mars Ketu		

Balance of Venus Dasa at birth : 9 years, 8 months and 3 days.

brilliance. The 10th house is occupied by the fighting planet Mars who also aspects the Lagna. The 10th lord the Sun occupies a martian Navamsa which made the native a fighter in every sense. He was also an advocate of Swaraj during the regime of the British.

Lawyer : Chart No. 172 is of a well-known bar-at-law. The 10th house is Capricorn aspected by Mars who gets cancellation of debility and the 3rd and 6th lord Mercury. The 6th house rules courts, litigation, while Mars is the natural ruler of strife and quarrels. The 10th lord Saturn is with the Moon aspected by Jupiter. Saturn is the natural law-dealer and Jupiter indicates the judiciary. The Lagna being a fiery sign, the native was a forceful and militant lawyer.

Major (Army) : The native of Chart No. 173 is a medical doctor in the armed forces. The 10th house is occupied by the planet of war, Mars. The 10th house falls in the sign Scorpio which rules healing and is aspected by the 12th lord Saturn. The 12th house rules hospitals and sickness. The Lagna and Lagna lord being both aspected by Mars from the 10th house gives a career connected with the armed forces.

Managing Director: The native of Chart No. 174 is the director of a firm dealing in automobile parts. The 10th house is Taurus aspected by the Moon. The 10th lord Venus is in Aquarius aspected by Mars from the Lagna. Mars not only rules mechanical articles but also conveyances being the ruler of the 4th house. The Moon obtains *neechabhanga* due to Mars being in Lagna and forms a Raja Yoga. The mutual aspects of Venus and Mars as rulers of quadrants and trines forms a Raja Yoga elevating the native to a position of authority. The aspect of 7th lord Saturn on 5th lord Jupiter is another important yoga fortifying the chart in general.

Chart No. 173.—*Born 31–1–1907 at 8–29 a.m. (I.S.T.) at 16 N 29, 81 E 3.*

		Jupit.		Ketu Venus Saturn Lagna		Mercury Moon Sun
Saturn Lagna		Rahu			NAVAMSA	
Mercury Sun Ketu	RASI	Moon	Jupit.			Mars
Venus	Mars				Rahu	

(Rasi chart marked RP-199/4)

Balance of Ketu Dasa at birth: 3 years, 5 months and 24 days.

Chart No. 174.—*Born 29–1–1916 at 8–30 p.m. (I.S.T.) at 16 N 15, 81 E 15.*

Jupiter		Sat.	Sat.	Mars Venus		Sun Rahu
Venus Mercury		Ketu			NAVAMSA	
Sun Rahu	RASI	Lagna Mars				Jupiter
	Moon		Ketu		Lagna Mercury	Moon

(Rasi chart marked RP-115/4)

Balance of Saturn Dasa at birth: 12 years, 4 months and 15 days.

Chart No. 175.—*Born 23-10-1898 at 11-35 p.m. (L.M.T) at 9 N 10, 59 E 28.*

		Ketu	Ketu			
		Lagna Mars				
	RASI			NAVAMSA		
Moon	RP-108/2					Mars
Rahu	Venus Saturn	Mercury Sun Jupiter	Sun Merc. Sat.	Venus	Jupiter	Rahu Lagna Moon

Balance of Mars Dasa at birth : 4 years, 5 months and 20 days.

Managing Director : The 10th house in Chart No. 175 is Aries aspected by Mercury, the Sun and Vargottama Jupiter. The 10th lord Mars, though *neecha*, gets *neechabhanga* in Lagna Kendra and is aspected by Lagna lord Moon. The native is the Managing Director of a bank. Mercury and the Sun together with the 9th lord Jupiter aspecting the 10th house have given the native a top post in a commercial concern.

Monk : The 10th house in Chart No. 176 is Aries aspected by an exalted 10th lord Mars from a kendra and the 7th lord Saturn. The mutual aspects between the 10th and 7th lords, both malefics, involving the Lagna, the 7th and the 10th house resulted in a dispassionate monk. The 10th lord aspecting Lagna in exaltation made the native's aim in life the realization of his own self. 'If Saturn or the lord of the Lagna aspects the lord of the sign occupied by the Moon, the person will betake

Chart No. 176.— *Born 15–12–1888 at 8–17 p.m. (L.M.T.)*
at 23 N 30, 88 E 15.

		Moon		Jupit. Sat.	Sun Venus		Mars
			Rahu Lagna Sat	Merc.			Rahu
Ketu Mars Venus	RASI			Ketu Moon	NAVAMSA		
Sun	Mercury Jupiter				Lagna		

(RASI — RP-134/4)

Balance of Sun's Dasa at birth : 3 years, 4 months and 26 days.

himself to a religious order or mendicancy.' The Moon, who is also the Lagna lord, is exalted in Taurus. Venus, ruler of this sign, is in Capricorn aspected by Saturn in great strength generating a powerful yoga for asceticism. The Moon is well placed aspected by the spiritual planet as well as 9th lord Jupiter from the mystic sign, Scorpio. Mercury, the *gnanakaraka*, joins Jupiter, the gnanasthanadhipati. Lagna itself is influenced by Rahu and Saturn indicating burning dispassion. In this chart, the Lagna and the influences it comes under explain the vocation (?) of the native more clearly than the 10th house.

In Chart No. 176 is noteworthy for Rajayogas as well which made the native monk the general secretary of an international mission of spirituality and Vedanta. The 4th and 5th lords, Venus and Mars, joining the 7th, a quadrant, and being aspected by the 7th lord Saturn generates a powerful

Raja Yoga.   The Lagna lord is exalted in the 11th aspected by
2 benefics, Mercury and Jupiter. The 10th lord Mars is exalted
in a kendra aspecting the 10th house which gives the native a
position of great authority and equal responsibility.

Chart No. 177.— *Born 6–10–1894 at 11–17 p.m. (L.M.T.)
at 12 N, 77 E.*

			Lagna Jupit.	Lagna Ketu		
Rahu	Mars			Merc. Jupit.		Sun Mars
	RASI				NAVAMSA	
	RP-4/37		Venus			
Moon	Mercury Saturn	Sun Venus Ketu		Saturn	Moon	Rahu

Balance of Venus Dasa at birth :   6 years, 9 months and
18 days.

Monk : The 10th house in Chart No. 177 Pisces is the last
sign of the zodiac also called the Moksha-rasi. Its lord Jupiter
occupies the Ascendant aspected by the 2nd lord Moon. The
10th house is aspected by the atmakaraka Sun, 5th and 12th
ord Venus and occupied by Rahu.   The Moon is influenced by
2 spiritual planets, Jupiter and Saturn. These two are not only
the natural significators of spirituality but also being the 10th
lord and 9th lord respectively, give the native a spiritual goal in
life.   Chart No. 177 is of a highly evolved monk. The 9th lord
Saturn is exalted in the 5th (purvapunyasthana) aspected trinally

by the 10th lord Jupiter from a kendra. The 10th lord has no
afflictions whatsoever indicating a blemish-free career in the
native's spiritual life. 'If the Lagna lord or Saturn aspect the
lord of the sign occupied by the Moon, the native becomes an
ascetic.' Here the lord of the sign occupied by the Moon is
Jupiter and he aspects the Lagna lord Mercury. A trinal
relationship is established between the two planets signifying
spiritual moorings.

Musician : Lagna is the 3rd sign of the zodiac and is
occupied by 3 planets, Mercury, the planet of skill and versati-
lity, Venus the planet of music and art, the Sun in Chart No.
178. Mercury as Lagna lord in Lagna is very good while his
combination with the 5th lord Venus and 3rd lord the Sun has
given the native a rich, deep and beautiful voice charged with
fervour (Moon's aspect) making her a singer of great popularity
and charm. The Adhiyoga has reference to these planets in
Lagna and has made the native an authority and outstanding
figure in the world of music. Venus is free of any afflictions
which has therefore confined the native's talents to classical,
traditional music.

Newspaper Owner : The 10th house in Chart No. 179 is
Cancer aspected by Yogakaraka Saturn and 3rd and 6th lord
Jupiter both placed in their own signs. In Navamsa, the 10th
lord occupies a Jupiterian sign. The native is the owner of a
chain of newspapers. The 10th lord being Moon and Jupiter
aspecting the 10th house as 3rd lord has given a calling
which is directly related to the public (Moon) as a media of
communication (Jupiter as 3rd lord).

Shop-keeper : The 10th house in Chart No. 180 is Gemini
ruled by Mercury, the planet of trade. It is aspected by 2nd
and 9th lord Venus and 5th and 6th lord neecha Saturn. The

Chart No. 178.—*Born 2/3-7-1928 at 5-30 a.m. (I.S.T.) at 13 N 5, 80 E 15.*

	Jupiter Mars	Rahu	Lagna Venus Merc. Sun		Venus Sun	Rahu	
				Lagna Merc			
	RASI				NAVAMSA		Jupiter Mars
	RP-49/34		Sat.				
Moon	Saturn Ketu				Ketu		Moon

Balance of Venus Dasa at birth : 12 years, 9 months and 27 days.

Chart No. 179.—*Born 18–4–1904 at 5-46 p.m. (Madras Time) at 22 N 18, 83 E 00.*

Jupiter Venus Ketu	Sun Mars Mercury	Moon		Moon			Sun
				Rahu			
	RASI				NAVAMSA		Ketu
Saturn	GD-129			Jupit.			
		Lagna			Venus Mercury	Lagna	Mars Saturn

Balance of Sun's Dasa at birth : 1 year, 0 month and 13 days.

Chart No. 180.—*Born 6–2–1912 at 11 p.m. (I.S.T.) at 15 N 30, 73 E 51.*

	Saturn Rahu	Mars		Merc.	Mars	Moon Rahu	
Sun Mercury	RASI RP-206/4				NAVAMSA		Sun
Venus	Jupiter	Ketu	Lagna Moon	Jupit.	Ketu	Saturn	Lagna Venus

Balance of Moon's Dasa at birth : 5 years, 7 months and 6 days.

10th lord Mercury occupies the 5th house with 12th lord the Sun. Chart No. 180 is of a proprietor of a store that deals in articles of fancy and general use such as cosmetics, ladies' ware, trinkets and the like. Venus and the Sun indicate the nature of business while debilitated Saturn makes the native trade in common-place articles signified by Venus.

Philosopher : The Lagna Libra, the sign of the balance, in Chart No. 181 is *vargottama* and gains considerable vitality because of the aspect of Jupiter and association of the lord of Lagna with Mercury. Mark the disposition of the Sun and the Moon in benefic signs and association with spiritual planets. The Moon is the atmakaraka and is very strongly placed in *vargottama* aspected by Jupiter, the divine planet. The 10th lord Moon in an intellectual sign indicates the *jnani* the native was. The powerful Dharma Karmadhipa Yoga

Chart No. 181.—*Born 29/30-12-1879 at 1 a.m. (L.M.T.) at 9 N 50, 78 E 15.*

Saturn	Mars		Ketu Moon	Jupit.		Ketu	Moon
Jupiter	RASI			Merc.	NAVAMSA		Venus
	NH-46						
Rahu Sun	Mercury Venus	Lagna		Sat.	Rahu Mars	Lagna	Sun

Balance of Jupiter Dasa at birth : 4 years, 1 month and 20 days.

Chart No. 182.—*Born 13-3-1925 at 10-12 a.m. (I.S.T.) at 8 N 40, 77 E 41.*

Sun Mercury	Lagna Mars				Saturn Venus		
Venus	RASI	Rahu	Lagna Mars Rahu		NAVAMSA		Sun Ketu
Ketu	RP-36/101						
Jupiter	Saturn Moon				Jupiter	Moon	Mercury

Balance of Mars Dasa at birth : 2 years, 2 months and 21 days.

involving Saturn and Jupiter, the latter planet occupying the mystic sign of Aquarius which happens to be the 5th from Janma Lagna gives a clue to the spiritual heights to which the native rose.

Photographer : The 10th house is Aquarius in Chart No. 182 occupied by the Lagna lord Venus. The 10th lord Saturn is exalted in the 6th house with the Moon. There is a distinct *parivartana* or exchange of signs between Venus and Saturn. The native is a photographer with his own studio. This is appropriate to the nature of the planet in the 10th house, *viz.*, Venus. The 10th lord Saturn is also in a Venusian sign with the Moon. The Moon generally indicates callings that have to do with the public.

Physician : The 10th house in Chart No. 183 is occupied by Lagna lord Jupiter and aspected by Mars (influenced by Rahu) and Saturn from Cancer, the sign of healing. The 10th lord Mercury is with the 9th lord in Rasi and is *vargottama*. Mars and Rahu together produce skilled physicians and this combination relates to the 10th house powerfully. The native is a physician but consistent with the strength and the natural karakatwa of the 10th lord, the native is research-oriented.

Poet : Venus, the planet of poetry, is in the 2nd house in Chart No. 184. The native revealed unusual powers of intellect and a poetical genius of no mean order. The Sun and Mercury, planets of intelligence, are in the 2nd forming a powerful Budha-Aditya Yoga which found manifestation in intuitively inspired poetry. The Lagna is conspicuously strong as it is occupied by exalted Jupiter, gnanakaraka and the lord of the 9th or dharmasthana and Lagnadhipati Moon is in a benefic sign. Cancer rising gives intuition, benevolence, sympathy, usefulness and fondness for subtle things in life all of which found place in his inspired poems.

Chart No. 183.—*Born 13-9-1945 at 1-00 p.m. (Standard Time) at 16 S 30, 68 W 09.*

		Rahu Mars		Jupiter	
		Venus Sat.	Rahu Venus		Saturn
	RASI			NAVAMSA	Ketu Mercury Lagna
	G.IV-240	Sun Merc.	Mars		
Lagna Ketu	Moon	Jupit.	Sun Moon		

Balance of Mercury Dasa at birth : 16 years, 0 month and 16 days.

Chart No. 184.—*Born 15-8-1872 at 5-17 a.m. (L.M.T.) at 22 N 30, 88 E 20.*

		Rahu		Lagna	Sun		Rahu Moon Venus
			Lagna Mars Jupit	Jupit.			
	RASI				NAVAMSA		
	NH-43		Sun Venus Merc.				
Moon Saturn	Ketu			Ketu	Mercury Saturn		Mars

Balance of Ketu Dasa at birth : 3 years, 2 months and 22 days.

Chart No. 185—*Born 3-4-1905   at   2-34 p.m. (I.S.T.) at 14 N 13, 75 E 52.*

Moon Sun	Jupiter Veuus Mercury				
Ketu Saturn	RASI		Rahu	Ketu	NAVAMSA
	RP-18/145			Sun	
	Lagna Mars			Sat.	Venus

	Mercury
NAVAMSA	Lagna Jupiter Rahu Mars
	Moon

Balance of Saturn Dasa at birth : 12 years, 3 months and 2 days.

Politician : Aries, the sign of fighting, is strong in Chart No. 185 due to the occupation of 3 planets and the aspect of Saturn. Lagna is a martian sign occupied by Mars. The 10th house is occupied by Rahu and aspected by Saturn, planet of the masses. The native emerged as a political fighter and was voted to power and was a minister for some years.

Postmaster (Sub) :   The 10th house in Chart No. 186 is Pisces ruled by Jupiter and aspected by Saturn. The 10th lord Jupiter is in the 3rd, house of communication. Saturn occupies a constellation of the Sun, ruler of the 3rd house. . The native of Chart No. 186 is a sub-postmaster. The 3rd house influencing the 10th house has given a vocation that has to do with communication. Saturn's influence makes it a public service job.

Chart No. 186.—*Born 27–11–1920 at 8–37 p.m. (I.S.T.) at 17 N 45, 82 E 30.*

	Ketu		Lagna Moon		Mars		Mercury	Lagna
					Rahu			
Mars	RASI		Jupit.		Sat.	NAVAMSA		Ketu
	RP-187/4							
Venus	Sun	Mercury Rahu	Sat.			Moon Sun Jupiter	Venus	

Balance of Mars Dasa at birth : 0 year, 7 months and 7 days.

Chart No. 187.—*Born 8–8–9133 at 4–30 p.m. (I.S.T.) at 13° N 77, E 35.*

								Ketu Moon
Moon Rahu	RASI		Merc. Sun		Sun	NAVAMSA		Saturn
Saturn	RP-18/51		Ketu Venus		Jupit.			
Lagna			Jupit Mars		Rahu		Lagna Mercury Venus	Mars

Balance of Jupiter Dasa at birth : 5 years, 7 months and 28 days.

Public Prosecutor : Chart No. 187 is of a public prosecutor. Lagna is a fiery sign and the 10th house is occupied by Jupiter indicating the judiciary and Mars, indicating advocacy and militancy. The 10th and 9th lords combine in the 8th forming the Raja Yoga for success and fame. Saturn aspects the 10th lord and Jupiter aspects the former from the 10th house giving legal brilliance As 5th lord, Mars, *vargottama* in the 10th gives a forceful and hammering approach in the native's dealing with cases. The 5th and Lagna lord combining in the 10th is a beneficial yoga strengthening the chart as a whole. Jupiter in the 10th and 10th lord combining with the Sun have been responsible for being in Government service.

Chart No. 188.—*Born 17–10–1915 at 8–00 p.m. (I S.T.) at 25 N 23, 68 E 21.*

		Lagna	Sat.			Saturn	Jupiter
Jupiter	RASI		Ketu Mars	Lagna Merc. Venus Ketu	NAVAMSA		Rahu
Rahu Moon	RP-36/77						
		Venus Sun Mercury			Mars	Sun	Moon

Balance of Mars Dasa at birth : 4 years, 9 months and 10 days.

Publisher : The 10th house in Chart No. 188 is occupied by Jupiter and aspected by debilitated Mars who gets cancellation of debilitation. The native is the proprietor of a big publishing house with offices all over the country. Jupiter in relation to the 10th gives a career in publishing books while Mars aspecting involves printing and allied sectors of work as well. The relationship between the 11th lord Jupiter and 9th lord Saturn has resulted in very prosperous and successful business for the native. Saturn, the 10th lord, is in Gemini, an intellectual sign and Jupiter aspects him from the 10th making the native publish books which cater to a limited number unlike in Chart No. 179, where public involvement is greater.

Chart No. 189.– *Born 14–3–1879 at 11–30 a.m. (L.M.T)* at *48 N 24, 10 E.*

Sun Mercury Venus Saturn		Lagna		Rahu Lagna	
Jupiter	RASI NH–45	Ketu	Moon Mars Rahu	NAVAMSA	Sun
Mars Rahu					
	Moon		Jupit.	Saturn	Mercury Ketu

Balance of Mercury's Dasa at birth : 7 years, 10 months and 26 days.

Scientist: The intellectual sign Gemini rises in Chart No. 189 giving great sensitivity and intuitional ability. The Lagna is aspected by Gnanakaraka Jupiter from the mystic sign Aquarius suggesting the native's gift of *gnana* (knowledge) to the world by his scientific brilliance. Four planets having reference to the 10th house involving the lordships of the

Lagna, the 4th, the 5th and the 9th made the native a great scientist *(gnani)*. The *parivartana* between the 9th and 10th lords, Malavya Yoga in the 10th house caused by Venus, and Mercury's neechabhanga yoga in the 10th all acted to make the native a Nobel Laureate in Physics, Note Pisces. the sign of intuition, rises on the 10th house. The native's discoveries were intuitive and deeply significant in the world of science.

Scientist : The native of Chart No. 190 was a genius, physicist, inventor and also proved that there can be no sharp dividing line between the nervous life of planets and animals. All the three benefics Mercury, Jupiter and Venus, indicating intelligence, knowledge and wisdom have brought about a link between Lagna, the 2nd, 4th, 9th and 10th houses from the Moon. Saturn's aspect on the 10th house and Aquarius with Rahu on the 10th cusp made the native a scientific mystic. Both Rahu and Aquarius are idealistic and have great affinity for invention, research and invisible things. The 10th lord Saturn is in Cancer aspected by exalted Mars from an earthy sign and Lagna Taurus is also a fruitful sign indicating the native's sphere of work was related to plant life.

Script-writer : Virgo, a sign of Mercury, rises in the Ascendant in Chart No. 191. The 10th house is also an intellectual sign, Gemini. The 10th lord occupies Cancer with exalted Jupiter. In Navamsa, the 10th lord Mercury is in Sagittarius ruled by Jupiter. Chart No. 191 is of a script-writer who writes for films. The Mercury-Jupiter combination in the watery sign Cancer makes the native a prolific writer catering to emotional audiences. Venus in the 10th has made him write for the cinema.

Theatre—Owner and Money-Lender : In Chart No. 192 the 10th house Virgo is aspected by the 8th lord *vargottama*

Chart No. 190.—*Born 30–11–1858 at 4–25 p.m. (L.M.T.) at 23 N 33, 90 E 3.*

		Lagna Jupiter				Mercury	Moon Venus
Rahu			Sat.				Mars Ketu
	RASI			Lagna Rahu Sat.	NAVAMSA		
Mars	NH-33		Ketu				Jupiter
Mercury Venus	Sun		Moon	Sun			

Balance of Moon's Dasa at birth : 2 years, 3 months and 0 days.

Chart No. 191.—*Born 6-7-1920 at 12–17 p.m. (I.S.T.) at 10, N 50. 78 E 42.*

	Ketu		Venus Sun	Moon Jupit.	Rahu Sun	Venus	
Moon			Merc. Jupit.				Lagna
	RASI				NAVAMSA		
	RP-18/26		Sat.				Saturn
		Mars Rahu	Lagna	Mars Merc.		Ketu	

Balance of Rahu Dasa at birth : 3 years, 2 months and 2 days.

Chart No. 192.—*Born   21/22-3-1901   at   0-39 a.m. (L.M.T.) at 27 N 55, 68 E 45.*

Sun Moon		Ketu		Merc. Moon	Mars	Lagna	Venus
Venus Mercury	RASI RP-159/4		Mars	Ketu	NAVAMSA		Rahu
Lagna Saturn Jupiter					Saturn		Sun Jupiter

Balance of Mercury's Dasa at birth : 2 years, 8 months and 4 days.

Moon and 2nd and 3rd lord Saturn.   The 10th lord Mercury is with the 6th and 11th lord Venus aspected by 5th and 12th lord Mars and Saturn. The native of Chart No. 192 is a banker (money-lender) and also the owner of cinema theatres.   The 10th lord is influenced by Venus and Saturn, both planets ruling the cinema and similar types of cheap entertainment. The Lagna and Lagna lord are both influenced by 2nd lord Saturn (ruling monies) who, in turn, aspects the 10th lord and the 10th house.   The aspect of the Moon shows public involvement in the native's calling.   Both business of money-lending and running cinema-theatres   rely on public partici-pation.

University Lecturer : The 10th lord Mars in Chart No. 193 occupies his debility sign Cancer but gets cancellation of debility because Jupiter who gets exalted in Cancer is in a

Chart No. 193. – *Born 6/7-9-1936 at 4-30 a.m. (D.S.T.) at 35 N 0, 106 W 40.*

		Moon	Ketu		Venus	Moon	Mercury Rahu Saturn
Saturn	RASI		Lagna Mars	Lagna Mars Jupit.	NAVAMSA		
			Sun				
	RP-36/18						
Rahu	Jupiter		Merc Venus	Ketu		Sun	

Balance of Moon's Dasa at birth : 6 years, 11 months and 16 days.

Chart No. 194.—*Born 13-3-1948 at 10-30 a.m. (I.S.T.) at 11 N 06, 79 E 42.*

Moon Sun	Venus Rahu	Lagna		Lagna Mars Moon		Ketu Jupiter	
Mercury	RASI		Sat. Mars	Sat.	NAVAMSA		Sun
							Venus
	G.III-4						
Jupiter		Ketu			Rahu Mercury		

Balance of Mercury's Dasa at birth : 3 years, 9 months and 27 days.

quadrant from the Moon. The 10th lord is aspected by Jupiter. The native is a professor in a college. The Moon and Jupiter indicate teaching in a college or similar institution. In Navamsa also, the 10th lord Mars is with Jupiter.

University Lecturer : The 10th house from Lagna has the intellectual planet Mercury while the 10th house from the Sun and the Moon is occupied by Jupiter. These planets in Chart No. 194 indicate broadly the native's profession as a college lecturer. The Moon-sign is the strongest of the three and the 2nd lord from it is Mars in a Jupiterian Navamsa with the Moon indicating a teaching job and earnings therefrom.

Rajayogas or Combinations for Political Power

We reproduce below combinations for *Rajayogas* (lives of celebrity) produced from classical works.

Three or more planets in exaltation or own sign and at the same time in quadrants give rise to a widely known king. Five or more such planets make even an ordinary man a ruler of the earth. If a native with such combinations is born in a royal family without any malefic yogas or planets being combust, he becomes a ruler. People born in ordinary families with 3 planets placed as above become counsellors or equal to kings in power and authority but not kings themselves. Two or more planets with digbala make a royal native a king while 4 or more such planets make even an ordinary man a ruler. According to some writers like Yavanacharya, when the planets concerned are malefics, then the native becomes a cruel tyrant while benefics make one a just and virtuous sovereign.

By a combination and permutation, Varahamihira enumerates 32 kinds of Rajayogas arising under the following conditions :—

(1)   When Mars, Saturn, Jupiter and the Sun are exalted with one of them occupying the Ascendant (4 yogas).

(2)   When any three of the planets, Mars, Saturn, Jupiter and the Sun, are exalted with one of them being in the Ascendant (16 yogas).

(3)   When any two of these 4 planets are exalted, one of them being in Lagna and the Moon being in Cancer (12 yogas).

(4)   When any one of these 4 planets is exalted in the Ascendant and the Moon is in Cancer (4 yogas).

The Ascendant or the Moon in *vargottama* (occupying the same sign in Rasi and Navamsa) is aspected by 4, 5 or 6 planets (leaving out the Moon), 44 cases of Rajayoga are caused.

If the Lagna lord occupies a quadrant or the 9th house in Vargottama Navamsa and the 9th lord, in turn, is in exaltation, own sign or Vargottama Navamsa, a king is born. Jupiter exalted in Lagna, the Moon, Venus and Mercury in the 11th house and the Sun in Aries gives rise to a powerful king. If Mercury occupies Virgo which is also the Ascendant, Jupiter and the Moon be in Pisces and Saturn and the Moon occupy Capricorn, the native becomes a king.

If the Sun and the Moon occupy the Ascendant in Aries, Mars occupies Capricorn, Saturn is in Aquarius and Jupiter is in Sagittarius, the person born in a royal family becomes a king.

According to Varahamihira in his great classic *Brihat Jataka,* a kingdom is obtained during the Dasa or Bhukti of (1) the planet in the Ascendant, or (2) the planet in the 10th house from the Ascendant, or (3) the most powerful planet in the chart.

22

A kingdom is lost during the period (the major period or minor period) of (1) a planet in an inimical sign or (2) a planet that occupies the 7th from the sign it rules.

As we have several times pointed out, since Rajayogas occur in large numbers, a clever student should assess the worth of each combination taking into account the chart in its entirety.

In the horoscope of a ruler-king, dictator, president or prime minister—we have found in our experience Saturn's position when his rays are properly blended with those of Rahu can give rise to realization of objects, consolidation of the country, establishment of peace and economic prosperity and a happy and contented populace.

Chart No. 195.—*Born 4–6–1884 at 10–18 a.m. (L.M.T.) at 12° N, 76, E 38.*

Ketu		Sun Mercury Saturn		Lagna Ketu			Mars
	RASI NH-52		Lagna Jupit. Venus		NAVAMSA		Sun Venus Saturn
			Mars	Merc.			
		Moon	Rahu			Moon Jupiter	Rahu

Balance of Mars Dasa at birth: 1 year, 11 months and 16 days.

The horoscope of Chart No. 195 is typically illustrative of certain well-known principles of predictive astrology with regard to Rajayogas. Throughout his long and memorable reign of 40 years the native of Chart No. 195 showed a rare conscientiousness and disinterested zeal for the promotion of the welfare of his subjects. Note how balanced and constructive are the planetary positions. Mark the *vargottama* positions of the Moon, Rahu and Venus. Lagna occupied by exalted Jupiter confers Hamsa Yoga, a most beneficial combination while the Moon occupying Libra, the sign of the balance and causing *parivartana* with Venus, lord of the 4th, is a yoga *par excellence*. This suggests a personality which though royal is not suggestive of pomp. The conjunction of Saturn and the Sun in the 11th made him a constitutional monarch and the native exercised an influence more pervasive and lasting than any power that dictator or despotic monarch could have, because that influence proceeded from personal example and devotion to duty. The Hamsa Yoga has reference to the 10th house from Chandra Lagna which is also responsible for these noble traits. The Lagna lord in a kendra and *vargottama* and the 9th lord in exaltation is another powerful Rajayoga. The Full Moon's disposition in a kendra other than Lagna is itself a Rajayoga denoting the birth of a scion of a royal family. The Full Moon's *vargottama* position is yet another asset.

The Sun–Saturn combination is no doubt good regarding career but comes in the way of domestic harmony as 2nd and 7th lords and mutually bitter enemies.

Mars is a yogakaraka and he is in the 2nd house. Saturn and Mars are in mutual kendras and are not involved in mutual destructive aspects. Rahu is confined to an upachaya. Thus his "political career" was assured till the end, and no indications either for frustration or failure is seen in the horoscope. Chart No. 195 is of Krishnaraja Wadiyar IV, Maharaja of Mysore.

The following Rajayogas may be noted :—

(1)   The Moon being aspecting by exalted Jupiter

(2)   Jupiter's exaltation in the 10th from the Lagna and in the 9th from the Moon

(3)   Mercury occupying a Rasi other than Capricorn identical with the Lagna (or Chandra Lagna) aspected by Jupiter.

Chart No. 196. —*Born 14–12–1895 at 3-5 a.m. (G.M.T.) at 52 N 51, 0 E 30.*

			Merc. Sun	Saturn	
Rahu	RASI NH-66	Jupit.	Venus Rahu	NAVAMSA	
		Ketu			Ketu Moon
	Moon Sun Mercury Mars	Lagna Venus Saturn	Jupit. Lagna	Mars	

Balance of Saturn Dasa at birth : 18 years, 1 month and 22 days.

According to *Phaladeepika* "If out of the lords of the 11th, 9th and the 2nd houses, there be but one planet that occupies a kendra position in respect to the Moon, the person born becomes the ruler of a full-blown empire."

In Chart No. 196, the lords of the 2nd, the 9th and the 11th are Mars, Mercury and the Sun respectively. All the three planets are in a kendra from the Moon.

Chart No. 196 is of King George IV. The outstanding feature to be remembered and astrologically accounted for is

that in all the nativities of the British Sovereigns during the
past century—Queen Victoria, Edward VII, George V, Edward
VIII and George VI, Jupiter is angular; in all but one he is
either rising or culminating. When Mars and Saturn join in
Lagna, the 7th, the 8th or the 10th houses unrelieved by other
favourable aspects the person becomes aggressive, lacks tole-
rance for the adversary, and is fanatical and ruthless. When
Mars is not involved in such destructive aspects but is confined
to an insignificant position and has nothing to do with the 10th
house (from Lagna or the Moon) the man no doubt will be
clever, noble and generous but he will also be impractical,
contradictory, utopian, authoritative but lacking in practicality,
sensitive and will possess a tendency to assume the role of a
hero. Where the persistence of Saturn and the fire of Mars are
lacking one's political career becomes frustrated.

   Chart No. 197.—*Born 23–1–1897 at about 12 Noon
(L.M.T.) at 5 E 44, 20 N 38.*

	Lagna	Mars	Moon Merc.	Sun	Venus Lagna
Venus		Ketu	Ketu		Mars
Sun Rahu Mercury	RASI NH-68	Jupit.		NAVAMSA	Rahu
	Saturn	Moon			Jupiter Saturn

   Balance of Sun's Dasa at birth : 0 year, 4 months and
15 days.

Chart No. 197 is of Subhas Chandra Bose. Lagna is strongly disposed being powerfully aspected by Jupiter from Leo. There is on Lagna a certain blending of martian and saturnine influences denoting a frank outspoken and free-handed disposition and fiery enthusiasm. The situation of Jupiter in the 5th or house of emotions aspected by Mars and Saturn denotes that while the native was moved by the highest impulses of patriotism, there was a sense of frustration also. Fascist tendencies can be present only when the vibrations of Mars and Saturn combine in the 7th, 8th, 9th or 10th houses, but here since it has reference to the 2nd and 8th houses, the native was not a dictator in the sense of Hitler or the Duce.

The most noteworthy feature in Chart No. 197 is the presence of the Sun, Rahu and Mercury in the 10th or house of career and occupation. Rahu eclipsing the political planet Sun in the 10th house in a sign owned by Saturn is significant in as much as the native's entire life constituted one long battle against British Imperialism. His chequered political career is attributable only to Rahu's association with the Sun in the 10th house aspected by Saturn.

Mars is the lord of Lagna and the native was, therefore, a man of action. His daring, his energy, his uncompromising nature and his dynamic personalities are all the qualities of Aries.

Chart No. 198 is of Jawaharlal Nehru. It is in direct constrast with Chart No. 197. Here Lagna is Cancer a passive sign and the lord of Lagna is in Lagna—neither Lagna nor lord of Lagna have anything to do with Mars, Aries or Sagittarius. The native had all the characteristics of the Moon—emotional, passive, inconstant, changeful, compromising, indecisive, weak and vacillating. Owing to the insignificant position of Mars, the native could not, as an administrator, make that impression which he made as a thinker and politician.

Five planets—Jupiter, Sun, Mercury, Venus and Mars—aspecting the 10th were mainly responsible for making him the idol of India. Venus, Mercury and the Moon in kendras cause Rajalakshana Yoga making him an aristocrat.

Chart No. 198. *Born 14–11–1889 at 11–03 p.m. (L.M.T) at 25 N 25, 82 E.*

			Rahu	Merc.	Mars		
			Moon Lagna	Rahu Lagna			Sun Saturn
	RASI				NAVAMSA		
			Sat.				Ketu Jupiter
	NH-59						
Jupiter Ketu	Sun	Venus Mercury	Mars	Venus Moon			

Balance of Mercury's Dasa at birth : 13 years, 7 months and 6 days.

The 5th and 6th lords in mutual kendras cause Sankha Yoga. Venus in a kendra identical with his own sign causes a powerful Malavya Yoga, one of the Panchamahapurusha Yogas. Three planets the Moon, Venus and Jupiter are in their own houses These and the concentration of 5 planets on the 10th house made the native a ruler (prime minister).

Chart No. 199 is of Harry S. Truman. The 3rd and 8th lord Mars is in the 11th from Lagna and the Sun, ruling

Chart No. 199.—*Born 8-5-1884 at 4-26 p.m. (L.M.T. at 39 N 7, 94 W 30.*

	Sun Ketu	Mercury Saturn	Venus		Ketu Mercury		Saturn
			Mars Jupit.	Moon Mars			
	RASI				NAVAMSA		
				Venus			
	NH-51						
		Rahu Moon	Lagna	Sun		Rahu	Jupiter Lagna

Balance of Rahu's Dasa at birth :   7 years, 5 months and 27 days.

political power is in the 8th or house of death. This explain the fact Truman became President following the death of hi predecessor Theodore Roosevelt. Jupiter exalted is actuall in the 10th Bhava though in the 11th Rasi. Mars has obtaine cancellation of debility in the 10th from the Moon which i fortified by the occurrence of Chandramangala Yoga. Th Gajakesari Yoga has reference to the 2nd, the 10th, the 4t and the 7th houses and its effects are further augmented b the disposition of Venus, lord of the 2nd and the 9th (wealt and fortune respectively) in the 10th. It was therefore a frea of fortune for him the exalted office of a democratic President ship fell on him unexpectedly. This is indicated by the exa tation of the Sun in the 7th from the Moon and the associatio of the Sun with Ketu. The distance between Ketu and th

Sun is more than 27° so that there is no affliction. Saturn as the 5th lord conjoining with 10th lord Mercury constitutes a Rajayoga. Mark the disposition of the majority of planets in the second half of the zodiac. Stress is, therefore, laid on the 9th, 10th and 11th houses indicating fortune, action and realization, the last being restricted by the intermingling of jupitarean, martian and saturnine influences. The sun is very strong in Aries and Mars in the 10th has obtained neechabhanga and digbala.

The most important Rajayogas in our opinion are the exchange of houses between the 9th and 10th lords, the association of Mercury and Saturn in the 9th, exaltation of Jupiter in the 10th, neechabhanga of Mars in the 10th and nodes, *vargottama.*

The native became President during the sub-period of Venus in the Dasa of Ketu. Venus is the lord of the 2nd and the 9th and is posited in the 10th in *parivartana* with Mercury, the Lagna and the 10th lord. This is a unique combination. The Dasa lord Ketu is in the 7th house *vargottama.* He occupies his own constellation in the house of Mars. As such, he is capable of producing martain results. Mars, though bad by ownership, is well placed from Chandra Lagna. He owns the 2nd and 7th houses from the Moon and occupies the 10th in conjunction with exalted Jupiter. Mars is in the constellation of Mercury. All these favour acquisition of exalted political office.

The native's political career came to an end in Venus Dasa, Venus Bhukti. Venus is in the constellation of Rahu whose results he must give. Rahu is in Lagna Bhava aspected powerfully by 3rd and 8th lord Mars. Also in Navamsa Venus is afflicted due to papakartari. In addition, Rahu is a maraka and power is delegated to Venus.

Chart No. 200.—*Born 29–2–1896 at 1–00 Noon (L.M.T.) at 20 N, 36, 72 E 59.*

			Lagna	Sun		Venus	Saturn
Sun Rahu			Jupit.	Mars			Mercury Ketu
	RASI				NAVAMSA		
Mercury Venus Mars			Ketu Moon	Lagna Rahu			
	GD-137						
		Saturn			Moon		Jupiter

Balance of Venus Dasa at birth : 0 year, 4 months and 6 days.

Chart No. 200 is of Morarji Desai who became the prime minister at 81 years. Three planets—all major planets—Saturn, Jupiter and Mars are exalted in mutual kendras. The Moon is full. The 6th lord Mars in the 8th with 12th lord Venus generates a Vipareeta Rajayoga. This is further strengthened by a *parivartana* between Venus and yogakaraka Saturn, the 5th and 8th lords respectively. The Vipareeta Rajayoga occurring in the 8th house involves the Lagna lord Mercury and is aspected by an exalted 10th lord Jupiter who aspects the 10th house. Jupiter is himself aspected by the Rajayogakarakas Mars, Saturn and Venus, the first two being exalted and the latter two being in mutual *parivartana.*

The native became prime minister in Mercury Dasa, Venus Bhukti. The Bhukti lord Venus is the yogakaraka for Gemini Ascendant and is aspected by exalted 10th lord Jupiter. He

is also a constituent of the Vipareeta Rajayoga. The Dasa
lord Mercury is the Lagna lord but with the Rajayoga-causing
planets, Mars and Venus, aspected by 10th lord exalted
Jupiter.

Chart No. 201.—*Born 21–4–1926 at 1–40 p.m. (G.M.T.)
at 51 N 30, 0 W 05.*

Venus Mercury	Sun		Rahu		Rahu Sun
Jupiter	RASI GD-139		Moon	NAVAMSA	Saturn
Lagna Mars			Lagna Venus Moon		
Ketu	Saturn		Ketu	Jupiter Mercury	Mars

Balance of Mercury's Dasa at birth : 11 years, 9 months
and 23 days.

Chart No. 201 is of Queen Elizabeth II. The royal planet
Sun exalted in a kendra explains her constitutional status as
a monarch. The Lagna is *vargottama*, Ketu is *vargottama*
Lagna Bhava, the Moon occupies his own sign, Yogakaraka
Venus is exalted in the 4th Bhava and 4th and 11th lord Mars
is also exalted but in the 2nd house. According to classical
works, 3 or more planets in exaltation and at the same time in
a kendra make one a widely renowned king (monarch). Here
3 planets are in exaltation, two of them being in Lagna Kendra,
Lagna and the nodes are *vargottama* and the Moon occupies
own sign—constituting a powerful Rajayoga. The 9th lord

Mercury is neecha but gets neechabhanga and joins the 10th lord Venus. The Lagna lord and 11th lord, Saturn and Mars, are in *parivartana*.

The native's accession to the British throne took place in Venus Dasa, Rahu Bhukti. Venus, the Dasa lord, is a yoga-karaka exalted in a kendra. In Rasi he combines with 9th lord Mercury while in Bhava he joins the Rajyakaraka exalted the Sun. Rahu the Bhukti lord is *vargottama* in the 6th, the best place for him to occupy. He is in a mericurial sign and Mercury is the 9th lord constituting a Rajayoga.

An unsullied 10th house aspected by karaka exalted the Sun and a weak cuspal 3rd and 12th lord indicates a spotless reign and the deep affection of the people the native has secured for herself.

Loss of Power (Rajayoga Bhanga)

Chart No. 202.—*Born 1-12-1751 (N.S.) at 8 a.m. (L.M.T.) at 13° N, 77 E 35.*

	Moon	Jupiter Ketu		Mars		Ketu	Jupiter
Mars				Venus Sat.			
	RASI				NAVAMSA		
	NH-21						
Lagna	Sun Mercury Saturn Rahu	Venus		Sun Merc.	Moon Rahu		Lagna

Balance of Venus Dasa at birth : 3 years, 4 months and 24 days.

Chart No. 202 is of Tippu Sultan.

The Rajayogas are disposed in a peculiar manner. The Sun as lord of the 9th and Mercury as lord of the 10th are in exact conjunction. This Dharma-karmadhipa Yoga is highly significant. Mercury is combust and one can contend that this could be dangerous to the Rajayoga. But the sum total of the influences to which Mercury is subject must be considered. The term 'association' implies results that are of mutual significance. In other words, if Saturn and the Sun are together in association with say Mercury, the effects of the yoga generated by the Sun and Saturn are delegated or transferred to Mercury also. A thorough study of standard astrological works gives ample testimony in support of this statement. Here 4 planets—the Sun and Mercury within 2°, Rahu nearer Mercury and Saturn, a little away—have conjoined. Such grouping of planets causes collective influences.

A planet has 3 main functions to perform apart from the subsidiary ones. They are : (a) due to ownership, (b) due to karakatwa and (c) due to generation of yogas. The subsidiary functions are given rise to by virtue of association, aspect, etc.

Therefore the Sun's innate function of karakatwa, blended with the main function of Saturn–Sun combination plus Saturn's innate function of karakatwa—should render the combination taken above as quite effective. Almost all standard astrological works agree the Sun–Mercury combination is auspicious. According to *Saravali* it indicates "fluctuating wealth, polite speech, fame, respect, liked by the king, a great man, fair-looking, wealthy and strong". According to *Jataka-parijata* it makes "the person fickle-minded, but endowed with learning, beauty and strength". "The person will be clever, intelligent, famous and happy" according to Varahamihira.

Mercury, in addition, is subject to the powerful aspect of Jupiter, lord of Lagna. Mercury's combustion with the Sun is said to destroy a person's abilities rendering him superficial and devoid of judgement. But here since Jupiter aspects combust Mercury, the significance of combustion is greatly minimised resulting in a distinct Rajayoga. But as the Rajayoga occurs in the 12th or house of loss, he could not enjoy it fully.

The native succeeded to the throne in Jupiter Bhukti, Rahu Dasa. Dasa lord Rahu is in a constellation of Saturn who is the 10th lord from Chandra Lagna and has given rise to a Rajayoga in association with the 5th lord the Sun. The sub-lord Jupiter occupies an upachaya and is aspected by yoga-karaka planets the Sun and Mercury.

He lost his political power by death by decapitation, the Rajayoga having peculiar reference to the 12th house and involving the 9th and 10th lords (Rajayoga) and the 2nd lord (head).

Chart No. 203 is of Napoleon Bonaparte.

There are quite a number of Rajayogas which enabled the native to achieve a position that literally laid the whole of Europe under his feet. But the Rajayogas are loosely knit with the result the foundation of his career collapsed at the prime of his life.

Saturn the 4th and 5th lord in the 10th with the 9th lord causes a powerful Rajayoga. This is further reinforced by the aspect of the 10th lord the Moon who is in *parivartana* (interchange of houses) with the 4th lord Saturn. The lord of the Navamsa occupied by the Moon is in Lagna. All the important planets causing the various yogas are arrayed in the 9th, the 10th and the 11th. The royal planet the Sun ruling the 11th is in the 11th while the martial planet Mars owning the 7th (war

Chart No. 203.— *Born 15–8–1769 at about 10–28 a.m. (L.M.T.) at 41 N 55, 8 E 40.*

			Ketu Venus	Moon Venus	Sun Rahu	Jupiter	
	RASI		Sat. Merc.		NAVAMSA		
Moon	GD-141		Sun Mars				Saturn
Rahu		Jupiter Lagna			Mercury	Mars Ketu Lagna	

Balance of Sun's Dasa at birth : 1 year, 6 months and 6 days.

and foreign relations) is also in Leo but in the 12th Bhava. As a result the native raised colossal and mighty empire with his sword.

The afflictions to the Rajayogas subject to a series of evil directions resulted in the collapse of the empire during his lifetime. In the Rajayogas formed in the 10th, Mercury and Saturn are nearly 10° apart. While Saturn is really a benefic, 12th lordship of Mercury has imparted to Saturn the quality of loss or destruction. This is an instance of a powerful Rajayoga delicately balanced and the Dasa of the planets causing the yogas not operating.

In Mars Bhukti, Rahu Dasa, the native proclaimed himself Emperor. Rahu, the major lord, is pre-eminently disposed. He is strongly placed in the 3rd house aspected by Lagna lord Venus. He occupies the constellation of Ketu who is in the

9th or house of fortune. In Navamsa, he is with exalted Sun and aspected by Mars. Since Rahu is in a constellation of Ketu and Ketu should give the results of Mars in accordance with the dictum *Kujavad Ketu* and since Mars, in turn, is associated with the royal and imperial planet the Sun, the native became an emperor during the directional influences of Rahu and Mars. But Rahu and Mars are not without their elements of destruction. Rahu is in the sign of Jupiter and Mars in the 12th Bhava.

The native abdicated in Juipter Dasa, Venus Bhukti. Usually under Jupiter's major period and Venus sub-period, unfavourable results can take place. In addition, here the two planets have certain inherent defects. When the lord of Lagna occupying a trine is aspected by the 6th lord and is joined by Saturn, Mars, Rahu or Ketu, Bandhana Yoga is produced. Here the major lord Jupiter is afflicted as owning the 3rd and 6th houses. The Bhukti lord Venus though in the 9th is aspected by 6th lord Jupiter and is in association with Ketu. The native was finally vanquished at Waterloo during the Sun's sub-period. The Sun is rendered evil by association with Mars.

The Rajayogas in this chart have in them the very seeds of destruction. Saturn's situation exactly in the 10th Bhava plus the afflictions of the royal planet the Sun in the Navamsa by Mars, Rahu and Ketu foreshadowed the native's downfall.

In Chart No. 204, in order to obtain a first impression we must first of all consider the ruler of the nativity. The Lagna is Scorpio. The lord of Lagna Mars is in the 7th a malefic Saturn aspecting Lagna. In Navamsa, Lagna is Cancer and Mars is in debility but obtains cancellation of debility.

Chart No. 204.—*Born 29-7-1883 at 2 p.m. (L.M.T.) at 41 N, 16 E.*

	Ketu	Moon Mars Saturn	Jupit. Venus				Moon Venus Jupiter Saturn
			Sun Merc.	Rahu			Lagna Mars
	RASI				NAVAMSA		Ketu
	NH-50						
	Lagna	Rahu			Sun Mercury		

Balance of Moon's Dasa at birth : 3 years, 8 months and 26 days.

According to Hindu astrology if the 8th house is occupied by benefics—especially Jupiter and Venus—the combination goes under the name of *Asura Yoga*. This makes the native a tyrant taking pleasure in the sufferings of others. According to Mantreswara "one born in *Asura Yoga* will become mean, a tale-bearer, will spoil others' works and will always be intent on securing his own interests. He will be headstrong. He will do vile acts and become miserable as a result of his own evil and mischievous doings". The situation of Jupiter and Venus should be viewed from the Moon as it causes a powerful Dhana Yoga. Moreover from the Moon, Saturn is a yogakaraka and hence in his Dasa which commenced about 1928, the native reached the highest position as a dictator. Saturn aspects the 10th from the Moon, Saturn also aspects powerfully the 10th lord from Lagna, namely, the Sun. It is this aspect that was responsible for the native's fall.

Saturn is not a benefic from Lagna while from the Moon he is a benefic. The Dasa of Saturn ran upto 1947. He produced good results in the first half of his Dasa while in the second half he gave very unfavourable results.

The native entered the World War II in Saturn Dasa. Moon Bhukti. Mark the situation of both these planets in the 7th along with Mars. In Navamsa, Saturn owns the 7th and 8th houses and is situated in the 12th house while the sub-lord owning Lagna is also placed in the 12th house indicating loss. Lagna is also placed in the 12th house indicating loss. Saturn tempted him to sacrifice himself for greedy ambition and self-aggrandisement.

In Navamsa, there is a conglomeration of 4 planets—the Moon (lord of Lagna), Saturn (lord of 8), Venus (lord of 11) and Jupiter (lord of 6)—all occurring in the 12th or house of loss. This satelletium is full of significance and made the native over-forceful, restless and disruptive.

What we must note in Chart No. 204 is the presence of the Sun in the 9th and his being aspected by Saturn, Saturn-Mars association in the 7th with the Moon unrelieved by beneficial aspects and Mars aspecting the 10th which explain the native's rise from humble life, his becoming a dictator, and his final violent end. Mark also the position of 4 planets in the 12th from Navamsa Lagna.

Chart No. 205 is of Richard Nixon.

The Lagna being Leo, the 10th lord Venus and 7th lord Saturn are in mutual *parivartana*. The Lagna lord Sun is *vargottama* in the 5th in a friendly sign with 4th and 9th lord yogakaraka Mars, 5th lord Jupiter and 2nd and 11th lord Mercury. The grouping of 4 planets in a powerful sign with the sign lord Jupiter in his own sign in Rasi and excellently isposed in the Navamsa by his exaltation constitutes a owerful Rajayoga. The 12th lord Moon in the 6th generates partial Vipareeta Rajayoga.

Chart No. 205.— *Born 9–9–1913 at 9–30 p.m. (P.S.T.) t 33 N 53, 117 W 49.*

Rahu	Saturn			Ketu	Mercury Mars
Venus	RASI		Sat.	NAVAMSA	Jupiter
Moon	GD-143	Lagna	Venus		
Sun Jupiter Mercury Mars		Ketu	Sun	Lagna Rahu	Moon

Balance of Mars Dasa at birth : 4 years, 1 month and days.

The native was elected President in Mercury Dasa, lercury Bhukti. Mercury is in exact degree combination with ogakaraka Mars and in his own sign Navamsa. He continued or a second term in the Sun Bhukti of Mercury Dasa. The un as Lagna lord *vargottama* in the 5th with 9th lord Mars nd 5th lord Jupiter confers great fortune or kingdom.

The Rajayoga-causing elements are not without their bad oints. The combination of 4 planets occurs in the 12th from e Moon. Saturn in the 10th is not at all desirable for although confers initial success, it also gives defeat and humiliation politically oriented charts. The fall came about following a nocking scandal involving corruption charges in Moon

Bhukti of Mercury Dasa. Mercury though well placed b
association is in a constellation ruled by Ketu who occupies
marakasthana. The Bhukti lord Moon is the lord of the hous
of loss placed in the 6th house, a dusthana. This chart is typ
cal of the destruction of Rajayogas capable of being cause
by Saturn in the 10th house.

Chart No. 206. -- *Born 19–11–1917 at 11–13 p.m. (I.S.T.*
at 25 N 27, 81 E 51.

	Jupiter	Ketu	Moon Lagna
	RASI	Sat. Lagna	
Moon	GD-145	Mars	
Venus Rahu	Sun Mercury		

		Jupiter	
	NAVAMSA		Rahu
Sat. Ketu			Sun
	Mercury	Venus	Mars

Balance of Sun's Dasa at birth : 1 year, 3 month
and 25 days.

Chart No. 206 is of Indira Gandhi.

The Ascendant is Cancer aspected by its lord the Moo
who is in mutual exchange of signs with the 7th lord Satur
The 9th lord Jupiter and 3rd and 12th lord Mercury are
vargottama. The 11th and 6th lords, Venus and Jupiter respe
tively, are in *parivartana*. So also are 2nd and 5th lords, th
Sun and Mars respectively. 3 sets of planets in *parivartar*
yogas, two planets in *vargottama navamsas* and Rahu in th
6th are all powerful Rajayogas making the native a prim

minister. Further Mercury and Saturn are in *nakshatra-parivartana*, each occupying the other's asterism. Rahu and Ketu have also mutually exchanged their constellations.

The native became prime minister in the Sun Bhukti of Jupiter Dasa. The Sun has exchanged signs with 10th lord yogakaraka Mars. He is aspected by Mars and occupies Leo, the royal sign, in Navamsa. The Dasa lord is Pre-eminently placed to give Rajayoga results being *vakra vargottama* in the 11th house. Moreover both the Dasa and Bhukti lords are in mutual aspect. This chart carries with it latent seeds for Rajabhanga. The only aspect the 10th house receives is of Saturn, a maraka and malefic for Cancer Lagna. Further he is placed in a constellation ruled by Mercury, the 3rd and 12th lord. It was in Saturn Dasa, Venus Bhukti, that the native lost power overnight. Not only are the Dasa and Bhukti lords in *shashtashtaka* but by standard astrological rules the mutual periods of Saturn and Venus are fatal to Rajayogas. Venus, the Bhukti lord, is eclipsed in the 6th house. Saturn, the Dasa lord, occupies an unfriendly constellation.

There are yet other factors, primarily the parivartana yogas, which put the native back in power. This chart is illustrative of the power of the inter-periods of Venus and Saturn to damage Rajayogas. However, if the Rajayoga is powerful enough, the bhanga (loss of power) will be set right in appropriate periods.

Chart No. 207 is of Zulfikar Ali Bhutto.

The grouping of Venus, Saturn, Ketu and Mars in Scorpio aspected by swakshetra Jupiter and exalted Moon in a kendra from the Moon is a powerful Rajayoga. Considered from Lagna, the Lagna lord Mercury and the Sun, significator of kingship, in the 7th form a Budha-Aditya Yoga being very

Chart No. 207.—*Born 5-1-1928 at 4-29 p.m. (L.M T.) at 27 N 27, 68 E 8.*

Jupiter		Rahu Moon	Lagna	Mars			
	RASI			Ketu	NAVAMSA		
				Lagna Sat.			Rahu Jupiter
	GD-153						
Sun Mercury	Venus Saturn Ketu Mars					Venus Sun Mercury	Moon

Balance of Mars Dasa at birth : 3 years, 9 months and 27 days.

closely placed to each other. Jupiter, the 10th lord, occupies a kendra in his own sign. From Lagna, the 5th lord Venus, the 11th lord Mars and yogakaraka Saturn in association from a formidable combination for an autocratic birth and background. The Adhi-yoga generated by Venus and Mercury being in the 7th and 8th respectively from Lagna is of added significance because the pivot of the Yoga is exalted. It gains extra vitality being the centre of a Ruchaka Yoga caused by Mars in Scorpio and a Sasi-Mangala Yoga formed by powerful Moon and Mars.

The native became prime minister in Mercury Bhukti of Saturn Dasa. Saturn is a yogakaraka both from Lagna and the Moon and in the constellation of Lagna lord Mercury. Mercury is in the 7th with Rajayogakaraka Sun in a quadrant and in the 8th from the Moon which confers dominion over a land.

The Rajayoga occurs in the 6th house from Lagna and therefore must suffer *bhanga*. Further, the nodes eclipsing the Rajayoga are a great danger to the sustenance of the yoga results. Consequently the native was ousted out of power in Moon Bhukti of Saturn Dasa. The Dasa lord is not only the 9th lord but also the 8th lord and in a malefic house. Bhukti lord the Moon, the crux of the yogas, occupies dusthana with Rahu bearing inherent defects for Rajayoga-bhanga.

Neechabhanga Rajayogas

In the study of career two important sets of planetary combinations are to be noted. There are some men born in the lap of luxury and wealth but who go down suddenly or gradually and lead a most miserable life. There are others born in the midst of abject misery and poverty but who reach very eminent social or royal positions. The first set of conjunctions is called Rajabhanga Yogas and the second, Neechabhanga Rajayoga. The word *bhanga* means breaking away, loss or ruin. Those who are usually styled usurpers of the thrones of others may generally, if not always, be taken to be men from humble ranks. The careers of some of the world's greatest men show clearly the set of combinations that go under the name of Neechabhanga Rajayogas.

Chart No. 208 (Hyder Ali) is a typical case of Neechabhanga Rajayoga. The native rose from the lowest position of almost nothing to very great power. The Lagna lord Venus occupies the 4th house. The lord of the Moon-sign Mars occupies it with benefics Jupiter and Mercury as well as Saturn and the Sun. This strange combination of 6 planets in the house of wealth and speech produced a man of extraordinary abilities. The second house holds a very powerful combi-

Chart No. 208. – *Born 8-2-1722 (N S.) at 2–15 a.m. (L.M T.) at 13° N, 77 E 35.*

			Rahu	Jupit. Sun Sat.	Venus	Ketu	
	RASI				NAVAMSA		
Venus	NH-19						
Ketu	Sun Moon Mars Mercury Jupiter Saturn	Lagna		Moon	Rahu	Mars Lagna	Mercury

Balance of Mercury's Dasa at birth: 15 years, 8 months and 6 days.

nation. The Moon is debilitated but the debilitation is distinctly cancelled. Starting with absolutely nothing in his pocket and no claims to any education, the native founded an empire, trained an army before which the disciplined and armed troops of Europe could make no head, collected a fortune which ranked second to none and exhibited a statesmanship which ran without a parallel.

The following are some important combinations for Neechabhanga Rajayoga :—

(1) If benefics are in the 10th, 11th and 3rd houses, Rajayoga arises.

(2) If a planet is in debility and the lord of this sign or the planet who gets exalted there is in kendra from the Moon or Lagna, Rajayoga results.

(3) If a planet is *neecha* (debilitated) in Rasi but gets exalted in Amsa, Rajayoga is formed.

(4) Jupiter in the 12th and Saturn in the 11th (in debilitation) cause Rajayoga.

(5) If Mercury is exalted in Lagna, Jupiter is in Pisces, Saturn is in Cancer, Venus is in Sagittarius and the Sun and Mars are in debilitation, Rajayoga is caused. In this combination, it will be noted that the Sun and Mars are lords of dusthanas (malefic lords) and, therefore, if weak, produce Rajayoga.

XV

Concerning the Eleventh House

The eleventh house refers to gains, elder brother, friends, acquisitions, freedom from misery, and happy tidings. An affliction to the 11th house may result in the loss of brother, friends, loss of wealth, misery or unhappy news. The exact nature of the result can be gleaned only after an assessment of the whole chart and the afflicting planets. To some extent the eleventh also concerns marriage.

Primary Considerations

In analysing the significations of the eleventh Bhava or house the general strength of the following factors must be studied : (a) the Bhava, (b) its lord, (c) the karaka, and (d) the occupants. Yogas in the chart bearing on the 11th house must also be taken into account.

We shall first study the general combinations and the effects of planets of severally.

Results of the Lord of the Eleventh House Occupying Different Houses

First House :—The native will be born in a rich family. He will earn much wealth. According as the 11th lord in Lagna is strong, middling or weak, the native will be born in a very rich, fairly rich or well-to-do family. He will lose an elder brother early in life.

Second House :—The native will live with his elder brothers. Benefics there give harmonious relations. Malefics cause domestic bickerings but common residence. The native will earn through commercial concerns and banking business. Business with friends will bring good profits but if malefics join, the native may suffer heavy losses on account of friends.

Third House :—The person will be a concert-singer or musician and will earn thereby. Gain through brothers is also indicated. He will have many friends and helpful neighbours. Afflictions give contrary results.

Fourth House :—One acquires profits through landed estates, rentals and products of the earth. His mother will be a cultured and distinguished lady. He will be renowned for his learning and scholarship of various subjects. He will live in comfort and enjoy all joys in life. He will have a devoted and charming wife.

Fifth House :—The native will have many children who will come up well in life. He will indulge in speculation and gain much money. If the 11th lord is afflicted, he will be a gambler and indulge in foolish ventures. If 11th lord is beneficially disposed, the native will be pious and observe many resolves and vows which will enhance his prosperity.

Sixth House :—The person gains money through maternal relatives, litigation and running nursing-homes. If the 11th lord is afflicted in the 6th, the native thrives on setting person against person, involve himself in other peoples' quarrels and anti-social activity. If malefics afflict the 11th lord, the native may lose through similar sources.

Seventh House :—The person marries more than once. He prospers in foreign countries. If there are afflictions to the 11th lord, the native carries on liaisons with women of ill-repute. He will indulge in trading in flesh and similar immoral activities. If the 11rh lord is fortified, the native marries only once but a rich and influential woman.

Eighth House :—The native though rich at birth suffers many calamities and loses much of his money. He will suffer from the *depracies* of thieves, cheats and swindlers. If the 11th lord occupies a malefic constellation, the native will be forced to eke out of his living by begging.

Ninth House :—He inherits a large paternal fortune and will be very lucky in life. He will possess many houses, conveyances and every other kind of luxury. He will be religious-minded and disseminate religious literature. He will be charitable and set up charitable institutions.

Tenth House :—The native prospers very well in his business and makes good profits. His elder brother will also help him in his business. He will earn some prize-money for original contributions to the subject of his study or profession. Depending upon the benefic or malefic nature of the planet he will earn through fair or foul means.

Eleventh House :—The native will have many friends and elder brothers who may help him throughout life. He will have a happy life with the blessings of wife, home, children and comforts.

Twelfth House :—He will suffer losses in business. His elder brother will be ailing and much expenditure will be incurred on account of his illness. The native may also lose an elder brother by death. He will have to pay fines and penalties frequently and will be burdened with many domestic responsibilities.

These results are very general and must not be applied directly without weighing other factors. According to Satyacharya if the 11th lord is placed in an evil constellation such as the 3rd, 5th or 7th from that occupied by the Moon, the native suffers penury and misery. If the 11th house is flanked on both sides by benefics or otherwise favourably disposed, one will have a powerful elder brother. The native will earn fabulous wealth through his mother. Benefics in the 11th house augment the significations of the Bhava while malefics diminish them both qualitatively and quantitatively.

Important Combinations

If a benefic planet occupies the 11th Bhava, the native acquires wealth through honest and noble means. If malefics be in the 11th Bhava, the native resorts to unfair and unscrupulous methods of earning. If both benefics and malefics are there, sometimes unjust means and sometimes just methods will be resorted to. Fortified planets in the 11th house confer fortunate conveyances, bungalows, and all comforts. He will have a noble and beautiful wife and will be fond of good clothes, food and enjoyments.

If the 11th house be occupied by a weak planet—eclipsed, depressed or defeated in planetary war, or occupying inimical vargas—even if one is born in an affluent family will lose everything and he will have to wander about without self-respect.

The source of gains is indicated by the nature of planet in the 11th house. If the Sun is in the 11th house, the native gets a fortune as an inheritance ; if the Moon—earns through mother, sea-products, pearls, milk, farms, fruit orchards and breweries ; if Mars—income is augmented through factories, litigation, lands and rentals and through self-exertion ; if Mercury—earns through teaching, writing, friends or uncles ; if Jupiter—gains through knowledge—scientific, religious, literary—and through well-placed sons ; if Venus—earnings increase through dance, drama, cinema, fine arts, music and women ; and if Saturn—wealth through industries, labour and agriculture.

If the Lagna, 2nd and 11th lords are friendly, the earnings are used for honourable ends such as legitimate expenses and charity. If the 2nd and 11th lords are afflicted and inimical to the Lagna lord, money is squandered on wine and women. The 11th lord well placed in a kendra or trikona from the Ascendant or malefics strong in the 11th make the native immensely wealthy.

When Mars occupies the 11th house and Lagna is a movable sign aspected by the 6th lord, one suffers physical ailments and fever due to spells and charms set into operation by black-magic and similar means. If malefics aspect the 11th, 5th, 9th and the 3rd houses without any benefic aspect, the native suffers from ear-troubles and deafness. If the afflictions are heavy and the 3rd and 11th houses are hemmed in between malefics, he may become stone-deaf. If benefic aspects feebly, only slight deafness is indicated. Both benefic and malefic aspects on the 11th and 3rd give irritating ear-ailments but not deafness.

If the Lagna lord is in a quadrant, the 10th lord is in the 4th and the 9th lord is in the 11th, one enjoys Rajayoga and becomes long-lived and even a ruler. If the Moon and Saturn join the 11th house, one can become a ruler even if born in humble circumstances. Similar results happen if the 2nd, 9th or 11th lord occupies a kendra from the Moon and Jupiter owns 11th.

Lord of the Navamsa occupied by the Lagna lord in a kendra or trikona from the Lagna or in exaltation, or the 11th house in strength makes the native happy after his 30th year. Lords of Lagna, the 2nd and the 11th in their own houses confer much wealth. If the 2nd and 11th lords being friendly planets occupy the Ascendant or if they occupy the 11th house in strength (such as one of them being in own sign, or friendly sign or exaltation) or if the lords of Lagna, the 2nd and the 11th combine preferably in a trine or quadrant, the native gets fabulous wealth.

If the 2nd and the 11th lords exchange houses or if the Lagna lord occupies the 2nd house and the 2nd lord occupies the 11th house, or if the 11th lord is in the Lagna, the native acquires much property.

If the 1st, 2nd, 9th and 11th attain their exalted Navamsa or Vaiseshikamsa (occupying own moolatrikona or exaltation or same varga three or more times, one becomes a millionaire.

Planets in the Eleventh House

The Sun :—The person lives for a long time and becomes wealthy. He will have wife, children and many servants. He gets royal and governmental favours, and achieves success without much effort. He will be sagacious and principled.

The Moon :—One will be noble, generous and blessed with riches, wife and children. Introspective by nature and quiet-going, he will become famous making good profits in business. He will acquire vast lands and be helped in his endeavours by the fair sex.

Mars :—The native will be an eloquent and forceful speaker, clever and rich but lustful, will acquire landed properties and wield considerable influence in top circles.

Mercury :—One becomes learned in many sciences. He will possess a keen and sharp intellect, will be wealthy, truthful and happy, will have many faithful servants and will prosper in engineering ventures.

Jupiter :—The native will be long-lived. He will have a limited number of issues, will be bold and wealthy with a piercing intellect and will become renowned. He will be fond of music, will accumulate riches and will have many friends.

Venus :—He will be of a wandering nature, will make immense profits possessing all kinds of comforts and luxuries. He will have a weakness for women and long for their company. He will be popular having many friends.

Saturn :—The native earns through employing many men and women. He will have few friends, will be fond of enjoyment and will earn through Government sources. He will have a long and healthy life, and will be involved in politics commanding great respect.

Rahu :—The native distinguishes himself in the army or navy, will become famous, wealthy and learned ; will have few children, will suffer from ear afflictions and will earn much wealth in foreign countries.

Ketu :—The native will have the habit of hoarding. He may get monetary wind-fall through speculation such as lottery, horse-racing and the stock exchange. Noble and possessed of many good qualities of head and heart, he will succeed in all his ventures, and will participate in charitable and similar works of beneficence.

Time of Fructification of the Results of the Eleventh House

The following factors must be taken into account in timing events pertaining to the eleventh house :-(*a*) Lord of the 11th house, (b) Planet of planets aspecting the 11th house, (c) planet or planets occuyping the 11th house, (d) planets aspecting the 11th lord, (e) planet or planets in association with the lord of the 11th house, and (f) the 11th lord from the Moon.

These factors may influence the 11th house either as the lords of the main periods or as the lords of sub-periods. (1) The sub-periods of planets capable of influencing the 11th house in the major periods of those who are also capable of influencing the 11th house produce rasults pertaining to the 11th house *par excellence.* (2) The sub-periods of planets associated with the 11th house in the major periods of planets, who are not associated with the 11th house, will produce results pertaining to the 11th house only to a limited extent. (3) Similarly the sub-periods of planets who are not associated with the 11th house in the major periods of planets who are associated with the 11th lord will produce results pertaining to the 11th house only to a feeble degree.

The factors capable of influencing the 11th house are :—

(a) Lord of the 11th house—Mars ;

(b) planet or planets aspecting the 11th house—Saturn and Jupiter ;

(c) planet or planets posited in the 11th house—the Sun, Mercury and Rahu ;

(d) planet or planets aspecting the lord of the 11th house —Jupiter.

(e) planet or planets in association with the lord of the 11th huose—nil ; and

(f) lord of the 11th house from the Moon—Venus.

24

Chart No. 209.—*Born 29–4–1948 at 9–48 a.m. (I S.T.) at 12 N 52, 74 E 53.*

	Sun Mercury Rahu		Venus Lagna		Mars Ketu		Jupiter
			Sat.	Sat.			
	RASI			Lagna	NAVAMSA		
	G.IV-106		Mars				
Moon Jupiter		Ketu			Moon	Venus Rahu	Sun Mercury

Balance of Venus Dasa at birth :   2 years, 10 months and 6 days.

Therefore in this chart Mars, Saturn, Jupiter, Mercury, the Sun, Rahu and Venus are capable of producing the results of the 11th house much more than the remaining planets. The sub-period of Jupiter in the major period of Rahu was important in the life of the native. It was during this period that the native started his own business having given up his job some months before.

Nature of the Results

The exact nature of results produced by a planet who is capable of influencing the 11th houss in its Dasa (major period) or Bhukti (sub-period) is qualified by its ownership, aspect and position. The general principles enunciated with regard to other Bhavas hold good here also.

The following results are likely in the Dasas of the different planets with reference to the 11th Bhava. *The Sun :* The native succeeds in his ventures without much effort. He will become famous and as a result many enemies will spring up. He acquires through fair means. *The Moon :* The person will get children. He will cultivate interest in literary and artistic pursuits. He will have a good reputation and will be charitable. He will earn through lands. *Mars :* The native's education will fare well. He acquries property and influence. But he will indulge in crafty schemes. *Mercury :* The person acquires knowledge of mathematics and astrology. He gets famous for his scientific studies and discoveries. He succeeds in trade. *Jupiter :* The person will be fond of music. He will be a good statesman. He will be religious and God-fearing. But will be slightly dependent on others and will get many good friends. *Venus :* The native will acquire conveyances. His friends will increase. He will earn through the theatre, dance, music and women. *Saturn :* The native's education will be disrupted. He will take part in political activity and succeed in politics. He acquires lands and other immovable properties. *Rahu :* The native becomes a leader of the lower classes. He acquires wealth and earns through farming and agriculture. He will go abroad. *Ketu :* The native will be happy and intelligent. He will be full of mirth and will travel to many places in great comfort. But he will be licentious and wanting in scruples.

Predictions regarding acquisition of money should be made after assessing the strength of the 11th house and the 11th lord and the source of acquisition can be judged from the planet in the 11th house or the planet associating with the

11th lord.   During the major and sub-periods of these planets, gain of wealth can be anticipated.

The following results are likely during the Dasa of the lord of the 11th house :

During the major period of the lord of the eleventh house when he is placed in the Ascendant with the Ascendant lord, one leads a happy and prosperous life. If the 11th lord is related to the 10th lord, he has a successful career. His merit is recognised and he gains many distinctions. If related to the 2nd house or lord, his business fares well and fetches him huge profits. If afflicted, he may lose an elder brother. Or, an elder brother may suffer many troubles and bad health.

If the lord of the eleventh occupies the 2nd with the 2nd lord, the native earns large sums of money. If Mars and the Sun are involved, prosperity as a dentist or throat specialist is shown, 9th and 2nd lords with the 11th lord in exaltation or own vargas, makes one a millionaire. If the 11th lord is in the 6th, the 8th or the 12th from Navamsa Lagna, results will be moderate.

Lord of the eleventh in the 3rd with the 3rd lord gives one both elder and younger co-borns. He will take on his brothers as partners in business and secure much wealth. Ability of writing will be acquired. If malefics afflict the 11th lord, the native's brother incurs losses and suffers in other ways. The native will have to face obstacles from competitors in his field of activity.

If the lords of the eleventh house occupies the 4th house with the 4th lord, one will be fortunate in his mother. She will be a cultured and refined lady who will influence the native greatly. He will acquire an excellent education during this period, will become famous and will get many awards and distinctions. He will also earn through lands, vehicles, houses and be very happy. Domestic harmony and bliss will prevail.

If the lord of the eleventh house is posited in the fifth house with the 5th lord, the native progresses fast in his spiritual sadhana. He will have excellent children. He will earn through investment (crops, edibles and drinks, depending upon the nature of sign and planets involved). Malefics here cause, during the period of the 11th lord. death of a child or intense mental anguish on account of one's progeny. Great anxiety and monetary loss due to a child may happen. Troubles will be minimised if the 11th lord is well fortified in the Navamsa.

Lord of the eleventh in the 6th with the 6th lord enables the native to succeed as a lawyer and through litigation. He will be generally healthy during the entire period. No amount of skill or treachery on the part of his ill-wishers can do him any harm. His earnings will be good. The bussiness of a maternal uncle or a close relative may fall in his favour. If afflicted, the native suffers from troubles in the legs, expenditure on medical bills and law-suits.

Lord of the eleventh in the 7th with the lord of the 7th gives one a rich wife. If the Sun is strong, he may go abroad as an ambassador. He will have many powerful and influential friends, and will engage himself in partnership ventures which may prove successful. If malefics afflict the 11th lord, both the native and his wife seek to earn money by questionable means. If Lagna lord is strong but the 7th house is weak, the native's wife may desert him.

If the lord of the eleventh joins the 8th lord in the 8th house, one suffers from pecuniary losses and incurs mounting debts. His business will not thrive well. He will suffer mental aberration and domestic disharmony. He will, however, succeed in small ventures engaging manual labour. His sense of right and wrong will be warped and he will be forced to indulge in unrighteous acts. He will also suffer from bodily weakness and pain.

Lord of the eleventh in the 9th house with the 9th lord indicates exalted and aristocratic father and background. He hails from a rich family and will continue the family business extend it beyond expectations. He will have a colourful social life and move on equal terms with rulers and other dignitaries. His regard for religion will increase and he will be virtuous and of good conduct. Foreign collaboration in business may bring the native both distinction and money.

Lord of the eleventh in the 10th with the lord of the 10th confers a highly successful and distinguished career. The native will have more than one occupation, the nature of the planet involved determining the nature of his means of earning. If malefics afflict the 10th, the native no doubt becomes powerful and rich, but he will be unscrupulous indulging in every kind of despicable act to achieve his ends. If the affliction is heavy, the native will be known for his monstrous nature and suffer grave repercussions. He may lose all his wealth and power.

If the lord of the 11th house occupies the eleventh, the native succeeds without much effort. Fair in his dealings and earning the goodwill of the people, he will be a dutiful son. Money will be spent only on legitimate account and for charitable purposes. The native's elder brother will be a very famous person. If Jupiter is the 11th lord, the native's business will be connected with books, publishing, religion and charity ; if

Saturn   it will be through industries, brick-kilns, printing press, hardware business, oil refineries, quarries, etc. ; if Venus — earnings will be through women, hoteliering, cosmetics, show-business, films, coffee, beverages and art ; if Mercury — writing, teaching, educational and research foundations and similar sources ; if Mars — financial dividends through drugs, chemicals, lands, timber, orchards, minerals, metals, match-sticks, sports goods and sports ; if the Sun – earnings through photography, hereditary professions, wool industry, gold and jewellery, banking, auditing and the stock-exchange ; if the Moon — farm · ing, milk-dairy, wines, coffee and snack bars, pearls and fish.

Lord of the 11th house in the twelfth with the ruler of the 12th house gives losses through varied expenditure. If malefics afflict the 12th house, wealth will be squandered. The elder brother of the native may pass through a troubled phase suffering much monetary loss.   The 11th lord in the 6th, 8th or 12th from Navamsa Lagna makes the native run into debts.

Let us study a few examples relating to the eleventh house.

Brothers

Although there is no karaka as such for elder brothers Mars who is the karaka for 'brothers' according to Vaidyanatha Dikshitar and other classical writers can also be considered for the 11th house.   Benefic aspects and associations on the 11th house give elder brothers and ensure their happiness and long life .   Malefic aspects and associations on the 11th house and 11th lord deny elder brothers or give them short lives or other-wise mar their prosperity.   When the 11th lord is in the 6th, 8th or 12th house and if Mars is afflicted, the native may not have any elder brother or may lose him by death.

According to one theory a native may have as many elder co-borns as the number of planets taken together in the 11th and 12th houses. This rule cannot be applied verbatim. It is subject to qualifications and students should test its veracity for themselves,

Chart No. 210.—*Born 16-8-1937 at 8-31 a.m. at (I.S.T.) at 13 N, 77 E 35.*

Saturn		Ketu	Venus		Sun Venus		Ketu
				Lagna			
	RASI				NAVAMSA		
			Sun Merc	Moon			
	G.I-10						
Jupiter	Mars Rahu Moon		Lagna	Jupit. Merc. Rahu		Mars Saturn	

Balance of Mercury's Dasa at birth: 6 years, 0 month and 8 days.

The Eleventh House: In Chart No. 210 Cancer, a fruitful sign, is the 11th house neither aspected nor occupied by any planet.

The Eleventh Lord: The Moon is debilitated in the 3rd house with 3rd and 8th lord Mars and Rahu. In Navamsa, the Moon occupies the 12th from Navamsa Lagna aspected by 3rd Mars. The Moon is badly afflicted.

Karaka: Mars is in his own house with 11th lord the Moon and Rahu.

Considered from the Moon : The 11th house is Virgo and the 11th lord Mercury is in the 12th therefrom with the 12th lord the Sun. Saturn, a malefic, aspects the 11th house.

Conclusion : The native has no surviving elder brother. The association of karaka Mars with the 11th lord Moon gave one elder brother. The afflictions to the 11th house and 11th lord are quite severe both from Lagna and the Moon without any benefic aspects. The aspect of Jupiter on the 11th lord from the Moon did not deprive the native totally of an elder brother but the afflictions did not let him live long. But he died in the native's Venus Dasa, Saturn Bhukti. Venus, the Dasa lord, is in the 12th from the 11th house and is the 7th and 12th lord from the 11th lord Moon. The Bhukti lord is the 7th lord from the 11th house and a natural maraka.

The Eleventh House : Aries the 11th house in Chart No. 211 is occupied by debilitated 8th and 9th lord Saturn and 7th and 10th lord Jupiter. It is hemmed in between malefics Ketu on one side and the Sun and Mercury on the other.

The Eleventh Lord : Mars ruling the 11th occupies the Lagna with Venus, 5th and 12th lord, and is aspected by debilitated Saturn. He is exalted in the 3rd house in Navamsa aspected by well-placed Moon.

Karaka : Mars is also the 11th lord placed with a benefic Venus and aspected by malefic Saturn.

Considered from the Moon : The 11th house is Virgo occupied by Rahu and aspected by the 6th lord Mars. The 11th lord Mercury is in the 7th from the Moon with the 12th lord the Sun. He is between both malefics (Saturn and Mars) and benefics (Jupiter and Venus).

Conclusion : The native has an elder sister while an elder brother died. Jupiter in the 11th is welcome but 8th lord

Chart No. 211.—*Born 21-5-1940 at 7-50 a.m. (I.S.T.) at 13 N 77, E 35.*

Ketu	Jupiter Saturn	Sun Mercury	Lagna Mars Venus	Sun Venus Merc.			Jupiter
							Moon
	RASI			Ketu	NAVAMSA		
				Mars			Rahu Saturn
	GI-12						
	Moon		Rahu	Lagna			

Balance of Jupiter's Dasa at birth :   1 year, 6 months and 22 days.

Saturn debilitated there and the *papakartari* to the 11th house does not augur well for elder co-borns. The 11th lord Mars associating with benefic Venus who is a female planet has given an elder sister. Malefic Saturn afflicting the male planet Jupiter in the 11th house has killed the elder brother. The death occurred in Mercury Dasa, Ketu Bhukti. Dasa lord Mercury is in the 2nd from the 11th house in a constellation ruled by the Sun who is also in a *marakasthana*. Mercury is also in the 12th from the 11th lord Mars. The Bhukti lord Ketu is in the 12th from the 11th house. He is in a sign ruled by Jupiter who is in the 11th house but afflicted by malefic Saturn.

In Chart No, 210, the number of planets in the 11th and 12th from the Lagna is two (the Sun and Mercury in the 12th)

while from the Moon it is nil. The average would be one
who, due to the heavy afflictions, died.

In Chart No. 211, the total number of planets in the 11th
(Jupiter and Saturn) and the 12th (the Sun and Mercury) from
Lagna is four while from the Moon it is nil, Rahu being
ignored, as a shadowy planet. The average would be 2 which
gave the native two elder-borns. In Chart No. 210, the 11th
lord Moon is in the 12th from Navamsa aspected by a malefic
Mars while in Chart No. 211, the 11th lord Mars is exalted in
the 3rd from Navamsa Lagna aspected by a benefic Moon,
allowing one elder co-born to survive.

The Eleventh House : In Chart No, 212 Libra, a fruitful
sign, rises on the 11th house. It is occupied by Lagna lord
Jupiter, Mars, Venus and the Moon. It is hemmed between
Ketu on one side and the Sun and Mercury on the other side.
It is quite strong.

The Eleventh Lord : Venus occupies the 11th, his moola-
trikona with benefics, Jupiter, Mars and the Moon. He is in
Gemini in Navamsa with the Moon and aspected by Jupiter.
Venus becomes very powerful.

Karaka : Mars occupies the 11th house with benefics
Jupiter, 11th lord Venus and the Moon and is also between
Ketu and the Sun—Mercury.

Considered from the Moon : The 11th house is Leo
hemmed between Saturn and the Sun while the 11th lord Sun
occupies the 12th house with exalted 9th and 12th lord
Mercury. He is aspected by Yogakaraka Saturn.

Conclusion : The native has 3 elder co-borns surviving
while one elder brother died. The presence of benefics in the
11th house and the 11th lord Venus beneficially disposed with
the fertile Moon are responsible for the elder co-borns. The

Chart No. 212.—*Born 29-9-1946 at 11-58 a.m. (I.S.T.) at 13 N, 77 E 35.*

		Rahu				Lagna Sun	Venus Moon
			Sat.	Ketu	NAVAMSA		
	RASI						Mercury Rahu
	GI-20			Mars			
Lagna	Ketu	Jupiter Mars Venus Moon	Sun Merc.	Jupit.	Saturn		

Balance of Jupiter's Dasa at birth : 5 years, 5 months and 1 day.

11th house is occupied by karaka Mars while the 11th house from the Moon is between malefics resulting in the death of a brother. The death occurred in the Sun's Bhukti of Saturn's Dasa. Both the Dasa and Bhukti lords cause a *papakartari yoga* to the 11th house from the Moon. In addition, the Dasa lord Saturn is the 7th lord from the 11th and placed in the 12th therefrom. The Sun is with the 2nd lord in the 2nd house from the 11th house.

There are four planets in the 11th house from Lagna and two planets in the 12th from the Moon. The average would be 3 indicative of the surviving co-borns. Also, the strongest planet in the 11th house is the 5th lord Mars who occupies his exaltation sign in a trine in Navamsa. Mars is in the 4th Navamsa indicating 4 elder co-borns. Malefic Saturn aspecting Mars destroys one elder co-born.

Chart No. 213—*Born 6-1-1974 at 12-40 noon (I.S.T.) at 13 N, 77 E 35.*

	Lagna Mars	Moon	Ketu Sat			Lagna	Rahu	Venus
		RASI				NAVAMSA		Mars Moon
Jupiter Venus		G.II-204						Jupiter Sun
Sun Mercury Rahu					Sat.	Ketu	Mercury	

Balance of Moon's Dasa at birth : 0 year, 11 months and 16 days.

The Eleventh House : It is not occupied or aspected by any planet in Chart No. 213.

The Eleventh Lord : Saturn is in the 3rd house aspected by 3rd lord Mercury and 5th lord the Sun. Saturn is with Ketu and blemished.

Karaka : Mars occupies a quadrant from Lagna, his own sign and is not aspected by any planet. He is debilitated in Cancer in Navamsa and associated with the sign-lord Moon.

Considered from the Moon : The eleventh is Pisces aspected by Saturn while the 11th lord Jupiter is debilitated in the 9th Moon-sign lord Venus.

Conclusion : The 11th lord Saturn in the 3rd house aspected by the Sun and Merecury and with Ketu, and Saturn aspecting the 11th house from the Moon give limited number of elder co-borns. The Moon's influence on karaka Mars in

Navamsa cannot deny elder co-borns. The native has a lone
surviving elder sister.

Chart No. 214. — *Born 30-12-1943 at 9-19 p.m. (L.M.T.)
at 27 N 36, 75 E 15.*

		Mars	Sat.			Jupiter Ketu Mars	
Moon			Rahu	Merc.			Lagna
	RASI				NAVAMSA		
Mercury Ketu	G II-64		Lagna Jupit.				Venus Sun
Sun	Venus				Rahu Moon	Saturn	

Balance of Mars Dasa at birth : 0 year, 10 months and
19 days.

The Eleventh House : In Chart No. 212 Gemini the 11th
is occupied by 6th and 7th lord Saturn and aspected by the
Lagna lord the Sun. The 11th is hemmed between malefics
Mars and Rahu.

The Eleventh Lord : Mercury is in the 6th house with Ketu.
He occupies the 8th house in Navamsa aspected by the Sun
and Venus.

Karaka : Mars occupies the 10th house aspected by 10th
lord Venus.

Considered from the Moon : The 11th is occupied by the
7th lord the Sun and aspected by 11th lord Jupiter, Moon-sign
lord Saturn and karaka Mars.

Conclusion : Saturn's influence as a malefic lord on the 11th house must give a limited number of elder brothers. The aspect of the Sun on the 11th house prevents denial of elder co-borns. The native has one elder brother.

Chart No. 215.—*Born 26–2–1953 at 9–20 p.m. (I.S T.) at 13 N, 77 E 35.*

Venus Mercury Mars	Jupiter			Venus		
Sun		Ketu Moon	Ketu Sun	NAVAMSA		
Rahu	RASI		Moon Mars			Rahu Mercury
	G II-78					
		Saturn	Lagna		Saturn Jupiter	Lagna

Balance of Mercury's Dasa at birth : 7 years, 10 months and 26 days.

The Eleventh House : Cancer, a fruitful and feminine sign, happens to be the 11th occupied by Ketu and sign-lord the Moon in Chart No. 215. It is aspected by exalted 5th and 6th lord Saturn.

The Eleventh Lord : The Moon is in his own sign in the 11th with Ketu aspected by exalted Saturn. The Moon occupies Capricorn Navamsa with karaka Mars exalted and aspected by sign-lord Saturn.

Karaka : Mars occupies the 7th house with Yogakaraka Venus exalted and *vargottama* and Lagna lord Mercury.

Considered from the Moon : Taurus is the 11th. It is neither aspected nor occupied by any planet. The 11th lord Venus is powerfully placed in a feminine sign with Mars and Mercury.

Conclusion : The predominance of feminine signs and the powerful influence of Venus on the karaka has given more elder sisters than brothers. The native has 3 elder sisters and one elder brother. The Moon is aspected by exalted Saturn which has prevented more elder co-borns warranted by the other planetary factors. The 11th lord Moon has gained 7 Navamsas but it aspected by 5th and 6th lord Saturn, a malefic in dignity. This has, therefore, instead of killing any co-borns, reduced their number to 5 in all (including the native himself). The Moon in Navamsa is acted upon by 2 malefics, Mars and Saturn, reducing the total number by 2.

Chart No. 216.—*Born 12–5–1925 at 7-30 a·m. (I.S.T.) at 13 N 04, 80 E 17.*

	Mercury Sun	Venus Lagna	Mars	Sat.		Mercury	Ketu
			Rahu	Venus			
	RASI			Jupit Mars	**NAVAMSA**		Lagna
Ketu Jupiter	GD-127						
Moon		Saturn		Sat. Rahu			Moon

Balance of Venus Dasa at birth : 13 years, 9 months and 9 days.

The Eleventh House :   In Chart No. 216 Pisces the 11th is neither occupied nor aspected by any planet.

The Eleventh Lord :   Jupiter is debilitated in the 9th house and afflicted by Ketu. He is aspected adversely by the 7th and 12th lord Mars.

Karaka :   Mars is in the 2nd house aspected by 3rd lord the Moon from the 8th house. In Navamsa he is exalted and joins debilitated Jupiter.

Considered from the Moon :   The 11th house is occupied by exalted Saturn 3rd lord and aspected by 7th and 10th lord Mercury and the exalted 9th lord Sun. It is superficially well disposed. Venus, the 11th lord, occupies his own sign Taurus aspected by Moon-sign lord Jupiter.

Conclusion :   The 11th lord Jupiter is debilitated and obtains *neechabhanga* but is eclipsed by Ketu. Mars, the karaka, no doubt aspects him but adversely. Further the 11th house from the Moon being influenced by powerful planets is nevertheless not free from affliction.   The Sun and Saturn, both powerful malefics, influence it in mutual aspect destroying it. The 11th lord Venus is subjected to a heavy *papakartari yoga* caused by the Sun and Mars.   The karaka Mars is aspected by the Moon but from a *dusthana.* These factors have all contributed to deny the native any co-borns, elder or younger. He is the only son of his parents.

The 11th lord Jupiter has gained only one Navamsa deny-ing the native any elder brothers. In addition, Jupiter occupies a *dusthana* in the Navamsa chart. So does karaka Mars.

Gains

The 11th house rules gains. These may be financial gains mostly but they also include gains by way of taking over
25

management of property, acquisition of a post of honour, trusteeship, respect of distinction and inheritance of properties. Jupiter, Dhanakaraka, can also be taken as the karaka for *labha* or gains.

The Dasa of a weak or depressed planet causes loss of 'labha' or gains. The 11th house necessarily comprises the 2nd also so that timing of results due to benefic dispositions or afflictions to the 11th house will have to be made taking into account the 2nd house factors as well.

Thus a person acquires gains in the periods (major period or sub-period) of the planet or planets in the 11th house, the 11th lord or of the planet or planets aspecting the 11th house or 11th lord. The same result may also be expected in the major period or sub-period of the planet occupying the 2nd house, the planet aspecting it or of the planet owning it.

Conversely, a person suffers loss of the 11th Bhava significations during the periods of the planets cited above and which are afflicted by malefic planets, or are combust or depressed, eclipsed or with inimical planets.

Gains may also be predicted in the following Dasas (major periods) and Bhuktis (minor periods) :—(a) Lords of the 2nd and 5th houses or the 2nd and 11th houses if they have mutually exchanged places ; (b) lords of the 5th and 9th when they are in the 5th and 9th respectively.

If the 11th lord is associated with the 12th lord, loss can be expected during their mutual periods. If the Lagna lord, 4th and 9th lords are in the 8th house, financial stress is possible during the major and minor periods of these planets. If the 5th lord is in the 8th house or the 8th lord occupies the 5th house, then also losses can occur.

Chart No. 217.—*Born 28–10–1922 at 8–40 p.m. (I.S.T.) at 9 N 55, 78 E 7.*

Ketu	Lagna		Mars		
Moon Mars	RASI GD-135		Rahu / Sun	NAVAMSA	Saturn / Ketu Mercury Lagna Moon
Venus	Jupiter Sun	Rahu Sat Merc.	Jupit. Venus		

Balance of Mars Dasa at birth : 6 years, 1 month and 17 days.

The Eleventh House : In Chart No. 217 Pisces is the 11th house aspected by 9th and 10th lord Saturn and 2nd and 5th lord exalted Mercury and occupied by Ketu. It is strongly disposed.

The Eleventh Lord : Jupiter lord of the 11th is in the 6th from Lagna in an inimical sign with debilitated Sun. The Sun's debility is cancelled by Venus occupying a kendra from Lagna. Apparently the 11th lord is not very strongly placed. But his occupation of a constellation ruled by Rahu who, in turn, is strongly placed in the 5th house strengthens him. In Navamsa, Jupiter is well placed in his own sign.

Karaka : Jupiter occupies an inimical sign in the 6th house with debilitated Sun and the same discussion as above applies since the karaka is also the 11th lord in this case.

Considered from the Moon : The 11th house is Scorpio occupied by an excellent benefic and yogakaraka Venus. The 11th house is aspected by Saturn lord of the Moon-sign and the 2nd lord therefrom. Saturn is in conjunction with exalted 9th lord Mercury. The 11th lord Mars is exalted in the Moon-sign with the 7th lord Moon generating a Sasi-Mangala Yoga.

Conclusion : Note the powerful Dhana Yoga in Chart No. 217 generated by exalted 2nd and 5th lord Mercury combined with Yogakaraka Saturn in a trine in the 5th house and with Rahu. The chart is strongly placed for financial gains. The 11th house being aspected by Mercury and Rahu and Saturn has given the native engineering (Mercury and Rahu) industries (Saturn) worth several crores.

Chart No. 218.—*Born 18-4-1904 at 5-57 p.m. (L.M.T) at 25 N 18, 83 E 0.*

Jupiter Venus Ketu	Sun Mars Mercury	Moon		Moon			Sun
Saturn	RASI			Rahu	NAVAMSA		Ketu
	GD-129			Jupit.			
		Lagna	Rahu		Venus Mercury	Lagna	Mars Saturn

Balance of Sun's Dasa at birth : 1 year, 0 month and 13 days.

The Eleventh House : In Chart No. 218 Leo the 11th house is neither aspected nor occupied by any planet.

The Eleventh Lord : The Sun occupies a kendra in exaltation joining the 2nd lord Mars and 9th lord Mercury. The Sun is well placed.

Karaka : Jupiter occupies his own sign in company with exalted Lagna lord.   His malefic lordship is turned into a benefic yoga by his association as 3rd and 6th lord with exalted 8th lord Venus in the 6th house generating a partial Vipareeta Raja Yoga enhanced further by the aspect of Yogakaraka Saturn.

Considered from the Moon : The 11th house is Pisces occupied by the 11th lord,   exalted Moon-sign lord Venus and Ketu and is aspected by Yogakaraka (9th and 10th lord) Saturn from his own house.

Conclusion : The powerful combination of the 2nd, 7th, 9th and 11th lords in the 7th house, a kendra, has generated

Chart No. 219.—*Born 30–7–1863 at 2 p m. (L.M.T.) at 42 N 5, 83 W 5.*

	Ketu		Ketu Saturn		Mars
RASI	Sun Merc.		NAVAMSA		Moon Lagna
Moon	Mars	Venus			
NH-38					
Rahu Lagna	Venus Jupit. Sat.		Sun	Mercury Rahu	Jupiter

Balance of the Moon's Dasa at birth : 2 years, 4 months and 6 days.

a very strong yoga for gains. The same situation obtains from the Moon-sign also. The native is a newspaper magnet with editions in different parts of the country.

The Eleventh House : In Chart No. 219 Virgo is the 11th house occupied by 2nd and 5th lord Jupiter, 3rd and 4th lord Saturn and 7th and 12th lord Venus in debility. Venus gets neechabhanga since his sign dispositor Mercury is in the 7th house from the Moon. The 11th house is fortified.

The Eleventh Lord : Mercury occupies the 9th house with 10th lord Sun aspected by a powerful 9th lord Moon.

Karaka : Jupiter is also the 2nd and 5th lord placed in the 11th with Saturn and Venus.

Considered from the Moon : The 11th house Scorpio is occupied by Rahu and aspected by 11th lord Mars and Moon-sign lord Saturn. The 11th lord Mars is in the 8th from the Moon. The 11th house is strong and the 11th lord is not weak being in Leo.

Conclusion : Saturn in the 11th is significant as giving gains through mines, iron, labour and so on. Jupiter, lord of wealth, is suggestive of influx of wealth. Vahanakaraka Venus advanced the fortune of the native through the manufacture and sale of automobiles The 2nd and 5th lord in the 11th aspecting the 9th lord, Full Moon, in turn aspected by 11th lord Mercury resulted in fabulous gains to the native.

The advent of Jupiter Dasa advanced the fortunes of the native. Jupiter is the 2nd and 5th lord placed in the 11th house and so the Dasa and Bhukti of the 2nd and 5th lord paved the way for the native's future gains. It was in Mars Bhukti, Jupiter Dasa that the native founded an automobile manufacturing company. The sub lord Mars is the Lagna lord placed in the 10th house. He also owns the 11th from the Moon. The subsequent Dasas of Saturn (11th occupant) and Mercury (11th lord) continued to add immensely to the native's position, wealth and influence.

Chart No. 220. - *Born 7–4–1893 at 9–31 a.m. (L.M.T.) at 20 N 56, 75 E 55.*

Sun Venus Mercury	Rahu Jupiter	Mars	Lagna			Moon	Mars	Saturn Rahu
	RASI			Sun		NAVAMSA		Jupiter
	NH-62			Venus				
Moon		Ketu	Sat.	Ketu	Mercury	Lagna		

Balance of Ketu Dasa at birth : 6 years, 4 months and 4 days.

The Eleventh House : In Chart No 220 the 11th house is Aries occupied by Rahu and the 7th and 10th lord Jupiter. It is not aspected by any planet and quite strong.

The Eleventh Lord : Mars occupies the 12th house but is *vargottama*. He is also not aspected by any planet.

Karaka : Jupiter is with Rahu in the 11th house and exalted in Navamsa gaining strength thereby.

Considered from the Moon : The 11th house is Libra aspected by Jupiter lord of Chandra Lagna. It is occupied by Ketu. Venus the 11th lord from the Moon is exalted and occupies the 4th with the 9th lord Sun and the 7th and 10th lord Mercury aspected by 2nd and 3rd lord Saturn. Mercury is debilitated but gets cancellation of debility due to his occupation of a kendra both from Lagna and the Moon.

Conclusion : The native of Chart No. 220, born in humble circumstances, became a big industrialist and one of the wealthiest men in the country. Financial gains depend not only on the 11th house but also on a strong Lagna, the 9th (fortune), the 10th (profession) and the 2nd (wealth) houses. There is a blending of all these significations both from Lagna and Chandra Lagna. Mercury is in the 10th in a kendra from the 2nd lord Moon in association with exalted 5th lord Venus and aspected by Saturn, lord of the 9th or house of fortune. The 10th lord Jupiter is in the 11th with Rahu who rules over industries and aspects the 2nd lord Moon. From Chandra Lagna also, the 2nd, 9th, 10th and 11th houses are all fortified. The Moon is aspected by its sign-lord Jupiter and 5th lord Mars. The 2nd lord Saturn is in the 10th aspected by 9th lord Sun, 10th lord Mercury and 11th lord Venus—an ideal combination denoting immense wealth.

The native started Sugar Mills in the Moon's Dasa. The Moon is lord of the 2nd and occupies the 7th aspected by Jupiter lord of the 10th and Mars lord of the 11th. In Mars Dasa, the native started cement industry. Mars is the 11th lord. In Jupiter's Bhukti of Rahu Dasa, the native purchased a big managing agency comprising of airways, coal mines, etc. Both the Dasa and Bhukti lords are in the 11th house.

The Eleventh House : In Chart No. 221 Libra, being the 11th house, is occupied by an exalted 2nd lord Saturn. It is not aspected by any planet. The 11th house is very strong.

The Eleventh Lord : Venus occupies Lagna with 5th lord Mars and is aspected by exalted 2nd lord Saturn from the 11th house. Venus gets highly fortified.

Chart No. 221.—*Born   30/31-1-1896   at   4-30 a.m.*
(L.M.T.) at 22 N 20, 73 E.

RASI				NAVAMSA			
			Moon Jupit.				Sun Venus Saturn
Mercury Rahu				Moon			Mars Ketu
Sun			Ketu	Rahu			
Lagna Mars Venus		Saturn			Mercury	Jupiter	Lagna

(RASI center: NH-67)

Balance of Mercury's Dasa at birth : 5 year's, 1 month and 6 days.

Karaka : Jupiter is also the Lagna lord exalted in the 8th house with the 8th lord and aspected by 9th lord the Sun and 2nd lord exalted Saturn. This indicates a sudden windfall in life.

Considered from the Moon : Taurus, a sign ruled by Venus, is the 11th house. It is not occupied by or aspected by any planet. The 11th lord Venus occupies the 6th with Yoga-karaka Mars and aspected by exalted Saturn lord of the 7th. The 11th house is quite strongly disposed.

Conclusion : The 2nd lord Saturn is exalted in the 11th house (gains). The 2nd house is occupied by 9th lord Sun aspected by an exalted Ascendant lord Jupiter and the Moon forming a Gajakesari Yoga. The Lagna and 9th lords are mutually aspecting and the 11th lord Venus and 2nd lord Saturn are interrelated forming a strong yoga for gains. The native of

Chart No. 221 was an industrialist having to do with labour, iron, steel, aluminium factories, etc. Saturn has predominantly to do with labour so that gain through employing labour on a large scale was the important source of wealth.

The Eleventh House : In Chart No. 222 Taurus the 11th is not occupied. But it is aspected by 2nd lord Sun, 5th lord Mars and 9th lord Jupiter.

The Eleventh Lord : Venus is in the 5th house with 7th lord Saturn, 3rd and 12th lord Mercury and Rahu.

Karaka : Jupiter is a benefic lord as well and occupies the 5th house, a trine, with 2nd lord the Sun and 5th lord Mars. In Navamsa he is exalted and becomes very powerful.

Considered from the Moon : The Moon is in Virgo. The 11th lord is the Moon himself. He is aspected by 5th lord Saturn. The 11th house is aspected by 4th and 7th lord

Chart No. 222.—*Born 26-11-1899 at 10–27 p.m. (L.M.T.) at 10 N 50, 79 E 36*

			Ketu		Rahu Saturn Venus Mercury		
			Lagna	Mars			Saturn
	RASI			Lagna Moon	NAVAMSA		
	RP-2/180						
Rahu Mercury Venus Saturn	Sun Mars Jupiter		Moon		Sun	Ketu	

Balance of the Sun's Dasa at birth : 4 years, 2 months and 9 days.

Jupiter.   The 2nd and 9th lord Venus, lord of Moon-sign and the 10th therefrom, *viz.,* Mercury and the 5th lord Saturn have all combined in a quadrant.

The native grew very rich with many investments and businesses but could not come anywhere near the financial level of Chart Nos. 221 and 222.   Though the 11th house and other factors bearing on it are quite well placed they are not particularly strong.   The 11th house being Taurus, the native amassed a fortune through soaps.   Mars and Rahu Dasa saw the native build his soap-business into a national monopoly. Mars is a Yogakaraka and joins the 9th and 2nd lord, Jupiter and the Sun respectively, in the 5th house (investments). Rahu occupies a Jupiterian sign and should therefore give his results.

Chart No. 223.—*Born 3-6-1939 at 10-30 p.m. (I.S.T.) at 24 N 51, 67 E 4.*

Jupiter	Saturn Venus Ketu	Mercury Sun			Mars	Saturn Mercury	Moon
				Rahu			Sun
	RASI				NAVAMSA		
Mars							Ketu
	RP-F/278						
Lagna Moon		Rahu		Lagna	Venus	Jupiter	

Balance of Ketu Dasa at birth :   2 years and 3 months.

The Eleventh House :   In Chart No. 223 Libra the 11th is occupied by Rahu and aspected by the 11th lord Venus and

the 2nd lord Saturn.   Saturn is debilitated but gets cancellation
of debility due to his exaltation and debilitation lords, Mars
and Venus, being in mutual kendras.

The Eleventh Lord :   Venus is the 11th lord.   He is in the
5th with the 2nd lord Saturn and also Ketu and is aspected by
exalted 5th lord Mars.   The 2nd and the 5th lords having
exchanged signs and involving 11th lord Venus fortify him.

Karaka :   Jupiter is the Lagna lord and occupies his own
sign in a quadrant.   He is favourably disposed due to his
lordship of both Rasi and Navamsa Lagnas.

Considered from the Moon :   The same picture emerges,
the Moon being in Lagna.

Conclusion :   The Lagna is *vargottama.*   The Lagna lord
Jupiter occupies his own sign in the 4th house.   In addition,
Jupiter becomes extremely powerful securing his own vargas
4 timse out of 5.   The interrelationship between the 2nd lord
Saturn, the 5th lord Mars, and the 11th lord Venus involving
all the three houses as well as generated a powerful Dhana
Yoga.   Rahu in the 11th made the native own a chain of
industries.

The Eleventh House :   In Chart No. 224 Libra the 11th
house is neither occupied nor aspected by any planet.   It has
no afflictions.

The Eleventh Lord :   Venus occupies the 3rd house aspected by the lord of the 2nd and the 3rd, Saturn, and 5th lord
Mars.   He is with the 7th and the 10th lord Mercury, and
well fortified.

Karaka :   Jupiter is well placed in Lagna which happens
to be his moolatrikona sign.   He is in association with the
2nd lord Saturn.   Further he occupies the constellation of the
11th lord Venus.

Chart No. 224.– *Born 22–3–1901 at 1–29 a.m. (I.S.T.) at 27 N 57, 68 E 40.*

Sun Moon	Ketu		Moon Merc.	Mars		Venus
Mercury Venus	RASI		Ketu	NAVAMSA		
		Mars				Rahu
Saturn Jupiter Lagna	G.IV-94 Rahu			Saturn		Lagna Jupiter Sun

Balance of Mercury's Dasa at birth : 2 years, 8 months and 26 days.

Considered from the Moon : The 11th house Capricorn is hemmed between benefics Jupiter on one side and Mercury and Venus on the other. It is neither occupied nor aspected by any planet. The 11th lord Saturn is with the Moon and the 10th lord Jupiter is in his own sign.

Conclusion : The association of the 11th lord Venus with Mercury has given the native considerable earnings through the business of money lending. The 11th lord Venus, the 2nd lord Saturn and the 5th lord Mars are all interrelated generating a powerful Dhana Yoga. Further the association of karaka Jupiter with the 2nd lord in the constellation of 11th lord Venus is favourable for acquisition of wealth.

The Eleventh House : In Chart No. 225 Leo the eleventh house is occupied by the 10th lord Moon and lord of the

Chart No. 225. —*Born 16–10–1892 at 7–12 a.m. (D.M.T.) at 13 N, 76 E.*

			Jupit. Ketu	Lagna	Saturn	
Jupiter	Rahu					
	RASI			NAVAMSA		Moon
Mars	GD-155	Moon Venus				
		Sun Mercury Ketu Lagna	Sat.	Merc.	Sun	Mars Venus Rahu

Balance of Ketu Dasa at birth : 1 year and 9 months.
Ascendant Venus. It is aspected by an exalted Mars, lord of the 2nd. It is fortified.

The Eleventh Lord : The Sun is the 11th lord. He is debilitated in the Ascendant but obtains cancellation of debility. He is also *vargottama* and joins the 9th lord Mercury and Ketu in Rasi.

Karaka : Jupiter is in his own sign Pisces, is *vargottama* and is aspected by Saturn lord of the 4th and 5th from the 12th house.

Considered from the Moon : The eleventh house is aspected by Saturn. The 11th lord Mercury joins the Sun lord of the Moon-sign, and Ketu in the 3rd house.

Conclusion : The eleventh house as well as karaka Jupiter are very favourably disposed. In addition, the Lagna lord Venus occupies his own constellation and is in *parivartana* with the 11th lord Sun, also strong due to neechabhanga and his *vargottama* position. The presence of karaka Jupiter in Pisces, a spiritual sign together with the aspect of Yoga karaka Saturn from the 12th house (mokshasthana) is of significance in as much as the native was the head of a religious Mutt. This is suggested by the 9th lord Mercury combining with the Atmakaraka Sun, which not only indicates great spirituality but also ascension to a seat of spiritual power and responsibility.

It was in 1912 in Mercury's Bhukti of Venus Dasa that the native was installed as a pontiff which, in addition to making him the spiritual head of millions, brought vast properties all over the country under his control. The Bhukti lord Mercury is the 9th lord combining with 11th lord Sun in Lagna while the Dasa lord Venus is the ruler of Lagna, placed in the 11th house in *parivartana* with 11th lord Sun. Venus, the

Chart No. 226. – *Born 26–5–1914 at 7-28 p.m. (I.S.T.) at 9 N 40, 78 E 37.*

		Sun Mercury Saturn	Moon Venus	Lagna Rahu	Sun		
Rahu Jupiter		RASI	Mars		NAVAMSA		
			Ketu	Mars			Mercury
	GD-165						
	Lagna			Venus		Moon Jupiter	Ketu Saturn

Balance of Mars Dasa at birth : 3 years, 4 months and 15 days.

Lagna lord, the 10th lord Moon and the 2nd lord Mars are all interrelated generating a formidable yoga for riches.

The Eleventh House : In Chart No. 226 the eleventh house is free from aspects and is not aspected by any planet.

The Eleventh Lord : Mercury owning the 11th occupies the 7th house, with 3rd and 4th lord Saturn and the 10th lord the Sun.

Karaka : Jupiter is in the 4th house aspected by Lagna lord Mars who, though debilitated, gets cancellation of debility. Jupiter is also aspected by 4th lord Saturn. The karaka is quite strong, though his association with Rahu blemishes him slightly.

Considered from the Moon : The lord of the 11th house Mars has neechabhanga. He occupies the 2nd house from the Moon and is aspected by the 9th lord Saturn. The 11th house and lord are considerably strong.

Conclusion : The Lagna lord in the 9th house and the 11th lord combining with the 10th lord in the 7th house give the chart much vitality. From the Moon, the 11th lord is powerfully placed signifying the devolution of a trusteeship of a spiritual centre and its administration on the native. This was in Saturn's Dasa, Saturn's Bhukti. The Dasa and Bhukti lord combines with the 11th lord Mercury and the 10th lord the Sun and reflects their results. The trusteeship has been the native's main occupation as indicated by the involvement of the 10th lord Sun with the planets in the 7th house.

The Eleventh House : In Chart No 227 Scorpio the 11th is occupied by Lagna lord Saturn. It is not aspected by any planet.

The Eleventh Lord : Mars, the 11th lord, is exalted in Lagna and has exchanged signs with the Lagna lord Saturn.

Chart No. 227.—*Born 21-4-1926 at 1-40 a.m. (G.M.T.) at 51, N 30, 0 W 5.*

Venus Mercury	Sun		Rahu
Jupiter	RASI		Moon
Mars Lagna	GD-139		
Ketu	Saturn		

			Rahu Sun
	NAVAMSA		Saturn
Lagna Venus Moon			
Ketu	Jupiter Mercury		Mars

Balance of Mercury's Dasa at birth :   11 years, 9 months and 23 days.

He is aspected by the 7th lord Moon.   The house and lord are both powerfully disposed.

Karaka : Jupiter occupies the 2nd house.

Considered from the Moon : The 11th house is Taurus. It is aspected by the 7th lord Saturn while the 11th lord Venus is exalted in the 9th house with Mercury, lord of the 3rd and 12th houses.

Conclusion : The exchange of signs between Lagna and the 11th lords and the 11th lord in exaltation is of great significance.   Mars occupies his own constellation and forms a *sasimangala yoga* being in mutual aspect with the 7th lord Moon.

The native of this chart acquired the titular monarchial rulership of a country in Rahu Bhukti of Venus Dasa.   Venus is a yogakaraka for the chart and conjoins the 9th lord Mercury

26

forming a Raja Yoga in the 3rd house. The Bhukti lord Rahu is in a kendra from the Dasa lord Venus and is in Gemini ruled by Mercury. Mercury, in turn, forms a Neechabhanga Raja Yoga with Dasa lord Venus.

The Eleventh House : In Chart No. 228 Virgo happening to be the 11th house is aspected by an exalted 7th lord Venus and Lagna lord Mars. It is quite strong.

The Eleventh Lord : Mercury, ruler of Virgo, occupies the 4th house, in association with 10th lord the Sun. He is not aspected by any planet.

Chart No. 228.—*Born 19/20-2-1253 at 19-10 a.m. (I.S.T.) at 12 N 20, 75 E 39.*

Mars Venus	Jupiter Moon			Mercury		Rahu
Mercury Sun	RASI GD-179		Ketu	Venus	NAVAMSA	Lagna
Rahu						
	Lagna	Saturn		Sun Moon Ketu Mars	Saturn	Jupiter

Balance of the Sun's Dasa at birth: 5 years, 9 months and 4 days.

Karaka : Jupiter occupies the 6th house with the 9th lord the Moon and has exchanged signs with the Lagna lord Mars. He is aspected by an exalted 3rd and 4th lord Saturn. The karaka is fairly well placed though in the 6th house.

Considered from the Moon : The 11th house is Aquarius. It is occupied by the 3rd and 6th lord Mercury and the 5th lord the Sun. The 11th lord Saturn is exalted in the 7th aspected by Mars and Jupiter lords respectively of Chandra-Lagna and the 9th therefrom.

Conclusion : The 2nd and the 5th lord Jupiter and the 9th lord Moon combining in the 6th house generate a powerful yoga for gains. This is enhanced by the aspect of a well-placed Lagna lord Mars on the 11th house. The presence of Lagna lord in the 5th house is a noteworthy factor for riches.

The native acquired immense properties as heir to an erstwhile prince in Jupiter's Dasa, Jupiter's Bhukti. Jupiter, the ruler of the major and the sub-periods, is the 2nd and 5th lord associating with the 9th lord the Moon and aspecting the 2nd house.

Chart No. 229.—*Born 19–11–1917 at 11–12 p.m. (I.S.T.) at 25 N 27, 81 E 51.*

		Jupiter	Ketu	Lagna Moon		Jupiter	
			Sat Lagna				Rahu
	RASI				NAVAMSA		
Moon			Mars	Sat Ketu			Sun
	GD-145						
Venus Rahu	Sun Mercury				Mercury	Venus	Mars

Balance of Sun's Dasa at birth : 1 year, 3 months and 25 days.

The Eleventh House : In Chart No. 229 Cancer being the Ascendant, the 11th house is Taurus. It is occupied by a very powerful 9th lord Jupiter who is also *vargottama.* It is aspected by the 2nd lord Sun and 3rd and 12th lord Mercury who is *vargottama.* The eleventh house is very powerful.

The Eleventh Lord : Venus occupies the 6th house in exchange of signs with 6th lord Jupiter. He is with Rahu which blemishes him slightly.

Karaka : Jupiter is *vargottama* in the 11th house and is aspected by the 2nd lord the Sun and the 3rd and the 12th lord Mercury, who is also *vargottama.*

Considered from the Moon : The eleventh house is equally strong being Scorpio tenanted by the 8th lord Sun and the 9th lord Mercury. It is aspected by the sign-dispositor Mars and the 3rd and the 12th lord Jupiter. The 11th lord Mars is not so strong being in the 8th from the Moon.

Conclusion : The outstanding features of Chart No. 229 is the extremely powerful *parivartana yogas* involving powerful planets. The Lagna is powerful being aspected by Lagna lord the Moon who is in *parivartana* with 7th lord Saturn. The 9th lord Jupiter is *vargottama* and aspects the 2nd lord Sun who, in turn, has exchanged signs with Yogakaraka Mars. This is a powerful yoga for fabulos financial gains. The 11th lord has exchanged signs with the 6th lord Jupiter and occupies his own constellation.

The native acquired an immense fortune in Jupiter's Dasa, Sun's Bhukti in the form of immovable properties, book-royalties and other assets following the death of her father. The Dass lord Jupiter owns the 9th, a constituent of the Dhana Yoga, involving the 11th house. The ruler of the sub-period, *viz ,* the Sun is the 2nd lord aspected by the 9th lord Jupiter and Yogakaraka Mars, causing the native inherit large estates in his period.

Loss or Gain

The Eleventh House : In Chart No. 230 Scorpio being the eleventh house is aspected by Yogakaraka Venus and the 3rd and the 12th lord Jupiter from the 5th house. The Lagna lord Saturn is *vargottama*. He aspects the 11th from the 9th house. The 11th house is powerfully placed.

Chart No. 230.—*Born 23-6-1894 at 10 p.m. (L.M.T.) at 51 N 30, 0 W 05.*

Mars Rahu		Jupiter Venus	Sun	Lagna	Ketu	

Mars Rahu		Jupiter Venus	Sun		Lagna	Ketu	
Moon	RASI NH-64		Merc.		NAVAMSA		Mercury
Lagna				Sun Moon Venus			
			Sat. Ketu			Rahu	Saturn Mars Jupiter

Balance of Rahu Dasa at birth : 9 years, 5 months and 12 days.

The Eleventh Lord : Mars occupies the 3rd house in association with Rahu. He is aspected by Lagna lord Saturn who is also with a node, Ketu. The 11th lord is blemished.

Karaka : Jupiter as karaka occupies a benefic sign in association with Yogakaraka Venus aspecting the 11th house.

Considered from the Moon : The 11th house is Sagittarius. Its lord Jupiter joins the Yogakaraka Venus in a kendra from the Moon. The 11th house is aspected by the political planet, the Sun, who is the 7th lord. The 11th house is favourably disposed.

Conclusion : The house of gains being extremely strongly disposed, the native inherited a royal throne in Rahu Bhukti of Saturn Dasa. Saturn occupies the 9th house in *vargottama* aspected by the 11th lord Mars and his Dasa must result in acquisition of a great fortune. But the 11th lord Mars occupies a malefic constellation and is eclipsed by Rahu who occupies the same asterism. As such, the gains acquried during Saturn's Dasa could not last long and the native had to abdicate the throne in the next Bhukti of Jupiter. Jupiter is the 3rd and the 12th lord. He is in the 5th house aspecting the 11th and the Dasa lord Saturn. He associates with Venus, the Yogakaraka, afflicting him as well. The 9th house is afflicted severely by malefics. Although Saturn as Lagna lord is a benefic, his association with Ketu and his being aspected by the 11th lord Mars (who himself is afflicted by his association with Rahu) renders him a malefic.

Note the powerful situation of Lagna lord in the 9th or house of fortune aspected by 11th lord Mars. Yogakaraka Venus occupies his own sign and aspects the 11th house. The 9th lord Mercury occupies the 7th house. These factors indicate birth in affluent and aristocratic circumstances forming as they do strong yogas for financiel prosperity.

The Eleventh House : In Chart No. 231 Libra is the house of gains. It is not occupied by any planet. The 2nd and 3rd lord Saturn aspects it from the 9th house. The 11th house is fairly strong.

The Eleventh Lord : Venus is in the 9th house joining the 2nd and the 3rd lord Saturn and 7th and 10th lord Mercury. His occupation of Leo is not welcome.

Karaka : Jupiter occupies the 8th house in exaltation. As 4th lord he is in *parivartana* with 8th lord Moon. He associates with the 9th lord Sun. He is flanked on both sides by malefic Mars and Saturn. Saturn's maleficence is checked through his association with Venus.

Chart No. 231.—*Born 18-7-1919 at 6-17 p.m. (I.S.T.) at 12 N, 76 E 38.*

Moon		Ketu	Mars	Ketu	Mercury	Saturn	
			Sun Jupit.				
	RASI		———		NAVAMSA		———
			Merc. Venus Sat.				Jupiter Sun
	GD-181						
Lagna	Rahu			Lagna			Moon Venus Rahu

Balance of Saturn's Dasa at birth : 11 years, 6 months and 24 days.

Considered from the Moon : The 11th house is Capricorn. It is aspected by exalted Jupiter lord of Chandra Lagna and the 6th lord the Sun from the 5th house. The 2nd and the 9th lord Mars also aspects the 11th house adversely. The 11th lord occupies the 6th house with the 3rd and the 8th lord Venus and the 4th and the 7th lord Mercury. The 11th house is quite well disposed but the 11th lord suffers heavy affliction.

Conclusion : The 5th lord Mars aspecting Lagna, Lagna itself *vargottama*, Lagna lord Jupiter exalted and in association with the 9th lord, the Sun, and the 11th lord Venus

How to Judge a Horoscope

joining the 2nd lord Saturn in the 9th house are indicative of power, wealth and riches by birth.

However, note the simultaneous planetary dispositions indicative of loss of power. The Lagna lord is in the 8th, a malefic place. Karaka Jupiter has exchanged signs with 8th lord the Moon. The 9th lord the Sun occupies the 8th house. The 11th lord Venus though apparently well placed in his own constellation suffers loss of strength due to his neecha position and affliction by the 8th lord Moon and Rahu in Navamsa.

Chart No. 231 is of an erstwhile prince who lost many privileges in Mercury Bhukti of Venus Dasa. The Dasa lord Venus is a malefic for Sagittarius Ascendant, made worse by his occupation of an inimical sign Leo which happens to be the 9th house causing yoga-bhanga. Venus is equally malefic from Chandra Lagna also. The Bhukti lord Mercury is in the constellation of a Node. Both the Dasa and Bhukti lords are blemished.

The Eleventh House : In Chart No. 232 Pisces, the 11th house, is aspected by the 4th lord the Sun, the 2nd and 5th lord exalted Mercury and the 11th lord Jupiter. The 11th house is strongly disposed.

The Eleventh Lord : Jupiter occupies the 5th house joining exalted Mercury, lord of the 5th and the 2nd, and the 4th lord Sun. The 5th lord is well placed.

Karaka : Jupiter is also the karaka as well as the 11th lord.

Considered from the Moon : The 11th house is Scorpio occupied by the 11th lord Mars. It is not aspected by any planet. The 11th lord being Mars is in his own sign. The house of gains is quite strong.

Chart No. 232.—*Born 29-9-1933 at 10-15 p.m. (I.S.T.) at 10 N 50, 78 E 42.*

		Lagna			Jupiter	Sun Venus Ketu	Saturn
Rahu	RASI				NAVAMSA		Lagna Mars
Moon Saturn	R.P. 18/90		Ketu				Moon
	Mars	Venus	Merc. Sun Jupit		Rahu		Mercury

Balance of Mars Dasa at birth : 6 years, 5 months and 18 days.

Conclusion : The combination in Chart No. 232 of the 11th lord Jupiter and Mercury, exalted lord of the 2nd and 5th house has generated a powerful Dhana Yoga. This is reinforced by the *vargottama* position of Mercury. In addition the combination occurs in the 5th house. The 11th lord Jupiter from the 5th house aspects Yogakaraka Saturn in the 9th house. Saturn, in turn, generates a Sasa Yoga. These yogas enabled the native to emerge as a powerful industrialist during Mercury's Dasa, his financial position consistently shooting up during this period.

A significant negative feature in an otherwise strong chart is the position of Venus in a *dusthana* in the 6th house hemmed in between malefics Mars and the Sun even though he occupies his own sign both in Rasi and Navamsa. The 11th lord Jupiter is combust which indicates that his malefic lord-ship can gain an upper hand during adverse planetary periods. As soon as Ketu Dasa began, the native's financial empire came crashing down. Ketu occupies his own constellation and afflicts the 10th house through Rahu. He is in Leo ruled by the Sun who afflicts the 11th lord Jupiter and the 5th house. During Ketu Dasa, the native suffered every kind of loss including that of prestige and reputation.

XVI

Concerning the Twelfth House

The twelfth house signifies losses, extravagance, expenditure, confiscation, *sayana sukha* (pleasures of the couch), left eye, feet, incarceration, divine knowledge and piety and Final Emancipation (Moksha). As in the case of previous Bhavas, the factors to be considered in analysing this Bhava are : (*a*) the Bhava, (*b*) its lord, (*c*) its occupants and (*d*) the karaka. A proper assessment of the indication of the twelfth house rests on a balanced examination of these factors.

Results of the Lord of the Twelfth House being Posited in Different Houses

First House :—The native will have a weak constitution and will be feeble-minded. He will, however, be handsome and sweet-tongued. If the sign is common, the native will generally be travelling about. If the 6th lord joins the 12th lord in Lagna, the native will live long. But if the 8th house is afflicted, he will be short-lived. This also indicates imprisonment and living abroad. If the Lagna and 12th lords exchange signs, the native will be a miser, hated by all and devoid of intelligence.

In the Second House :—The person will suffer financial losses. He may contact debts and get involved in nefarious activity. He will not eat timely meals. His eye-sight will be poor and his family life, marked by lack of harmony. If the twelfth lord is a benefic and in dignity, these evil indications will be greatly reduced and the native will have financial stability. He will be a tactful speaker. If the twelfth lord is ill-disposed, the native indulges in gossip and quarrelling.

In the Third House :—He will be timid and quiet. Loss of a brother is shown. He will be shabbily dressed. If malefics afflict, he may develop ear-ailments. He may have to spend much money on younger brothers. As a writer he may be unsuccessful. He may work in some commonplace job and earn very little. If the 12th lord joins the 2nd lord in the 3rd and is aspected by Jupiter or the 9th lord, one may have more than one wife.

In the Fourth House :— Early death to mother, mental restlessness, unnecessary worry, enmity of relatives and living abroad are some of the results. Suffering constant harrassment from the landlord, his residence will be in an ordinary house. But if the twelfth lord is well placed, these adverse indications get mitigated to a large extent. If Venus is strong, the native may own his own conveyance but it will always give trouble.

In the Fifth House :—Either difficulty to beget progeny or unhappiness from children will be experienced. He will be religious-minded and may undertake pilgrimages. Weak-minded and suffering mental aberrations, he feels he is miserable. He will not succeed in agriculture as his crops will suffer from pests and disease.

In the Sixth House :—The native will be happy and prosperous, live long, enjoy many comforts, possess a healthy and handsome physique, and vanquish his enemies. But he may become involved in litigation which may come to an end to his advantage. But if malefics afflict the 12th lord, the person will be unscrupulous, sinful and ill-tempered, hating his mother suffering from unhappiness on account of his own children. Womanising will land him in distress.

In the Seventh House :—The wife may come from a poor family. Married life will be unhappy and may end in separation. Later on he will take to asceticism. Weak in health and suffering from phlegmatic troubles, he will be without learning or property.

In the Eighth House :—The native will be rich and celebrated, will enjoy a luxurious life with many servants waiting on him. Gain through deaths and legacy is indicated. Interested in occult subjects and devoted to Lord Vishnu, he will be righteous, famous and a gentle speaker being endowed with many good qualities of head and heart.

In the Ninth House :—Residence abroad and prosperity are shown. He may acquire much property in foreign lands. Honest, generous and large-hearted he may not have any spiritual leanings. Not liking his wife, friends and preceptor, and interested in physical culture, he loses his father early in life.

In the Tenth House :—Hard-working and having to undertake tedious journeys for his occupation he will be a jailor, doctor or work in the cemetery and such places. He spends money on agricultural pursuits in which he makes profits. The native will derive no happiness or physical comforts from his sons.

In the Eleventh House :—He will engage himself in business, but does not make much profit. He has few friends but many enemies. Troubled by extravagant brothers, some of whom may be invalids, the native's funds may dwindle on this account. He will earn well by trading in pearls, rubies and other precious stones.

In the Twelfth House : — The native spends much on religious and righteous purposes. He will have good eye-sight and enjoy pleasures of the couch. He will be engaged in agriculture. If malefics afflict the twelfth lord, the native will be restless and always roaming about.

These results are general and must be adopted to suit individual cases. If the twelfth lord is a benefic, his occupation of the twelfth house gives generally favourable results. If the 12th house is a movable sign and contains the Moon or Mercury, the native will do lot of travelling. Benefics aspecting this combination give residence abroad, delightful journeys and general good fortune. If malefics afflict by *papakartari yoga* or by aspect, the native may leave the country for fear of the law or life, and leave vagrant life as an incognito.

If the Lagna lord is in the 12th house and the trines or quadrants are not occupied by benefics, the native will be a man of mediocre or poor means leading a monotonous life.

General Combinations

We give below some important combinations bearing on the twelfth house and its significations drawn from various standard classical works.

When the lord of the twelfth house occupies benefic vargas, the native spends his wealth in honourable and approved ways. If the 12th lord is aspected by or is with a malefic or depressed or eclipsed planet, the native spends his money in illegal and questionable ways. Depending upon the planet afflicting the 12th lord, one may expend his wealth on wine, women, illegal gratification, races, gambling or other vices. If benefics aspect or occupy the 12th house, the native may have a good father to take care of his wants to spend any amount of money. If malefics afflict the 12th, one's earning get dissipated in many ways. Lords of malefic houses such as the 6th or the 8th in the 12th result in loss of prestige and money provided the 10th house, its lord, the 2nd house, the 11th house and their lords also get afflicted.

If the 12th lord is exalted or in a friendly sign, the person will be generous ; if related to a well-placed 9th lord, fortunate. A benefic in the 12th makes one thrifty and careful with his money. Lord of the 12th aspected by Jupiter, the 9th lord in the 4th, and the 10th lord in a kendra, indicate a charitable disposition. The Ascendant and the 9th lords in *parivartana* make the native engage himself in charitable and virtuous deeds. One will be keen on undertaking pilgrimages and also charitably disposed if the 9th lord is in the 12th. The 9th lord, occupying a benefic sign in Navamsa with a benefic planet, makes one spend lavishly on charity. Exalted Mercury posited in a quadrant or the 11th and aspected by the 9th lord makes one a philanthropist.

The 9th lord in *simhasanamsa* (occupying the same varga 5 times) aspected by the lords of the Lagna and the 10th ; or the 9th lord aspecting the Ascendant and the Ascendant lord disposed in a quadrant ; or a benefic planet in the Ascendant and the 9th lord in a malefic Navamsa or shashtyamsa ; one spends large sums on charity out of ostentation.

If the 12th house and Venus are both beneficially disposed, the native, wherever he be, will have bed comforts. Similar results will happen if the lord of the twelfth house is conjoined with or aspected by a benefic and occupies a benefic sub-division (varga). One will not enjoy such pleasures under the following combinations :

If the Lagna lord occupies the 6th, 8th or the 12th : the Lagna lord is debilitated or joins Saturn, Mandi or Rahu ; or if the 12th lord is afflicted by malefic aspects or associations. Depending upon the other planets and the Lagna in a horoscope, such denial or deprivation of bed-pleasures may be due to force of circumstances, poverty, ill-health, physical deformity or continence due to spiritual inclinations.

The nature of the planet in the twelfth house gives us a clue as to how one's wealth is lost, dissipated or spent.

The native's wealth is spent on fines or will be confiscated by the Government when the afflicted Sun occupies the 12th. Mars in the 12th gives expensive litigation and dangerous enemies. Money will be lost through ransom, cheating and swindlers. Reckless investment in shares and trade and business are likely when Mercury is placed in a similar situation. Family litigation will also dwindle wealth. Venus causes loss of money through women of ill-fame, scandals or black-mail. Saturn and Mars create expenditure on account of co-borns. Saturn and Rahu cause heavy expenses on deaths and similar calamities. The Moon and the Ascendant lord in the 12th result in dissipation of money through medical and hospital bills, sureties, bail-amounts, etc. These results are possible *in toto* only if there are appropriate indications in the chart as a whole and the particular Bhava concerned to show such loss. One should be very careful in weighing the afflictions correctly.

The native's mother is instrumental in his losing money when the afflicted 12th lord joins the 4th lord. The 12th lord so connected with the 6th lord, Mars, Venus, 5th lord, 3rd lord, 7th lord and the 10th lord shows loss of money through their respective significations, namely, enemies, litigation, women, children, co-borns, married partner and father.

The 12th lord with a malefic suggests embezzlement tendencies. An exchange of houses between the 2nd and 12th lords and affliction by Lagna lord in the 6th house indicates criminal proceedings against the native leading to loss of wealth. Similar effects can happen when the 12th lord occupies the 2nd, the 11th lord is in the 12th and the 2nd lord is debilitated or occupies the 6th, the 8th or the 12th house; when the 2nd lord is combust, debilitated or afflicted in the 12th and the Ascendant lord is weak ; or the 10th lord is in the 11th combining with the Lagna lord in a malefic shashtyamsa ; or when the 2nd lord is debilitated, joins a malefic or is combust in the 6th ; or if Venus, Rahu and the Sun are in the 12th, such expenditure will be due to courts, litigation, fines, etc.

If the lord of the Navamsa occupied by the 2nd house is aspected by the Lagna lord and is in the 6th, the 8th or the 12th houses, the native incurs expenditure on account of fines. This combination may also indicate losses through theft and fire.

If Mars aspects the weak 2nd and 11th lords who also occupy inimical Amsas ruled by malefics and are at the same time afflicted by malefics, theft, outbreak of fire or fines could lead to loss of wealth. If the afflicted 10th lord is in the 6th with the 2nd and 11th lords in an evil shashtyamsa, the natiive suffers public censure and thereby loses his wealth.

If the luminaries occupy the 12th, loss of wealth takes place through tax raids, government enactments or confiscation. Jupiter in the 12th makes one honest and pay taxes and tolls properly.

Lord of the Navamsa occupied by the 11th lord with a benefic but in a malefic shashtyamsa in the 6th, the 8th or the 12th houses may plunge one in debts. If the 10th lord be either aspected or conjoined with the 11th lord, a malefic occupies the 2nd house and the Lagna lord occupies the 12th house, then the native will get involved in debts. Involvement in debts may be anticipated under the following combinations :

Lagna lord joins the 2nd or the 7th lord is either eclipsed, debilitated or in an inimical sign in any of the dusthanas (the 6th, the 8th and 12th houses) while the 9th lord does not receive any benefic aspects ; the 2nd lord is eclipsed and conjoins a malefic in the 2nd or the 8th house ; the 2nd lord is both combust and debilitated and occupies a malefic shashtyamsa ; the Ascendant lord is afflicted both by a malefic planet and the lord of either the 6th, 8th or 12th.

If the lords of the Navamsa occupied by the rulers of the drekkanas occupied by the 2nd and 11th houses are in *vaiseshikamsa* and be in a trine or quadrant, the native will be able to clear off his debts during his life time.

Poverty is indicated when Jupiter is in the 12th, 6th or 8th from the Moon and the Moon is in a trine or a quadrant, debilitated or occupying an inimical varga. The Sun in debility in the 9th and Mars in the 8th cause appalling poverty. If the Sun in Aries is aspected by a malefic and is in debility in Navamsa ; or if Venus occupies Virgo both in Rasi and Navamsa, a beggar is born. When the Ascendant is Sagittarius, Pisces, Leo or Taurus and Jupiter is stronger than the 9th lord and the 11th lord is weak and combust and occupies any

Bhava other than a kendra, the native will generally be in indigent circumstances.

If a malefic occupies the 2nd, 4th or the 5th house from Jupiter, one will be poor. The same result is indicated if the luminaries in the Lagna are aspected or associated with the 2nd or the 7th lord. The 9th lord in the 12th, the 12th lord in the 2nd and malefics in the 3rd cause penury and suffering.

If the Lagna lord is in the 8th house while the 8th lord joins the 2nd or the 7th lord in Lagna, the native will never earn enough for even bare subsistence. Benefics in the 10th and malefics in the 2nd denote poverty. The Moon, Jupiter and Saturn in quadrants and Mars and Mandi in the 5th, the 8th or the 12th bestow poverty. Most of these combinations can be found in the charts of slum-dwellers, servant-maids, flower-sellers, show-shine boys and similar categories of vocation where life is lived from day-to-day.

The Ascendant, its lord and planets in *papakartari yoga* usually give rise to imprisonment. If the Lagna and the 6th lord combine with Saturn in a kendra or kona, the native will suffer imprisonment. Malefics in the 2nd, 5th, 9th and 12th houses cause captivity, the exact nature of which is determined by the nature of the sign rising on the Ascendant. If Aries, Taurus or Sagittarius is rising, the native is said to be bound by ropes. If Scorpio is the Lagna, the native will be thrown into an underground cell. If Gemini, Libra or Virgo is ascending, one may be put in fetters. Imprisonment will be in a large protected building if the Lagna is Pisces, Cancer or Capricorn.

The 6th and Lagna lords in a trine or quadrant, joining Rahu or Ketu, cause incarceration. Death in captivity may occur when the Moon, Mars. Saturn and the Sun occupy the 10th,

9th, 1st and 5th houses respectively. If the rulers of (a) the
2nd and the 12th houses, (b) the 5th and 9th houses, (c) the
6th and 12th houses, (d) the 3rd and 11th houses or (e) the
4th and 10th houses are equal in strength, the native may face
criminal action provided there are no other mitigating factors.

If Lagna lord Venus is in the 6th, one suffers from diseases
in the left eye. The 2nd and 12th lords conjoining Venus and
the Lagna lord in any of the *dusthanas* (the 6th, the 8th or the
12th) makes one born blind. Combination of the Lagna lord,
the Sun and Venus gives the same results. The Moon afflicted
by a malefic planet and Venus in the 2nd house can cause loss
of vision. The Sun, the Moon and Venus are the natural
significators of the eyes. Afflictions to these and the 12th
house cause defective vision.

The Moon and Venus in the 6th, the 8th or the 12th cause
night-blindness. One will have weak vision if the waning
Moon is aspected by Saturn, or if the Moon in Cancer is aspected
by malefics from the 7th or the 10th house. Eye troubles are
foreseen when Venus occupies the Lagna or the 8th house
afflicted by malefics. If the Sun aspected by Mars or Saturn or
afflicted by Rahu occupy the 12th house or any trine, the
native will have defective vision.

If the Lagna and 2nd lords occupy the 6th, 8th or the 12th
houses, one's eye-sight may be affected. Mars in the 12th
injures the right eye. If the Sun and the Moon occupy the
6th and the 12th from Lagna, one may lose one of his eyes.
If the Moon and Venus occupy the 12th house, or if Venus
along with a malefic occupy the 12th house, the left eye will
be affected.

Defective vision and eye-ailments are not so serious today
as they were when the classical works were written. In those

days. defective vision made one handicapped and depend on
the mercy of others.   As such, natives whose charts indicated
such defects were rejected for marriages and generally looked
upon as a burden. Now-a-days things have changed totally and
defective vision is of little consequence except in certain vocations.   Most cases of defective vision can be set right through
prescribing proper lenses or through simple surgical operations.
Blindness is also no longer a handicap since blind people are
taught to be self-reliant.

If the 12th house be aspected or occupied by Saturn or
Mandi and the 12th lord be in a Vipat (3rd), Pratyak (5th) or
Naidhana (7th) constellation reckoned from Janma Nakshatra
(birth-constellation), the native may face untold calamities
and hardships. He will enter upon a vicious code of conduct,
commit sins and go to hell after death.

If a malefic planet in combustion, debilitation or a state of
eclipse afflicts the twelfth Bhava, one may go to lower planes
such as hell after death. When the 12th lord occupies a
malefic *shashtyamsa* and is aspected by a malefic planet or
when Rahu is in the 12th house with Mandi and the 8th lord
is aspected by the 6th lord, the person descends into the
infernal regions after mortal death.

If the 12th house is occupied by a benefic or is subject to
a *shubhakartari yoga*, the native goes to heaven. If Jupiter as
the 10th lord occupies the 12th house or is aspected by Venus,
waning Moon or well placed Sun, one becomes a celestial
after death.

The same state occurs if a benefic planet in strength occupies the 12th house in benefic vargas and is aspected both by
benefics and malefics. If powerful Jupiter occupies Cancer
and his moolatrikona sign in Navamsa and 3 or 4 planets are

in kendras, the native is said to attain Brahmaloka after his mortal death. When Sagittarius is the Ascendant, Aries is the Navamsa Lagna, Venus occupies the 7th house in Gemini and the Moon is in Virgo, the native is said to attain Liberation (Moksha) after death. Ketu in the 12th from karakamsa gives Kaivalya or Final Emancipation. If the 10th lord joins 4 other planets in a trine or quadrant, the native attains Final Liberation. Mars and Mercury in Pisces and Gemini as Ascendant give Moksha.

These combinations culled out from authoritative works on astrology by ancient writers indicate the next stage of the soul's journey after its release from the human body. This is a very deep subject and involves a profound understanding of deep studies in the doctrine of Karma. There is no way of veryfying predictions bearing on the state of the soul after it shakes off the physical body. But some clues can be had by studying the twelfth Bhavas of great saints such as Sri Ramakrishna Paramahamsa, Ramana Maharishi and Sri Aurobindo.

There is a little known but practically applicable dictum in *Bhavartha Ratnakara* bearing on the twefth house. According to it a person will be fortunate in respect of that house whose karaka is situated in the 12th house from the Ascendant. The following are the important karakas for the different Bhavas :

Thanubhava or 1st house	— The Sun
Dhanabhava or 2nd house	— Jupiter
Bhratrubhava or 3rd house	— Mars
Matrubhava or 4th house	— The Moon
Putrabhava or 5th house	— Jupiter
Satrubhava or 6th house	— Saturn
Kalatrabhava or 7th house	— Venus
Ayurbhava or 8th house	— Saturn

Pitrubhava or 9th house   —   The Sun
Karmabhava or 10th house   —   Jupiter
Labhabhava or 11th house   —   Jupiter
Vyayabhava or 12th house   —   Saturn

Thus if the Sun is in the 12th house, the native will be fortunate in respect of the 9th house indications ; if the Moon is in the 12th house, in respect of the 4th house indications ; if Venus is in the 12th house, in respect of the 7th house indications and so on.

Chart No. 233.—*Born 12-2-1856 at 12–21 p.m. (L.M.T.) at 18 N, 84 E.*

	Moon Rahu	Lagna	Sat.		Lagna Jupiter	Rahu	
Sun Mercury Ketu							
	RASI			NAVAMSA			
	NH-29						
Venus	Mars Ketu		Merc.	Ketu	Sun Saturn Venus Mars	Moon	

Balance of the Venus Dasa at birth : 12 years, 5 months and 21 days.

In Chart No. 233, the Moon, karaka for the 4th house, occupies the 12th from the Ascendant. The native was extremely fortunate in respect of his mother who was a genteel, refined and highly spiritual lady. But also note that the Moon is with Rahu aspected by Mars. The mother died in the native's 12th or 13th year.

Planets in the Twelfth House

The Sun : The native may take to an immoral life and engage himself in vile occupations. He will not be quite successful in his life and may feel neglected by all. He will suffer the loss of some limb and have weak eye-sight. He will, however, be energetic and have sons.

The Moon : The native may suffer from some deformity. He will be narrow-minded, hard-hearted and mischievous. He prefers to lead on obscure life in solitude. Eye-sight will be weak. If the Moon is waning and combines with Saturn, sloth and lethargy will be the result.

Mars : The person may lose his wife. He will be selfish, hateful and suffer diseases due to excess of heat in the body. He is liable to deception and may lose his money. If Mars and Saturn occupy the 12th and the 2nd houses respectively, the Moon be in Lagna and the Sun in the 7th house, he may suffer from leucoderma. If Mars in the 12th house is aspected by the Sun, danger from fire and wicked people is indicated. Malefics in the 7th and the 8th and Mars in the 12th denote that one will have another wife even when the first is alive.

Mercury : Capricious and wayward, the person will indulge in extra-marital relations and suffer penury, and perverted thinking will make him unhappy. He will also have a few children.

Jupiter : The native may deride religion and be evil-minded. He will commit fearful deeds and lead a lascivious life. Later on he repents and reforms himself. The native will always be anxious about his vehicles, ornaments and clothes.

Venus : Desertion by relatives ; hankering after comforts without success and penury will make the native's life miserable.

He will indulge in lying and associates with low women. His eye-sight will be poor. If Venus is exalted, contrary results will happen.

Saturn : The native will be dull-headed and lose all his money. He will have squint eyes and a deformed limb, make many enemies, suffer losses in trade, be a pessimist and commits sins in secret.

Rahu : The native will be prosperous, immoral, but of a helpful nature. He will have eye troubles. If the Sun is in the 7th, Mars is in the 10th and Rahu is in the 12th Bhava, the native's father will die early.

Ketu : The native will have a restless and wandering mind and leave his country of birth. The lower classes will befriend him. All his inherited property may be lost.

Time of Fructification of the Results of the Twelfth House

As explained in the previous chapters, here also the following factors must be considered in timing events : (*a*) Lord of the 12th house, (*b*) planet or planets aspecting the 12th house, (*c*) planet or planets posited in the 12th house, (*d*) planets aspecting the lord of the 12th house, (*e*) planet or planets in association with the lord of the 12th house, and (*f*) the lord of the 12th house from the Moon. The position of Saturn is also of significance as he is the karaka of loss, sorrow, after-life as well as renunciation and Emancipation or Moksha.

The factors mentioned above may influence the 12th house either as the lords of main periods or as lords of sub-periods. (1) The sub-periods of planets capable of influencing the 12th house in the major periods of those who are also capable of influencing the 12th house produce results pertaining to the

12th house *par excellence*. (2) The sub-periods of planets associated with the 12th house in the major periods of whose lords are not associated with the 12th house, will produce results relating to the 12th house only to a limited extent. (3) Similarly, the sub-periods of planets who are not associated with the 12th house in the major periods of planets associated with the 12th house will produce results pertaining to the 12th house only to a feeble extent.

Note the Bhava ruled by the planet occupying the 12th, and also the Bhava occupied by the lord of the 12th house. During the periods of these lords, loss or trouble in respect of these Bhavas can be expected.

Nature of Results

If the 12th lord is well placed with beneficial aspects and associations, his Dasa will make the native benevolent. He becomes virtuous and acquires merit. The native will be honoured by the rulers. If the lord of the 12th is weak due to association with malefics, debilitation or combustion, one will face much suffering. His health will break down and he may face calumny from all sides, and even suffer captivity. His earnings will dwindle.

The exact nature of results depends upon the ownership, etc., of the planets connected with the 12th lord. The following results may be expected during the periods of the different planets when they are connected with the twelfth house :—
Sun : Becomes unsuccessful in all ventures. Takes to study and practice of occult sciences. Children will cause much un-happiness. *Moon :* The native meets with obstacles in all his undertakings. Becomes cruel and evil-minded. Loses power and is deceived by trusted colleagues. Leads an obscure life. *Mars :* Contracts many diseases. May meet with accidents.

Loses popularity and career deteriorates. Becomes dishonest—
will be duped. Liable to be defrauded. *Mercury:* Becomes
philosophical. Suffers initiality, mental delusions and worries.
Acquires new skills. Will beget limited progeny. Mother will
face danger. *Jupiter:* Becomes poor and unlucky. Suffers loss
of children and becomes a sadist. Commits sins and gradually
takes to a life of piety. *Venus:* Associates with women of
ill-repute. Loses or separates from the married partner. Takes to
unscrupulous ways and means of gaining money. Becomes
miserly. *Saturn:* Business fails and debts mount. Litigation
and loss of prestige. Eye-sight fails. Becomes dispassionate
if Dasa occurs late in life. *Rahu:* Suffers loss of limbs through
violent accident. Begets limited progeny. Earns well through
unconventional means. *Ketu:* Mental disturbance and wandering habits. Will reside abroad and work amidst servile classes.

Dasas of planets in the 12th house generally produce untoward results or else give interest in spirituality and religion.
If, however, there are benefic yogas, benefic results can also
be expected on a material level such as distinction in profession, financial prosperity, acquisition of wife, children, comforts,
jewels, clothes and other objects of luxury.

The following results are likely, in a general sense, during
the periods (Dasa or Bhukti) of the 12th lord. But these results
must be modified by the nature of the sign and planets influencing the 12th house and its lord. The results of the Dasa
must be predicted taking into account the karaka and lordship
of the house occupied by the 12th lord.

When the lord of the 12th is placed in the Ascendant with
the Ascendant lord, one will generally lose the affection of
others during the period of the 12th lord. His intelligence will
grow dull and he may become miserly. He loses his wealth

through short-sighted schemes, associates with evil persons and becomes addicted to bad habits. If the 12th lord is a benefic, the evil is reduced. Even if the native loses all his money, he will try to work hard and regain it.

If the lord of the 12th house occupies the 2nd house with the 2nd lord, domestic peace will be lacking. There will be constant bickerings in the family. He will not be able to eat good food or he may even develop some ailment of the tongue or throat. He will be ill-tempered and commit many indiscretions. His eye-sight will be affected. If the 12th lord is strongly afflicted, the native may have to live at others' expense and doled out food. If the 12th lord is favourably disposed, the malefic indications will be greatly reduced.

If the 12th lord occupies the 3rd house with the 3rd lord, the brothers of the native will face hardships. They will take recourse to evil ways. The native's expenditure will keep mounting. If the 12th lord occupies the 6th, 8th or 12th house from Navamsa Lagna or is aspected by benefics, the contrary results can be expected. The person will have to undertake many journeys within the country. If the 10th lord is also involved, his job may require him to constantly move about. If the 12th lord combines with the 6th and 8th lords, the native enjoys good food, riches, conveyances, luxuries and prosperity of every kind.

If the lord of the 12th house occupies the 4th with the 4th lord, the mother may die early. If benefics influence the 4th lord, the native will be happy and own substantial immovable property and many conveyances. He will evince growing interest in spiritual literature. If malefics afflict the 12th lord, the native's mother suffers a crisis in life. She will have unhappy days. The native gets trouble on account of his properties, which may get lost or destroyed. If both benefics and malefics aspect or associate with 12th lord in the 4th house, the native will face troubles but will be able to overcome them.

If the lord of the 12th occupies the 5th along with the 5th lord, the native gets progeny in the former's periods. He will suffer mental aberration and his friends will desert him. He may lose the association of an influential person. If malefics afflict the 12th lord, his children may face trouble or the native suffers much unhappiness and pain on their account. His father will pass through difficulties while he himself may rouse the wrath of a powerful man. His life will be disrupted due to political disturbances. The native will face many troubles in his work (occupation).

If the lord of the 12th house occupies the 6th with the 6th lord, the Dasa of the 12th lord will be filled with joyous festivities. The person becomes fortunate in all walks of life, gets much wealth, marries a noble and good woman and his children will be a source of happiness. If the 12th lord combines with the 8th lord, the native will get political power, fame and honour. If malefics afflict the combination, he may be troubled by adverse criticism and enemies.

The native's wife may have to face some danger or the other if the lord of the twelfth occupies the seventh with the 7th lord. If a maraka period is on, he faces danger to his life. Wife may live abroad. Acquisition of money and the wife surviving a crisis will be the result of benefics aspecting the 12th lord. If malefics afflict the 7th house and the 12th lord, one may wander aimlessly, get tired, lack physical comforts, be beet with sorrows and ailments and his married life may be marred by slanderous talk.

If the lord of the twelfth is placed in the eighth with the 8th lord, one enjoys luck and at the same time some troubles. But generally, during the period of the 12th lord, he will have happiness, succeed in his ventures, though results may be slow in coming. Marriage and other happy celebrations will take place and much money and authority will be secured. The 6th lord joining the 12th lord confers results *par excellence,* the native enjoying honour, recognition, distinction and prosperity. The 12th lord being related to 5th lord makes one deeply devoted to God. A steady career is vouchsafed if the lord of the 12th occupies the 9th with the 9th lord. Affliction of the 9th lord leads to the loss of job and luck. If benefics aspect the 9th house, one develops interest in piety and leads a virtuous life. His material prosperity will be on a low keel. These results can be expected in the Dasa or Bhukti of the twelfth lord.

If the lord of the 12th occupies the 10th with the 10th lord, one will spend money for charitable purposes. Paternal property may slip out of the native's hands or get spoilt through fire or other accident. Benefics aspecting the 12th lord makes one detached and develop spirituality. If malefics afflict, one may resort to propitiation of lower deities or Kshudra Devatas and goblins for a living. If there is a *papakartari yoga*, he will be dreaded for his evil powers.

Lord of the 12th in the 11th with the 11th lord causes financial set-backs. Trade may bring in losses. Benefics aspecting the 12th lord make the person expend much money on religious and charitable deeds even at the cost of his own well-being. Loss of money through theft, fire or accident occur if malefics afflict. If one is a businessman, loss may occur due to misunderstanding with elder brothers or partners who are in the business. The nature of the afflicting planet gives a clue to the source of loss. If Jupiter or the 5th lord afflicts the 12th lord in the 11th house, the native's wealth may be dissipated by a bad son.

Lord of the 12th in the 12th makes his period bring in much wealth. There will be no untoward expenditure. A benefic planet combining with the 12th lord indicates the native incurs honourable expenditure during the period of the former. The Ascendant and its lord well-placed results in income far exceeding expenditure. The native will be religiously inclined, will feed many holy men and seek their company, will always be engaged in spiritual thoughts and talks and will lead a comfortable life. Malefics afflicting the 12th house and the Ascendant weak, make one, though born in an illustrious family, become obscure, take to evil ways and lead a miserable existence. He will eke out of his livelihood through serving as a menial.

Summing up when the 12th lord is in any Bhava subject to malefic aspects and associations, his period causes debts, expenses, involvement in unhealthy and wicked company and pursuits. When both benefics and malefics influence the 12th lord, mixed results can be expected in the period of the 12th lord. If the 12th lord combines with or is aspected by benefics, religious piety and legitimate and charitable expenditure can be expected in his period.

In Chart No. 234, the Ascendant lord Mercury occupies the 8th house. The 12th lord Venus is in the 8th with exalted Mars lord of the 6th and the 11th. The native took to a life of celibacy after the birth of his children when he was in his thirties. The presence of Lagna lord in a *dusthana*, and of karaka Venus who is also the 12th lord afflicted by Mars is

Chart No. 234.—*Born 29–2–1896 at 1·00 p.m. (L.M.T.) at 20 N 36, 72 E 59*

			Lagna	Sun		Venus	Saturn
Sun Rahu			Jupit.	Mars			Mercury Ketu
Mercury Venus Mars	RASI GD-137		Ketu Moon	Lagna Rahu	NAVAMSA		
		Saturn				Moon	Jupiter

Balance of Venus Dasa at birth : 0 years, 4 months and 6 days.

responsible for it. Jupiter's aspect gave the native conjugal life until he voluntarily renounced it.

We can also note the exaltation of the 10th lord Jupiter in a spiritual sign aspected by the 12th lord Venus which has made the native a Karmayogi-*cum*-Jnani. The Lagna lord Mercury is in a *dusthana* in the 8th with the 6th lord Mars and 12th lord Venus. The native suffered jail terms many a time during the pre-Independence period.

Saturn, the 12th lord, is exalted in the 8th in Chart No. 235. As lord of *mokshasthana* in a *dusthana*, he has made the native a great mystic of a high spiritual order. The 9th lord Mars occupies the 12th house giving the native decidedly spiritual leanings. Mars with Rahu in the 12th is significant as favouring destruction of happiness of the couch (*sayana-sukha*). Even from childhood she had been lost in spiritual trances and

Chart No. 235.—*Born 30-4-1896 at 4-08 a.m. (L.M.T.) at 23 N 45, 91 E 30.*

Lagna	Sun Venus	Mercury		Venus Mars	Saturn	Ketu
Rahu Mars	RASI		Jupit.	NAVAMSA		
	GD-137		Ketu	Lagna Merc Sun		
	Mercury	Saturn		Rahu	Jupiter	Sun

Balance of Mercury's Dasa at birth : 10 years, 10 months and 24 days.

the formal rite of marriage was never consummated. Her spiritual celibacy continued untainted

The 12th house in Chart No. 236 is occupied by Mars and Saturn. The native's wife died soon after marriage and he never married again. He became deeply philosophical and spiritual. The 12th lord Jupiter, though in the 2nd, is in Aquarius, a spiritual sign and the centre of a powerful *pravrajyaka yoga* (yoga for renunciation). The 12th lord is hemmed inbetween malefics which denied the native both the pleasures and comforts of a bed.

In Chart No. 237, the 12th lord aspects the 12th along with the Lagna lord Mars. Jupiter and Saturn also aspect it. The native was a staunch Christian who spent most of his life in propagating its teachings. Saturn aspecting the 12th from the 10th is responsible for this voluntary missionary work.

28

Chart No. 236.—*Born 20/21–2–1879 at 5 a.m. (L.M.T.) at 13 N 5, 80 E 2.*

Saturn				Rahu		Lagna Venus
Ven. Sun Moon Mercury Jupiter	RASI		Ketu		NAVAMSA	
Lagna Rahu				Sun		
Mars			Moon		Mars Mercury Jupiter Sat , Ketu	

Balance of Rahu's Dasa at birth : 11 years, 8 months and 28 days.

Chart No. 237.—*Born 8–4–1919 at 7–00 p.m. (G.M.T.) at 19 S 40, 30 E 00.*

Sun Mercury	Mars Venus	Ketu	Jupit.		Saturn	Ketu Mars
	RASI		Moon	Merc. Jupit. Sun	NAVAMSA	
	RP-3/32		Sat.			
	Lagna Rahu			Venus Lagna	Rahu	Moon

Balance of Saturn's Dasa at birth : 6 years, 6 months and 20 days.

Chart No. 238.--*Born 10-10-1917 at 10-21 p.m. (L.M.T.) at 27 N 30, 77 E 43.*

		Jupiter	Lagna Ketu		Mercury		
			Sat. Mars Moon	Lagna Ketu Mars Moon			Jupiter
	RASI				NAVAMSA		
				Sat.			Sun Rahu
	RP-3/67						
Rahu	Venus		Merc. Sun				Venus

Balance of Mercury's Dasa at birth : 4 years, 9 months and 19 days.

Chart No. 238 is of a dedicated mass leader who worked zealously for the nation. He was a man of spartan habits and spiritually much evolved. The 12th house is occupied by the spiritual planet Jupiter who is also the 10th lord. This indicates the nature of his life's work which was reorienting the thought of youth to ancient values of purity and renunciation. The 12th lord Venus aspects the 12th house from the 6th house. The native led a life of celibacy.

The 12th lord Venus in Chart No. 239 is exalted and is with the Lagna lord and the Sun aspected by the 9th lord Saturn Mercury who gets *neechabhanga* occupies the 10th house, a kendra, aspected by 9th lord Saturn. The native spent fabulous sums in charity. At the same time note that the 12th lord Venus is exalted powerfully with the result the

Chart No. 239.—*Born 7-4-1893 at 9-31 a.m. (L.M.T.) at 20 N 56, 75 E 55.*

Sun Venus Mercury	Jupiter Rahu	Mars	Lagna			Moon	Mars	Saturn Rahu
	RASI NH-62				Sun Venus	NAVAMSA		Jupiter
Moon		Ketu	Sat.		Ketu	Mercury	Lagna	

Balance of Ketu's Dasa at birth : 6 years, 4 months and 4 days.

native enjoyed comforts of the bed. It was rumoured he had more than 3 wives.

There is also *bandhana yoga* present in this chart, which led to the native's conviction in Jupiter's Dasa, Jupiter's Bhukti. Mercury, the Lagna lord, is in a kendra with 12th lord Venus aspected by 8th lord Mars. The Dasa lord Jupiter is hemmed in between malefics Mars (the 6th lord) and the 3rd lord Sun which led to the native's arrest.

Chart No. 240 is that of a trustee of a temple whose fabulous family properties have been set aside for feeding of pilgrims and other charities. The 12th lord Venus occupies his *moolatrikona* sign in the 5th house (a trine) with the spiritual planet Ketu and is aspected by the 9th lord Saturn. The 12th house is aspected by the Atmakaraka Sun and the Lagna lord Mercury.

Chart No. 240.—*Born 25–11–1948 at 7–28 p.m. (I.S.T.) at 13 N 20, 74 E 48.*

	Rahu		Lagna			Mars
				Moon		Jupiter Mercury Rahu
	RASI			NAVAMSA		Saturn
	RP-49/60		Sat.	Ketu		
Mars Jupiter	Sun Mercury	Venus Ketu	Moon	Venus	Lagna Sun	

Balance of the Sun's Dasa at birth : 2 years, 9 months and 12 days.

Chart No. 241.—*Born 30/1-4/5-1898 at 1-23 a.m. (L.M.T.) at 13 N 20, 74 E 49.*

Mars	Sun Mercury	Venus		Venus	Jupiter	Moon
Lagna			Ketu		NAVAMSA	Ketu
Rahu	RASI		Moon	Sat. Rahu		
	RP-29/47				Lagna Mars Mercury	Sun
	Saturn		Jupit.			

Balance of Ketu's Dasa at birth : 1 year, 11 months and 15 days.

438

The 12th house in Chart No. 241 is occupied by *moksha-karaka* Rahu and aspected by Jupiter and Saturn. The native was a dedicated social worker and built a national banking concern starting from scratch. Saturn as Lagna lord and benefic Jupiter aspecting the 12th house made him a selfless worker whose projects of philanthropy proved a boon to countless numbers. The 12th lord Saturn is aspected by a well-placed blemish-free Venus who is also the 9th lord.

Chart No. 242.—*Born 6-6-1901 about midnight at 7 S 15, 112 E 45.*

		Ketu Sun	Venus Merc.			Lagna Moon	
Lagna		RASI		Merc.	NAVAMSA		Rahu
Moon		RP-P II/14	Mars	Ketu			Sun
Saturn Jupiter	Rahu				Saturn	Venus	Jupiter Mars

Balance of the Moon's Dasa at birth : 7 years, 0 month and 27 days.

The 12th house in Chart No. 242 is occupied by the 6th lord Moon while the 12th lord Saturn occupies the 11th house. The 12th lord is aspected by Venus and Mercury. The native was a President of an Asian country. He married many wives and had many mistresses as indicated by the Moon in the 12th house, the influence of Venus on the 12th lord and the preponderance of common signs.   The native spent fabulous sums on his private life.

Chart No. 243. *—Born 15–2–1934 at 9-15 a.m. (I.S.T.) at 12 N 18, 76 E 39.*

Lagna			Mars Moon Ketu	Mercury		Venus
Mercury Sun Mars Moon	RASI	Ketu		NAVAMSA		
Venus Saturn Rahu	RP-42/50					
		Jupiter	Lagna	Sun	Jupiter	Saturn Rahu

Balance of Rahu's Dasa at birth :   0 year,   5 months and 28 days.

Chart No. 243 has a badly afflicted 12th house. Mars, Mercury, New Moon and the Sun occupy it. The 12th lord Saturn is afflicted by Rahu and Venus also joins them. The native spends extravagantly on drink and has an extra-marital life as well. The affliction to Venus and the 7th lord Mercury afflicted in the 12th house are also responsible for it.

Chart No. 244 has Rahu and the Moon in the 12th aspected by the 12th lord Venus. Born in an aristocratic family the native lived a reckless private life with many mistresses. There was no dearth for pleasures of the bed as many beautiful women vied for his favour. The 12th lord Venus and the 12th house are both heavily afflicted indicating extravagant expenditure on sensual gratification. There are Bandhana Yogas also present.

Chart No. 244.—*Born 5–1–1928 at 5–26 p.m. (I.S.T.) at 27 N 27, 68 E 8.*

Jupiter		Rahu Moon	Lagna	Mars			
	RASI RP-3/181			Ketu	NAVAMSA		
				Lagna Sat.			Jupiter Rahu
Sun Mercury	Venus Saturn Ketu Mars					Mercury Venus Sun	Moon

Balance of Mars Dasa at birth :   3 years, 9 months and 27 days.

Mark the 12th lord Venus in the 6th house with 6th lord Mars and 8th lord Saturn. The yoga is stronger from the Moon occurring in a quadrant in an insect sign. The native was in jail for over a year before he was hanged.

The 12th house, in Chart No. 245, is occupied by Venus, Saturn and its own lord Mercury. It is aspected by Mars and Lagna lord the Moon. The native wasted money in pleasures and lost heavily in racing. The affliction by malefics to the 12th house and its lord led the native to squander money in the pursuit of pleasures. But the 12th lord in the 12th with Venus also gave him the benefit of his pursuits.

Venus, lord of the 12th house, in Chart No. 246, occupies the 11th house in debility aspected by Saturn, Mars and the Moon. This weakens the 12th house and gives wasteful expenditure. The native took delight in horse-racing in which

Chart No. 245.—*Born 4-7-1738 at 7—46 a.m. (L.M.T.) at 51 N 30, 0 W 05.*

			Venus Sat. Merc.		Jupiter	Rahu	
Mars	Jupiter	Sun					
Ketu			Lagna				
	RASI				NAVAMSA		
			Rahu	Venus			Sun
	RP-3/123						
Moon				Mars Merc. Sat.	Ketu Lagna	Moon	

Balance of Venus Dasa at birth : 6 years, 8 months and 12 days.

Chart No. 246.- *Born 7–8–1887 at 1–21 p.m. (L.M.T.) at 11 N, 77 E 1.*

			Mars	Rahu		Mars	
Moon							
			Sun Merc. Rahu Sat	Sun Venus			Moon
	RASI				NAVAMSA		
Ketu							
	NH-56						
	Lagna	Jupiter	Venus	Jupit.		Lagna Mercury	Saturn Ketu

Balance of Jupiter's Dasa at birth : 0 year, 8 months and 5 days.

Chart No. 247.—*Born   2-10-1869   at   7-45 a.m.*
(L.M.T.) at 21 N 37, 69 E 49.

		Jupiter			Moon Ketu	Venus	Sun Mars
			Rahu				
Ketu	RASI			Jupit Lagna Merc.	NAVAMSA		
	NH-41		Moon				
	Saturn	Mars Mercury Venus Lagna	Sun	Sat.		Rahu	

Balance of Ketu's Dasa at birth :   6 years, 10 months and
28 days.

he lost sometimes. However the 12th house itself is occupied
by benefic Jupiter so that the native's reputation was untar-
nished.   It also gave him a philosophic outlook on life.

Chart No. 247 has the Sun in the 12th powerfully aspected
by Jupiter, a natural benefic, which made the native spiritual.
The chart is more significant for the prison-terms the native
underwent during the Indian Independence days. It was Rahu's
Dasa and part of Jupiter's Dasa that the native was arrested
several times.   Rahu occupies the 12th house from the Moon
while Jupiter is the 3rd and 6th lord from Lagna placed in the
8th house. The Lagna lord Venus is related to the 12th lord
Mercury.   Venus is also the 8th lord and is subject to a *papakartari yoga* between Saturn and the Sun. The presence of the
8th lord and the 12th lord in a kendra has resulted in a Bandhana
Yoga.

Chart No. 248.— *Born 28-5-1883 at 9–25 p.m. (L.M.T.)* *at 18 N 23, 73 E 53.*

	Mars Ketu Venus	Sun Saturn	Jupit. Merc.	Rahu Sat		Sun	Mars
Moon		RASI		Jupit	NAVAMSA		
							Venus
		NH-49					
Lagna		Rahu		Lagna	Moon	Mercury	Ketu

Balance of Mars Dasa at birth : **1 year, 1 month and 26 days.**

Chart No. 248 has a number of Bandhana Yogas, the most important ones being the association of the Lagna and 7th lord in a quadrant from the Moon ; Ketu's disposition in Navamsa in the 10th from Lagna aspected by three malefics—Mars, Saturn and Rahu— and the 8th lord the Moon occupying the constellation of Mars (12th lord) causing confinement in chains. The affliction to the 12th house from the Sun and Saturn—two bitter enemies in the same sign—made the native a revolutionary who was interned for political reasons. The conjunction of the 6th and the 12th lords Venus and Mars respectively are also responsible for the native's incarcerations.

The native of Chart No. 249 was a celebrated jail-bird. The Ascendant Cancer and the Ascendant lord Moon are hemmed in between malefics Rahu and Saturn. Mercury and Venus are also between malefics Mars and the Sun and are

Chart No. 249.—*Born 14–11–1889 at 11–03 p.m. (L.M T.) at 25 N 25, 82 E.*

RASI

		Rahu	Merc.
	RASI		Moon Lagna
	NH-59		Sat.
Ketu Jupiter	Sun	Mercury Venus	Mars

NAVAMSA

Mars			
Rahu Lagna	NAVAMSA		Sun Saturn
			Ketu Jupiter
Venus Moon			

Balance of Mercury's Dasa at birth : 13 years, 7 months and 6 days.

Chart No. 250.—*Born 19-5-1910 at 8-29 a.m. (I.S.T.) at 18 N 31, 73 E 52.*

RASI

Venus	Saturn	Mercury Sun Rahu	Lagna Mars
	RASI		
	NH-72		
	Ketu		Moon Jupit.

NAVAMSA

Mars Lagna Rahu	Moon	Jupiter Mercury	Saturn
Sun	NAVAMSA		
Venus			
			Ketu

Balance of the Moon's Dasa at birth : 9 years, 5 months and 16 days.

aspected by 6th lord Saturn. The Sun is in a Keeta Rasi or insect sign in a quadrant from the 6th lord Saturn. These yogas gave the native many terms in prison. Malefics in the 2nd, 5th, 9th and 12th houses cause captivity. Saturn is in the 2nd, the Sun is in the 5th, Mars aspects the 9th house and Rahu occupies the 12th almost fulfilling all the requirements of Bandhana Yoga.

The 12th house in Chart No. 250 is occupied by Mercury the Lagna lord, the Sun and Rahu. It is further afflicted by a *papakartari yoga* caused by debilitated 8th lord Saturn and the malefic 6th lord Mars. The native committed a grave murder. Affliction to the 12th house is aggravated by the affliction to the Lagna as well. The native was incarcerated and then hanged. The 6th and 8th lords affect not only the Lagna but also the Lagna lord Mercury forming a powerful Bandhana Yoga.

Chart No. 251.—*Born 24-3-1883 at 6 p.m. (L.M.T.) at 13 N, 77, E 35.*

Lagna Sun	Ketu	Saturn	Jupit.	Mars	Mercury Rahu	Moon	
Mercury Mars		RASI			NAVAMSA		
Venus				Sat.			
		Rahu	Moon			Lagna Ketu Sun Jupiter	Venus

RASI — NH-48

Balance of the Moon's Dasa at birth : 6 years.

In Chart No. 251 the 2nd and 12th houses are heavily afflicted. The Sun, the natural significator of the eye, is subject to *papakartari yoga* between Ketu and Mars. The Moon is powerfully but adversely aspected by Mars. The 2nd lord Mars is in the 12th house. The 2nd and the 12th houses have the evil influences of all the planets centered on them. Mars and Mercury are in the 12th house aspected by Saturn while Rahu-Ketu conjointly act on the 2nd house. Further the second house is hemmed in between 2 malefics, the Sun and Saturn. The native initially suffered from night-blindness and later lost his vision completely.

In Chart No. 252, the 12th lord Venus, though *vargottama*, is afflicted by the nodes both in Rasi and Navamsa. He is also with Saturn, a malefic. The 2nd lord occupies the 6th house in *parivartana* with 6th lord Mars. The 12th house is

Chart No. 252.—*Born 9–12–1608 (O.S.)* at about 6–30 a m. at 51 N 31, 0 W 05.

Mars	Jupiter	Moon			Moon		
			Rahu				Saturn Sun Ketu
Ketu Saturn Venus	RASI			Rahu Venus	NAVAMSA		
	NH-16						
Sun Mercury	Lagna			Merc.	Lagna		Mars Jupit.

Balance of the Moon's Dasa at birth : 8 years, 3 months and 9 days.

Chart No. 253.—*Born 1-8-1947 at 10-10 p.m. (I.S.T.) at 14°N 49, 74 E 15*

Lagna		Rahu Mars	Merc.		Rahu	Moon	Jupiter	Mercury
	RASI		Venus Sat. Sun			NAVAMSA		
Moon	RP-42/118			Sat.				
	Ketu	Jupiter				Sun	Lagna	Mars Venus Ketu

Balance of the Moon's Dasa at birth : 7 years, 10 months and 24 days.

aspected by Saturn and Jupiter. More than anything else the heavy affliction to Venus both in Rasi and Navamsa was responsible for making the native totally blind.

The native of Chart No. 253 has weak eyes which water under even slight strain. The 12th lord Saturn is in Cancer in close conjunction with his bitter enemy and 6th lord the Sun. Venus, the karaka for eyes, is also with Saturn. The 2nd lord Mars is also afflicted by Rahu. The 12th lord and the karakas, the Sun and Venus, occupying Cancer, a watery sign and aspected by the watery Moon have given eye affliction of a similar nature.

The native of Chart No. 254 suffers from weak eye-sight. In addition, he sees a blinking aura before his eyes. The 12th lord Venus occupies an inimical sign with Ketu and is subject to a *papakartari yoga* caused by the Sun and Saturn. The

Chart No. 254.—Born 2–8–1951 at 1–35 p.m. (I.S.T.) at 13 N, 77 E 30.

			Mars	Rahu Sat.			Mars
Jupiter							
Rahu			Moon Sun				
	RASI		Merc. Venus Ketu	Jupit.	NAVAMSA		Lagna Mercury
	G II-234						
	Lagna		Sat.	Sun	Venus	Moon	Ketu

Balance of Saturn's Dasa at birth : 8 years, 5 months and 14 days.

2nd house is aspected by Mars while the 2nd lord Jupiter, though occupying his own sign Pisces, is aspected by Saturn. Venus, the karaka, is afflicted by a blemished Mercury so that the root of the trouble is traceable to the nervous system.

The 12th house in Chart No. 255 is aspected by the 12th lord Mars and the divine planet Jupiter. The 9th house is occupied by 9th lord Saturn who aspects the Sun, the Moon and Mercury—all three planets ruling soul, mind and intellect in the spiritual sign Cancer. The Lagna lord Venus is in the 4th house with *kaivalyakaraka* Ketu and the spiritual Jupiter, The native is a spiritual aspirant, who, in spite of high academic qualifications, has taken to a line of austerity and *sadhana*.

Chart No. 255.—*Born 23/24–7–1933 at 1–40 a.m. (I.S.T.) at 21 N 9, 79 E 9.*

		Lagna				Lagna Venus	Mars Ketu
Rahu	RASI	Sun Moon Merc.			NAVAMSA		Saturn
Saturn	G.II-200	Venus Ketu Jupit.	Moon				
		Mars	Merc. Jupit. Rahu				Sun

Balance of Mercury's Dasa at birth : 9 years, 11 months and 10 days.

Chart No. 256.—*Born 19–9–1936 at 10-50 a.m. (I.S.T.) at 10 N 30, 78 E 45.*

			Ketu			Mars	Saturn Rahu
Saturn	RASI		Sun Jupit.		NAVAMSA		
	RP-42/141		Mars	Moon			Mercury
Rahu	Lagna Jupiter	Moon	Sun Venus Merc.	Ketu		Lagna	Venus

Balance of Rahu's Dasa at birth: 9 years and 3 months.

The native of Chart No. 256 is spiritual-minded. The 9th lord Moon occupies the 12th house or *mokshasthana* and hemmed in between benefics, Jupiter on one side and Venus and Mercury on the other. The 12th lord Venus also receives no malefic aspects. He is in Virgo, *vargottama* and debilitated, with the Sun and Mercury. The native is a full-time *sadhaka*.

In Chart No. 257 the 12th house is occupied by the 9th lord the Moon and Atmakaraka the Sun who is also the 10th, lord. The Lagna is under the influence of Mercury, the planet of wisdom and Jupiter, a significator of philosophical and spiritual inclinations while Lagna lord Mars' aspect only strengthens it. The chart belongs to the occupant of the highest seat of spirituality and religion in the illustrious line of Sri Adi Sankaracharya. The 12th lord Venus is in Sagittarius with *mokshakaraka* Rahu. The native is a *jeevanmukta*.

Chart No. 257.—*Born 13-11-1917 at 8-30 a.m. (I.S.T.) at 12 N 58, 77 E 35.*

	Jupiter	Ketu		Lagna			Jupiter Sun
	RASI		Sat.		NAVAMSA		Rahu
	RP-42/102	Mars		Sat. Ketu			Mercury Venus Mars
Venus Rahu	Mercury Lagna	Moon Sun		Moon			

Balance of Rahu's Dasa at birth : 13 years, 9 months and 7 days.

Chart No. 258.—*Born 16–10–1892 at 7–12 a.m. (L.M.T.) at 13 N, 76 E.*

				Jupit. Ketu	Lagna	Saturn	
Jupiter	Rahu						
							Moon
	RASI				NAVAMSA		
Mars			Moon Venus				
	RP-239/PN						
		Sun Mercury Ketu Lagna	Sat.	Merc.		Sun	Mars Rahu Venus

Balance of Ketu's Dasa at birth :   1 year and 9 months.

In Chart No. 258 the 12th house is occupied by yogakaraka Saturn and aspected by the planet of spirituality, Jupiter, who not only occupies the mystic sign of Pisces but is also *vargottama*. The native was an exalted sage also coming in the glorious line of Sri Adi Sankaracharya. The 12th lord Mercury is also the 9th lord in Lagna associating with the Sun, ruler of the soul, and *kaivalyakaraka* Ketu. The 12th house is hemmed in between Lagna lord Venus and Atmakaraka the Sun who are in mutual *parivartana* indicating the blazing spirituality of the native.

XVII

Some Practical Illustrations

We have seen so far how to assess the nature of results of each of the twelve Bhavas or houses beginning from the seventh (marriage) to the twelfth (emancipation) in this volume. The principles of astrology provide us with a tool to estimate the general worth of an individual and what life has in store for him in its various sectors such as marriage (7th), suffering and death (8th), parentage, prosperity, travel (9th), fame, success, distinction and occupation (10th), friends, brothers, gains (11th) and expenditure, incarceration and final release (12th) after death. Although the planetary configurations can give a broad outline of the future of an individual, it is only an intuitional perception that can help us to assess the real worth of a horoscope. It is no easy job to draw conclusions. The astrologer has a duty in dressing up his predictions in such a way that the truth is revealed without adversely affecting one psychologically.

If the Lagna lord, the Moon or Mercury is afflicted, a negative prediction may drive the native to melancholia and frustration. Hence one must be careful in revealing the truth. On the contrary, a native with strong Ascendant, the Moon or Mercury will be able to digest any prediction without reacting strongly. This mental maturity of a native must be assessed before the astrologer gives his comments on any chart.

Coming to the question of interpretation, the Rasi, Navamsa and Bhava charts must all be taken into account. Malefic afflictions cause denial or lack of happiness or positive misery in a particular sector of life. On the contrary, benefic dispositions through aspects, associations and occupation give happiness and success in the relevant aspects of life. A proper assessment and balancing of all factors must be made before coming to any conclusion. The Dasa-Bhuktis are of very great importance since if appropriate periods do not operate in the life-time of an individual, he may not experience the results in their entirety.

We shall analyse in a general way the several Bhavas in the following two charts :

Chart A.—*Birth details with-held for obvious reasons :*

RASI				NAVAMSA			
Mercury Moon Rahu	Mars Sun		Venus	Lagna Merc.	Mars Saturn		
	RASI		Jupit.	Jupit. Ketu	NAVAMSA		Rahu
Saturn	GD-202						Moon
	Lagna		Ketu		Venus		Sun

Balance of Saturn's Dasa at birth : 17 years, 2 months and 1 day.

Marriage

The seventh house falls in Taurus. It is not occupied or aspected by any planet and therefore, quite unafflicted. The seventh lord Venus occupies the 8th house and is free of aspects, good or bad. Hence the seventh Bhava is fairly strong. The 7th house from the Moon is Virgo occupied by Ketu and aspected by the 7th lord Mercury. He is *neecha* (debilitated) but gets cancellation of debility due to Venus, who gets exalted in Pisces, being in a kendra (quadrant) from the Moon. Mercury is afflicted by Rahu and aspected by exalted Moon-sign lord Jupiter and 11th lord Saturn from his own sign (Capricorn).

The 9th house is occupied by an exalted Jupiter who is a benefic for Scorpio Ascendants. He is aspected by powerful Saturn, a malefic.

The presence of Venus in the 8th house, both as Kalatrakaraka and 7th lord, is not desirable since it gives a sickly husband. Further Mercury, the 8th lord, occupies the 5th house with a benefic the Moon but malefic Rahu.

The 7th house has no afflictions *prima facie*. Neither the 7th lord nor the Bhava is aspected or associated with Saturn. The 9th house is fortified by a *parivartana* (exchange of signs between 5th and 9th lords). An early marriage is therefore, possible. The strength of the 9th house indicates a fortunate match and great prosperity in life.

Timing Marriage: The following planets would be capable of giving marriage in their periods (Dasas or Bhuktis):–

(1) The lords of the Rasi and Navamsa occupied by the 7th lord namely, Mercury and Mars.

(2) Venus.

(3) The Moon.

(4) The lord of the sign occupied by the 2nd lord Jupiter—the Moon.

(5) The 10th lord—the Sun.

(6) The 9th lord—the Moon.

(7) The 7th lord—Venus, there being no planets occupying or aspecting the 7th house.

(8) The 7th lord from the Moon—Mercury.

That is, Mercury, Mars, Venus, the Moon, and the Sun become capable of giving marriage in their periods.

The native finished her Saturn's Dasa when slightly over 17 years and Saturn having no marriage-giving power did not give her matrimony. The next Dasa would be of Mercury. Early marriage being indicated, the Dasas of Venus, the Sun, the Moon and Mars could not be considered at all since Venus Dasa would begin in her 42nd year, the Sun's Dasa by the 48th year, the Moon's Dasa by the 58th year and Mars Dasa by her 65th year. So Mercury's Dasa would be most appropriate for marriage. In addition, Mercury is with the 9th lord, the Moon and aspected by exalted Jupiter (2nd lord and *Kutumbasthanadhipati*) so that within 6 months from the commencement of the Dasa, the native got married.

Applying the method of adding the longitudes of the Lagna Bhava (223° 11') and the seventh house (43° 11'), the sum would be 266° 22' or Sagittarius 26° 22'. Transit Jupiter was in Capricorn when the marriage took place in January 1950. Jupiter from here was aspecting natal 7th house and natal Jupiter who is also the ruler of the sign signified by the sum.

The 9th house is extremely strong involving the 9th lord Moon and the 2nd and the 5th lord Jupiter as well as the 11th lord Mercury and gives rise to a powerful Dhana Yoga. The marriage occurring in the commencement of the Dasa of the

11th lord Mercury gave a very rich husband. The 7th lord Venus occupying Gemini, a sign ruled by Mercury, and Mercury being strong with *neechabhanga* gave a highly intelligent husband. Venus occupies a martian constellation in a mercurial sign so that the partner turned out to be an expert in technology.

Mercury being very well placed with 9th lord the Moon (*sowbhagya*) and aspected by the 2nd lord (*kutumba*) and the 5th lord (*progeny*) Jupiter from the 9th house (general fortune) gave happiness in married life with the birth of children and prosperity of husband in his Dasa.

Widowhood

The 8th house is occupied by the 7th lord Venus which is not a good feature. Ketu afflicts the 7th house from the Moon with no relieving influences. The presence of the 7th lord in the 8th house gives a sickly husband. Venus, further, occupies a constellation ruled by Mars who is in the 6th house.

The native's husband developed prostrate trouble about the end of Mercury's Dasa. It aggravated after several operations during Saturn's sub-period, the last in Mercury's Dasa. By the time Ketu's Dasa began, it had become so complicated that normal conjugal life was no longer possible. The Rahu–Ketu axis afflicts the 9th lord from Lagna and the 7th house from the Moon causing vicissitudes in married life. Ketu Dasa continued in this manner. After prolonged illness and several more surgical operations, the native's husband died in the sub-period of Mars in Venus Dasa. The Dasa lord Venus is in a *dusthana* so that his karakatwa (natural significations) suffered until the end. Venus occupies *mangalyasthana* from the Ascendant and is the 8th lord from the Moon. Mars is the 7th lord from the 7th and becomes a maraka. He is in the

12th from the 7th. The chart indicates widowhood and this occurred in the sub-period of the 6th lord in the Dasa of the 7th lord placed in the 8th causing Kalatra-bhanga.

Foreign Travel

The ninth house is Cancer, a watery sign, occupied by exalted 2nd and 5th lord Jupiter. The 9th lord Moon is in Pisces, another watery sign, and with 8th and 11th lord Mercury. The Moon is aspected by the 3rd lord Saturn and the 5th lord Jupiter. Rahu associates with the Moon. The Lagna lord Mars being in a moveable sign, the 9th house being a moveable and watery sign, the 9th lord Moon occupying a common sign and being aspected by the 3rd lord Saturn from his own sign Capricorn which also happens to be a moveable sign are all indicative of foreign travel and journeys to distant places in the appropriate Dasas (periods) and Bhuktis (sub-periods).

The following factors must be considered in timing foreign journeys, namely,

(a) lord of the 9th house – the Moon ;

(b) planet or planets aspecting the 9th house—Saturn ;

(c) planet in the 9th house—Jupiter ;

(d) planets aspecting the 9th lord—Saturn and Jupiter ;

(e) planets in association with the 9th lord—Mercury, Rahu and Ketu ; and

(f) the 9th lord from the Moon—Mars.

Therefore, the Moon, Saturn, Jupiter, Rahu, Ketu, Mercury and Mars become qualified to give foreign travel in their periods. The presence of Lagna lord Mars in a moveable sign and the 9th lord Moon in a dual sign aspected by a well-placed 3rd lord Saturn indicate several journeys abroad. Mars, the lord of the Lagna, in the 6th house cannot, however, give foreign residence or prolonged stay abroad as would have been the case if he were in the 9th or 12th house.

Venus is the 12th lord as well as the 7th lord and is also capable of travel abroad more particularly because of his occupation of a common sign.

The native first went abroad in Venus Bhukti of Mercury Dasa. Venus, as we have just seen, is the 12th lord and so qualified for giving travels. The Dasa lord Mercury is in association with the 9th lord in Pisces. The second time Saturn Bhukti in Mercury Dasa took her abroad. Saturn is the 3rd lord aspecting the 9th lord Moon and Dasa lord Mercury from the 3rd house. Ketu, the next Dasa lord, is in the 11th house in a common sign, aspected by 9th lord Moon. The Bhuktis of Venus, Mars, Jupiter and Mercury took her abroad in this Dasa. Venus Dasa also gave her many journeys abroad.

We can also apply the *Saham* tests.

Paradesha Saham = 9th house—9th lord + Ascendant lord
= 103° 11'—334° 27' + 0° 25'
= 129° 9' or Leo 9'.

The lord of the Saham is the Sun who is exalted in the 6th house in association with the 9th lord Mars from the Moon.

Jalapatana Saham = Cancer 15°—Saturn + Ascendant
= 105° − 283° 10' + 223° 11
= 45° 01' or 15° Taurus 1'.

The lord of the *Jalapatana Saham* is Venus who is the 7th and 12th lord occupying a common sign. The lords of the two Sahams being connected with the 12th and 9th houses, the chart can be said to indicate foreign travel.

Father : The Sun is the karaka for father. He is exalted in the 6th house with Lagna lord Mars who occupies his moolatrikona sign. The Sun is fairly strong except for his

occupation of a *dusthana*. The 9th lord, the Moon, occupies
the 5th house, a trine, in exchange with 5th lord Jupiter.
The Moon is closely placed to Rahu and is with 8th lord
Mercury. Malefic Saturn aspects him but this is countered by
the aspect of an exalted sign dispositor and benefic, Jupiter.

Considered from the Moon, the 9th lord Mars occupies a
maraka house (2nd house) with exalted 6th lord the Sun who
is also *pitrukaraka*.

Chart B.—*Birth details withheld for obvious reasons* :

Ketu		Lagna		Mars			
	RASI GD-135			Rahu	NAVAMSA		Saturn
Moon Mars				Sun			Mercury Moon Ketu
	Venus	Jupiter Sun	Rahu Sat. Merc.	Jupit. Venus			Lagna

Balance of Mars Dasa at birth :   6 years, 0 month and
17 days.

The exaltation of the Sun gave the native a well-placed
father. His death occurred in Saturn Bhukti of Mercury Dasa.
Saturn is the 7th lord from the 9th house as well as the 12th
lord from the 9th lord Moon. The Dasa lord Mercury is 3rd
and 12th lord from the 9th house. He is also the 7th lord
from the 9th lord the Moon. The exaltation of the *karaka*
and the *parivartana* between the 5th and 9th lords gave a
fairly long-lived father.

Marriage

The 7th house, *viz.*, Scorpio is occupied by Venus lord of Lagna and 6th. It is aspected by yogakaraka Saturn. This has both good and bad significance. The 7th lord Mars is exalted and occupies the 9th house with the 3rd lord the Moon. He is not aspected by any planet. The 7th lord is well placed. Karaka Venus, though well placed in a quadrant in the 7th house, is partly benefic being the lord of the Lagna and partly not welcome being the 6th lord. This has a mixed influence on his *karakatwa* (natural signification). The 7th house from the Moon, *viz.*, Cancer, is aspected by the Moon himself and exalted Mars, a *badhakadhipati* and lord of the 4th and 11th.

Timing Marriage: The following planets become qualified to give marriage: Venus, Jupiter, Moon, Mercury, Saturn and Mars. The 7th house is occupied by Lagna lord Venus which is good. Saturn is a yogakaraka and aspects the 7th house. This has a delaying effect but since he happens to be a functional benefic and his sign dispositor Mercury is exalted, he cannot push the event too far ahead. The native got married in Saturn's Bhukti of Jupiter's Dasa when about 27 years old. In the late 40's and early 50's, this could not be said to be an early marriage nor even a very late one The Dasa lord Jupiter is the ruler of the Navamsa occupied by the 7th lord while the Bhukti lord Saturn is lord of both the 9th and 10th houses and aspects the 7th house. Adding the longitudes of the Lagna and the 7th Bhava we get 56° 47′ + 236° 47′ = 293° 34′ or Capricorn. Jupiter in transit was moving over this sign as well as 7th lord Mars at the time of marriage.

The 7th house is occupied by Venus, the planet of beauty. The 7th lord Mars is exalted in the 9th house (good fortune) with the Moon. The native married a beautiful and intelligent woman. Venus in the 7th house made the couple deeply devoted to each other. The association of the 7th lord Mars with the Moon gave a wife, many years younger—almost ten —than the native.

The 7th lord is in the 9th and karaka Venus with no afflictions gave a long lease of married life. There are no indications in the chart for loss of wife.

Longevity

The Ascendant is aspected by its lord Venus. The eighth lord Jupiter is in the 6th house with debilitated 4th lord Sun. The Sun gets *neechabhanga* (cancellation of debility) since his sign-lord Venus is in a kendra (quadrant) from Lagna. The eighth house receives no other aspects. From the Moon, the eighth house is Leo aspected by exalted Mars. The 8th lord Sun occupies the 10th house with 3rd and 12th lord Jupiter. *Ayushkaraka* Saturn is in the 5th house with exalted Mercury. At the same time, he is afflicted by the Nodes. The 3rd lord the Moon aspects the 3rd house. This is good. Considered from the Moon, the 3rd lord Jupiter is in the 10th with the 8th lord Sun. The 8th lord Jupiter in a *dusthana* and the 8th lord Sun (with reference to the Moon) being strong in a kendra are not very good for longevity. On the other hand, the presence of Venus in a kendra gives some strength. Since both benefics and malefics are in a kendra (quadrant) and kona (trine) and 8th lord is in a malefic Bhava, the span of life can be said to be medium or *madhyayu*. Another reason for medium life is the exaltation of maraka planets, namely, 2nd lord Mercury and 7th lord Mars in trines.

The Dasas that operate during *madhyayu* (32 to 75 years) are of Jupiter (in part), Saturn and Mercury. Of these three

Dasa lords, Jupiter is the 8th lord from Lagna and the 3rd and·12th lord from the Moon combining with 8th lord Sun. Saturn is not a maraka from Lagna. He is the natural maraka and combines with the 2nd lord Mercury. From the Moon, he is the 2nd lord. Mercury is the 2nd lord from Lagna placed with karaka Saturn. He associates with the 2nd lord from the Moon, namely, Saturn. Of these three planets, Jupiter does not have sufficient maraka power, either due to lordship or association. Between Saturn and Mercury, the latter is the 2nd lord and powerful due to his exaltation. But Saturn who associates with Mercury takes over the *marakatwa* from him and becomes a first-rate killer. Since Lagna lord aspects Lagna, Saturn cannot be expected to kill in the beginning of his Dasa. This would not be warranted by the planetary dispositions. Hence he can kill only in the closing part of his period. Rahu who is with Saturn (maraka) and 2nd lord Mercury and who should also reflect the results of Saturn becomes quite capable of proving fatal. The native died in Saturn's Dasa at the fag end of Rahu Bhukti.

Nature of Death

The 8th house is Sagittarius and falls in the 3rd drekkana of the sign, ruled by ths Sun.

The 8th house is free of aspects, malefic or benefic, while the 8th lord joins the Sun (4th lord) in the 6th house (*rogasthana*). The Sun as lord of the 2nd drekkana occupying the 6th house gives a clue to the cause of death. Death came after an attack of pneumonia followed by a fatal heart-attack. Death was sudden and natural since there are no malefic aspects on the 8th house or 8th lord.

Foreign Travel

The ninth house is Capricorn, a moveable sign, occupied by the Moon lord of the 3rd and exalted 7th and 12th lord Mars. The lord of the 9th house is in a trine in a common sign with Rahu and exalted Mercury, lord of the 2nd and 5th houses. The Lagna lord Venus occupies a watery sign Scorpio in the 7th house. Considered from the Moon, the 9th house is Virgo occupied by Rahu and Moon-sign lord Saturn. The 9th lord Mercury is exalted in the 9th house itself. These factors are indicative of foreign travel. Applying the *Saham* tests, we get *Paradesha Saham* = 211° 20′ or 1° Scorpio 20′. *Jalapatana Saham* comes to 19° 3′ or 19° Aries 33′. Both Sahams have Mars ruling them. He is not only the 7th and 12th lord from Lagna but is exalted in the 9th house.

The native went abroad first in Jupiter's Dasa, Jupiter's Bhukti. Jupiter is with the 4th lord Sun so that it was for reasons of education. Jupiter, the Dasa lord, is in a moveable sign in the 6th house. He occupies the constellation of Rahu who associates with the 9th lord Saturn. The second time the native went abroad was in Saturn's Dasa, Saturn's Bhukti. Saturn as the 9th lord in the 5th house in a common sign is well placed to give foreign journeys. After that there were innumerable journeys abroad in the rest of Saturn Dasa until death.

Father

The Ascendant being Taurus, the ninth house is Capricorn occupied by 3rd lord the Moon and the 7th and 12th lord exalted Mars. The presence of a ruler of a *dusthana* (twelfth) house in the 9th is not so good. The 9th lord Saturn is in the 5th house with 5th lord Mercury and Rahu. Although Saturn as 9th lord in a trine is good for father, his association with Mercury who is also the 2nd lord is not desirable.

Considered from the Moon, the 9th house is Virgo occupied by an exalted 9th lord Mercury, Moon-sign lord Saturn and Rahu. The karaka Sun is in the 6th debilitated and with 6th lord Jupiter. The Sun gets cancellation of debility due to his sign-dispositor Venus being in a kendra from Lagna. This explains the humble beginnings in life of the native's father. The karaka being in an *upachaya* lifted him to the rank of a leading industrialist as indicated by the exalted planets in the 9th both from the Lagna and the Moon.

Death of the native's father occurred in Venus Bhukti of Jupiter's Dasa. Jupiter is the 7th lord from the 9th house from the Moon. He is in the 2nd from the 9th house. He is the 2nd occupant from the 9th lord Saturn associating with the 12th lord the Sun, therefrom, gaining maraka powers. Venus, ruler of the sub-period, is the 2nd lord from 9th lord Saturn and the 9th house from the Moon and in the 2nd house from the karaka Sun.

Occupation

The 10th house is Aquarius aspected by 8th and 11th lord Jupiter. The 10th lord Saturn is also the 9th lord and occupies the 5th house, a trine, with exalted 2nd and 5th lord Mercury and Rahu. The link-up between the 2nd and 5th lords and the 9th and 10th lords in the 5th house is powerful yoga for success and financial prosperity.

The 9th and 10th lord happening to be Saturn and associating with 2nd lord Mercury, the native joined the family business. This was in Saturn's Bhukti of Jupiter's Dasa. Jupiter is the 11th lord and aspects the 10th house. Saturn, the lord of the Bhukti, is a yogakaraka and owns the 10th house. Venus incidentally is in the 7th house in a kendra ahead of the Sun so the native's career began following marriage.

The 10th lord Saturn combines with Rahu (engineering) in the 5th house (investment) with a powerful Mercury (industry). The business was connected with a chain of engineering industries. The 11th lord who signifies gains is in a venusian sign (conveyance) with 4th lord Sun (vehicles) so that the major business was dealing with automobiles.

Jupiter being the 11th lord and Saturn, the Yogakaraka and both planets being related to the 11th houses, these Dasas saw the native's business prosper and expand considerably.

Elder co-borns

The 11th house is Pisces, a fruitful sign and is aspected by Yogakaraka Saturn and exalted benefic Mercury. It is occupied by Ketu.

The 11th lord Jupiter is in a *dusthana*, the 6th house, which is also an *upachaya*, with the 4th lord Sun. Jupiter occupies his own sign in Navamsa with a benefic Venus. The 11th house and lord are fairly well placed.

Considered from the Moon, the 11th house is Scorpio occupied by Yogakaraka Venus. The 11th lord Mars, in turn, is exalted in the Moon-sign itself. In Navamsa, Mars occupies a benefic sign Pisces. Mars, who is also the karaka, is in the 9th house with the fertile Moon.

The 11th both from Lagna and the Moon are fortified by the influence of the respective Yogakarakas, Saturn and Venus. The 11th lord Jupiter occupying a *dusthana* is the only blemish on the 11th house.

Saturn and Mercury, functional benefics from Lagna, who act on the 11th house, have moved 6 and 7 complete Nav-

30

amsas respectively. From the Moon, Venus who is in the 11th house has moved 5 whole Navamsas. Saturn who aspects the 11th house from the Moon has covered 6 whole Navamsas. The average number of Navamsas covered by these planets is $(6 + 7 + 5 + 6) = 24$ divided by 4. This would give 6 Navamsas. The native had four elder brothers and two elder sisters. The Rahu–Ketu axis afflicts the 11th house from Lagna. Rahu has covered one Navamsa. Jupiter, the 11th lord, is afflicted by debilitated Sun in the 6th house. These two afflictions on the 11th Bhava resulted in the loss of two elder co-borns, leaving an equal number of brothers and sisters alive.

While eunuch planets, Mercury and Saturn, aspect the 11th house from Lagna, the eleventh house from the Moon is subject to the equally strong influence of a female planet, Yogakaraka Venus and a male planet exalted Mars with the result two elder brothers and two elder sisters continued to live during the native's life-time.

The death of an elder brother came about in Jupiter's Dasa, Saturn's Bhukti. The Dasa lord Jupiter is the lord of the eleventh house and placed in the 8th (a *dusthana*) from the 11th house. Jupiter, in addition, occupies the constellation of Rahu who occupies a *maraka* place from the 11th house. The Bhukti lord Saturn is in *dwirdwadasa* (2/12 position) from Dasa lord as well as 11th lord Jupiter. He is in the 7th house from the 11th house combining with the 7th lord Mercury which makes him an extremely powerful maraka.

Another elder brother died in Mars Bhukti of Saturn's Dasa. Mars, the sub-lord, is the ruler of the 2nd from the 11th house. He is a maraka from the 11th lord Jupiter, being the 2nd and 7th lord therefrom. Saturn in the 7th with a maraka planet is a powerful killer with reference to the 11th house as already analysed.

Sayana-sukha—Conjugal life

The twelfth house is a barren sign Aries aspected by the 10th lord Mars, 8th and 11th lord Jupiter, and another fiery planet the Sun, the last two occupying a malefic place, viz., the 6th house. The 12th house is quite blemished except for the aspect of the 12th lord Mars, who occupies the 9th house, with the 3rd lord Moon and hence fairly well placed.

Considered from the Moon, the 12th house is Sagittarius, neither occupied nor aspected by any planet. The 12th lord Jupiter occupies the 10th house with the 8th lord Sun.

The karaka Venus is in a quadrant. As Lagna lord in the 7th house he is good but as 6th lord, not so feasible so far as Kalatrabhava is concerned. He is aspected by Saturn, a hermaphrodite, whose characteristics are further enhanced by association with another similar planet, an afflicted Mercury. Moreover, Venus occupies a mercurial constellation and as we have already seen, this is not a welcome situation.

The 12th house from Lagna being afflicted by planets in the 6th house (*rogasthana*) and the karaka being ruler of the 6th house and afflicted resulted in health troubles that prevented the native from having a normal married life.

But since the 12th lord Mars is well placed and Venus is also a benefic due to his ownership of Lagna and occupies a kendra, this state of affairs began only after the native had lived a normal life for about 15 years. The next 15 years approximately, until his death, were filled with complicated health problems that did not allow *sayana-sukha*. This is a unique instance of how both benefic and malefic influences on a particular Bhava have been equalised and given good and bad results in an equal measure.

Expenditure

The 12th house indicates acts of piety, charity and expenditure.

The 12th house is aspected by a natural benefic Jupiter, atmakaraka Sun and exalted 12th lord Mars. The 12th lord Mars occupies the 9th house in great strength. Considered from the Moon also, the 12th lord Jupiter occupies a kendra with the Sun. He receives no aspects, good or bad. The native was extremely generous and charitable. There are no malefic aspects on the 12th house. The native spent large sums of money on bettering the living conditions of his workers and on many projects of social welfare.

INDEX OF TECHNICAL TERMS

Bhratrukaraka	— Mars, the natural significator of brother
Bhukti	— Sub-period
Budha	— Mercury
Budha-Aditya Yoga	— A combination for intelligence and learning
Budha Dasa	— Mercury's major period
Buddhi	— Intelligence
Buddhisthana	— The house of intelligence
Chandra	— The Moon .
Chandra Dasa	— The Moon's period
Chandra-Mangala Yoga	— Angular disposition between the Moon and Mars
Chara Rasis	— Moveable signs
Chatushpada Rasis	— Quadrupedal signs
Dasa	— Major period
Dhanakaraka	— Jupiter, the natural significator of wealth.
Dhanus	— Sagittarius
Dharma	— Right living or the first of the 4 aims of life according to Sanatana Dharma
Divya Drishti	— Supersensuous perception
Dosha	— Affliction
Drekkana	— One-third division of a sign
Dusthana	— An evil place, namely, the 6th, 8th and 12th house
Dwikalatra Yoga	— A combination for two wives
Dwirdwadasa	— 2nd and 12th houses from each other
Dwiswabhava Rasis	— Common signs
Gangasnana	— A dip in the River Ganga

Ghati	— Equivalent to 24 minutes or 1/60th of a day
Gnanakaraka	— Jupiter, the natural significator of knowledge
Graha	— Planet
Gopuramsa	— Occupying the same varga four times
Guru	— Jupiter
Guru Dasa	— Major period of Jupiter
Guru Bhukti	— Sub-period of Jupiter
Hora	— One-half division of a sign
Jaimini	— A Maharishi of India. Author of works on Astrology and Philosophy
Jalapatana Saham	— Sensitive point relating to voyage
Janma Rasi	— Sign occupied by the Moon at birth
Jathaka	— Horoscopy
Jeevanmukta	— One who has attained self-realisation
Kalatrakaraka	— Venus, the natural significator of wife or husband
Kanya	— Virgo
Karaka	— Natural significator
Karako bhavanasaya	— The karaka in that particular Bhava destroys it
Karma	— Activity
Karmasthana	— The 10th house
Kataka	— Cancer
Kendra	— The 4th, 7th and 10th houses, a quadrant
Kendradhipati	— Quadrangular lord

Ketu	— Cauda or Dragon's Tail
Krishna Paksha	— Dark half of a lunar month
Kuja	— Mars
Kuja Bhukti	— Sub-period of Mars
Kuja Dasa	— Major period of Mars
Kuja Dosha	— Affliction caused by Mars occupying the 2nd, 4th, 7th, 8th or 12th houses
Lagna	— Ascendant or rising sign
Lagnadhipati	— Ascendant lord
Madhyayu	— Medium span of life
Mangalya	— Coverture
Mangalyasthana	— The 8th house
Makara	— Capricorn
Mandagraha	— Superior or slow-moving planet
Mandi	— A sensitive point in the horoscope
Maraka	— Death or death-inflicting planet
Matrukaraka	— The Moon, the natural significator of the mother
Meena	— Pisces
Mesha	— Aries
Mithuna	— Gemini
Mitra	— Friend
Mitravarga	— The varga or the place of a friendly planet
Moksha	— Final Emancipation
Moolatrikona	— A sign of well-being for a planet
Naisargika	— Natural
Nararasis	— Human signs
Navamsa	— 1/9th division of a sign
Neecha	— Debilitated